Place, Pedagogy and Play

Place, Pedagogy and Play connects landscape architecture with education, psychology, public health and planning. Over the course of thirteen chapters it examines how design and research of places can be approached through multiple lenses – of pedagogy and play and how children, as competent social agents, are engaged in the process of designing their own spaces – and brings a global perspective to the debate around child-friendly environments.

Despite growing evidence of the benefits of nature for health, wellbeing, play and learning, children are increasingly spending more time indoors. Indeed, new policy ideas and public campaigns suggest how children can become better connected with nature, yet linking outdoor space to pedagogy is largely overlooked in research. By focusing on three themes within these debates, place and play; place and pedagogy; and place and participation, this book explores a variety of angles to show that best practice requires dialogue between research disciplines, designers, educationists and psychologists, and a move beyond seeing the spaces children inhabit as the domain only of childhood professionals.

Through illustrated case studies this book presents a wider picture of the state of childhood today, and offers practical solutions and further research avenues that promote a more holistic and internationally focused perspective on place, pedagogy and play for built-environment professionals.

Matluba Khan PhD is a Lecturer in Urban Design at Cardiff University. She is an architect and landscape architect from Bangladesh and her doctoral research at the University of Edinburgh focused on co-design, development and evaluation of outdoor learning environments in elementary schools in Bangladesh. She co-founded the charity A Place in Childhood (APiC) with Dr Jenny Wood in 2018.

Simon Bell PhD, CMLA studied forestry at the University of Bangor, landscape architecture at the University of Edinburgh and took his PhD at the Estonian University of Life Sciences. He is co-director of the OPENspace Research Centre at the Edinburgh School of Architecture and Landscape Architecture at the University of Edinburgh and Chair Professor of landscape architecture at the Estonian University of Life Sciences. He was president of the European Council of Landscape Architecture Schools (ECLAS) between 2012 and 2018.

Jenny Wood PhD is a Research Associate in the Institute for Social Policy, Housing and Equalities Research (I-SPHERE) at Heriot-Watt University. She gained her PhD in children's rights and the Scottish town planning system in 2016, and currently contributes to research on homelessness and poverty. She co-founded A Place in Childhood (APiC) with Dr Matluba Khan in 2018.

Place, Pedagogy and Play

PARTICIPATION, DESIGN AND RESEARCH WITH CHILDREN

Edited by Matluba Khan, Simon Bell and Jenny Wood

LONDON AND NEW YORK

First published 2021
by Routledge
2 Park Square, Milton Park, Abingdon, Oxon OX14 4RN

and by Routledge
52 Vanderbilt Avenue, New York, NY 10017

Routledge is an imprint of the Taylor and Francis Group, an informa business

British Library Cataloguing-in-Publication Data
A catalogue record for this book is available from the British Library

Library of Congress Cataloging-in-Publication Data
Names: Khan, Matluba, editor. | Bell, Simon, 1957 May 24– editor. |
Wood, Jenny, 1991– editor. | Researching With and For Children: Place,
Pedagogy and Play (Conference) (2017: University of Edinburgh)
Title: Place, pedagogy and play: participation, design and research
with children / edited by Matluba Khan, Simon Bell and Jenny Wood.
Description: New York: Routledge, 2020. |
Includes bibliographical references and index.
Identifiers: LCCN 2020006197 (print) | LCCN 2020006198 (ebook) |
ISBN 9780367086367 (hbk) | ISBN 9780367086374 (pbk) |
ISBN 9780429023477 (ebk)
Subjects: LCSH: Children and the environment. |
Play environments. | Place-based education.
Classification: LCC BF353.5.N37 P53 2020 (print) |
LCC BF353.5.N37 (ebook) | DDC 155.9/1–dc23
LC record available at https://lccn.loc.gov/2020006197
LC ebook record available at https://lccn.loc.gov/2020006198

ISBN: 978-0-367-08636-7 (hbk)
ISBN: 978-0-367-08637-4 (pbk)
ISBN: 978-0-429-02347-7 (ebk)

Typeset in Univers
by Newgen Publishing UK

To all the children who have been denied their human rights.

CONTENTS

Notes on contributors ix

Foreword
Robin Moore xi

Preface
Catharine Ward Thompson xiii

INTRODUCTION
Simon Bell, Matluba Khan and Jenny Wood 1

PART 1 PLACE AND PLAY

1 MANUFACTURED PLAY EQUIPMENT OR LOOSE PARTS? EXAMINING THE RELATIONSHIP
BETWEEN PLAY MATERIALS AND YOUNG CHILDREN'S CREATIVE PLAY
Reyhaneh Mozaffar 11

2 NO TIME FOR PLAY: CHILDREN'S DAILY ACTIVITIES DURING SUMMER HOLIDAYS IN THE
BEIJING CENTRAL AREA
Pai Tang and Helen Woolley 31

3 AN EXPLORATION OF HOW PLAYGROUND DESIGN AFFECTS THE PLAY BEHAVIOUR OF
KINDERGARTEN CHILDREN IN TARTU, ESTONIA
Bhavna Mishra, Simon Bell and Himansu Sekhar Mishra 41

4 DESIGN OF SENSORY GARDENS FOR CHILDREN WITH DISABILITIES IN THE CONTEXT OF
THE UNITED KINGDOM
Hazreena Hussein 63

5 CAN ACTIVE PLAY ENCOURAGE PHYSICAL LITERACY IN CHILDREN AND YOUNG PEOPLE? 77
Patrizio De Rossi

PART 2 PLACE AND PEDAGOGY

6 TURNING THE CLASSROOM INSIDE OUT: LEARNING AND TEACHING EXPERIENCES IN AN
EARLY CHILDHOOD SETTING
Muntazar Monsur 93

7   BECOMING NATURISH: WAYS OF COMING TO KNOW NATURE IN THE PRIMARY SCHOOL   108
    Cathy Francis

8   CLOSING THE ATTAINMENT GAP IN SCOTTISH EDUCATION: THE CASE FOR OUTDOORS AS
    A LEARNING ENVIRONMENT IN EARLY PRIMARY SCHOOL   124
    Jamie McKenzie Hamilton

9   SCHOOL GROUND INTERVENTIONS FOR PEDAGOGY AND PLAY: HOW CAN WE EVALUATE
    THE DESIGN?   143
    Matluba Khan, Simon Bell and Sarah McGeown

PART 3 PLACE AND PARTICIPATION

10 CHILDREN AS HETEROTOPIANS: TOWN PLANNING WITH AND FOR CHILDREN   165
    Jenny Wood

11 THE CHAIR PROJECT: CO-CREATION THROUGH MATERIAL PLAY   180
    Simon Beeson

12 CHILDREN'S PERSPECTIVES ON GREEN SPACE MANAGEMENT IN SWEDEN AND DENMARK   194
    Märit Jansson and Inger Lerstrup

13 A VIEW FROM CHINA: REFLECTING ON THE PARTICIPATION OF CHILDREN AND YOUNG
    PEOPLE IN URBAN PLANNING   209
    Yupeng Ren

    CONCLUSIONS   222
    Matluba Khan, Jenny Wood and Simon Bell

    Index   *230*

CONTRIBUTORS

Simon Beeson ARB, BA, DipArch, M.Arch, FHEA studied architecture at Manchester, Hull and Minnesota. He has practiced as an architect, public artist and teacher. In 2007 he moved to the Arts University Bournemouth to establish a new undergraduate architecture course as Principal Lecturer and Course Leader.

Simon Bell PhD, CMLA studied forestry at the University of Bangor, landscape architecture at the University of Edinburgh and took his PhD at the Estonian University of Life Sciences. He is co-director of the OPENspace Research Centre at the Edinburgh School of Architecture and Landscape Architecture in the University of Edinburgh and Chair Professor of landscape architecture at the Estonian University of Life Sciences. He was president of the European Council of Landscape Architecture Schools (ECLAS) between 2012 and 2018.

Cathy Francis is a Lecturer in education and PhD candidate at the University of Aberdeen. Previously, for almost 30 years, she was a primary school teacher in England, Germany and Scotland. Her doctoral studies focus on school children's embodied experiences, gathered while at the beach in north east Scotland.

Hazreena Hussein PhD is an Associate Professor at the University of Malaya, Kuala Lumpur. Her research interests are environment–behaviour interactions and multisensory environments. The particular focus of her doctoral work was on accessible design in relation to the use of sensory gardens, particularly by children with special educational needs.

Märit Jansson PhD is an Associate Professor in landscape planning at the Swedish University of Agricultural Sciences. Her research concerns the management and functions of urban green spaces with a focus on social aspects for sustainable urban development. She has particularly studied children's perspectives on neighbourhoods, playgrounds and school grounds.

Matluba Khan PhD is a Lecturer in urban design at Cardiff University. She is an architect and landscape architect from Bangladesh and her doctoral research at the University of Edinburgh focused on co-design, development and evaluation of outdoor learning environments in elementary schools in Bangladesh. She co-founded the charity A Place in Childhood (APiC) with Dr Jenny Wood in 2018.

Inger Lerstrup PhD has a background as an agronomist and scientific writer with a PhD in landscape architecture. Her research is focused on human perception and use of green spaces, mainly related to children. With a basis in ecological psychology and the concept of affordance, she is concerned with learning, well-being and health.

Jamie McKenzie Hamilton PhD is a professional co-creation consultant and facilitator. He studied psychology and environmental decision-making at the Open University, and took his doctorate at Heriot Watt University on relationships between primary school task settings and cognition. He is a board trustee of A Place in Childhood.

Bhavna Mishra MSc is an architect, landscape architect and a doctoral student at Aalto University now working as a landscape designer at Ramboll Finland Oy. Her master-level research into kindergarten children's outdoor play in Estonia was conducted at the Estonian University of Life Sciences.

Himansu Sekhar Mishra, MSc, is an architect, planner and landscape architect and a doctoral student at the Estonian University of Life Sciences, where he is currently researching the links between blue spaces and human health and wellbeing.

Muntazar Monsur PhD is an Assistant Professor in the Department of Landscape Architecture in the College of Agricultural Sciences and Natural Resources, Texas Tech University, USA. His teaching and research activities are focused on enhancing the quality of children's lives by improving/modifying environments with special emphasis on schools, preschools and childcare centres.

Reyhaneh Mozaffar PhD is an Associate Lecturer at Edinburgh Napier University. She gained her PhD from the University of Edinburgh, where she developed the Creative Play Taxonomy, a tool measuring children's creativity in play, and focused her research on educational outdoor spaces and which environmental features can encourage creativity among children. She has an MA (Hons) and BA (Hons) in Design.

Yupeng Ren PhD is a Lecturer at Yantai University, China. He was taught and trained in both China and the UK, building up a range of knowledge in architecture and spatial planning. He earned his PhD in town and regional planning at the University of Dundee. His research interests include youth participation in planning decision-making, planning governance and sustainable urban design.

Patrizio De Rossi is an ERSC-funded PhD student in education at the University of Stirling, looking at how adolescents and adults might co-create opportunities for active play in secondary schools. He worked for several years as a PE teacher, in early years and primary schools, and as a sports coach.

Pai Tang is a PhD student in landscape architecture at the University of Sheffield. Her research is focused on children's daily use of their surrounding environments in the rapidly developing Chinese cities, helping to bring forth suggestions for creating the child-friendly city.

Catharine Ward Thompson, PhD, FLI is Professor of Landscape Architecture and directs OPENspace – the research centre for inclusive access to outdoor environments at the University of Edinburgh. Her work focuses on inclusive access to outdoor environments and links between landscape and health.

Jenny Wood PhD is a Research Associate in the Institute for Social Policy, Housing and Equalities Research (I-SPHERE) at Heriot-Watt University. She gained her PhD in children's rights and the Scottish town planning system in 2016, and currently contributes to research on homelessness and poverty. She co-founded A Place in Childhood (APiC) with Dr Matluba Khan in 2018.

Helen Woolley BSc BPhil FLI is a Reader in Landscape Architecture and Society, University of Sheffield. Her research on children's outdoor environments relates to policy, practice and use and has an increasing focus on how this is facilitated or constrained by individuals, structures, organisations and society.

FOREWORD

When children play, do they learn? "Yes," would be the expected answer from child development experts and early childhood educators, and hopefully, parents. Positive responses from professionals not directly engaged with children and the public at large are probably less likely. Perhaps the question should be more often asked. If we agree that children do learn through play, are *where* they play and the physical characteristics of those places important? This question is seldom asked and poorly understood.

Recently, I tagged along with a half-dozen four-year-olds, their teacher and a student intern, in a small remnant woodland situated just beyond the boundary fence of the licensed area of a large child development center. In the quarter-acre paradise, informal paths had been cleared and edged with pieces of tree trunks and limbs, which sometimes ballooned out to form additional activity areas. Some were equipped with large tree trunk slices, laid horizontally to support kids' investigations. "Research tools" included recycled plastic receptacles, bottles, hand-lenses, and steel-bladed scissors. The teachers let kids roam freely, solo or in groups, exploring and discovering whatever attracted their attention. Within moments, kids were digging in the leaf litter, turning over logs, peeling decomposing bark, digging into rotting wood with scissors, clearly fascinated by the material transformations they made and the small animals they found.

Teachers stayed in the background keeping a watchful eye, joining in when the children's attention focused on something specific, using Socratic, inquiry-based probing. What did you find? What color is it? What's that along the edge of the body? Legs? How many? Are they all used at once? Children trap the centipede-like insect in a bottle for closer inspection. The student teacher discusses with another child the curvy grooves on the inside of bark separated from a fallen log and asks what made them.

The two-fold advantage of the woodland was its easy access from the childcare center and the fact that it was an unkempt landscape, with a mix of deciduous trees and conifers, some fallen and left to decompose, together with a diverse understory—a biosystem of readable markers of seasonal cycles and the passage of time. To the casual observer the place would appear similar to any patch of Piedmont woodland in North Carolina. However, through the play and learning experiences of children with their teachers, the woods have been psychologically transformed into a well-loved place full of meaning, reinforcing the childcare center's bio-identity. Intervention was a looping, rough-and-ready pathway to help children discover some of the infinite affordances of the place. The freedom and imagination of these children was also expressed in natural shelter constructions, pretend animal habitats, and homes for other imagined beings.

Teachers facilitated, extended, and deepened discovery, encouraging close observation, responding to questions, inventing ways to capture, observe, describe, count, and use words related to animal and plant parts, sounds of nature, qualities of ever-changing light, the sensation of air on one's face, and the behavior of autumn leaves floating gently to the ground. Play and learning experiences were taken back to the classroom for further steps in the learning process: observing more closely, making drawings, listening to a related teacher-read story. Each woodland trip adds layers of individual meaning and collective meaning for the class. A new kid, just arrived from a foreign land, experiences the woodland as a social link with another child as they explore wordlessly together, then starting a conversation as they share discoveries, co-creating the pedagogy of the place. Social-emotional learning is palpable when observed first-hand, although not yet well represented in the literature.

The above example of place pedagogy lies at one end of the place biospectrum as a diverse, multi-layered, well-established habitat, requiring minimalist intervention to activate childhood wonder and its extension by mindful teachers. The other end of the place biospectrum is more challenging to activate because it involves the re-naturing of existing childhood spaces to create biodiversity from scratch. Nonetheless, a positive aspect is the possibility of engaging children and youth in the design and management processes that strengthen place affiliation and a sense of ownership. As the majority of children live in cities, conserving local natural places and re-naturing them are equally important. Nature facilitates equity and inclusion by affording many points of entry, offering diverse possibilities for interaction and rich social relations at ground level, regardless of individual special needs or disabilities.

Possible place pedagogy outcomes include health promotion via increased time outdoors as a proxy for physical activity and reduction of sickness (reduced exposure to indoor germs). Adding nature can dramatically increase body-in-space affordances and thus fitness. The adaptability of nature can support wide-ranging learning styles, especially for kids intolerant of sitting in classroom chairs for long periods. For them, outdoor hands-on learning can be transformed through memory and applied to new situations back in the classroom and beyond. Tacit, experiential learning through play in nature supports cognitive development. Children know things because they confidently perform actions on their environment and observe the results—in other words gain agency, now recognized as crucial to successful human development. Hands-on science happens in front of their eyes. Diverse action in nature motivates literacy.

As human society enters the Anthropocene and faces the enormous challenges of climate change, guided by OECD's *Future of Education and Skills 2030*, we must re-examine the role of learning, education, and schools in the volatile digital era, where acquiring social values may be more important than learning skills. In this regard, the timely publication of *Place, Pedagogy and Play* must be applauded. The book's interdisciplinary contents bridging research, practice, and policy take us a long step forward towards a new vision of holistic childhood based on the integration of play, learning, and education; and, I would emphasize, the need for place pedagogies intimately entwined with nature. Supportive, international policy already exists in the form of the UN Convention on the Rights of the Child and the UN Sustainable Development Goals. Together, they provide portals for national and local policy to shape the long-term health of Planet Earth and its human inhabitants. Action is imperative!

Robin Moore
Natural Learning Initiative
North Carolina State University
Raleigh, USA

PREFACE

The inspiration for this book comes from a vision about researching with and for children, to learn how to enhance the opportunities offered by the environments in which they spend their days to provide for stimulating, healthy and playful child development. Remarkably, given the success of the vision – culminating in this book – it was initially developed by a group of Landscape Architecture and Architecture doctoral (PhD) students at the University of Edinburgh, who then reached out to their colleagues in other disciplines, including Design and Education, to develop and obtain funding for an international conference. The organising committee, many of whom were already professionals in academia or practice as well as being research students, brought together an international group of researchers and practitioners working on diverse aspects of children's environments for an interdisciplinary conference held at the University of Edinburgh in May 2017. The conference, entitled 'Researching with and for Children: Place, Pedagogy and Play', combined these three important themes of childhood, often explored only in disciplinary silos.

To enhance these links, the conference was designed so that all participants attended every presentation across the wide range of topics. The diverse contributions, ranging from experiences of children's play in China to considerations of learning and creativity in primary school classrooms and nursery playgrounds in the UK, spawned much debate and fruitful discussion. It was a particular pleasure to engage with so many dedicated and enthusiastic colleagues at this conference, given the track record of research into supportive outdoor environments for children and young people undertaken by the OPENspace research centre, to which I and co-editor Simon Bell belong. We are delighted that this book can now expand and reflect on the rich range of research, and its practical implications, that continues to be needed in the ever-changing world of childhood today.

The book presents 13 chapters that reflect varied aspects of children's lives in different contexts. Part 1 focuses on the dynamic between places and children's play; Part 2 focuses on how place affects children's learning and their experience of this learning; and Part 3 reflects on the role of children in place making and how we may work to counter some of the barriers currently in place for children's participation. The conclusion then draws out the differences and commonalities in the range of approaches, identifies learnings for academia and practice, and considers how we may use interdisciplinarity to illuminate approaches and understandings in different parts of the world.

The outcome of this volume is a call to action for further collaboration between individuals and organisations that believe in the primacy of children's environmental experience for better understanding and shaping our world. We hope that lessons contained in this book will be of use both to researchers and to practitioners. Several contributions come from practitioners engaged in research and many chapters report on an action research approach that worked with communities and other child-focused organisations. The aim is to draw out the links between current research and practice and inspire future collaborations.

Catharine Ward Thompson
OPENspace
University of Edinburgh

INTRODUCTION

Simon Bell, Matluba Khan and Jenny Wood

In 2005 the American child advocacy expert Richard Louv published a book which was to have reverberations around the world. *Last Child in the Woods: Saving our Children from Nature Deficit Disorder* (Louv 2005) became a best-seller, bringing together a body of research and demonstrating through this the importance of giving children direct experiences of and exposure to nature (in its widest sense). This serves a vital contribution to their development in terms of physical and mental health and well-being. As well as presenting the evidence, Louv also offered solutions. It therefore seems strange that in the almost 15 years since then children appear to be spending less time outdoors than ever before. Louv's call has largely fallen on deaf ears, despite the uptake of his ideas and the continuing references to his work. Is knowing about the problem enough to solve it?

Since 2005 we have seen the inexorable rise of the internet, and social media in particular has attracted children to the indoor world of the screen. Smartphones have become entrenched and strongly intermingled with both child and adult cultures worldwide, and with the wealth of content now at our fingertips, it is proving irresistible to many, if not most, children.

The massive increase in urbanisation across the globe is a further contributing factor to children's increasingly indoor lives. Since 2008 over 50% of the world's population has been living in cities, and the poor quality of many urban environments – replete with traffic, air and water pollution, poor housing and a lack of green areas – means that many children grow up in places devoid of nature, so that even if they wanted to make direct contact, it is not easy to do so. Add to that the perception that urban areas are child-unfriendly and full of risks – ranging from traffic to stranger danger – and children are often not allowed out on their own to play freely.

Compounding the above factors, children in many societies face pressures to succeed in their education and lead programmed lives where almost every minute is taken up with some activity which is supposed to increase their chances of getting into a good school or succeeding in sports, music or art (as well as in the classroom). Clearly this pressure varies from society to society, but it has a major negative impact on the development of young children in ways other than those measurable by educational or sporting attainment.

The United Nations Convention on the Rights of the Child (UNCRC) was adopted in 1989 and came into force in 1990. 196 counties ratified the UNCRC, including all eligible member states of the United Nations except the USA. There are three aspects which concern us in this book: play, pedagogy and participation. Regarding play, the convention contains a single major clause on this in Article 31 where it states:

> States Parties recognize the right of the child to rest and leisure, to engage in play and recreational activities appropriate to the age of the child and to participate freely in cultural life and the arts.
>
> (UN 1989)

Other articles also contain statements which link to this, such as Article 15, which gives children the right to gather, assemble and organise their own activities. Signatory countries have in many cases taken on the task of creating a set of guidelines on play which refer to both the letter and spirit of the convention. As an example, the Play England Charter for Children's Play states:

> Play is an essential part of every child's life – vital to his or her development. It is the way that children explore for themselves the world around them; the way that they naturally develop understanding and practice skills. Play is essential for healthy physical and emotional growth, for intellectual and educational development, and for acquiring social and behavioural skills.
>
> (Play England 2009)

However, such moves are usually led by Non-Governmental Organisations, and there continues to be a lack of strategic thought from governments (with some exceptions) across the world as to how to protect children's declining freedoms to play on their own terms.

Regarding pedagogy, the UNCRC declares a right for all children to receive an education in Article 28, and stipulates qualities of that education in Article 29. This includes education that helps children learn about the world around them, and respect for their own and other people's rights. While new policy ideas and public campaigns suggest how children can become better-connected with nature, linking outdoor space to pedagogy is largely overlooked in both research and practice. An exception may be Scotland's new 'Learning for Sustainability' aspect of the school curriculum. However, it is too early to measure the impact of this.

Participation is explicitly mentioned in the UNCRC in Article 12 section 1:

> States Parties shall assure to the child who is capable of forming his or her own views the right to express those views freely in all matters affecting the child, the views of the child being given due weight in accordance with the age and maturity of the child.
>
> (UN 1989)

Indeed, this is an underpinning principle of the UNCRC, and one that challenges many existing societal structures. The other two underpinning principles are 'non-discrimination' (Article 2), and 'best interests of the child' (Article 3). In relation to the concept of place – a specific geographic location or space which can be connected to a person, and with which they identify an attachment – children frequently grow up in and form strong links to their home environment. This is not just their residence but their immediate neighbourhood, local parks, their school, shops, religious centres and other places which form their world. Ideally this place-attachment leads to a feeling of safety and security; enabling children to play freely; to be concerned about and develop care for the environment; and to wish to be consulted or to participate in certain decisions which may affect their space. Thus, the place in which rights are enacted are vital, and children are likely to have important insights to contribute around what makes a place good or bad – for them and also for others.

Place can be changed for the better by design and, for example, play equipment or educational tools at the micro scale. At the meso and macro scale, play or educational space (whether indoor or outdoor classrooms or other environments such as forests) can be improved with the participation of children who are the beneficiaries of the design.

This book is the first to link place, pedagogy and play, by connecting landscape architecture with education, psychology, public health and planning. It looks at how children, as competent social agents, can participate in the process of designing their own spaces, and brings a global perspective to the debate around child-friendly environments. It also considers how research in these fields (obviously done *for* children as beneficiaries) should be undertaken, where possible and ethically acceptable, *with* children. This reverses traditional approaches of conducting research *on children.* Readers will find that this is a central theme in the book.

This book started life at an interdisciplinary conference held at the University of Edinburgh in May 2017. The conference, entitled "Researching with and for Children: Place, Pedagogy and Play" combined three important interconnected themes of childhood often explored only in mono-disciplinary silos. To enhance these links, the conference was not split into different themes as is usual, but all attendees sat in on every presentation across the diverse range of topics. From researching the experiences of children's play in China, to how the layout of a primary school classroom in the UK affects children's learning, the structure and collegiate nature of the gathering spawned fruitful and energising discussion. We are delighted that this book can now draw out the commonalities in these areas and reflect the diverse range of research that has been carried out to date and should continue to benefit future generations of children.

A key aspect of the conference is that it was entirely planned, organised, and the funding acquired by PhD students led by Matluba Khan following the submission of her PhD thesis in landscape architecture to the University of Edinburgh. A large proportion of the papers were also presented by doctoral students from a range of locations. Many of these, while conducting their research in Scotland or the UK, were from overseas and this is reflected in the authorship. When inviting and selecting papers to include in the book – and for a range of reasons not all submitted papers from the conference were suitable, nor could some authors commit to a book chapter – we also took the opportunity to identify other work which fit the theme and invited these authors to submit a chapter. Thus, the book adheres to the themes as presented in the three well-balanced sections, while the actual range of chapters is rather eclectic.

This collection shows the range of issues of interest to researchers, and a wide variety of research methods and contexts for research. Moreover, the chapters are more discursive, reflective and hopefully make interesting and stimulating reading for the non-expert. By focusing on three themes within these debates, this book takes a variety of angles and shows that best practice requires links between research disciplines, designers, educationists and psychologists, and a move beyond seeing the spaces children inhabit as the domain only of childhood professionals. We hope that lessons contained in this book will be of use to both researchers and practitioners, and while chapters present academic research, all authors have brought out implications for policy and practice through their exploration. Indeed, several contributions come from practitioners engaged in research and even more chapters take an action research approach where authors worked with communities and other organisations. The aim is that, far from research taking place in ivory towers away from the gaze of those shaping the world we live in, we can draw out the connections for current practice and future collaboration.

Collaboration is increasingly important in focusing these wide-ranging debates, as while changing pedagogical models favour innovation, the design of the pedagogical "place" remains largely static. As noted on p. 2, the UNCRC has transformed the way child-focused researchers and practitioners view children; however, practitioners of environmental design continue to eschew these rights in spatial practice. This means:

- the place for play and the place for pedagogy are thought of as mutually exclusive;
- spaces for play are often segregated from the rest of the public realm;
- practice fails to acknowledge children's capabilities to participate in design and planning.

The book draws together a wider (but necessarily partial) picture of the current state of childhood research, grouped into the three themes, and offers both practical solutions and further research avenues to promote a more holistic and internationally focused perspective on place, pedagogy and play. This reflects the foci of the young researchers who had the foresight and ambition to hold the conference (and that of their senior supervisors who supported them and who of course saw their research come to fruition).

We present here 13 chapters that reflect different aspects of children's lives in different contexts. Part 1 focuses on the dynamic between places and children's play; Part 2 examines how place affects children's learning and their experience of this learning; and Part 3 reflects on the role of children in place-making and how we may work to counter some of the barriers currently in place for children's participation. The conclusion then draws out the differences and commonalities in the approaches presented and lessons for academia, practice and how we may combine approaches and understandings in different disciplines in different parts of the world.

As Catherine Ward Thompson writes in the Preface, the outcome of this volume, taken as a whole, is a call to action for further collaboration between individuals and organisations that believe in the primacy of children's experience for better understanding and shaping our world.

PART 1: PLACE AND PLAY

This section comprises chapters that explore the ways outdoor environments can be designed to foster children's rich play opportunities and behaviour and, through this, affect their learning. Chapters address:

- which playground features encourage more creative play among children;
- whether natural play elements and loose materials have an impact on children's active play;
- how architects and other designers can understand how a play space for younger kindergarten children functions and how it can be improved;
- how the play experiences – or lack of them – of primary school children affect their lives;
- how we can design for equity and for children with special educational needs;
- how we can improve physical literacy among children, given the crisis with low levels of physical activity.

The section starts with an important question for planners and designers, posed by Reyhaneh Mozaffar in Chapter 1: given the current state of play provision in many areas, should we provide manufactured play equipment or loose parts? This is examined in the context of a need acknowledged by UNICEF to ensure children's cognitive development, and the author believes this to be in part achieved by creative play. Her chapter reviews the nature of creativity and how to measure it, and defines creative play and related theories. Her research explored the creative possibilities of provided equipment and loose parts (all sorts of things such as blocks of wood, tyres, cloth and sand) through an experiment at a cooperative nursery for pre-school children in a small town in Scotland. The results showed how the loose parts led to much more creativity, with differences between boys and girls. It would be a straightforward task to apply the findings by simply providing such materials – cheap and versatile – in a nursery, with potentially important results, and this has implications transcending geographical boundaries.

From a project aiming to maximise creative play, we move to Chapter 2 where Pai Tang and her supervisor Helen Woolley study children's daily activities during summer holidays in the Beijing central area, China. Here, due to a competitive educational environment, the amount of time for children's free play is very limited and little of this takes place outdoors. This is ground-breaking research in a society which places great importance on education. The situation is not helped by the summer climate of inner Beijing which is hot and humid. This chapter shows that problems of lack of time and space for play are not only features of western societies, which have so far been the predominant focus of play research.

We next move to Estonia, one of the Baltic states which were part of the Soviet Union between 1944 and 1990. In Chapter 3, Bhavna Mishra, with her supervisor Simon Bell, and Himansu Sekhar Mishra, explored how playground design affects the play behaviour of kindergarten children in Tartu, Estonia. Bhavna describes how she chose four different kindergartens in the city, all reflecting in varying degrees the somewhat out-of-date approach to their function following decades of Soviet theories and practices. She undertook detailed observations of children playing in the outdoor spaces of each kindergarten and interviewed the staff. This revealed the specific ways in which the layout and equipment of each space was used by small children and which elements and designs have the most play value for them. The research revealed how different settings provided affordances for different types of play, which differed between girls and boys. It draws out the shortcomings and opportunities for improving the design and for making the most of natural spaces and loose materials with less reliance on manufactured equipment – so it fits well alongside the results of the study presented in Chapter 1.

Chapter 4 moves from small, able-bodied children or the specific geographic focus of China or Estonia, to explore landscapes for children with disabilities. Hazreena Hussein examines the design of sensory gardens for children in the context of the United Kingdom. She conducted case-study research using mixed methods in order to understand better how two sensory gardens in special schools work and the benefits they provide for children. She focuses very much on drawing out design principles for landscape architects but also notes that such gardens could have pedagogic as well as play potential if integrated into mainstream schools.

This section ends with the rather compelling Chapter 5, in which Patrizio De Rossi investigates and reveals a critical understanding of the role of active play in promoting physical literacy. Physical literacy refers to the motivation, confidence, physical competence, knowledge and understanding for engagement in physical activities throughout the life course. This chapter considers the perspectives of children and adolescents in rural Gloucestershire in an investigation into the relationship between play and physical literacy. Patrizio asked four boys and three girls to create their own 'play diary' for a week using a disposable camera, and then held interactive discussions with children around the 99 photographs. The narrative analysis of the data gathered in meetings with children reveals that free, unstructured and semi-structured (traditional playground games) active play activities have the potential to encourage the development of physical literacy. The chapter ends with recommendations for creating opportunities for active play.

PART 2: PLACE AND PEDAGOGY

This theme is addressed in chapters that explore the relationship between the design of physical environments and pedagogy. Physical environments, when designed with the learning needs of children in mind, can enhance the teaching and learning process. Teachers, if aware of the role of the environment, can integrate the outdoor context in teaching of the curriculum. The chapters in this section address:

- how teachers can work towards new models of curriculum planning by recognising and harnessing the active role places can play in learning;
- how educators can make learning more purposeful by involving nature;
- how children transition between key stages of school and navigate the differential balance of 'work' and play in primary classrooms;
- the role of the indoor–outdoor relationship of space in teaching and learning in early childhood classrooms;
- how an outdoor learning environment can be designed and evaluated to foster both children's play activities and learning of the curriculum;
- the role of outdoor learning in reducing the attainment gap between children from the richest and poorest socio-economic backgrounds.

This section starts with Chapter 6, in which Muntazar Monsur explores the role of the indoor–outdoor relationship of space in teaching and learning in an early childhood classroom in the USA. The intersection between indoor and outdoor environments is rarely explored in research as an important aspect of children's environments. Indeed, it is 'much more than just the size and number of windows and doors' as the author put it while investigating the answer to the question, "Can the design of windows, doors and desk spaces become effective tools for teaching and learning?". Inspired by the educational philosophies of Montessori and Reggio Emilia, the author discusses the importance of critically examining the built environment in terms of learning outcomes and behaviour, and the special attention the indoor–outdoor relationship deserves in this discourse. The results show how a better view from the window, i.e. a view of nature, resulted in more motivated teaching, more engaged children, and more nature-based learning inside the classroom. This therefore indicates the importance of better landscape design in early childhood settings. Results also indicate how a simple design intervention like wider window sills, with wider views from the windows, can offer more opportunities for learning activities like growing plants, drying artworks, conducting science experiments, etc., which has potential application beyond the USA.

From an architect's exploration of elements for better teaching and learning, we move next to a pedagogue's account of how children's connection with nature can be instated through learning in nature in Chapter 7. Inspired by a love of nature, this chapter reflects on Cathy Francis's thirty years' experience as a primary teacher working with children who seemed increasingly distanced from nature. The chapter particularly draws on weekly excursions of eight to nine-year-old children from the north east of Scotland to a local beach with their class teacher. Cathy begins the chapter by expressing her personal motivation to connect with nature, defines 'nature' in the context of the chapter and proposes a theoretical framework comprising four elements: encounter, touch, affiliation and surrender, to describe a process by which children may secure a positive, mutually beneficial connection with Nature. This chapter principally addresses teachers, but has implications for planners and landscape architects in terms of finding a balance between natural and built elements when designing and planning environments.

Chapter 8 by Jamie McKenzie Hamilton, also situated in Scotland, explores the impacts of indoor and outdoor settings on children's education, and provides recommendations for environmental qualities for engaging pre-schoolers in learning. Jamie's PhD research involved three primary schools, and compared the performance of 71 pupils on curriculum tasks between indoor and outdoor settings, categorised for their natural richness. He used multiple mixed methods including observations, questionnaires carefully designed for young children, focus group interviews with teachers and teachers' answers to the child-focused questionnaires. The results show general individual and group performance was superior outdoors and related to natural richness, including significant impacts on memory, attention, motivation and social interaction. Effects on underachievers were especially notable, bringing their engagement, contribution and self-confidence to levels which matched their peers. Jamie argues that stronger policy on outdoor learning could help close the attainment gap in Scottish education and beyond.

From the description of aspects of environmental qualities in early childhood settings, Chapter 9 poses an important question: 'Can we bridge the gap between research and practice?', and moves to discussing a comprehensive approach for evaluation of interventions in school grounds as both places for play and for pedagogy. The approach proposed by Matluba Khan, her supervisor Sarah McGeown and Simon Bell can be used by both researchers and professionals: architects, landscape architects and planners. It is based on Matluba's action-focused and experimental design and research projects (prior, during and post-PhD) in the context of Bangladesh. The authors first illustrate the theoretical framework that underpins the approach, and continue by discussing the usefulness and challenges of using different methods by referring to several case studies. In particular, the authors focus on a design project at a primary school in a small town about 80 km from the capital city, Dhaka. The chapter ends by providing a framework for the analysis of school ground settings based on the designers' intentions as potential affordances, i.e. opportunities for a behaviour or activity offered by a setting or object, affordances actualised by children and new affordances discovered by children.

PART 3: PLACE AND PARTICIPATION

This theme highlights and explores how children are often excluded from decisions about places and spaces. While co-production and community engagement are increasingly important to planners, designers, and other policymakers, it remains the case that including children is still seen as 'innovative'. Aspects under discussion include:

* how children are currently involved in the design and planning of their spaces through both active participation and playful manipulation of everyday space;
* how children could be more effectively involved in design;

- what methods we might use to encourage creative participation;
- challenges and opportunities of engaging children in the design process;
- children's perspectives on the management of space and place.

This section offers a critical commentary on contemporary issues regarding children's participation in a number of matters that affect them. Attempts at integrating Article 12 of the UNCRC have thrown up a number of challenges for nations across the world, but when it comes to place-based issues there are significant gaps in policy, practice and research. The four chapters here explore a variety of issues in the UK, Sweden, Denmark and China.

The section opens in Scotland, with a take on children in town planning through Jenny Wood's empirically supported, theoretical discussion of children's participation in urban environments in Chapter 10. She takes participation in this context to be an inalienable combination between participation both in the processes and the outcomes of planning. Drawing on the views of children in one area of a Scottish city, she links their insights with theories of power and spatial organisation, as proposed by Foucault. The result is an untangling of power in the outcomes of planning, and a route forward through the use of Foucault's heterotopia to see children as heterotopians – always seeking their own playful opportunities in every and any space. Through this theorisation, planners can come to understand that children not only need specific facilities, but also places where they are unconfined without their activities being dictated by adults. Children have agency in their own use of place; planners could do better by reducing the dominance of cars on urban environments, improving active travel infrastructure and taking a less interventionist approach to open and 'leftover' space.

The section continues with Chapter 11 by Simon Beeson, a chapter that truly embodies the interconnection of play, pedagogy and participation with regard to children and place. Beeson reflects on his long standing, playful pedagogic practice where children co-create ideas for public art and architecture by manipulating simple but adaptable chair-shaped blocks. Offering a comprehensive historical analysis on this and similar practices, he situates his work as distinctly Froebelian in nature. While the initial work was never intended to be more than exploratory educational practice, Beeson reflects on the ongoing impact of the children's ideas in his own practice. The chapter thus embodies the impact that listening and engaging with children can have on adult approaches, allowing us to reflect on our own views, assumptions and worldviews, and often resulting in a more playful and pleasing result.

As we move away from public art and architectural practice, Märit Jansson and Inger Lerstrup, in Chapter 12, move the conversation to Sweden and Denmark to consider green space management and its relation to children. While these nations undoubtedly offer greater independence for many children than others in Europe, the authors note that regard for children's rights is not always consistent or sustained and that many of the same problems around reductions in children's independence are occurring. They document and compare the views of children aged 10–11, gathered primarily through child-led walks. This simple and situated method allows for the rich collection of data and true insights that relate directly to place as children interact naturally with their surroundings. Importantly, the experiences detailed in this chapter show the high regard children have for their local environments, and their strong wish to have them well-maintained, attractive and interactive. While many of the children felt they could not have a say in green space management, it was clear from their reflections that children's involvement here is equally, or perhaps even more important than their participation in wider planning processes. Management issues can have direct impact on children's everyday lives, and are often more easily rectified than planning issues that work to more complex arrangements and time frames.

Staying on the planning theme, we end 'Place and Participation' by looking at the emerging opportunities and challenges for youth participation in Chinese urban planning. Yupeng Ren, in Chapter 13, introduces the tensions created by a nation that on the one hand has ratified the UNCRC, and on the other operates through centralised state control with cultural principles of both Confucianism and Communism (or arguably state-run capitalism). Yupeng takes us through the implications of a human rights instrument which emphasises individualism in a context that emphasises collectivism. With increasing access to western media and values through the internet, as well as rising knowledge of environmental problems, the chapter supposes that youth participation is endowed with both major challenges and opportunities. This first critical look may well springboard further academic research into young people's participation in environmental matters in China. These tentative and fascinating insights are an exciting place to end our initial discussions of the interaction between Place, Pedagogy and Play, with plenty of work to continue in future across these emerging themes.

WHO SHOULD READ THIS BOOK?

The multidisciplinary nature of this book lends itself to a wide readership. Indeed, since contributors take a range of research methodologies and examine a range of contexts rarely brought together in a single volume, we anticipate a readership not only from Europe, but North America and Asia. This extends the debate beyond its usual confines, bringing in new voices that allow for a more global conversation about children's lives today. We hope that it will be picked up and read by people interested in the field from all over the world. Moreover, as this book will be the first volume to present wider evidence on child-centric design to designers, educators and environmental psychologists, we feel sure that such disciplines will find something of value.

Architects and landscape architects can use the book as a guide for designing school grounds and other outdoor environments, while educators can use it to understand the role of environment in pedagogy and play, with suggestions on how to implement it into their practice. It is also pertinent that government policies in Scotland and Scandinavian countries encourage outdoor learning and reinforce this through their curricula, which provide policymakers from other countries rich insights. Meanwhile, children's rights are increasingly supported by governments across the world, with genuine interest from policymakers in how to care for and prepare children for a rapidly changing world.

Naturally, we hope that students of the disciplines noted above will find it of use, to stimulate their own thoughts and research into children and help them to realise that children, their environments, play and educational needs are of vital importance and that we cannot continue to create child un-friendly cities, to ignore children in decision making, to restrict their freedom to play or to keep applying limited pedagogical approaches.

REFERENCES

Louv, R. (2005) *Last child in the woods: Saving our children from nature-deficit disorder.* Chapel Hill, NC: Algonquin Books.
Play England (2009) *Charter for children's play.* London: Play England.
UN (1989) *Convention on the rights of the child.* New York: UN Secretary-General.

Part 1
PLACE AND PLAY

1

MANUFACTURED PLAY EQUIPMENT OR LOOSE PARTS? EXAMINING THE RELATIONSHIP BETWEEN PLAY MATERIALS AND YOUNG CHILDREN'S CREATIVE PLAY

Reyhaneh Mozaffar

INTRODUCTION

UNICEF (2001) states: "The early years from conception through birth to eight years of age are critical to the complete and healthy cognitive, emotional and physical growth of children" (p.2). In order to have a healthy future generation, we need to value these golden years and consider how to facilitate these developments in the best ways and how to equip children for a better future. One of the important aspects that can help reach these goals is encouraging creative thinking among children. It is the creative people's innovations in history which have built today's wealth (Runco 2004), and for an even better future, we need this empowering force to be concentrated even further. Creativity as a part of cognitive development is a vital feature for people's performance, personal development and academic success (Kim and Zabelina 2011, Besançon et al. 2013, Kandler et al. 2016). It is an important aspect that needs to be encouraged among individuals, as new issues are raised in today's society that need to be solved through original ideas (Lubart and Sternberg 1995, Amabile 1996a, 1996b). The golden age of childhood is highly influential on individuals' creativity (Krippner 1999).

One of the major things that can promote creativity in children is play. Play not only supports children's physical, emotional and social development, it is highly supportive of children's cognitive development and particularly creativity (Piaget 1962, Vygotsky 1978, Moore 1986, Titman 1994, Lansdown 1996, Russ 1996, Moore and Wong 1997, Burdette and Whitaker 2005, Ginsburg 2007, Kopp 2010, Wilson 2012, Mayesky 2014, Oncu 2015). The Association for Childhood Education International (ACEI) has argued that children of all ages need to play (Isenberg and Quisenberry 2002), so in a dense contemporary environment where children are under pressure from adults to learn different skills and to gain knowledge in various fields, ensuring sufficient time to engage in free play becomes increasingly important for children's development. The more opportunities they have to engage in free play, the more children can free their minds and develop creative thoughts.

Children's time is increasingly devoted to structured and educational activities instead of free play (Lester and Russell 2008, Hofferth 2009), even when most people recognise that play is crucial to children's development. Peter Gray (2011) argues that over the past half century, children's engagement in free play has declined significantly. In her study, Sue Palmer (2008) found that the large number of technology-based entertainment games as well as manufactured play equipment and the ease of access to these are distancing children from free play, resulting in less creativity and imagination among them. Clements (2004), in a survey of mothers, found that 85% of them believed that modern technology is the main reason why children spend less time engaged in free play activities (and back in 2004 these were not so highly developed as in 2019). Between 1981 and 1997, children spent 25% less time in free play and instead engaged more in structured play over this time period, according to a study by Owens and Hofferth (2001).

Based on the importance of creativity and the fact that children's engagement in free play can strongly encourage their creative thinking, there is a need to offer sufficient play spaces that provide children with more creative play activities and opportunities. In fact, the settings in which play takes place are very influential on children's creative play, but knowledge in relation to children's creativity is usually held by psychologists and educationists, and brings with it a lack of attention on how physical environments can actually affect children's creative play behaviour from an architectural and environmental design point of view. Thus, many psychologists argue that physical environments can influence the development of creative abilities and have an important role in supporting individuals to express creativity in different ways (McKellar 1957, Amabile 1988, Sternberg and Lubart 1996, Stokols et al. 2002, Simonton 2003, Lubart et al. 2013, Berlin et al. 2016, Kandler et al. 2016). Accordingly, the study presented in this chapter aimed to understand how different play contexts can encourage creativity among children. This chapter will compare two different play contexts, one facilitated with manufactured play equipment and the other facilitated with loose parts play materials, to understand which of the two will encourage creative thinking among children more than the other. It then presents what features within the play elements of these contexts encourage creative play behaviours among children.

WHAT IS CREATIVITY?

While creativity has been a neglected subject in the past, with only 0.2% of psychological abstracts before 1950 and 0.5% between 1975 to 1994 focused on creativity (Guilford 1950, Sternberg and Lubart 1996, Coulter 2004), since 1990 the topic of creativity has risen up the research agenda (Feist and Runco 1993, Sternberg and Lubart 1996, Sternberg and Lubart 1999, Coulter 2004). Now there are over 100 different definitions of creativity (Treffinger et al. 2002).

For this study, a definition of creativity defined by Lubart and partners (Barbot et al. 2011, Lubart et al. 2012) is used. This definition was chosen not only because it is one of the most up-to-date definitions, but also, and most importantly, it covers several aspects of thinking processes, unlike many other definitions which only focus on divergent thinking as creativity. This model recognises two general thinking processes, namely divergent thinking and convergent thinking. Divergent thinking refers to the ability to produce lots of ideas and answers for solving a problem, so it has a quantitative nature. Convergent thinking refers to the capability to put different ideas together in new and original ways, so it is related to the quality of the concept or production (Sternberg and Lubart 1991, Sternberg and Lubart 1992, Barbot et al. 2011).

While many theorists in the past such as Guilford (1950), Torrance and Kim (Torrance 1966, Torrance 1968, Torrance 1998, Kim 2006a, Kim 2006b) believed that creativity is only related to divergent thinking and that convergent thinking is related to intelligence, Lubart and his colleagues (Barbot et al. 2011, Lubart et al. 2011, Lubart et al. 2012, Barbot et al. 2016), believe creativity includes both of these processes which occur in cycles. Based on this theory, they have also designed a creativity assessment test known as the Evaluation of Potential for Creativity.

Accordingly, creativity refers to the ability to grow an original and useful idea or product, meaning it is new or unexpected as well as appropriate to its context (Lubart 1994, Lubart and Mouchiroud 2003, Runco and Jaeger 2012). Hence, creativity is defined as:

> the capability of an individual to produce work that is original (i.e. new, different from that which we can usually see) and adaptive to the context and the constraints of the situation
>
> (Lubart et al. 2012, p.15)

THE CREATIVE PLAY TAXONOMY: HOW CHILDREN'S CREATIVITY IS MEASURED IN PLAY

Amabile (1996) believes that "Creativity is a concept that is difficult to define and even more difficult to measure." As preschool children have limited verbal and drawing skills (Reisman et al. 1981, Zachopoulou et al. 2009), most of the tools that are developed to measure creativity are not designed for application to children (Mottweiler and Taylor 2014). Thus, there are limited studies on the creativity of preschool children (Ward 1968, Busse et al. 1972,

Manosevttz et al. 1977, Mottweiler and Taylor 2014). Among those tests that are designed to assess children's creativity, they either only measure aspects of divergent thinking (Reisman, Floyd et al. 1981) or only measure children's verbal and graphical creativity, such as the Evaluation of Potential for Creativity (Barbot et al. 2011, Lubart et al. 2012, Besançon et al. 2013, Barbot et al. 2016). In fact, there is no currently available test that could measure children's creativity when engaged in play.

Accordingly, as a part of my PhD I designed the "Creative Play Taxonomy" based on my observations of children's play, the chosen theory of creativity and the existing assessment tools of creativity. The Evaluation of Potential for Creativity (Lubart et al. 2012) was chosen as the theoretical framework for developing the Creative Play Taxonomy. Studying this tool in detail resulted in the identification of three parameters associated with creative thinking, which cover both divergent–exploratory thinking and convergent–integrative thinking. These are integration, flexibility and originality.

- Integration refers to the number of different elements integrated together. Thus, integration is noted when a child integrates two or more elements together (Besançon et al. 2013).
- Flexibility is related to the element's functionality and refers to the unexpected way in which items are used. Thus, flexibility takes place when a child uses an object differently from its intended design (Besançon et al. 2013).
- Originality is associated with the way the child acts compared to the other children. It is found when the child engages in an activity differently to other children (Lubart et al. 2012).

This taxonomy introduces eight different possibilities for a child's play, based on how many of the above factors are included in it. These eight possibilities are built in four levels of creative play behaviour depending on how many and which of these three factors occur together:

a) the highest level of creativity; which includes all three factors;
b) a relatively high level of creativity where two of the three factors are included;
c) a low level of creativity where the child only engages in one of the three factors;
d) no level of creativity when none of the factors are seen in child's play.

Table 1.1 shows the four different levels and eight stages of creativity in play with a description of each.

This taxonomy was applied and tested in my research (see p. 14).

WHICH TYPES OF PLAY ARE CREATIVE?

When talking about encouraging children's creativity in play, it is important to know how play can be creative and which type of play includes creativity. Russ (2004) argues that one of the types of play highly associated with creativity is pretend play. Fein (1987) defines pretend play as the process where "one thing is playfully treated as if it were something else" (p.282). In her study, Russ (2004) found that children who engaged in more positive affects in pretend play did better in their storytelling, which was more creative, imaginative and enjoyable. She argued that those who were more imaginative in play were more creative in telling a story (Russ and Grossman-McKee 1990, Russ 2004). She counted five ways in which children are encouraged to engage in more creative behaviours with play (Russ 2004):

1. play engages practice in making relations, which is vital in divergent thinking processes;
2. play encourages experiencing and expressing of positive effects, which are vital to creativity;
3. using symbols, manipulating elements and integrating different ideas are led by pretend play. These relate to insight abilities and the ability to transform, which both relate to creativity;
4. pretend play encourages the child to think about negative and positive affect themes, which results in building relations and memories, thus encouraging problem-solving skills;
5. pretend play leads to cognitive development in containing, integrating and controlling affect.

TABLE 1.1 The creative play taxonomy

LEVEL	STAGE	ABBREVIATIONS	DESCRIPTION	FLEXIBILITY	INTEGRATION	ORIGINALITY
D	1	NO	Playing with one or no element, as per its function and similarly to others			
C	2	INT	Playing by integrating **various types of elements** as per their function		▓	
	3	FLEX	Playing with an element in an **unexpected way**	▓		
	4	ORI	Playing with an element as per its function, but **differently to others**			▓
B	5	FLEXINT	Playing by integrating **various types of elements** in an **unexpected way**	▓	▓	
	6	INTORI	Playing by integrating **various types of elements** as per their function, but **differently to others**		▓	▓
	7	FLEXORI	Playing with an element in an **unexpected way** and **differently to others**	▓		▓
A	8	FLEXINTORI	Playing by integrating **various types of elements** in an **unexpected way** and **differently to others**	▓	▓	▓

Another type of play that includes creativity is dramatic play (Hughes 2013). In a study, Sutton (2011) found that adding loose parts to children's play spaces encouraged them to become involved in higher levels of dramatic play. The children engaged in thematic play where they could build a story by using these materials and then engage in dramatic play. In her study, Kirkby (1989) found that children engaged in dramatic play for 68% of their whole play time in natural settings, compared to 42% of their whole play time in manufactured settings.

In another study, Maxwell et al. (2008) compared the way two different play contexts would encourage children to engage in specific play types. Their first context was facilitated with manufactured play equipment and fixed structures. For their second play context, they added some loose parts and junk materials to the same play setting. They particularly focused on constructive play, referring to children's engagement in building something with a specific aim, and dramatic play, referring to children imagining being something or someone else. In this study, they found that adding loose materials to the play context encouraged children to engage in constructive play where they built their own spaces and play features, which then resulted in dramatic play in the setting. Again, when they removed the loose parts, the dramatic and constructive play behaviour reduced considerably (Maxwell, Mitchell et al. 2008).

The Scottish Curriculum for Excellence also supports the idea that children should be encouraged to engage in "active play", including creative play and imaginative play (Kidner 2013). Neill (2013) believes that facilitating play settings with loose parts encourages various types of play among children. These are creative play, dramatic play, exploratory play, cooperative play and constructive play. He believes that they are supportive as they are flexible and the children can adapt them in their play based on their own abilities and preferences (Neill 2013).

Adventure playgrounds include loose materials that are movable, where the children get to decide how they want to use them (Hayward et al. 1974). Children give meaning to these materials by their play behaviour through exploring, building and breaking (Kozlovsky 2008). Also known as Junk Playgrounds, they were first suggested by Carl Theodor Sørensen, a Danish landscape architect, in 1931 (Kozlovsky 2008). He suggested, "Perhaps we should try to set up waste material playgrounds in suitable large areas where children would be able to play with old cars, boxes, and timber." (quoted by Allen of Hurtwood 1968).

Loose parts refer to adjustable materials that can be used in various ways in children's play through invention and experiment (Nicholson 1972). Sutton (2011) defines loose parts as:

> any collection of fully movable elements that inspire a person to pick up, re-arrange or create new configurations, even realities, one piece or multiple pieces at a time. Loose parts require the hand and mind to work in concert; they are catalysts to inquiry. Loose parts are the flexible edge of an inviting open-ended interactive environment that allows participants to make an imprint of their intention. Experiences with loose parts provide a profound yet playful way for children to form associations between learning and pleasure.
>
> (Sutton 2011, p. 409)

Neill (2013) defines them as:

> materials with no specific set of directions, and they can be used alone or together with other materials. They can be moved, carried, combined, redesigned, lined up, taken apart, and put back together in multiple ways. The child, rather than a manufacturer or other adult, determines how the materials are used. Loose parts are the opposite of the battery-operated toys that require only that children push a button.
>
> (Neill 2013, pp.2–3)

The Theory of Loose Parts is built upon two parameters (Nicholson 1972):

1. no evidence supports the idea that some children are born creative while other children are not;
2. there is evidence that supports the idea that all children desire to interact and play with variable surroundings including flexible materials and shapes.

The study which forms the core of this chapter was conducted as a field experiment – where an experiment is performed in real life environments on a small group of participants with a well-focused research question (Neuman 2004, Bryman 2015). Accordingly, this study involved observation of 15 preschool children (aged between 3 and 5) while they were playing in two play contexts: a manufactured play context and a loose parts play context. The independent variable was the play context and the dependant variable was children's creative play behaviours (Goddard and Melville 2004).

Children were closely observed in each of the two contexts. Observation is an appropriate method to help understand people's behaviour in different settings (Bechtel and Zeisel 1987). For this research I was a recognised outsider, as it was important to observe children's behaviour from a close distance, so all the detailed behaviours could be recorded. I had several previous visits to the nursery and acted as their play supervisor, so the children got used to my presence and played as usual during the actual research observations.

For the observation recording procedure, I used empirical duration recording which covers accurate measurement and is a detailed recording method, so the data can be studied and analysed independently (Skinner et al. 2000). Duration recording also helps to record the amount of time during which the behaviour happens (Skinner, Rhymer et al. 2000), so I could collect reliable data of the length of the time each child spent in each of the stages of creative play in each of the play contexts.

Children's play sessions were video recorded, so their play behaviours were able to be looked at individually and coded later. All the coding was undertaken using behaviour coding software and each recorded video was reviewed several times as needed, in order to track all the children and note all the types of behaviour, no matter how fast they occurred and how short they were. The observations took place between March and June 2017, where the weather was partly cloudy to sunny and dry in all sessions.

The site and the play contexts

The study was conducted in Bilston Nursery in Loanhead, a small town located south of Edinburgh, Scotland. Both of the play contexts were held in the nursery's playground, where one was facilitated with manufactured play equipment and the other with loose materials. The nursery's playground is a rectangular space approximately 16 metres long by 5 metres wide, with access from the back of the nursery via a path (see Figure 1.1). It includes a fixed climbing frame in the centre with artificial grass on the ground underneath (see Figure 1.2). The play space has a hexagon-shaped sandpit as well as several plant boxes with flowers growing in them. The rest of the area is covered with tarmac. Two sides of the playground are wire-fenced, with the other two sides formed by the building. The building has two windows with wide windowsills and a door that is always locked.

The manufactured play context

The manufactured play context was facilitated with manufactured playing equipment: different types of bikes and toy cars; balls; sticky balls and a target sheet; musical instruments such as mini maracas; mini tambourines; a xylophone and drums; bucket stilts; toy telephones and cars; dolls with a buggy; a barbecue and picnic set including plates, cups and toy food; and a sandpit with buckets, spades and rakes (see Figure 1.3).

FIGURE 1.1 An overview of the nursery's outdoor setting
Source: the author

FIGURE 1.2 Timber climbing frame
Source: the author

Six play sessions were held in this play context. The sessions were of different lengths with different numbers of children taking part. A total of 105 minutes of observation took place. The minutes of observation multiplied by the number of children observed in each session makes a total of 1106 minutes (18 hours 26 minutes) of child creative play observations (see Table 1.2).

The loose parts play context
The loose parts play context was in the same playground; however, it was facilitated with junk elements and loose materials. These consisted of: plastic boxes; tyres; wooden slabs; wooden bricks; some cloth and carpet pieces; timber logs; a bucket full of small, different shaped pieces of wood; pipes; tubes; chalk; some vertically cut tubes with stands and a few balls; a sandpit with buckets, spades and rakes (see Figure 1.4).

FIGURE 1.3 Elements of the manufactured play context
Source: the author

TABLE 1.2 Manufactured play context implementation

Manufactured Play Context sessions	1	2	3	4	5	6	total
No. of Children	13	12	8	13	8	11	65
Duration	09:33	23:46	29:00	17:00	13:21	12:25	105
TOTAL	124	285	232	221	107	137	1106

There were also six different play sessions in this play context, again of different lengths and with different numbers of children taking part in each of the sessions. A total of 99 minutes of observation took place, with a total of 63 child observations, making an overall total of 1069 minutes (17 hours and 49 minutes) of child creative play observations (see Table 1.3).

FIGURE 1.4 Loose parts play context
Source: the author

TABLE 1.3 Loose parts play context implementation

Loose Parts Play Context sessions	1	2	3	4	5	6	total
No. of Children	11	14	9	9	11	9	63
Duration	29:00	19:00	7:30	13:00	12:30	18:00	99
TOTAL	319	266	68	117	137	162	1069

How creatively did children play in each context?

Figure 1.5 compares the duration of engagement for each of the three creativity factors introduced on p. 13, in the manufactured play context and the loose parts play context, across all of the sessions. As shown, flexibility was the most common creativity factor happening in children's play in both play contexts and it happened significantly more often in the loose parts play context compared to the manufactured play context. However, originality happened rarely in both play contexts, and, interestingly, there was not a major difference in original play among the two play

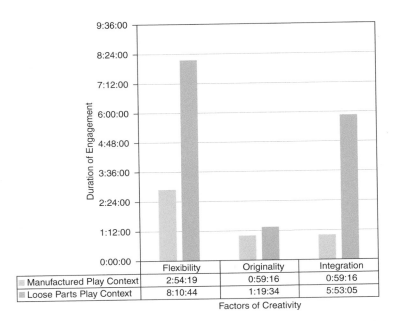

FIGURE 1.5 Flexibility, originality and integration in all sessions in the manufactured play context and the loose parts play context
Source: the author

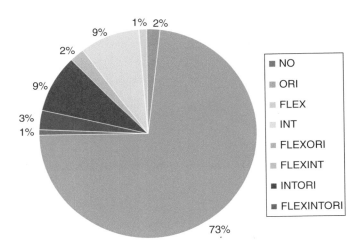

FIGURE 1.6 Children's engagement in the different stages of creative play in the manufactured play context
Source: the author

contexts. This shows that although the loose parts play context is more supportive of the two factors of integration and flexibility, when it comes to originality, both play contexts are fairly similar.

In order to analyse each of the play contexts in relation to their supportiveness of creative play behaviour, they were analysed separately according to each of the levels and stages of creativity. This helped to understand the level of creativity of which each play context was more supportive.

Creative play behaviour in the manufactured play context
Figure 1.6 shows that nearly 75% of the play in the manufactured play context included no level of creativity and only 2% engagement was at the highest level of creative play, "FLEXINTORI". The majority of the children's play, which, as the figure shows, fits into level D of the Creative Play Taxonomy, included activities such as riding the cars

and bikes, playing with musical instruments such as maracas, tambourines and xylophones as they were designed to be played, playing with balls by throwing them around, playing on the climbing frame and running around. The FLEXINTORI mainly happened with the wooden pieces, picnic toys or in the sandpit. This was, for example, when a child started filling the trucks with sand, moving them and making a "beep beep" sound, and finally pouring the sand to build a house. Another child started mixing different picnic pieces together to make a bowl of soup and some juice to invite others to the picnic. A third child was seen to play with a musical instrument, banging it on a bucket filled with wooden pieces to produce a new sound.

Only 13% of the play sessions were engaged in level D creativity and within this category, 9% was related to integration. The INT mainly happened when children were provided with picnic toys. Many of them started integrating different parts of the picnic equipment together and pretended they were having a real picnic. Also, some children played with balls and ball catchers. On a few occasions, some of the children were seen playing with the musical instruments while riding in the cars. FLEX play was noted when some children used the ball catchers as shields in play, or when they tried climbing the side of the climbing frame.

The remaining 12% showed children's engagement in level B creativity, and most of that was when integration and flexibility happened together. A lot of the play in FLEXINT occurred when the children combined the picnic toys with some pieces of wood. Some of them pretended that the pieces of wood were also foods, such as lettuce, and pretended to eat them, while others mixed different pieces with some of the toys in a bucket to make a pudding. Some children were engaged in FLEXINT play while they were playing with different trucks or spades and buckets in the sandpit.

FLEXORI was noted when a child was pretending that the ball catcher was her pudding and that she was eating from it, or when another child was spreading sand out of the sandpit.

Creative play behaviour in the loose parts play context

Figure 1.7 shows the percentage of children's engagement in each of the creative play stages in the loose parts play context across six sessions. Just over half of the play session included some level of creative play. In the 48% that the children were not engaged in any creative play, they were mainly playing on the climbing frame, sliding on the slide or running around the frame and playing tag.

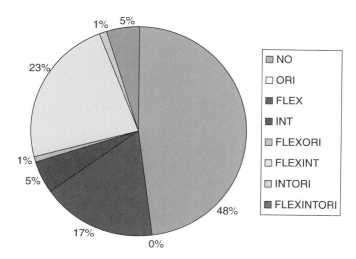

FIGURE 1.7 Children's engagement in the different stages of creative play in the loose parts play context
Source: the author

22% of children's engagement was level C, the majority of which was in FLEX, and a small portion was INT, with no engagement in stage ORI. Some of the examples of play that only included flexibility were when the children used the plastic and cardboard boxes to sit inside, or when they used the brooms to ride on or pretend they were flying around space as witches. Many of the children just enjoyed walking on the junk materials that other children had previously put next to each other and used it as a path.

The 5% engagement in INT included putting different parts of a loop together, or when some of the children put a carpet underneath the climbing frame and a cloth around them and sat on the carpet. These materials were used together, but they were all used as per their usual function.

The percentage of engagement in level B was 25%. Most engagement in level B was FLEXINT, which is the stage of creativity where integration and flexibility occur together.

There was a lot of building in this context. Children put together the plastic boxes, wooden slabs, bricks, carpet pieces and other loose materials and made many different structures. Some children sat on the plastic boxes holding the broom and started singing songs. Some of them also placed loose materials such as tyres or plastic boxes beside the climbing frame to make a more secure space under it and played there. The sandpit was also used in some of the sessions, and the children started making things with sand and wooden pieces. In some sessions, chalks were also provided, and some children used them to colour the small wooden pieces and mix them in a metal bucket with other materials such as strings or tiny stones and feathers that they found, making an interesting mixture.

An example of INTORI was when one of the children sat inside a boat that others had made, got some pieces of paper and a pencil and started making tickets to sell to the other children. Here, flexibility was not noted, because the paper in that context did not have a specific function and was there to be used to support children's play, as it did. But as only this child came up with the idea of using pencil and paper to make tickets, she was scored as original.

In this play context, 5% of children's play was engaged in the highest level of creative play, FLEXINTORI. One of the examples of FLEXINTORI play was when a child started making a ship by putting three plastic boxes beside each other with some wooden bricks inside it. He then started sailing the boat and others joined his ride.

Another child started making a very developed structure by putting together bricks and slabs with plastic boxes. He was also successful in making a small shed with slabs and plastic boxes. In one of the sessions, one child started individually putting the different loose materials on and around the slide and finally said he had made an aeroplane, which was unique. Another child started placing the wooden logs beside the climbing frame to close a path and make a den underneath the stage of the frame. In all of these examples, there was only one child making the structure, so it was scored as original; the materials were used differently to their usual function, so it was scored as flexible; and finally there were different elements integrated with each other, which scored as integration. Accordingly, they were classified as FLEXINTORI.

Comparison of girls' and boys' creative play behaviour percentages in the manufactured play context

To understand how the two play contexts influenced creative play among the different groups of children, I wanted to know whether the two contexts might influence the groups of boys and girls differently or whether they followed the same pattern. To test this, the boys' and girls' play behaviour in both contexts were initially scored separately. Among the 15 participants, nine were boys and six were girls. Different participants may have been absent during the 18 different sessions, but as the data is shown in percentages, the number of each gender does not influence the outcome.

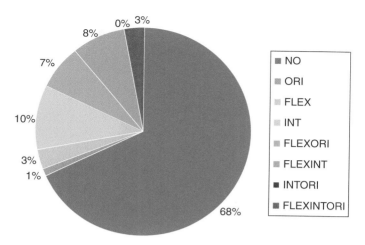

FIGURE 1.8 Girls in the manufactured play context, 24 observations across all sessions
Source: the author

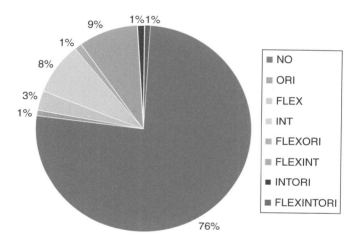

FIGURE 1.9 Boys in the manufactured play context, 43 observations across all sessions
Source: the author

Different genders' creative play in the manufactured play equipment context

In the manufactured play context, girls showed 8% more engagement in some level of creative play than boys (see Figures 1.8 and 1.9). Overall, they were seen to be able to engage in more original play behaviours than boys, as they had an average of 11% engagement in play that included originality, while boys only had 3% engagement in originality. For flexibility and integration, girls had 21% engagement in each, while boys had only 14% engagement in flexibility and 19% engagement in integration.

Different genders' creative play in the loose parts play context

In the loose parts play context, both genders had exactly the same percentage of engagement in some level of creative play (see Figures 1.10 and 1.11). However, the interesting finding was that, in this context, it was the boys who had more engagement in original play than the girls. While girls only had 2% engagement in FLEXINTORI and no other engagement in any stage of creative play that included originality, boys had 8% engagement in originality, 7% of it at the highest level of creative play. This showed that the loose parts play context was a suitable context for fostering originality as a factor of creative play among boys, which resulted in them being engaged more at the highest level of creativity than girls.

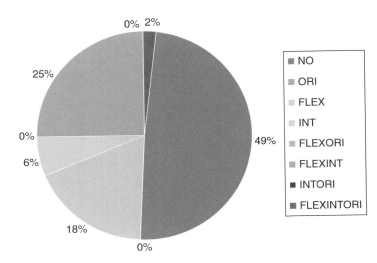

FIGURE 1.10 Girls in the loose parts play context, 17 observations across all sessions
Source: the author

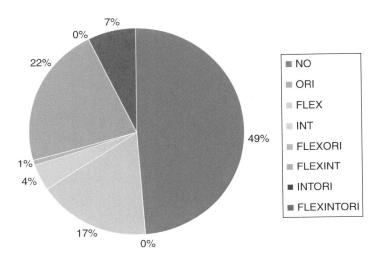

FIGURE 1.11 Boys in the loose parts play context, 46 observations across all sessions
Source: the author

How manufactured play equipment supports creativity

As the findings show, with all of the different play equipment provided over six different sessions, only 27% of play overall included some level of creativity. The available literature suggests that play contexts that include manufactured play equipment solely support physical play and, compared to adventure playgrounds that include loose materials, they are not very supportive of dramatic play (Hayward et al. 1974, Frost and Campbell 1985, Maxwell et al. 2008).

Among the different kinds of play equipment, the cars, the bikes and even the buggies did not result in any specific creative play behaviour among the children. Studying them in more detail showed that all three pieces of equipment were movable; however, their movement was based on a specific function and a certain way: they only moved on their wheels, and this was part of their initial function, which was transportation. In other words, they were not flexible enough in movement to give the children the opportunity to think of using them creatively. Their function, which was riding, was so obvious that they did not support any creative play behaviour.

There was a scooter in some sessions. This was the one piece of riding equipment that resulted in creative play on occasion, as a child sat on it to ride. This seemed to be because its design was not as straightforward as the bike or the car, which had seats and handlebars or a wheel, which showed the child where to sit and which way to move.

Another piece of equipment in this play context was the picnic playset. This had different parts such as different fruits, plates and cutlery. The elements were not interchangeable, so each part was predetermined. Also, it was clear what each of the elements were, so the design was not flexible. However, the set did have diversity of shapes and elements, so it gave the children the opportunity to integrate them in different ways. Also, as they were movable, this helped the children to put them together in any way they could imagine.

These findings are in line with the literature showing that manufactured play equipment is less supportive of creative play behaviour. This is because they have pre-existing functions that guide children on how to use them, and thus provide fewer constructive and dramatic play opportunities (Maxwell et al. 2008).

The sandpit and the two sets of play equipment within it, the buckets, spades and rakes and the toy cars and trucks, were sets of elements that did provide some level of creative play. A lot of it seemed to be related to the flexibility, formability, movability and looseness of the sand. The children used the trucks and other toys in the sandpit to move the sand from one side to another. They also used the spades and buckets to move and build shapes with the sand. These play behaviours not only included integration of the use of different elements, but on some occasions resulted in flexibility and even originality. Even though the trucks and the spades and rakes were not flexible on their own, they were equipment that supported children's play with sand.

In some of the sessions the teacher also brought some pieces of chalk and some cut pieces of wood. A lot of the scoring for some level of creative play in this context related to children's engagement with these elements. The chalk provided the opportunity to create an effect when integrated with a surface. As it was movable, it was also used in different parts of the space, integrating with different surfaces.

The cut pieces of wood were also supportive of creative play. They were movable as well as flexible, so they did not convey a very clear function. Thus, different children could think of using them in flexible ways. Some made different shapes and statues with them while others integrated them with other elements in the playground, such as the picnic toys, to develop new things (such as soups or puddings).

One of the manufactured play equipment pieces that resulted in some creative play behaviour was the ball catcher. Although designed to catch balls with its sticky surface, it seemed that, because of its simple shape, the ball catcher gave the children another chance to think of different ways to use it. It was also movable, so the children could take it around the playground. Some of them used it as a shield, and one child used it in an original way by pretending it was a pudding.

Children also seem to avoid becoming highly involved and attracted to very structured types of play equipment. In their book *The Impossible Playgrounds*, Norén-Björn et al. (1982) present the results of studies conducted in order to compare how different play contexts support children's play. Their findings showed that the children were not interested in using the manufactured play equipment in playgrounds when they had the option to engage with other play features, such as loose materials, which they preferred to use instead.

How loose parts support creativity

The findings of the study showed that the loose parts play context was far more supportive of creative play than the manufactured play context. Nearly all the loose elements had some characteristics in common, which seemed to support creative play. The elements did not have a specific function in the play setting, so they were flexible, which resulted in flexibility in play. For instance, a tyre did not suggest a specific use in the play context. It could be used to roll or sit on or could be laid next to the frame to make a den. Similarly to what has been found in the current study, Neill (2013) also suggests that loose parts encourage creativity due to their flexibility and because different groups of children can use them based on their own abilities and individual developments. He states, "When children have access to loose parts, it frees their creativity and imagination to change the world around them in infinite ways. The more flexible are the materials in their environment, the greater the level of creativity and inventiveness they express" (p.3).

All of the loose materials were movable by the children, so they could be placed in different positions and be used in flexible ways; they could integrate them with each other, which could even result in building original structures. Oncu (2015) also carried out a study exploring how loose parts can influence preschool children's divergent thinking abilities, and suggests that these materials encourage flexibility among children as they could be used in many different ways. These materials allow children to play with them using their own interpretations; thus, instead of playing in structured play settings with designed play equipment and certain play rules, the children can decide what the object could be and how it could be used (see also Szekely 2015).

The loose elements had diversity of material and shape, which gave the children the opportunity to play with them in different ways. They could be integrated together based on their different shapes: for instance, the wooden blocks could fit well into the plastic boxes, and through this integration new structures were built. A long wooden slab placed on the sides of some plastic boxes laid on top of each other resulted in a very original aeroplane. According to Nicholson, who developed the theory of loose parts (Nicholson 1972), the level of creativity and inventiveness and the chance to discover are related to the number and type of elements in the environment. Similarly, in my research I found that, when more elements that could be put together are available, children can engage in more integration, resulting in more creativity among them.

The findings show that the loose parts play context was more supportive of creative play overall, and it was more supportive when it came to the highest level of creativity. These findings show that high levels of flexibility, movability and some level of diversity in shape among play elements could be supportive of creative play taking place.

While some research has looked at the relationship between loose parts and children's play behaviour (Maxwell, Mitchell et al. 2008, Sutton 2011), other research has mainly focused on the effects of the use of loose parts on children's creativity. Oncu (2015) promotes the use of loose materials for children's play activities as well as artwork, as he believes it can result in creative thinking and that the children are encouraged to engage in innovative thinking processes when deciding how to use the materials. Szekely (2015) has also found that providing loose materials in outdoor settings results in more creative play as well as fostering artistic abilities among children. He suggests moving from conventional playgrounds, including climbing frames, to adventure playgrounds where children can "interact freely" and have the opportunity to "choose for themselves what and how to play" (Szekely 2015).

Marshall (2011) believes that loose parts have a very positive impact on creative play as well as meeting educational goals. However, similar to what was found in this study, some schools do not use such materials for play purposes (Wardle 2000). There are four main reasons for this:

1) some adults believe there is a "mess" left after the use of these materials (Hurwitz 1999, Nicolson and Shipstead 2002);
2) using loose materials in the play setting shows a lack of principles (Kylin 2003);
3) in free play, children often lack teamwork (Kylin 2003);
4) some adults believe that large play structures are more suitable and satisfying for children's play (Armitage 2005, Knowles-Yánez 2005).

It is clear by now, from both the literature and my own research, how crucial play is for children and the important role it has in nurturing their creative thinking. However, my work emphasises the fact that not all play settings provide the same level of supportiveness in terms of creative play. Many environmental designers and child-carers think of the most straightforward ways of designing and providing play contexts for children by installing structured and manufactured play equipment. Although these do provide play opportunities for children, they are not the best option for nurturing creativity. While some researchers have already found that loose materials encourage certain types of play related to creativity, there has been no study examining all possibilities for creative play in relation to different play contexts. Thus, my study looked in detail at two different play contexts and the extent to which they supported each of the possible creative play behaviours. The findings could give a clear understanding to designers and carers of why certain play contexts are more supportive of creative play, and what design parameters should be considered when choosing play equipment for children to encourage creative thinking among them.

This study has shown that play spaces supplied with loose parts are supportive environments for all stages of creative play and encourage the highest level of creativity among children, while manufactured play equipment is not found to be very supportive of children's creative play behaviour overall. When providing play materials for children, what must be taken into account is the amount of flexibility, originality and number of integration options that the elements may provide for play. Based on the findings of this study, overall flexibility occurred more often than integration and integration happened more often than originality in both play contexts, so originality is a harder factor to reach in play. However, the take away message from this study is that flexibility and integration happen far more often with loose parts and that is what makes the main difference between the two contexts.

An interesting contribution to knowledge by this study is the different types of creative play behaviour between girls and boys. I found that girls can be more creative than boys when playing with manufactured play equipment. They had 7% more engagement in originality and 7% more engagement in integration than boys did with these play elements. However, when it comes to loose parts play contexts the results showed the opposite. Here, although both girls and boys were engaged in the same percentage of some level of creative play overall, when it came to the highest level of creative play, boys were 5% more engaged than girls. Boys' percentage of engagement in originality was also 6% higher than girls in the loose parts play context. So, on the one hand, these findings show that although manufactured play contexts are not very supportive to creative play overall, girls can come up with more creative play with them than boys. On the other hand, loose parts not only support creative play among all children, but boys' original thinking abilities are triggered even more with these elements.

Looking in detail at the elements which provided more creativity in children's play in both contexts revealed some guidance as to what design specifications are necessary in order to provide creative thinking opportunities to children. Play elements that are flexible give the children the chance to think of different ways of playing with them. They can use their imagination to use them in unexpected ways. Elements which have clear functions and use guides do not provide such opportunities. Changeability and movability are other specifications that encourage creative play behaviours among children; when elements are able to move in various ways, they can be integrated with other elements, they can be used in different ways and even result in original ways of playing with them. Mouldability of materials has the same result, as children can form them into what they think of, not limited to a certain way but in any original way that they can come up with. Another design specification that could result in creative play behaviour is to provide both diverse play elements and elements that express diversity in different ways; diversity gives children the opportunity to integrate different elements together in different ways, and if they are well designed, they could even result in flexible and original behaviours by children.

Overall, manufactured play contexts have fewer of these design specifications, so, as the findings of this study show, children spent little of their time in creative play. These contexts are not found to be very supportive of children's creative play behaviour overall, while in loose parts play contexts, most of the materials are flexible, movable, mouldable and changeable, and diverse in different ways. According to the findings of this study, children spent over half of their play session in some level of creative play, which shows these play settings are supportive environments for creative play and can even encourage the highest level of creativity among children, more effectively than manufactured play equipment.

REFERENCES

Allen of Hurtwood , Lady (1968). *Planning for Play*. Cambridge, MA: MIT Press.

Amabile, T. M. (1988). A model of creativity and innovation in organizations. *Research in Organizational Behavior* **10**(1): 123–167.

Amabile, T. M. (1996a). *Creativity in Context: Update to the Social Psychology of Creativity*. New York, London: Westview Press.

Amabile, T. (1996b). *Creativity and Innovation in Organizations* **(Vol. 5)**. Boston: Harvard Business School.

Armitage, M. (2005). The influence of school architecture and design on the outdoor play experience within the primary school. *Paedagogica Historica* **41**(4–5): 535–553.

Barbot, B., et al. (2011). Assessing creativity in the classroom. *The Open Education Journal* **4**(1): 58–66.

Barbot, B., et al. (2016). The generality-specificity of creativity: Exploring the structure of creative potential with EPoC. *Learning and Individual Differences* **52**: 178–187.

Bechtel, R. B. and J. Zeisel (1987). Observation: The world under a glass. In R. Bechtel, R. Marans and W. Michelson (Eds), *Methods in Environmental and Behavioral Research*, pp. 11–40. New York: Van Nostrand Reinhold.

Berlin, N., et al. (2016). An exploratory study of creativity, personality and schooling achievement. *Education Economics* **24**(5): 536–556.

Besançon, M., et al. (2013). Creative giftedness and educational opportunities. *Educational and Child Psychology* **30**(2): 79–88.

Bryman, A. (2015). *Social Research Methods*. Oxford: Oxford University Press.

Burdette, H. L. and R. C. Whitaker (2005). Resurrecting free play in young children: Looking beyond fitness and fatness to attention, affiliation, and affect. *Archives of Pediatrics and Adolescent Medicine* **159**(1): 46–50.

Busse, T. V., et al. (1972). Testing conditions and the measurement preschool children of creative abilities in lower-class. *Multivariate Behavioral Research* **7**(3): 287–298.

Clements, R. (2004). An investigation of the status of outdoor play. *Contemporary Issues in Early Childhood* **5**(1): 68–80.

Coulter, K. A. (2004). Classroom structure as an environmental effect on creative production of College students. *Honors Projects*. Paper 26. http://digitalcommons.iwu.edu/psych_honproj/26 (accessed 1 July 2020).

Fein, G. G. (1987). Pretend play: Creativity and consciousness. In D. Gorlitz and J. Wohlwill (Eds), *Curiosity, Imagination, and Play*, pp. 281–304. Hillsdale, NJ: Lawrence Erlbaum Associates.

Feist, G. J. and M. A. Runco (1993). Trends in the creativity literature: An analysis of research in the *Journal of Creative Behavior* (1967–1989). *Creativity Research Journal* **6**(3): 271–283.

Frost, J. and S. Campbell (1985). Equipment choices of primary-age children on conventional and creative playgrounds. In J. L. Frost and S. Sunderlin (Eds), *When Children Play: Proceedings of the International Conference on Play and Play Environments*, pp. 89–92. Wheaton, MD: Association for Childhood Education International.

Ginsburg, K. R. (2007). The importance of play in promoting healthy child development and maintaining strong parent-child bonds. *Pediatrics* **119**(1): 182–191.

Goddard, W. and S. Melville (2004). *Research Methodology: An Introduction*. Lansdowne: Juta and Company Ltd.

Gray, P. (2011). The decline of play and the rise of psychopathology in children and adolescents. *American Journal of Play* **3**(4): 443–463.

Groves, L. and H. McNish (2011). Natural Play: Making a Difference to Children's Learning and Wellbeing. Edinburgh: Forestry Commission Scotland.

Guilford, J. P. (1950). Creativity. *American Psychologist* **5**: 444–454.

Hayward, D. G., et al. (1974). Children's play and urban playground environments: A comparison of traditional, contemporary, and adventure playground types. *Environment and Behavior* **6**(2): 131–168.

Hofferth, S. L. (2009). Changes in American children's time – 1997 to 2003. *Electronic International Journal of Time Use Research* **6**(1): 26–47.

Hughes, B. (2013). *Evolutionary Playwork*. Abingdon: Routledge.

Hurwitz, S. (1999). The adventure outside your classroom door. *Child Care Information Exchange* **127**: 55–57.

Isenberg, J. P. and N. Quisenberry (2002). A position paper of the Association for Childhood Education International PLAY: Essential for all children. *Childhood Education* **79**(1): 33–39.

Kandler, C., R. Riemann, A. Angleitner, F. M. Spinath, P. Borkenau, and L. Penke (2016). The nature of creativity: The roles of genetic factors, personality traits, cognitive abilities, and environmental sources. *Journal of Personality and Social Psychology* **111**(2): 230–249.

Kidner, C. (2013). *Curriculum for Excellence*. Edinburgh: Scottish Parliament.

Kim, K. H. and D. L. Zabelina (2011). Mentors. In M. A. Runco and S. R. Pritzker (Eds), *Encyclopedia of Creativity* (2nd edn), pp. 102–106. Oxford: Elsevier.

Kim, K. H. (2006a). Can we trust creativity tests? A review of the Torrance Tests of Creative Thinking (TTCT). *Creativity Research Journal* **18**(1): 3–14.

Kim, K. H. (2006b). Is creativity unidimensional or multidimensional? Analyses of the Torrance Tests of Creative Thinking. *Creativity Research Journal* **18**(3): 251–259.

Kirkby, M. (1989). Nature as refuge in children's environments. *Children's Environments Quarterly* **6**(1): 7–12.

Knowles-Yánez, K. L. (2005). Children's participation in planning processes. *Journal of Planning Literature* **20**(1): 3–14.

Kopp, T. A. (2010). Learning Through Play. Master's Dissertation, University of Wisconsin-Platteville.

Kozlovsky, R. (2008). *Adventure Playgrounds and Postwar Reconstruction*. New Brunswick, NJ: Rutgers University Press.

Krippner, S. (1999). Dreams and creativity. *Encyclopedia of Creativity* **1**: 597–606.

Kylin, M. (2003). Children's dens. *Children, Youth and Environments* **13**(1): 30–55.

Lansdown, R. (1996). *Children in Hospital: A Guide for Family and Carers*. Oxford: Oxford University Press.

Lester, S. and W. Russell (2008). *Play for a Change*. London: National Children's Bureau.

Lubart, T. (1994). *Creativity*. San Diego, CA: Elsevier.

Lubart, T. I., et al. (2011). Assessing creativity in the classroom. *Open Education Journal* **4**(1): 58–66.

Lubart, T., M. Besançon and B. Barbot (2011). *Evaluation du Potentiel Créatif (EPoC)*. Paris: HOGREFE.

Lubart, T., et al. (2013). Creative potential and its measurement. *International Journal for Talent Development and Creativity* **1**: 41–51.

Lubart, T. I. and C. Mouchiroud (2003). Creativity: A source of difficulty in problem solving. In J. E. Davidson and R. J. Sternberg (Eds), *The Psychology of Problem Solving*, pp. 127–148. Cambridge: Cambridge University Press.

Lubart, T. I. and R. J. Sternberg (1995). An investment approach to creativity: Theory and data. In S. M. Smith, T. B. Ward and R. A. Finke (Eds), *The Creative Cognition Approach*, pp. 269–302. Cambridge: MIT Press.

Manosevttz, M., et al. (1977). Imaginary companions in young children: Relationships with intelligence, creativity and waiting ability. *Journal of Child Psychology and Psychiatry* **18**(1): 73–78.

Marshall, D. (2011). *Boosting Creative Play Through Loose Parts*. Altarum Institute: Health Policy Forum. Retrieved from http://altarum.org/formu/post/boosting-creative-play-through-loose-parts (5 Nov. 2012).

Maxwell, L. E., et al. (2008). Effects of play equipment and loose parts on preschool children's outdoor play behavior: An observational study and design intervention. *Children, Youth and Environments* **18**(2): 36–63.

Mayesky, M. (2014). *Creative Activities and Curriculum for Young Children*. Stamford: Cengage Learning.

McKellar, P. (1957). *Imagination and Thinking: A Psychological Analysis*. London: Basic Books.

Moore, R. (1986). *Children's Domain: Play and Play Space in Child Development*. London: Croom Helm.

Moore, R. C. and H. H. Wong (1997). *Natural Learning: The Life of an Environmental Schoolyard: Creating Environments for Rediscovering Nature's Way of Teaching*. Berkeley, CA: MIG Communications.

Mottweiler, C. M. and M. Taylor (2014). Elaborated role play and creativity in preschool age children. *Psychology of Aesthetics, Creativity, and the Arts* **8**(3): 277–286.

Neill, P. (2013). Open-ended materials belong outside too! *High Scope* **27**(2): 1–8.

Neuman, W. L. (2004). *Basics of Social Research: Qualitative and Quantitative Approaches*. Boston: Pearson Education.

Nicholson, S. (1972). The Theory of Loose Parts: An important principle for design methodology. *Studies in Design Education, Craft and Technology* **4**(2): 5–14.

Nicolson, S. and S. Shipstead (2002). *Through the Looking Glass*. Columbus, OH: Merrill Prentice Hall.

Norén-Björn, E. (1982). *The Impossible Playground: A Trilogy of a Play*. Human Kinetics: Champaign, IL.

Oncu, E. C. (2015). Preschoolers' usage of unstructured materials as play materials divergently. *Education Journal* **4**(1): 9–14.

Owens, T. J. and S. L. Hofferth (2001). *Children at the Millennium: Where Have We Come From? Where Are We Going?* Amsterdam: JAI.

Palmer, S. (2008). *Detoxing Childhood: What Parents Need to Know to Raise Happy, Successful Children*. London: Hachette UK.

Piaget, J. (1962). *Play, Dreams and Imitation in Children*. New York: W. W. Norton and Co.

Reisman, F. K., et al. (1981). Performance on Torrance's "Thinking Creatively in Action and Movement" as a predictor of cognitive development of young children. *Creative Child and Adult Quarterly* **6**(4): 205–209.

Runco, M. A. (2004). Creativity. *Annual Review of Psychology* **55**: 657–687.

Runco, M. A. and G. J. Jaeger (2012). The standard definition of creativity. *Creativity Research Journal* **24**(1): 92–96.

Russ, S. W. (1996). Development of creative processes in children. *New Directions for Child and Adolescent Development* **1996**(72): 31–42.

Russ, S. W. (2004). *Play in Child Development and Psychotherapy: Toward Empirically Supported Practice*. New Jersey, London: Lawrence Erlbaum Associates.

Russ, S. W. and A. Grossman-McKee (1990). Affective expression in children's fantasy play, primary process thinking on the Rorschach, and divergent thinking. *Journal of Personality Assessment* **54**(3–4): 756–771.

Simonton, D. K. (2003). Creative cultures, nations, and civilizations. In P. B. Paulus and B. A. Nijstad (Eds), *Group Creativity: Innovation through Collaboration*, pp. 304–325. Oxford: Oxford University Press.

Skinner, C. H., K. N. Rhymer and E. C. McDaniel (2000). Naturalistic direct observation in educational settings. In E. S. Shapiro and T. R. Kratochwill (Eds), *The Guilford School Practitioner Series: Conducting School-based Assessments of Child and Adolescent Behavior*, pp. 21–54. New York: The Guilford Press.

Sternberg, R. J. and T. I. Lubart (1991). An investment theory of creativity and its development. *Human Development* **34**(1): 1–31.

Sternberg, R. J. and T. I. Lubart (1992). Buy low and sell high: An investment approach to creativity. *Current Directions in Psychological Science* **1**(1): 1–5.

Sternberg, R. J. and T. I. Lubart (1996). Investing in creativity. *American Psychologist* **51**(7): 677–688.

Sternberg, R. J. and T. I. Lubart (1999). The concept of creativity: Prospects and paradigms. *Handbook of Creativity* **1**: 3–15.

Stokols, D., et al. (2002). Qualities of work environments that promote perceived support for creativity. *Creativity Research Journal* **14**(2): 137–147.

Sutton, M. J. (2011). In the hand and mind: The intersection of loose parts and imagination in evocative settings for young children. *Children, Youth and Environments* **21**(2): 408–424.

Szekely, I. (2015). Playground innovations and art teaching. *Art Education* **68**(1): 37–42.

Titman, W. (1994). *Special Places; Special People: The Hidden Curriculum of School Grounds*. Surrey: ERIC.

Torrance, E. P. (1966). *The Torrance Tests of Creative Thinking: Norms – Technical Manual Research Edition: Verbal Tests, Forms A and B – Figural Tests, Forms A and B*. Princeton: Personnel Press.

Torrance, E. P. (1968). *Torrance Tests of Creative Thinking*. Princeton: Personnel Press.

Torrance, E. P. (1998). *Torrance Tests of Creative Thinking: Norms – Technical Manual: Figural (streamlined) Forms A and B*. Bensenville: Scholastic Testing Service.

Treffinger, D. J., et al. (2002). *Assessing Creativity: A Guide for Educators*. Storrs: University of Connecticut, National Research Center on the Gifted and Talented.

UNICEF (2001). Early Childhood Development – The key to a full and productive life. https://docplayer.net/15966001-Early-childhood-development-the-key-to-a-full-and-productive-life.html (accessed 24 April 2020).

Vygotsky, L. S. (1978). *Mind in Society: The Development of Higher Mental Process*. Cambridge, MA: Harvard University Press.

Ward, W. C. (1968). Creativity in young children. *Child Development* **39**(3): 737–754.

Wardle, F. (2000). Supporting constructive play in the wild. *Child Care Information Exchange* **5**: 26–29.

Wilson, R. (2012). *Nature and Young Children: Encouraging Creative Play and Learning in Natural Environments*. Abingdon: Routledge.

Zachopoulou, E., et al. (2009). Evaluation of children's creativity: Psychometric properties of Torrance's "Thinking Creatively in Action and Movement". *Early Child Development and Care* **179**(3): 317–328.

2

NO TIME FOR PLAY: CHILDREN'S DAILY ACTIVITIES DURING SUMMER HOLIDAYS IN THE BEIJING CENTRAL AREA

Pai Tang and Helen Woolley

INTRODUCTION

It is now 40 years since the Chinese economic reform of 1979, which has had a profound influence on the living conditions of urban families in China. In addition, since 1980, the introduction of the one-child policy has had great significance for individuals, families and communities in urban areas. These dramatic economic and social transformations mean that the childhood experience of urban Chinese children is distinctive and different, even unique, compared to many other parts of the world. Rapid urban development in some parts of the world, including the Netherlands, Norway, Japan and the UK, have resulted in children's experience of outdoor environments changing as a result of influences such as increased traffic and parental fears (Karsten, 2005; Kinoshita, 2009; Skår and Krogh, 2009; Woolley and Griffin, 2015). However, is this the same in the Chinese context? Or what are the dominant influences shaping Chinese children's daily routines and their use of outdoor environments for play?

The worldwide decline of children's outdoor play

Across many western countries, the phenomenon of children's outdoor play has been reported to have declined, with contemporary children spending less time playing outdoors compared with their parents' or grandparents' childhoods (Kimbro, Brooks-Gunn and McLanahan, 2011). The home range of children and their degree of independent mobility in outdoor environments is also shrinking (Kyttä, 2004; Fyhri and Hjorthol, 2009; Kyttä *et al.*, 2015; Woolley and Griffin, 2015). Reasons for these reductions are discussed in different social contexts, including increasing time spent in front of TV or computer screens in the USA (Kimbro and Ariela, 2011); parental concerns about neighbourhood safety (Kimbro and Ariela, 2011; Hand *et al.*, 2018); increasing car ownership, working parents and technology which is easy to access in New Zealand (Witten *et al.*, 2013); and the changing affordances of the outdoor environment in Finland and Belarus (Kyttä, 2002; Kyttä, 2004). However, the understanding of children's outdoor play is not evenly distributed across the world.

China has 90 million children aged 6 to 11 (UNICEF 2016). Children's outdoor play conditions and experiences have only been explored and recorded to a small extent. This is because the publications on the subject are written in Chinese and only a few papers are available to the international community. One piece of research, conducted in a *hutong* community (the traditional urban structure of courtyards – *sihe* – and alleys) in Beijing to understand the environmental and spatial needs of children, revealed the spaces that were identified as children's favourites for outdoor play in the high-density urban environments (Wang *et al.*, 2012). This research provides some insights into children's outdoor play behaviour in the central historical protected area in Beijing. However, more specific information about children's outdoor play, such as their daily use of outdoor environments, their daily routines and what they think and feel about their outdoor play is still unknown. In addition, there is no published evidence for the factors influencing children's use of outdoor environments in the current Chinese social context. No published research has given any insight into children's experiences of outdoor environments in China for contemporary children and in particular for changes over the generations. It is thus important to provide some additional understanding of the context of Chinese urban children's lives and especially the aspect which is most commonly discussed: educational pressure. In the next section we introduce the history of the importance of educational achievement and how this has influenced the current situation, with special reference to primary school children aged 6–12 years.

The historic and current academic context in China

The emphasis on academic achievement is deeply rooted in Chinese culture, where there is a strong link between educational success, financial success and social status (Quach *et al.*, 2013). This tradition stemming from the 'imperial exam system', which started in the 600s and continued for around 1300 years, ended in the 1910s. This exam system was the dominant method for selecting government officials during the long period of the feudal monarchy (Li and Li, 2010). Thus, for educated intellectuals, the desire to enter into the governing class by passing the examination and achieving top grades among all the competing candidates was the goal. To achieve this, they were educated and prepared for the examinations from a young age. This traditional education system was gradually transformed by borrowing educational concepts from western countries, starting after the Opium War in 1840 (Ruth, 1987). Subsequently, with the establishment of the republic in the 1910s, the 'imperial exam system' was abolished. Since then the apparent relationship between educational success, financial success and the improvement of social status has changed to some extent. However, the longstanding social value connected with academic achievement is still a very strong influence in Chinese culture.

Over the last 100 years, Chinese society has undergone dramatic transformations, and this also applies to the educational system. After many different models were tried, the university entrance examination system was resumed in 1978 and continues today. The ongoing importance of higher education can be summarised as: 'the university entrance exam, like a baton or magic spell relates all kinds of study closely to it' (Li and Li, 2010). The national university entrance examination takes place once a year at the national level. In order to be competitive in this annual exam, having received a better education in principal schools is crucial for the vast number of university candidates. Principal schools are defined by their better transition rate performance, which means that there is a higher percentage of students getting a university or top university admission from these than from other schools. A good education in a principal middle school or even a principal elementary school is the guarantee of admission to a top university. Each step in this lengthy process is critically important. Failure at any of these steps is unacceptable for Chinese urban families who usually have only one child. So, to some extent, the 'one child policy' has increased the academic pressure on urban Chinese children's lives.

The 'one-child policy' was implemented in 1979 and ended in 2016 with an adjustment to a new 'two children policy'. During the 30 years of the one-child policy, Chinese parents were anxious to prevent their children from, as a popular saying goes, 'losing at the starting line' (Hu, Kong and Roberts, 2014). For the parents, the one child carries all the hope of their families on their shoulders (Nakra, 2012). This desire for success is not only the children's aspiration but also, and to a larger extent, that of the whole family who wish to increase their standard of living. Becoming the focus and hope of the whole family means that the only child faces unprecedented pressure.

Taken together, these cultural, political and social factors create a Chinese social environment that has driven parents and children to prioritise academic performance in opposition to the promotion of children's outdoor play.

After-school classes in Chinese cities

The academic pressure on Chinese children is increased by the phenomenon whereby urban children are kept busy with various after-school classes. In addition to the emphasis on academic achievement, discussed above, the prevalent 'Quality Education' system, while reducing the academic pressure in mainstream schools, forces children to study more in after-school classes. The 'Quality Education' system became the dominant concept of elementary education implemented in Chinese cities from 1997. Before that, the 'Examination-Oriented Education', was criticised because of its excessive emphasis on theoretical knowledge (Li and Li, 2010). To achieve quality education, primary schools and secondary schools were ordered by the government to reduce teaching hours, to remove grade ranking lists and to increase art and physical education classes. However, the paradox is that enrolment in a higher school still depended on the grade ranking, art talents and other outside school awards obtained by children. Therefore, the reduction in school teaching hours meant that to maintain a competitive advantage over other students, after-school classes, which help to improve grades, talent and performances, are the best choice.

After-school classes take place both during school term times and the summer holidays, so that some children attend a summer school followed by after school classes.

The various after-school classes and their influence on children's daily lives are largely unknown to western researchers. In Chinese research, however, the phenomenon is so familiar that it is not usually discussed: it is taken for granted, as a social norm. The only recent research on after-school classes was conducted in Taiwan among senior high school students, and it identified that the so-called 'cram schools' help to improve students' exam scores at the cost of their leisure time (Jheng, 2013). In mainland China, especially the capital city Beijing, primary school children go to all kinds of after-school classes in order to increase their academic performances, which is different from the situation in Taiwan. However, the time the children spend on these after-school classes, and the extent to which these academic pressures influence Chinese children's lives are, surprisingly, still under-researched.

Therefore, the aim of the research presented in this chapter is to explore children's daily summer holiday routines in the central area of Beijing, in particular to understand the time children spend on learning compared with playing in outdoor environments. This will help develop an understanding of the relationship between children's academic pressure and their outdoor play.

METHODOLOGY

Target group

The target age group for the research was primary school children aged from 6 to 12, living in the central area (within the second ring-road) in Beijing. This is the area immediately to the north of the Forbidden City. One reason for choosing children in this age range is that they already possess basic reading and writing skills and can respond to the researcher's requests better than younger children. Another reason is that the 'university entrance examination' academic pressure is more for older children. So, compared with the older age groups at high school, primary school children are considered to encounter less academic pressure. That is to say: primary school children can be presumed to spend more time playing instead of studying and learning.

Data collection methods, ethics and practical issues

Daily activity logs were the main data collection method for recording children's daily routines and the length of time they spend on each activity. The daily activity logs act in a way similar to a questionnaire, the children being asked to record their activities in a table. This provides more information than a questionnaire might if asking general questions about daily activities. Children were asked to record in the log the activities they did for every hour over one sample day in the common school summer holiday; more precisely, children wrote down what they had done in the day before. They were asked to record what activity they did, who accompanied them and their perceptions of the activity.

The daily logs were used to provide information about the children's daily routines. In order to obtain a deeper understanding of the reason for these activities, semi-structured interviews were also conducted with the children who answered the daily activity logs and some of their parents who volunteered to share their opinions. Each interview was conducted one-to-one with the child or parent. During the semi-structured interviews with children they were given the opportunity to talk about their daily lives, their feelings and thoughts. Children were asked for their point of view, their feelings about outdoor play time and academic pressure; as far as we know, this is the first time that Chinese children have been invited to talk about these experiences. During the interviews with parents they also shared their concerns about their children's education and long-term development as well as their thoughts about current social issues. By using both daily activity logs and semi-structured interviews together, increased reliability of the data collected in this real-world setting was ensured.

To do any research on or with children requires ethical approval which was given by the authors' departmental committee. As the field research was conducted during the school summer holiday, it was not possible to obtain help from primary schools, so a different mechanism for gaining access to children was needed. After seeking help from the Xicheng District Committee, the field research proposal was approved by the local government. Then, with the help from the District Committee, the field researcher was introduced to several residential communities. Finally, the researcher was introduced to and guided by the staff working in the residential communities so that the data collection could begin. Fifty-eight children completed the logs and a further 100 other children took part in interviews. Fifteen parents of the interviewed children were also interviewed.

The residential communities are the primary department of the Chinese government system, which take charge of the many different neighbourhood affairs. Being introduced to the local people by the staff working in the residential communities had two advantages. First, the researcher was more easily accepted by the local residents and second, the safety of the researcher was guaranteed.

SOCIAL-SPATIAL BACKGROUNDS OF THE CASE STUDY SITE

After solving the ethical and practical problems, the formal data collection was conducted in the Shichahai Subdistrict and the Xinjiekou Sub-district, in Xicheng District (Figure 2.1). Within the premises of the second ring-road, this area adjoins the Forbidden City, which is the geographic centre of Beijing. Living in this area, the children are thus considered to live in the central area of Beijing City. The lifestyles of these children do not represent the typical childhood lifestyle within greater Beijing. Despite this, the research provides a new and significant perspective for beginning an understanding of the childhood experience of daily life in Beijing.

The case study site is a historically protected district within the Beijing old city area. It consists of several connected alleys and is occupied by courtyard houses (*siheyuan*), which is what makes it a *hutong*, and it occupies around 10 hectares in area with more than 30,000 registered residences. Because of the Historical Area Protection Policy, the narrow alleys and old courtyard houses maintain their historic appearance (Figure 2.2). However, these low-rise courtyard houses, designed and built hundreds of years ago, are deficient in infrastructure facilities, including the

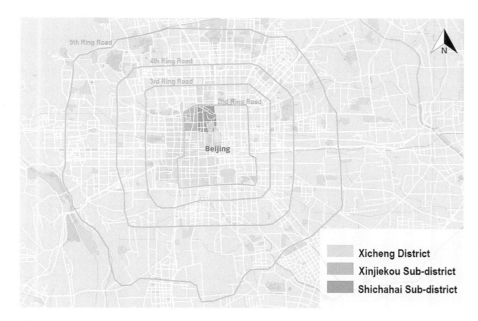

FIGURE 2.1 Location of the case study site
Source: Pai Tang

FIGURE 2.2 A view over the case study site showing the character of the housing
Source: Pai Tang

sewage system. The lives of people there are not that convenient and comfortable. Many of the local people who can afford higher-priced houses in newly built residential areas have already moved out. Therefore, the residents still living there are primarily older people who have spent nearly all of their lifetime here (which means that they have a strong sense of place attachment). Other residents are from the younger generations who work in the area.

Within this area, there is one principal primary school (for children aged 6 to 12) and four principal middle schools (for teenagers aged 13 to 16), which is far more than the average amount of high-level educational provision found in other sub-districts of Beijing. This abundance of good quality schooling has resulted in some families choosing to stay here, against the trend of families moving out of this central area.

FINDINGS

Children's daily activities in the summer holidays

For a primary school child living in Beijing, the school summer holiday comprises the months of July and August each year. The weather at this time is usually hot and humid. For the children, it can be boring and dull. Most children usually wake up before 8 am, then go to holiday school classes or stay at home for the whole day. In the evening, after having dinner with their parents, some of the children might play outside for a little while, accompanied by adults, either parents or grandparents, depending on who is available. The children then return home, have a shower and go to bed. The next day will be another similar day, repeating all these activities, until the two months' summer holiday ends.

Some of the children attended summer school, some attended after-school classes and some attended both summer school and after-school classes during the summer holidays. The children reported many activities in their logs, sometimes using different names for similar activities, which is not uncommon when children explain about their play and activities. These could be classified into ten categories, based on the content of the activity and the location in which each activity took place. The ten activity types are: learning at home; playing at home; resting at

TABLE 2.1 Children's daily activities

Category	Detail activities
learning at home	doing homework
	reading books
	practising musical instruments
playing at home	playing computer games
	playing on an I-pad
	playing on a smartphone
	playing with toys
	watching TV
resting at home	having a nap
	taking shower
household chore	cooking
	cleaning
	washing
outdoor free play	walking in park/plaza/courtyard/garden
	running in park/plaza/courtyard/garden
	cycling in park/plaza/courtyard/garden
playing in an indoor playground	playground in supermarket
	playground in shopping mall
doing sports in the gym	swimming
	fencing
after school classes	summer schools
	English course
	math course
	musical instrument course
	painting course
wake up and wash up	
time spent on travel	going to summer school
	going home
	going to some other place

home; doing household chores; outdoor free play; playing in an indoor playground; doing sports in the gym; going to after school classes; waking up and having a wash; and the time spent on travel (Table 2.1).

Different from the play activity categories proposed and used by other researchers, these categories are not limited to children's play activities but include all types of activities undertaken during their daily lives. These broader activity categories are generated from the children's self-reported activity logs which reflect their real life.

After-school classes and home learning take up most of the time
Among all the participant children, 47% go to after-school classes during the summer holiday. The average time spent on all kinds of after-school classes is 7 hours per day, every day. There are 60% of the children who also spend time studying at home, with an average duration of 3 hours and 24 minutes per day. The average waking time of these children is 13 hours and 40 minutes. Therefore, the 7 hours' class time and the 3 hours' home learning together take up almost all of the available daytime for those who both attend classes and have to study at home. From this perspective, it could be concluded that education and learning play the most significant role in children's lives, even during the summer holiday.

Some of the after-school classes also provide the summer schools in the summer holidays by holding intensive courses or training. In these summer schools, just like common mainstream schools, there is a timetabled curriculum for the whole of each day. Curriculum content includes English, art and advice about school homework. The summer schools play an important role in improving children's academic performance by giving additional training while also providing summer child-care for parents. Many working parents have no time to be with their children during the daytime in the school holiday and the summer schools, which provide well-arranged courses and professional teachers, seem to the parents to be the obvious best choice for their child. According to the father of an 8-year-old girl, the reason for sending her to the summer schools is that:

> Recently, the school course my daughter takes is really difficult for her age. What they are learning now in grade 2 is the same knowledge we learned when we were in grade 5. As a result, they need more time to understand this higher-level knowledge. So we sent her to the summer school in the summer holidays. On the one hand, she can spend more time on study, on the other hand, we don't have enough time to look after her.
>
> (Father of an 8-year-old girl)

Different from the all-day summer schools with a full curriculum, the after-school classes focus on the intensive training of a specific skill during a 40 or 50-minute lesson. These after-school classes include but are not limited to playing musical instruments, painting, sports and language training. With the parents expecting improvements in their children's performance in a particular skill, the learning and practising process can become boring and stressful.

Parental enthusiasm for all kinds of summer schools or after-school classes varies, but revolves around the parents' belief that such provision will help their children to develop in all areas:

> My daughter has Chinese zither, English, maths, Peking opera and some other classes. Some of them we enrolled her into but have no time to attend. We still want to send her to basketball class, but there is not enough spare time … we just want her to develop in an all-round way; I think that is the expectation of all parents.
>
> (Father of an 8-year-old girl)

However, from the children's perspective, only a small number could understand their parents' intentions regarding the summer schools. In the children's minds, though some of the after-school classes or summer schools can be interesting, most of them are boring and depressing. The reason they have to go to these classes is their parents' desire, not the children's. Usually the children passively accept that their lives should contain much home-work and many after-school classes. They do not reject these classes, but they do not enjoy them either. For the children, it is a part of their everyday and normal life. They have to get used to it, as the following quotes show:

> (in school days) After school, on Mondays and Wednesdays I go to Chinese zither classes, then I also need to go swimming classes in the evening. On Thursdays I have a painting class, on Fridays I have a dancing class … (Q. do you like them?) hum, it's hard to say, I like dancing, hum… I don't know…
>
> (7-year-old girl)

> I have after-school dancing classes on Mondays, Wednesdays and Fridays. I also have classes on Saturdays and Sundays outside the school. Saturdays are full, and so are Sunday mornings. (Q. do you like to go to after-school classes?) I like playing, but I have no time to play. I can play only on Sunday afternoons.
>
> (9-year-old girl)

> I have maths classes on Mondays and Thursdays. I also have Chinese on Tuesdays… on Wednesdays and Fridays. (Q. do you enjoy these classes) No! my mum makes me go to these classes!
>
> (6-year-old girl)

Of all the children involved in the research, 45% stated that they played outdoors for an average of 2.6 hours a day. They usually spend their outdoor time playing in parks, courtyards, plazas and streets. According to the interviews, most of the children prefer playing outdoors to playing indoors. However, there are some issues, apart from academic expectations, which prevent them from playing outside.

First, the weather can affect whether children can play outdoors. However, the weather conditions do not directly affect the children, but are instead one of the most important factors for parents when making decisions as to whether children are allowed to play outside or not. For example, the hottest weather in the summer or periods of particularly poor air quality can prevent parents from taking their children or allowing their children to play outdoors. Conversely, the children themselves are not usually bothered by the hot weather or poor air quality in the summer:

> If it is not raining or snowing, I can always play outdoors. Oh, on a snowy day I can play outside the house. So, except when it is raining heavily, I do play outdoors. (Question: how about the hot weather in summer?) Yes, I can still play outdoors.
>
> (10-year-old boy)

> The air quality is not always good in Beijing recently. In the hazy weather, I don't let my daughter play outside; even at school, their PE class would be cancelled.
>
> (Mother of an 8-year-old girl)

Additionally, heavy traffic and strangers are considered by parents to be serious safety/security problems which have negative influences on children's outdoor play. According to the interviews with the parents, when the children are playing outdoors, most of the parents accompany them to look after them. This makes the duration of the children's outdoor play time largely dependent upon parents' free time:

> Every time he plays outdoors, there should be an adult accompanying him. It never changes since he was young until nowadays.
>
> (Mother of a 9-year-old boy)

> We seldom take him to play at places far from home. He always plays in the yard downstairs. But even if he is in the yard, I am still worried about the safety issues… We never let him play alone. Sometimes when we don't have time to take him to play outdoors, he can play at home.
>
> (Mother of a 10-year-old boy)

Furthermore, children also reported that they need to finish their homework before they can go out to play. It is no surprise that in a society that places high values on academic achievement this is the basic requirement before children can outside to play:

> on school days, if I finish my homework quickly, then I can have more time playing. Otherwise, I have no time for playing. Recently (summer holidays), I can play outdoors from 7 pm to 9.30 pm…
>
> (10-year-old girl)

> (question: when do you play outdoors?) after I finish my homework…
>
> (8-year-old girl)

Children's play activities don't just take place in outdoor environments. They also play electronic games at home or play at indoor playgrounds when they are going to supermarkets or shopping malls with their parents. However, comparing play outdoors with play indoors, more than half of the children interviewed prefer to play in outdoor environments. Some of the parents also support their children playing more in outdoor environments, because they think outdoor play is good for them. However, the fact is that, as some of the parents say, outdoor play has more preconditions, such as time, weather and safety, than indoor play.

DISCUSSION

The daily activity logs and interviews with children allowed the main research questions about young children's daily activities in the school summer holiday in the centre of Beijing to be answered. In particular, they revealed that, despite the school holidays, a high percentage of children are still under immense academic pressure, expressed by the amount of time they spend in summer school classes and in doing homework at home during the daytime. The responses clearly indicate that the historic educational ethos in China is still very strong, despite changes to the educational systems and processes over the years. One of the results of this ongoing academic pressure is that children are not playing outside in the summer as much as they would like to. This finding is already known to some extent in China but, as far as we can tell, has not been identified in research about children before.

Other reasons for restricting children's ability to play outdoors in the summer include parental concerns about traffic and weather, including air pollution. Traffic has long been a parental concern with respect to children's outdoor play in many parts of the world (Karsten, 2005; Kinoshita, 2009; Skår and Krogh, 2009; Woolley and Griffin, 2015) as discussed in the introduction. So traffic being a parental concern in China is not a surprise, especially in the highly urbanised city of Beijing. However, the fact that the hottest weather and poor air quality resulting from severe air pollution are factors influencing parents' decisions to allow, or not allow, their children to play outdoors is a finding we believe has not been identified before. Children's social safety in the outdoor environment was also identified as a real concern by Chinese parents. In some parts of the world it is an issue mainly driven by the media, whereas in China it can be a lived reality for parents who only have one child who is considered to be very precious.

The limitations of this research in beginning to uncover the outdoor play experiences of Chinese children in central Beijing are mainly twofold. Firstly, the timing of this research was such that it only recorded activities during the summer and not at other times of the year, when patterns of activity might be different. However, we hypothesise and anticipate that the expression of the academic pressure in the lives of urban Chinese children in future research will also reveal most of the children's time to be spent in educational activities and less in outdoor play. Secondly, this study has focused on the central historic core of Beijing; the responses to time for play, places to play and restrictions on play may be different from other parts of Beijing, in different Chinese cities and in rural areas of China.

CONCLUSIONS

This research explored children's daily lives through the summer holiday in inner-city Beijing, giving new insights into the different amounts of time spent in educational and play activities. It also provides new insights into other reasons which influence the children's outdoor play opportunities.

The responses indicate that most of the children would like to have more time to play outside but have already become used to the study-oriented lifestyle and decisions that their parents make for them about outdoor play opportunities, both in time and space. From the parents' perspective, they seem to understand that there is something wrong with the educational system but can do nothing to change it. The only thing they can do is to help their children gain more useful skills and be more competitive among their peers. Parents are trying to make the best choice for their children's future from an educational perspective, but this does appear to be to the detriment of children's outdoor play. This research provides new insights into the daily lives of Chinese urban children. However, understanding these issues among older children would also be of interest because it could be expected that if primary school children's daily lives are already occupied by endless learning and studying, the daily lives of older children might be even more so.

REFERENCES

Fyhri, A. and Hjorthol, R. (2009) 'Children's independent mobility to school, friends and leisure activities', *Journal of Transport Geography*, **17**(5), pp. 377–384.

Hand, K. L. *et al.* (2018) 'Restricted home ranges reduce children's opportunities to connect to nature: Demographic, environmental and parental influences', *Landscape and Urban Planning*, **172**, pp. 69–77.

Hu, B. Y., Kong, Z. and Roberts, S. K. (2014) 'The policies and practice of preschoolers' outdoor play: A Chinese perspective on greeting the Millennium', *Childhood Education*, **90**(3), pp. 202–211.

Jheng, Y.-J. (2013) School as a Battle over Time: How Social Class Influences Taiwanese Senior High School Students' Use of Time in and after School. PhD Thesis, University of California.

Karsten, L. (2005) 'It all used to be better? Different generations on continuity and change in urban children's daily use of space', *Children's Geographies*, **3**(3), pp. 275–290.

Kimbro, R. T. and Ariela, S. (2011) 'Neighborhood poverty and maternal fears of children's outdoor play', *Family Relations*, **60**(October), pp. 461–475.

Kimbro, R. T., Brooks-Gunn, J. and McLanahan, S. (2011) 'Young children in urban areas: Links among neighborhood characteristics, weight status, outdoor play, and television watching', *Social Science and Medicine*, **72**(5), pp. 668–676.

Kinoshita, I. (2009) 'Charting generational differences in conceptions and opportunities for play in a Japanese neighborhood', *Journal of Intergenerational Relationships*, **7**(1), pp. 53–77.

Kyttä, M. (2002) 'Affordances of children's environments in the context of cities, small towns, suburbs and rural villages in Finland and Belarus', *Journal of Environmental Psychology*, **22**(1–2), pp. 109–123.

Kyttä, M. (2004) 'The extent of children's independent mobility and the number of actualized affordances as criteria for child-friendly environments', *Journal of Environmental Psychology*, **24**(2), pp. 179–198.

Kyttä, M. *et al.* (2015) 'The last free-range children? Children's independent mobility in Finland in the 1990s and 2010s', *Journal of Transport Geography*, **47**, pp. 1–12.

Li, W. and Li, Y. (2010) 'An analysis on social and cultural background of the resistance for China's education reform and academic pressure', *International Education Studies*, **3**(3), pp. 211–215.

Nakra, P. (2012) 'China's "one-child" policy', *World Futures Review*, **4**(2), pp. 134–140.

Quach, A. S. *et al.* (2013) 'Effects of parental warmth and academic pressure on anxiety and depression symptoms in Chinese adolescents', *Journal of Child and Family Studies*, **24**(1), pp. 106–116.

Ruth, H. (ed.) (1987) *China's Education and the Industrialized World: Studies in Cultural Transfer*, London: M. E. Sharpe, Inc.

Skår, M. and Krogh, E. (2009) 'Changes in children's nature-based experiences near home: From spontaneous play to adult-controlled, planned and organised activities', *Children's Geographies*, **7**(3), pp. 339–354.

UNICEF (2016) Annual Report 2016, New York: UNICEF Division of Communication. www.unicef.org/publications/files/UNICEF_Annual_Report_2016.pdf [accessed 4 May 2018].

Wang, F. *et al.* (2012) 'Stuck between the historic and modern China: A case study of children's space in a hutong community', *Journal of Environmental Psychology*, **32**(1), pp. 59–68.

Witten, K. *et al.* (2013) 'New Zealand parents' understandings of the intergenerational decline in children's independent outdoor play and active travel', *Children's Geographies*, **11**(2), pp. 215–229.

Woolley, H. E. and Griffin, E. (2015) 'Decreasing experiences of home range, outdoor spaces, activities and companions: Changes across three generations in Sheffield in north England', *Children's Geographies*, **13**(6), pp. 677–691.

3

AN EXPLORATION OF HOW PLAYGROUND DESIGN AFFECTS THE PLAY BEHAVIOUR OF KINDERGARTEN CHILDREN IN TARTU, ESTONIA

Bhavna Mishra, Simon Bell and Himansu Sekhar Mishra

INTRODUCTION

In the last few years, there has been an increasing amount of research published on children's outdoor education and the role of outdoor play in early childhood development. The benefits of outdoor and nature play range from improved early childhood development to enhanced problem-solving abilities and better preparation for skilled adult actions.

There has been a lot of research in the field of education and child development which has been used to design or renovate playgrounds in pre-schools. Introducing gaming equipment (Verstraete et al., 2006), paint markings on playgrounds (Stratton, 2000; Stratton and Mullan, 2005), assisted play or supervised play programmes or interventions (Pangrazi et al., 2003) have all proven to have improved child physical activity and mental development. Factors like age, gender and seasonal variability in physical activity in the playground have all proven to have varied results on children's development (Ridgers et al., 2006). It has also been argued that more research is required into the above interventions to find out which of these factors are most influential (Ridgers et al., 2006). There has been more research in urban school playgrounds regarding interventions of natural or green settings that have improved physical activity in children (Dyment and Bell, 2007).

Different aspects of children's play choices, their behaviour, improvements to physical activity through playground markings or equipment and the benefits of natural play are among those to have been studied in different contexts, but none of these have been conducted in Estonia. In this chapter we present a study which focused on the behaviour and development of children playing in different types of kindergarten playgrounds in Tartu, the second city of Estonia and the 'educational capital' with several venerable universities and a large academic population.

THE PRE-SCHOOL EDUCATION SYSTEM IN ESTONIA

We should start by briefly summarising the current situation in Estonia and the reasons for the lack of recent research. Estonia, while recently celebrating 100 years since the first Declaration of Independence in 1918, went through 47 years under Soviet occupation as part of the Soviet Union, starting in 1944, and regained independence in 1991. These Soviet years saw the imposition of a centrally-planned and highly regulated system of childcare and kindergartens with a very specific approach to the care and development of young children that focused less on play than on their development in other areas. All children had to belong to special youth organisations which started with the 'Little Octobrists' at 7 years of age, when children moved from kindergarten to elementary school, so there was already some preparation for political activity, or perhaps we could see this as the last period of innocence.

It took some time for the newly-independent Republic of Estonia to sort out and 'de-Sovietise' all aspects of government and society (in some ways a process still to be finally completed) and it was not until 1999 that the first national framework for a pre-school education curriculum was developed and came into force. Nine years later, by 2008, it was realized by the educational authorities that the pre-school or kindergarten curriculum did not meet the needs of a rapidly evolving society. Estonia was, by then, one of the fastest developing states of the new Europe in economic, political and creative terms, having joined the European Union in 2004. It has adopted a mostly Nordic model of development, looking largely to Finland as a source of inspiration, where among other areas the educational system is the envy of Europe. However, there are still echoes and remains from the Soviet time present in various guises, which still need to be resolved. Early childhood development and the role of kindergartens is one of these aspects.

Thus, in 2008, a new curriculum was established which emphasized the importance of children's comprehensive development (Lasteasutuse riiklik Öppekava, 2008). 'Play' was stated to be the main activity of children in the new curriculum. The rationale for this was that through play children develop communicative skills, emotional values, and socializing abilities. According to Tuul et al. (2011), during Soviet rule, play spaces in pre-schools were over-regulated and play was regarded as an isolated activity detached from more important tasks such as learning or practicing self-help skills. The first post-independence curriculum still contained too much of the Soviet model, largely because most of the people involved in its development had come through the Soviet system and had little if any experience of other, more contemporary, models. In this 2008 curriculum, still the one used currently across the country, the role of play aims to achieve a broad range of educational activities, self-determination, and freedom of play choice.

While the curriculum has changed, many of the kindergarten premises still date from Soviet times and the kindergarten outdoor playground and its design still remains, in essence, almost the same now as it was before 1991. While play itself is recognized as having a role, what exactly play consists of, what is a playful environment and what is the potential of the outdoors for play are not very well-understood concepts among kindergarten teachers. All kindergartens in Estonia cater to children in the 3–7 age group. There are state-run kindergartens with free places as well as private establishments, some of which accommodate the children of foreign academics and students (Tartu being a university city). There is strong competition for places.

A typical daily routine in an Estonian kindergarten is as follows:

  08.00 children are dropped off by parents and they have breakfast;
  09.00 the study hours and indoor play activities start;
  10.30–11.30 they are taken outside to play (weather permitting) and once outside have no free choice to go back indoors until the end of the session;
  11.30 they line up to go inside;
  12.00 they have lunch;
  13.00–15.00 they have nap time;
  15.00–16.00 they play/do gym activities indoors or outdoors depending on the planned schedule of each kindergarten (all have different strategies);
  16.30 to 17.00 they have dinner;
  After dinner, they are collected by their parents/guardians.

Another aspect specific to Estonia (as well as other Nordic and Baltic countries and also Russia) is the winter climate, which can result in very cold (down to -30°C on occasion) conditions with considerable amounts of snow. In the very coldest periods small children are not allowed outside for fear of damaging their lungs, while snow and ice may pose risks of slipping and getting hurt – although all children have very warm clothes suitable for these conditions and dry powdery snow is excellent for playing in!

Contemporary guidance on school ground design
New school grounds designed by landscape architects tend to include natural elements such as trees, butterfly gardens, ponds, and vegetable patches related to an understanding of childhood needs, depending on the site constraints. Gardening, naturalization, restoration, and greening are terms used in projects for school grounds where natural environments are thought to have positive benefits to children. The greening of playgrounds has

become prominent in Australia, Canada, Denmark, the United States, the United Kingdom, New Zealand, and South Africa, embracing natural settings in the school playground (Bell and Dyment, 2006). Natural playgrounds have been found to benefit the physical, emotional, mental, and social development of children (Kirkby, 1989; Greenwood et al., 1998; Barbour, 1999; Malone and Tranter, 2003). Green school grounds in Canada with trees, gardens, and various other natural elements have been found to have positive benefits on the health and physical activity of children (Dyment and Bell, 2007).

The concepts of 'playscape' (Frost, 1992) and 'affordance' (Gibson, 1979), which describe an awareness of the natural play environments and their functional significance in children's play, also provide strong support to this research. The playscape concept claims, with supporting evidence, that children playing in natural environments gain more benefits than from any other play environments. Gibson's affordance theory suggests that a wide range of elements in the playground helps stimulate many play activities, which are not necessarily specifically designed into the space, but occur due to the possibilities they offer. One example could be a tree with low, strong branches which can afford climbing on, swinging from or constructing in, another could be a small pebble which can afford grasping or throwing by a small child. Therefore, from the smallest elements in the playgrounds to the overall layout, all aspects of design influence children in their early developmental stages.

Kindergarten playgrounds in societies where pre-school care and preliminary education is an essential part of the overall curriculum, can play a very important role in early childhood health and development. Outdoor play by children in kindergartens has been strongly related to better learning of creative problem solving, cooperative behaviour, and logical thinking. Fisher (1992) found that play improved the progress of early childhood cognitive, linguistic, and affective-social development. There is a positive influence of well-designed playground features that afford high levels of physical activity through different play forms on the social, emotional, and cognitive development of children. Spacious preschool outdoor play areas have been found to trigger physical activity and development when there are diverse natural elements (Fjørtoft, 2009; Ozdemir and Yilmaz, 2008). Greener playgrounds or public playgrounds in a more natural setting have shown increased amounts of physical activity (Lucas and Dyment, 2010) and social interaction in children (Seeland et al., 2009).

Therefore, the purpose of the study described in this chapter was to test the degree to which the above evidence can be found in Estonian kindergarten playgrounds by determining the relationship between different types of playgrounds and the variety of activities and associated development in children.

THE APPLICATION OF THE BEHAVIOUR MAPPING METHOD IN THE RESEARCH

Researching small children, especially ones who are not very articulate, is extremely difficult and poses a number of ethical issues. In this study we decided to apply a mode of behaviour observation so that we could avoid any direct contact with children and also make sure our research did not affect their behaviour. In addition, we developed some innovative data recording and analysis methods which may have potential for similar research in the future.

Studying different, contrasting case studies is a research strategy with clear potential to produce new knowledge through projection of new variables and dynamics (Swaffield, 2011). We used four case studies in this research. Two were playgrounds which have existed since Soviet times and which had undergone very few changes since then, the third was a newly designed kindergarten playground, and the fourth a city park with a natural setting used as a kindergarten playground in the recess hours.

In Estonian kindergartens the children are divided into groups (or classes) according to their age ranges. As it was impossible to study all the children in each kindergarten a sample group was selected for observation and analysis – chosen to be representative of the age groups, 3½–4½, 4–5 or 4–6 years being the closest possible matches across all four case studies.

The target group of children in each case study kindergarten was observed for half an hour during the morning play hours (10.30 am to 11.00 am) over four days in one week in the month of October, through direct observation, videography and recording field notes wherever necessary. The timing of the observations in October and for the short period was a result of the available time in the semester for undertaking field research. Kindergartens are closed in the summer (from the start of June to the end of August) and in the deep winter outdoor play may be restricted, so this time was most practical.

The method combined the System of Observing Play and Activity in Youth (SOPLAY) with observation relating activity types to specific locations (behaviour settings) (Cosco et al., 2010) and to the playground types and target areas described by Cummins and Zamani (2017) to identify the affordances of the types offered. The recording method we used in this study involved systematic, two-minute scans of all the children in the 30-minute recorded video of the selected study group in the pre-determined target. The two-minute time lapse sampling used is similar to the SOPLAY time-lapse testing by McKenzie et al. (2000). It is a standard instrument for measuring macro-population data with proven validity in similar studies and was thus deemed appropriate for this study. In the SOPLAY testing, the target areas are scanned individually, whereas in this research the pre-categorised different types of playgrounds with different target areas were scanned.

A unique feature of this work was that instead of just recording a static picture at a point in time, a detailed analysis of how each child used the area and moved around within it was obtained and from it a series of time-lapse animations showing how the children moved around the site over the 30-minute period was generated. This complex recording could not have been undertaken by manual methods. Unfortunately we cannot show the animations in an illustration here.

Following the video recording in the field, the raw recordings were used to capture specific data for each two-minute scan: the number of boys and girls in each target area of the playground was counted and the dominant type of play activity observed for each child in their respective target areas was recorded. The categories of play types were selected according to play theory as being one of the three types: social play, motor play, and cognitive play (Bell, 2008) and the levels of play were analysed according to general child development theory as functional play, cooperative play, role play, rule game, symbolic play, or being sedentary; each were analysed separately since it is possible to link the play types with child development.

The use of a Geographical Information System (GIS) for behaviour mapping of pre-school children has already been widely practiced (Cosco et al., 2010). Behaviour mapping is an unobtrusive, direct observational method for recording both the location of subjects and measuring their activity levels simultaneously. It is also very practical when the researcher does not wish to affect the behaviour of study subjects or where no direct access is possible due to ethical concerns. By recording the precise location of a participant on a detailed plan of a place, and associating that point with a range of attributes, it is possible to undertake a variety of analyses of that behaviour and the affordances of the location in relation to it. We used the freely available Quantum GIS (QGIS) to record the information.

Before data entry we prepared charts based on observing each two-minute long recorded activity of each child, to classify activities prior to converting the video data into spatially resolved data in the GIS (Table 3.1). A base plan had also been prepared previously from spatially-referenced site plans and a detailed survey of each play area, in order to be able to locate each child in a precise spot. Then, for each two-minute segment, the precise location of each child (target area) was marked as a user-defined coordinate on the QGIS maps and for each point the gender of each child, the type of play, and type of physical activity levels were listed in the database.

At each case study kindergarten, a total number of 64 scans (one scan equalled a two-minute time lapse) of each target area was conducted over 30 minutes' time for four days during a week. Therefore, a total number of 256 scans (1 scan x 16 times x 4 days in one kindergarten x 4 kindergartens) was obtained and each one was interpreted

TABLE 3.1 Example of the chart showing the recorded activity of each child in every two-minute scan

SL. NO	CHILD IDENTIFICATION NAME	DATE-TIME	USER-DEFINED GIS COORDI-NATES	TARGET AREAS	TYPES OF PLAY	PHYSICAL ACTIVITY LEVEL	SOCIAL %	MOTOR %	COGNITIVE %
1	BOY1			TREES	CONSTRUCTIVE	LOW	40	25	35
2	BOY 2			PLAY HOUSE	ROLE PLAY	MODERATE	60	10	30
3	GIRL 1			GREEN PATCH	FUNCTIONAL	VIGOROUS	5	80	15
...	ETC.			ETC.	ETC.	ETC.			

into the QGIS and analysed to determine the type of play conducted in the target areas, which playground types produced most social, motor, or cognitive play, gender variation in play activities, physical activity levels in different types of playgrounds, etc.

THE PLAYGROUNDS USED IN THE STUDY

As the main intention of the study was to analyse child development while playing in different outdoor kindergarten playgrounds in Tartu it was necessary to find suitable examples as case studies with staff who were interested in and willing to participate in and facilitate the research. The selection of the playgrounds depended on their diversity and potential to qualify as comparative case studies. There are some 31 public and 11 private kindergartens in Tartu, 10 of which were very different from each other in terms of the playground features and showed potential for the proposed study. Following an ethical procedure for obtaining permission four of the 10 kindergartens gave their full approval for the research.

As the design or layout of the playgrounds differ in each case study kindergarten, it was necessary to categorize the different playgrounds before research began. Based on Cummins and Zamani's (2017) description of *play target areas*, the kindergarten playgrounds were categorized into one of three types: 1) Natural (Centre D), 2) Mixed (Centres A and B) and 3) Manufactured (Centre C), based on the similar target areas present in these kindergarten playgrounds (Table 3.2 and Figure 3.1). Furthermore, the target areas at each playground suggested many kinds of play-affordances with their potential contribution to development in children.

Centre A (Figures 3.1a and 3.2a) is a typical Soviet-era school and, while it has undergone a lot of change with the addition of newer play equipment, it still has a very traditional setting. The kindergarten caters to 160 children in total, allocated to 14 separate playgroups. Each playgroup uses an allocated section in the outdoor playground during the morning recess (10.30 a.m. to 11.00 a.m.). The target group played in a 500m² section of the playground and used the same patch every day. The study group comprised 16 children (9 boys and 7 girls) in the age group of 4–5 years. According to the playground categories selected, the target areas that describe the Centre A playground are: trees, hard-surfaced path, sand, play-house, green patches, table/chair, swing, play structure, and see-saw (Table 3.1) which fits the category of 'Mixed Playground'.

Centre B (Figures 3.1b and 3.2b) is also one of the typical Soviet-era kindergartens, but has had a recent renovation to its playground. It also has several earth mounds where children play with their sledges in the winter snow, which sets it apart from the others which are rather flat. The kindergarten has a total of 280 children divided into 14 playgroups. The children play in different allocated patches of play areas in the outdoor playground. The study target group plays in a very compact play area of 250m². The group consisted of 17 children (10 boys and 7 girls) in

TABLE 3.2 Description of play target areas and playground types, categorized according to the target areas described by Cummins and Zamani (2017)

	Target areas	Description	Centre A	Centre B	Centre C	Centre D
NATURAL	Hills	Slopes affording fast movement and challenging behaviour.				X
	Camp	Tree logs, small stones or trunk arranged in a circle.				X
	Stick Pile	Piles of sticks, leaves or logs encouraging collection and stacking.				X
	Trail	Naturally designed pathways with increasing ambiguity and mystery.				X
	Trees	Trees supporting hanging, leaning, jumping, climbing, etc.	X	X		X
MIXED	Hard surface Pathways	Pathways with gravel, tarmac, or concrete, etc.	X	X	X	X
	Sand	Sand boxes or sand pile	X	X	X	
	Play-houses	Play-houses encouraging family role plays such as cooking, cleaning, etc.	X	X		
	Green Patches	Bushes, grass covers, or meadows.	X	X	X	X
MANUFACTURED	Tables/Chairs	Table, bench, or picnic chairs.	X	X	X	
	Swing	Swings, whether circular or single seating.	X	X	X	
	Rockers	Equipment with rocking apparatus, moving as if riding a horse.			X	
	Gazebo	Wooden shaded structures encouraging children to sit, crawl, and mix loose materials.			X	X
	Platform	A perimeter or landmark affording sitting and gathering play opportunities.			X	
	Play structure	Structure affording climbing, sliding, hanging down, etc.	X	X	X	
	See-saw	The typical see-saw balancing weight.	X		X	

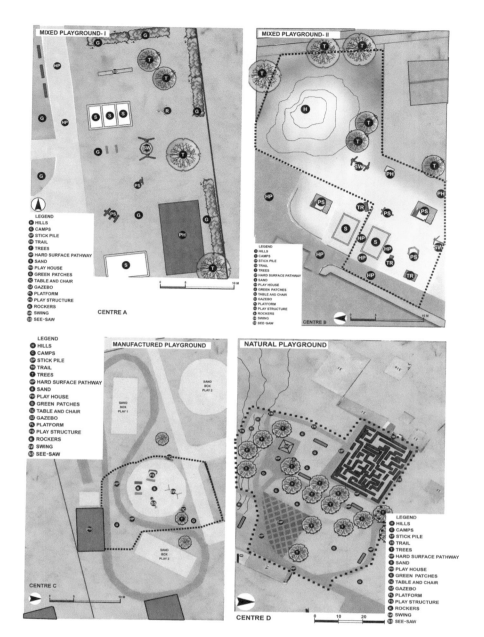

FIGURE 3.1 Illustrated maps showing the character of each playground at a) Centre A, b) Centre B, c) Centre C, and d) Centre D
Source: the authors

the age group of 3½-4½ years. According to the playground categories, the target areas that describe the Centre B playground are: trees, hard-surfaced path, sand, play-house, green patches, table/chair, swing, and play structure (Table 3.1), which fulfils the category of 'Mixed Playground'.

Centre C (Figure 3.1c and 3.2c) is a newly built kindergarten with a modern playground design. The kindergarten is smaller than Centres A and B and has 80 children in total, organised into six playgroups. The children play in different allocated patches of play areas in the outdoor playground. The target group studied had 13 children (6 boys and 7 girls) and in the age group of 4–6 years. According to the playground categories selected, the target areas that describes the Centre C playground are: hard-surfaced path, sand, green patches, table/chair, swing, platform, play structure, rockers, gazebo and see-saw (Table 3.1) and fulfils the category of 'Manufactured Playground'.

CENTRE A

CENTRE B

CENTRE C

CENTRE D

FIGURE 3.2 Photographs showing the character of each of the playgrounds at a) Centre A, b) Centre B, c) Centre C, and d) Centre D (intentionally blurred in order not to show any identification of the children)
Source: the authors

Centre D (Figure 3.1d and 3.2d) is different in that it uses a public park for its outdoor play area which can be considered as a natural play area, since it has no play equipment such as swings or sandboxes, etc. Even though the public park is managed and the grass is mown, nevertheless it still has quite a natural setting and feeling. This kindergarten is the smallest, with 35 children in total divided into 4 small playgroups (maximum of 11 children in a group). All the children can use the entire outdoor public park for play during the play time. The curriculum of outdoor play is different to the other 3 case studies. The boys and girls are looked after separately during outdoor play by different teachers. Unlike other kindergartens, the play groups also have a gym teacher helping them in assisted play in the outdoor play area once in a week. The target group studied had 8 children (6 boys and 2 girls) in the age group of 4–6 years. According to the playground categories selected, the target areas that describe the Centre D playground are: hills, camp, stick pile, trail, trees, hard surface pathways, sand, play-houses, and green patches (Table 3.1), matching the category of 'Natural Playground'.

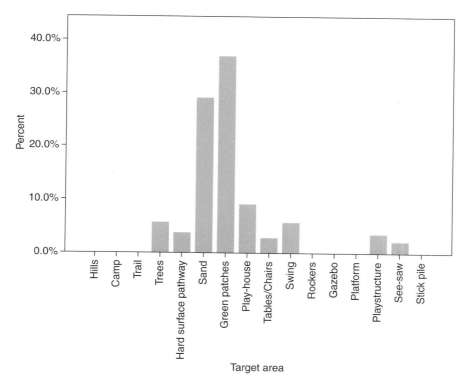

FIGURE 3.3 Favourite places observed in Centre A
Source: the authors

FAVOURITE TARGET AREAS

We found both similarities and differences in the popularity of the different target areas in each playground.

At Centre A

Centre A, categorised as a mixed playground, has all the play equipment evenly spaced across it. The play area for 16 children in the target group is 500m². The most popular space was the green patches (37.01% of observed children playing there) and the see-saw was the least popular (2.15%). The remaining seven target areas each contained between 2.93% and 29.39% of the children (see Figure 3.3).

At Centre B

Centre B is also a mixed playground with all the play equipment placed in a very small and compact space. The play area for 17 children in the target group is 250m², which is very densely occupied during the play time. The most popular space was the sand box (43.29% of observed children playing there) and the swing was the least popular (0.83%). The remaining 5 target areas each contained between 1.65% and 27.39% of the children (see Figure 3.4).

At Centre C

Centre C is a manufactured playground and all the play equipment is placed in a sand pit and surrounded by a low, thin bamboo-like edging/platform that children also use for balancing. The play area for the 13 children in the target group is 280m², which is also very compact. The most popular space was the sand (29.33% of observed children playing there) and the gazebo was the least popular (0.12%). The remaining eight target areas each contained between 0.84% and 19.35% of the children (Figure 3.5).

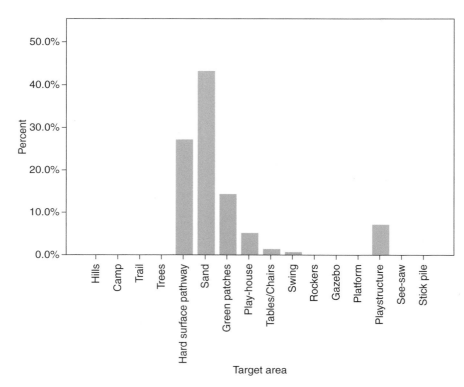

FIGURE 3.4 Favourite places observed in Centre B
Source: the authors

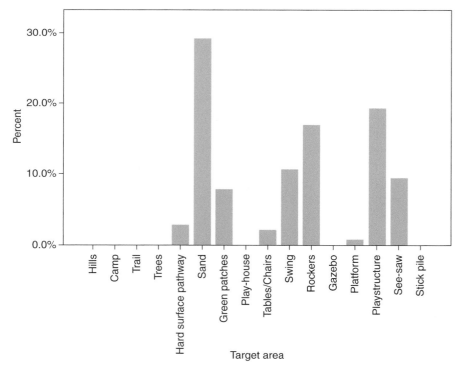

FIGURE 3.5 Favourite places observed at Centre C
Source: the authors

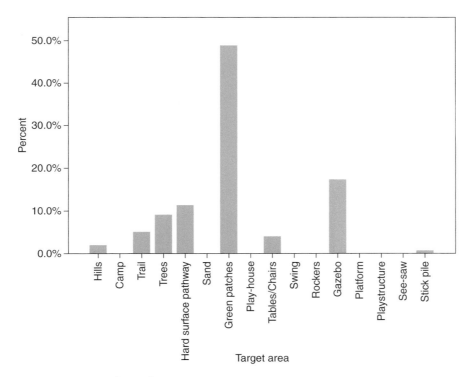

FIGURE 3.6 Favourite places observed at Centre D
Source: the authors

At Centre D

Centre D is a natural playground and has a natural setting with old trees, manmade green patches, gravel pathways (counted as hard-surfaced pathways), trails, maze bushes (seen in Figure 3.1), and a gazebo (as seen in most Estonian public manor parks). The play area defined for eight children in the target group is the entire park size of 3500m² which is relatively large compared with the other case studies. The most popular space was the green patches (49.02% of observed children playing there) and the stick pile was the least popular (0.98%). The remaining eight target areas each contained between 2% and 17.38% of the children (Figure 3.6).

DOMINANT PLAY TYPES IN DIFFERENT TARGET AREAS IN EACH PLAYGROUND

We also found similarities and differences in the dominant play types at each centre, clearly affected by the affordances of the facilities.

At Centre A

Across all the target areas at Centre A, children were mostly engaged in functional (29.97% of all scans) and cooperative play (22.48% of all scans) (see Figure 3.7). Although it is relatively small proportion, it is worth noting that the greatest proportions of constructive play (18.21% of all scans) and role play (17.94% of all scans) were observed at Centre A. The hard-surfaced pathway and swing promoted the highest proportion of functional play (82.05% and 55.10% of scans in each target area, respectively). In terms of constructive play, the lowest proportion of children was observed in the play-house (2.13% of scans in this target area) while the highest was observed in the area under the tree. At the see-saw, the scans revealed that children were engaged in the highest proportion of cooperative play (72.73% of scans in this target area) and, in the play-house, the highest proportion of role play (87.23% of scans in this target area) (see Figure 3.7).

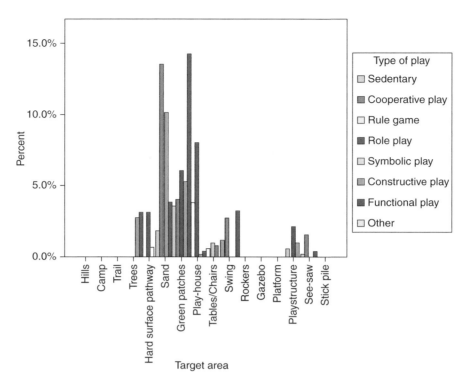

FIGURE 3.7 Dominant play types found in Centre A
Source: the authors

At Centre B

Irrespective of target area, the children were mostly observed engaging in functional play (44.35% of all scans) followed by cooperative play (29.45% of all scans). The play structure promoted the highest percentages of functional play, followed by the play-house and the swing (92.31%, 79.31% and 77.78% of scans in each target area, respectively). The table/chair promoted the highest percentage of cooperative play (72.22% of scans in this target area). No symbolic play was observed in any of the target areas. The sand area mostly promoted constructive and cooperative play (see Figure 3.8).

At Centre C

Irrespective of the target area, the scans revealed that the majority of children were engaged in functional play (35.04% of all scans), followed by cooperative play (20.55% of all scans). The sand feature had the highest percentage of constructive play (54.10% of scans in this target area). The rockers at Centre C engaged cooperative play in 97.16% of scans in this target area. Surprisingly, 21.27% of all scans observed sedentary activity, the highest of all the centres (see Figure 3.9).

At Centre D

Irrespective of target area, children at Centre D were engaged in functional play (39.32% of all scans) and cooperative play (21.71% of all scans).. All target areas, except the areas under the trees, promoted a high degree of functional play (e.g. the gazebo 84.27% of scans, hard-surfaced pathways 76.27% of scans, and hills 75% of scans in these target areas). Interestingly, the area under the trees promoted notably less functional play and more role play (see Figure 3.10).

The comparative analysis of the mixed playgrounds of Centres A and B shows that the compact and dense playground (Centre B) performed better in terms of the physical activity levels of the children. Children seemed to be influenced by their closer interaction with other children in the denser playground, which may motivate them to

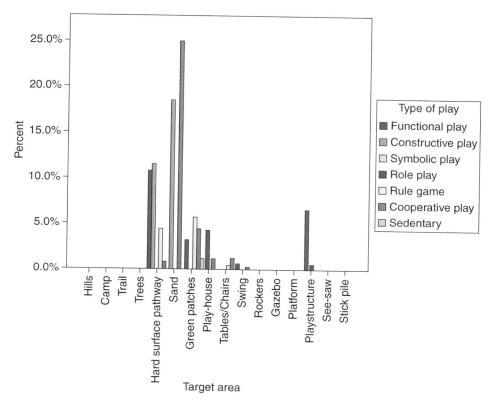

FIGURE 3.8 Dominant play types found in Centre B
Source: the authors

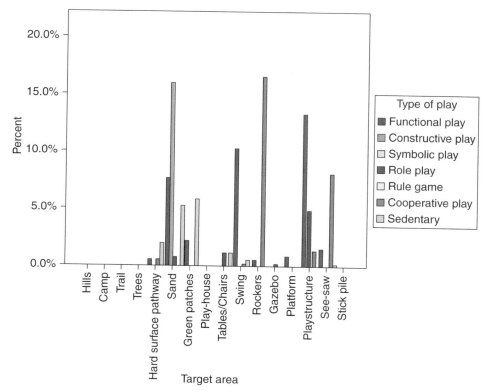

FIGURE 3.9 Dominant play types found in Centre C
Source: the authors

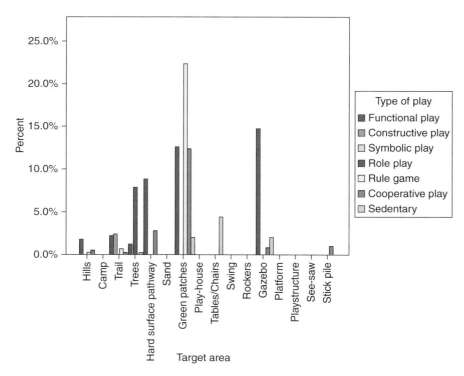

FIGURE 3.10 Dominant play types found in Centre D
Source: the authors

be more active compared with the children playing at the more open Centre A mixed playground. More functional and role play activities were identified as taking place in outdoor playgrounds in a study by Shim et al. (2001), and our findings also showed clear evidence of the same at the Centre A mixed playground, Centre C manufactured playground and Centre D natural playground; however, at Centre B the mixed playground, with its compact and denser play area, showed less evidence of role play. It might be because of the greater social interaction through cooperative play.

At centre D, the natural playground did not score very highly in terms of levels of physical activity, which goes against the trend observed by e.g. Muñoz (2009), that forest schools increase physical activities in children, maybe because although it is in a natural setting, this public park may not meet the criteria of a forest school or else the children are attracted to other aspects – we noted a lot more functional and role play there. Boldermann et al. (2006), Fjørtoft (2004), and Fjørtoft and Sageie (2000) also found that natural environments invited more physical activities than the traditional playgrounds, whereas we found the mixed playground with a very compact play area (Centre B) had the most physical activity of all the cases. In line with Johnson (2004), who found that the opportunity to engage in adventurous play, involving imagination and even an element of risk, was missing in many contemporary adult-designed play spaces, we found the same in the manufactured playground Centre C.

Also, in line with Frost and Campbell (1985) we found that functional play and rule games occurred significantly more on the traditional (or mixed) playgrounds, while role play and constructive play took place more often on the manufactured playgrounds. Moreover, Goldstein (2012) found that children tend to play longer when they are provided with suitable objects or activities. This was clearly seen in the fourth day of observations at Centre D, when the children were engaged in vigorous assisted play and they wanted to play longer. Dyment et al. (2009) point out that most vigorous physical activity occurs in manufactured playgrounds like Centre C and that most natural playgrounds invite moderate play like we found in Centre D.

When children play with loose parts or sand they tend to carry out more constructive play and are also encouraged to be involved in role play (Maxwell et al., 2008) which we also found in all the different types of playgrounds except the natural playground Centre D which had no sand. Equipment for games (Verstraete et al., 2006), painted markings on playgrounds (Stratton, 2000, Stratton and Mullan, 2005), and assisted play or supervised play (Pangrazi et al., 2003) interventions have been shown to promote improved physical activity and mental development. We found that these kinds of interventions were needed more at the Centre D natural playground and are organised there one day a week by the kindergarten.

PLAYGROUND TYPES AND PHYSICAL ACTIVITY LEVELS

The mixed playground Centre A showed a balanced physical activity level ranging from low to vigorous, as calculated from the scans. The mixed playground Centre B showed more moderate physical activity, while at Centre C there was much less vigorous physical activity seen from the scans. At the natural playground Centre D, there was a balance between low and vigorous physical activity levels (see Figure 3.11). The greatest social development score was shown by the Centre D natural playground (46% of all scans), followed by the Centre B and C mixed playgrounds (33% of all scans), while the Centre A mixed playground (32% of all scans) was slightly less.

The maximum degree of motor development was found at Centre B (39% of all scans) followed by the Centre A mixed playground (34% of all scans) with the lowest motor development score seen at Centre C (29% of all scans) – although it scored highest for cognitive development (43% of all scans). Surprisingly, the Centre D natural playground showed the least cognitive development (22% of all scans) compared with the other playgrounds. As already shown by Bradley (1985), the different types of factory-made toys placed in the compact manufactured playground such as the one at Centre C offered the most cognitive contribution to pre-school children. In a study by Driscoll and Carter (2009) the availability of toys increased social interaction in children, which is to some degree contradicted by the findings from the natural playground of Centre D, where the absence of toys and equipment led

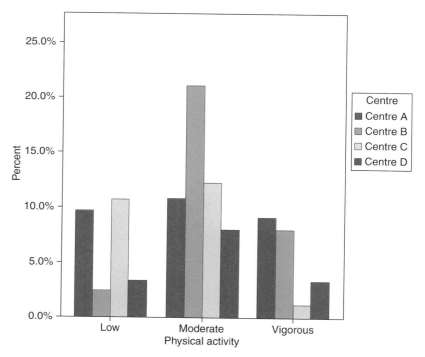

FIGURE 3.11 Levels of low, moderate and vigorous physical activity across all four centres
Source: the authors

to increased social interaction among children, possibly due to a greater dependency on each other to play. Studies have found that the natural environment contributes to the improvement of problem-solving abilities, increased creativity, and social interaction (O'Brien and Murray, 2005) and provides educational benefits that we also saw in the natural playground Centre D.

There is evidence that play activity behaviour and developmental aspects in a variety of outdoor play areas have a significant role in children's social, emotional, and cognitive development (Barbour, 1999; Shim et al., 2001; Fjørtoft, 2001; Dyment et al., 2009). This is reflected in the findings of the mixed playgrounds A and B, which are also more diverse compared to the other two playgrounds. Play in naturally designed areas, compared with traditional (mixed) playgrounds seems to have a positive influence on social competencies (O'Brien and Murray, 2007), which was also seen in the results obtained from the natural playground Centre D. The maximum motor development noticed at Centre B is most probably due to the diversity and the influence of close interaction between children who tend to run around or perform vigorous physical activities. Centre A scored 34% of all scans for motor development, in part because of the free movement possible in the open grassy patch and along the hard-surfaced path without any obstructions. Centre C saw less motor development, possibly due to the many obstructions to free movement.

The mixed playgrounds showed a balance between social, motor, and cognitive development, whereas the manufactured playground scored higher in the cognitive development and the natural playground scored higher in social development. At Centre A, target areas of sand and grassy patches showed a balance of social, motor, and cognitive development, possibly because they were more open and less dense play areas. At centre B, target areas of hard-surfaced paths and sand provided maximum benefits for social, motor and cognitive development. At Centre C, since the entire play area is on sand, it also showed high potential for social, motor, and cognitive skills. At Centre D, the grassy patches contributed to a greater degree to child development, due to the possibilities for free movement together with other opportunities for talking, playing, fighting, constructing, etc.

BOYS AND GIRLS PLAY DIFFERENTLY

Dyment et al. (2009) have demonstrated a clear variation in gender preferences for play choices in outdoor play activities which we also found in all the three types of playgrounds as follows:

At Centre A
Girls showed some favourite play target areas, such as the green patch behind the play-house, the swing, and the sand. Although girls and boys played in groups, the play activities differed due to different choices (Dyment et al., 2009). The data on physical activity levels showed that girls were either sedentary or involved in role play, whereas boys were mostly involved in vigorous functional activity (see Figure 3.12).

At Centre B
Here there is a clear picture of the most typical play choices in the dense playground. Girls were either playing with the sand and talking, were sedentary, or playing on the play structure with the slides. Girls tended to perform low to moderate physical activity, while the boys were moving or running around the whole playground uniformly, as it is a compact playground with lot of opportunities for playing with other groups, all activities being close to each other (Figure 3.13).

At Centre C
Surprisingly, at this manufactured playground, even though girls and boys play differently, and physical activity levels were different, the girls' play movements showed a very similar spread across the whole playground when compared to the boys' movements (Figure 3.14).

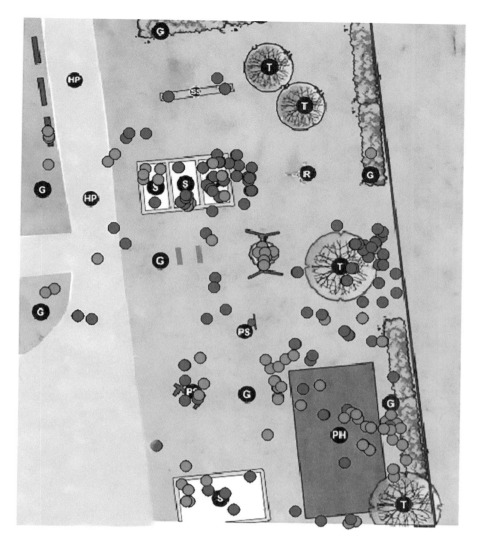

FIGURE 3.12 Play patterns of boys (blue) and girls (pink) at Centre A
Source: the authors

At Centre D

It was clear from the analysis that boys and girls played differently in the natural playground. The boys' activities covered 75% of the playground, moving to cosy places further away, but the girls tended to remain secure in the open areas at the centre of the playground. However, on the last day of the study here, we found that boys and girls played in almost the same manner when involved in adult-assisted play with rule games. Groves and McNish (2008) state that landscape intervention in a school playground may lead to increase in girls' levels of physical activity, so at the natural playground Centre D, there is an opportunity to add some temporary loose materials which might improve the girls' participation in motor activities (Fig 3.15).

CONCLUSIONS

The study revealed that the children were using the three types of playgrounds at Centres A, B, C, and D differently, while the outdoor play duration of all four kindergartens were the same according to the standard curriculum. While this study has only focused on the design of kindergarten outdoor playgrounds as a determinant of children's

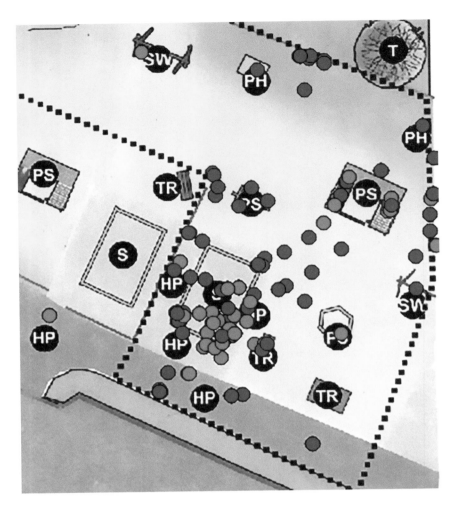

FIGURE 3.13 Play patterns of boys (blue) and girls (pink) at Centre B
Source: the authors

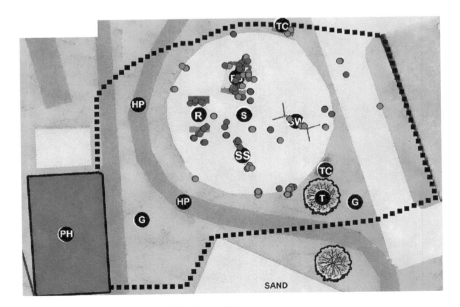

FIGURE 3.14 Play patterns of boys (blue) and girls (pink) at Centre C
Source: the authors

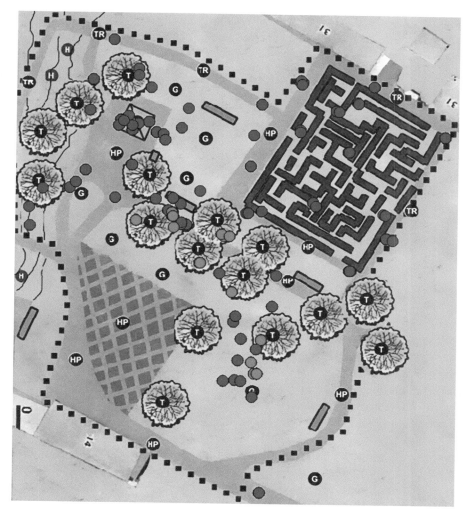

FIGURE 3.15 Play patterns of boys (blue) and girls (pink) at Centre D
Source: the authors

play behaviour and development, many other factors are also likely to influence where and how children play. For example, the age preferences for different types of outdoor play, physical competence levels, the climate (which is a major factor in Estonia but is not included in this study), cultural influences, and parental upbringing may all exert influence.

The centre staff and their role in the pre-school play space also have an important influence on how children play. Some teachers would see the outdoor play time as being equally important as indoor time and would engage and interact with children, while other teachers might see it as a time to have a break for both themselves and the children and would assume a primarily supervisory role with no direct interaction with the children during this time. Closely related to this point are teachers' physical and mental abilities, experience, training, and the pre-school curricula, which can also influence how teachers interpret the role of outdoor play in children's lives (Dowda et al., 2004; O'Connor and Temple, 2005). Growing research on children's play benefits through outdoor play, such as studies by Elkind (2007) and Fisher et al. (2005), have led to the introduction of outdoor play in the pre-school curricula and its inclusion in the curriculum of Estonian pre-schools since 2008.

Research has shown that interventions such as the introduction of loose parts and play equipment (Verstraete et al., 2006), the provision of rule games, assisted play, and symbolic play (Lawlis et al., 2008) as well as the use of playground marking (Cardon et al., 2009) can affect where and how children play outdoors. Finally, different climatic or environmental factors influence children's play choices, including very cold conditions, snow play or it being too sunny and hot to play (Boldemann et al., 2006), linked to general seasonality (Fisher et al., 2005) and shade provision (Dyment and Bell, 2007).

This study, however, sought to focus on the variables of design with a view to understand and analyze the relationship between playground design, children's play choices, behaviours, and development on four kindergarten playgrounds. Our research clearly suggests that the different playground designs could afford different kinds of play, which determined their potential to deliver different developmental benefits. Affordances of the landscape are what it offers to the child while playing, and these, whether few or many, have an impact on the child's behaviour and performance. Therefore, through the 256 separate observation scans of children playing in the different types of playground, we were able to demonstrate the range of possible play choices and behaviours. This enabled us to illustrate the various ways in which the playground target areas were used and types of play performed as a function of the affordances of the target areas.

Through the research findings, we found that the notions of preschool playground design commonly held in Estonia need to be reconsidered, especially aspects such as:

- the proportion of hard-surfaced paths;
- the spacing of the play equipment;
- having low tree canopies to provide shelter and shade for children;
- the importance of natural areas;
- the role of early childhood professionals;
- the benefits of manufactured equipment;
- the assumed popularity of sand boxes.

Our findings suggest a wide range of potential future research. They highlight the contribution of kindergarten playground design for promoting different types of play to support social, motor, and cognitive development. They also underline the limitations of some playground design in terms of, for example, play quality, lack of equipment, and ground surface obstructions for free play. The strength of the results indicates that the findings deserve further investigation. Nevertheless, children need opportunities that will encourage all types of play and diversity in kindergarten play landscapes. As stated by Paechter and Clark (2007), 'relatively small changes in playground arrangements and organization can also make a comparatively large effect on the activities open to children'.

REFERENCES

Barbour, A.C. (1999). The impact of playground design on the play behaviours of children with differing levels of physical competence. *Early Childhood Research Quarterly*, **14**(1), 75–98.
Bell, A., and Dyment, J.E. (2006). *Grounds for action: Promoting physical activity through school ground greening in Canada*. Toronto, Ontario: Evergreen.
Bell, S. (2008). *Design for outdoor recreation*. Abingdon: Taylor and Francis.
Boldermann, C., Blennow, M., Dal, H., Martensson, F., Raustorp, A., Yuen, K., and Wester, U. (2006). Impact of preschool environment upon children's physical activity and sun exposure. *Preventative Medicine*, **42**(4), 310–308.
Bradley, R. H. (1985) Play materials and intellectual development. In C. Caldwell Brown and A. W. Gottfried (Eds.), *Play interactions: The role of toys and parental involvement in children's development*, pp. 129–142. Lexington, MA: Lexington Books – Johnson & Johnson Pediatric Round Table series.
Cardon, G., Labarque, V., Smits, D., and De Bourdeaudhuij, I. (2009). Promoting physical activity at the pre-school playground: the effects of providing markings and play equipment. *Preventive Medicine*, **48**(4), 335–340.
Cosco, N. G., Moore, R. C., and Islam, M. Z. (2010). Behaviour mapping: a method for linking preschool physical activity and outdoor design. *Medicine and Science in Sports and Exercise*, **42**(3), 513–519.
Cummins, E., and Zamani, Z. (2017). Play environments and affordances. In Masiulanis, K., and Cummins, E. (Eds.), *How to grow a playspace: Development and design* (pp. 37–47). Abingdon: Routledge.

Dowda, M., Pate, R. R., Trost, S. G., Almeida, M. J. C., and Sirard, J. R. (2004). Influences of preschool policies and practices on children's physical activity. *Journal of Community Health*, **29**(3), 183–196.

Driscoll, C., and Carter, M. (2009). The effects of social and isolate toys on the social interaction of preschool children with disabilities. *Journal of Developmental and Physical Disabilities*, **21**(4), 279–300.

Dyment, J. E., Bell, A. C., and Lucas, A. J. (2009). The relationship between school ground design and intensity of physical activity. *Children's Geographies*, **7**(3), 261–276.

Dyment, J. E., and Bell, A. C. (2007). Grounds for movement: Green school grounds as sites for promoting physical activity. *Health Education Research*, **23**(6), 952–962.

Elkind, D. (2007). *The power of play: How spontaneous imaginative activities lead to happier, healthier children*. Da Capo Press.

Fisher, A., Reilly, J. J., Montgomery, C., Kelly, L. A., Williamson, A., Jackson, D. M., and Grant, S. (2005). Seasonality in physical activity and sedentary behavior in young children. *Pediatric Exercise Science*, **17**(1), 31–40.

Fisher, E. P. (1992). The impact of play on development: A meta-analysis. *Play and Culture*, **5**(2), 159–181.

Fjørtoft, I. (2004). Landscape as playscape: The effects of natural environments on children´s play and motor development. *Children, Youth and Environments*, **14**(2), 21–44.

Fjørtoft, I. (2009). Children in schoolyards: Tracking movement patterns and physical activity in schoolyards using global positioning system and heart rate monitoring. *Landscape and Urban Planning*, **93**(3–4), 210–217.

Fjørtoft, Ingunn (2001). The natural environment as a playground for children: The impact of outdoor play activities in pre-primary school children. *Early Childhood Education Journal*, **29**(2), 111–17.

Fjørtoft, Ingunn, and Sageie, Jostein (2000). The natural environment as a playground for children: Landscape description and analyses of a natural playscape. *Landscape and Urban Planning*, **48**(1–2), 83–97.

Frost, J., and Campbell, S. (1985). Equipment choices of primary age children on conventional and creative playgrounds. In J. Frost and S. Sunderlin (Eds.), *When children play: Proceedings of the international conference of play and play environments* (pp. 89–92). Olney, MD: Association for Childhood Education International.

Frost, Joe L. (1992). *Play and playscapes*. Albany, NY: Delmar.

Gison, J. J. (1979). *The ecological approach to visual perception*. Boston: Houghton Mifflin.

Goldstein, J. (2012). *Play in children's development, health and well-being*. Brussels: Toy Industries of Europe.

Greenwood, P. W., Greenwood, P. W., Model, K., Rydell, C. P., and Chiesa, J. (1998). *Diverting children from a life of crime: Measuring costs and benefits*. Santa Monica, CA: Rand Corporation.

Groves, L., and McNish, H. (2008). *Baseline study of play at Merrylee Primary School*. Glasgow: Forestry Commission Scotland.

Johnson, L. M. (2004). American playground and schoolyards – a time for change. Paper presented at the Open Space, People Space Conference.

Kirkby, M. (1989). Nature as refuge in children's environments. *Children's Environments Quarterly*, **6**(1), 7–12.

Koolieelse lasteasutuse riiklik Õppekava (2008). Estonian National Curriculum. Online at https://www.riigiteataja.ee/akt/13351772 (accessed 14 April 2020).

Lawliss, T., Mikhailovich, K., and Morrison, P. A. (2008). Physical activity in long day care and family day care settings. *Australian Journal of Early Childhood*, **33**(2), 27–31.

Lucas, A. J., and Dyment, J. E. (2010). Where do children choose to play on the school ground? The influence of green design. *Education 3–13*, **38**(2), 177–189.

Malone, K., and Tranter, P. J. (2003). School grounds as sites for learning: Making the most of environmental opportunities. *Environmental Education Research*, **9**(3), 283–303.

Maxwell, L. E., Mitchell, M. R., and Evans, G. W. (2008). Effects of play equipment and loose parts on preschool children's outdoor play behavior: An observational study and design intervention. *Children, Youth and Environments*, **18**(2), 36–63.

McKenzie, T. L., Marshall, S. J., Sallis, J. F., and Conway, T. L. (2000). Leisure-time physical activity in school environments: an observational study using SOPLAY. *Preventive Medicine*, **30**(1), 70–77.

Muñoz, S. A. (2009). *Children in the outdoors*. London: Sustainable Development Research Centre.

O'Brien, L., and Murray, R. (2005). Forest schools in England and Wales: Woodland space to learn and grow. *Environmental Education*, **80**, 25–27.

O'Brien, L., and Murray, R. (2007). Forest School and its impacts on young children: Case studies in Britain. *Urban Forestry and Urban Greening*, **6**(4), 249–265.

O'Connor, J. P., and Temple, V. A. (2005). Constraints and facilitators for physical activity in family day care. *Australian Journal of Early Childhood*, **30**(4), 1–10.

Ozdemir, A., and Yilmaz, O. (2008). Assessment of outdoor environments and physical activity in Ankara's primary schools. *Journal of Environmental Psychology*, **28**(3), 287–300.

Paechter, C., and Clark, S. (2007). Who are tomboys and how do we recognise them? *Women's Studies International Forum. Pergamon*, **30**(4), 342–354.

Pangrazi, R. P., Beighle, A., Vehige, T., and Vack, C. (2003). Impact of Promoting Lifestyle Activity for Youth (PLAY) on children's physical activity. *Journal of School Health*, **73**(8), 317–321.

Ridgers, N. D., Stratton, G., Clark, E., Fairclough, S. J., and Richardson, D. J. (2006). Day-to-day and seasonal variability of physical activity during school recess. *Preventive Medicine*, **42**(5), 372–374.

Seeland, K., Dübendorfer, S., and Hansmann, R. (2009). Making friends in Zurich's urban forests and parks: The role of public green space for social inclusion of youths from different cultures. *Forest Policy and Economics*, **11**(1), 10–17.

Shim, S.-Y., Herwig, J. E., and Shelley, M. (2001). Preschoolers' play behaviors with peers in classroom and playground settings. *Journal of Research in Childhood Education*, **15**(2), 149–163.

Stratton, G. (2000). Promoting children's physical activity in primary school: an intervention study using playground markings. *Ergonomics*, **43**(10), 1538–1546.

Stratton, G., and Mullan, E. (2005). The effect of multicolor playground markings on children's physical activity level during recess. *Preventive Medicine*, **41**(5–6), 828–833.

Swaffield, S. (2011). Research strategies in landscape architecture: Mapping the terrain. *Journal of Landscape Architecture*, **6**(1), 34–45.

Tuul, M., Ugaste, A., and Mikser, R. (2011). Teachers' perceptions of the curricula of the Soviet and post-Soviet eras: A case study of Estonian pre-school teachers. *Journal of Curriculum Studies*, **43**(6), 759–781.

Verstraete, S. J., Cardon, G. M., De Clercq, D. L., and De Bourdeaudhuij, I. M. (2006). Increasing children's physical activity levels during recess periods in elementary schools: the effects of providing game equipment. *European Journal of Public Health*, **16**(4), 415–419.

4

DESIGN OF SENSORY GARDENS FOR CHILDREN WITH DISABILITIES IN THE CONTEXT OF THE UNITED KINGDOM

Hazreena Hussein

INTRODUCTION

The term 'sensory garden' has been very much over-used in recent years, but in a therapeutic context, it explains the sensory landscapes that have been specially designed to fulfil the needs of people who want to be involved in active gardening and who also enjoy the passive pleasures of being outdoors among plants (Gaskell, 1994; Philips *et al.*, 2011). Lambe (1995:114) differentiated sensory gardens from any other garden by her statement, 'The only difference in a sensory garden is that all attributes of hard landscaping, soft landscaping, colours, textures and wildlife must be carefully chosen and designed to appeal to the senses in such a way that they provide maximum sensory stimulation'. Shoemaker (2002:195) added, 'Unlike traditional display gardens that are meant to be observed from a distance, sensory gardens draw the visitor in to touch, smell and actively experience the garden with all senses'.

The subject 'sensory garden' raised a number of preliminary questions for me as a researcher: *Are not all gardens sensory? What is a sensory garden composed of? How do people use or benefit from sensory gardens?* I undertook a review of the literature to find out how best to approach the subject of 'sensory gardens'. However, the review showed that there had been a lack of rigorous research on the subject and research issues could not readily be identified. I decided that the best approach would be to conduct preliminary site studies, mainly by visiting places that claimed to have or be sensory gardens (fourteen of them) and to find out what made them so through personal observations of the use of these gardens and interviews with the garden users, key experts and designers.

Six main findings arose from these preliminary site studies:

i)   Water is an important feature in that it provides users with the opportunity to respond to it through hearing and touch. In some sensory gardens, however, water is not fully accessible, therefore, such features are not of true benefit to the users. Some sensory gardens also lack this feature.

ii) Ramps, even with an accessible gradient, were not appreciated by the garden users, who were concerned about slippery surfaces. Steps were also not favoured, especially by wheelchair users and their carers.

iii) Loose materials on the surface of paths, such as gravel separated by wood edging, are inaccessible to wheelchair users. Therefore, such users are unable to appreciate significant features that can only be accessed in this way. (Not all features will be accessed by loose-surface paths. The loose surface is problematic for some users, particularly for students in wheelchairs, if it is the only form of access. On the other hand, if the school is unlikely to have wheelchair users, the use of loose surfaces can be sensorily stimulating and pleasant for users with other disabilities.)

iv) Regardless of who designs a sensory garden – a landscape architect or a joint community or school effort – challenges in terms of long-term maintenance should be addressed in the design plan. If they are not, a poorly maintained sensory garden will not benefit its users and it will lack aesthetic value.

v)   Sensory gardens which are designed as such, tend not to be entirely satisfactory from the users' perspective; some designers, apparently, may not interview the users to determine their needs and preferences before designing the garden in detail.

vi) There are no design guidelines for sensory gardens (although there are some publications on anthropometrics for a variety of users, including disabled people). The design of sensory gardens relies on the experience and attitude of designers.

This chapter presents the experience of children with special needs and their adult carers in the multi-sensory learning environment, which is based upon the walk-through interviews, personal observations and behavioural mapping of the case study examples I carried out for my doctoral research (Hussein, 2009; Hussein *et al.*, 2015). In this study, observation notes of the users' activities in the sensory garden were written up while undertaking the behaviour mapping. As a result, in order to interpret the results, a few significant occurrences were used as observations with the integration of a selection of photographs to illustrate these occurrences. The difference between how the landscape architects and school staff anticipated users would behave during the interviews, and what was recorded during the observation periods in the case studies, is an important finding to highlight in this study.

MULTI-SENSORY ENVIRONMENT

For the purpose of the study presented in this chapter, the term 'multi-sensory environment' will be used when describing the type of approach to which students with special educational needs could be exposed, namely, to an environment that is designed to offer sensory stimulation through all the senses using textures (touch), colours (sight), scents (smell), sounds (hearing), etc.

The evolution of multi-sensory environments began within indoor settings in the 1970s (Hulsegge et al., 1987; Hirstwood et al., 1995; Hogg et al., 2001). However, it was only in the late 1980s that designers started to take account of visual and aural ambiences and to install equipment that could accommodate, in special schools and nursing homes, the needs especially of people with profound and multiple disabilities (Mount et al., 1995). Hogg and Sebbas' (1986) and Longhorn's (1988) research examined the development of auditory, physical and visual impairments in people with profound and multiple learning disabilities and they developed appropriate multi-sensory curricula to address each. Longhorn suggested, 'without stimulation and an awakening of the senses, children with profound and multiple learning difficulties would find it almost impossible to make sense of their experiences and to begin to learn' (quoted in Mount *et al.*, 1995:52). As a result, a multi-sensory curriculum was integrated into the special needs educational system to satisfy the United Kingdom's national curriculum (Byers, 1998).

Following on from the recognised positive benefits of multi-sensory indoor experiences, outdoor sensory gardens have logically developed (Nebelong, 2008). The only functional difference between them is that the cost of a sensory garden is considerably less and it is a truly natural multi-sensory environment compared to a manufactured multi-sensory or '*snoezelen*' room (Lambe, 1995).

> Each adult working with a child with multiple disabilities has an important role in ensuring that the child is able to make sense of the environment using appropriate information from a range of sensory channels. In attempting to provide the child with a balanced understanding of the environment, the adult will need to structure on appropriate learning environment which can be both reactive to the child's actions and responsive to the child's needs.
>
> (Bell, 1993, quoted in McLinden, 1997:321)

Nowadays, multi-sensory design in the context of a garden is becoming increasingly popular for educational purposes in special schools (*Building Bulletin* 102, 2008; Westley, 2003; Woolley, 2003; Frank, 1996; Stoneham, 1996; Titman, 1994; Winterbottom *et al.*, 2015), for rehabilitation purposes in hospitals (Cooper Marcus *et al.*, 1999; Tyson, 1998; Cooper Marcus *et al.*, 2014; Winterbottom *et al.*, 2015) and for health benefits in nursing homes (Stoneham, 1997; Stoneham *et al.*, 1994; Winterbottom *et al.*, 2015).

Having a multi-sensory environment in a special school is beneficial for both teachers and students as it provides a two-way learning process. *Learning through Landscapes*, an association formed in 1990 in the United Kingdom, has conducted research concerning children with special educational needs in outdoor areas. The findings made it apparent that teachers appreciate outdoor areas a foundation for the education of children with special educational needs. As their paper in *Building Bulletin* 77 (1992:49) outlined, 'Outdoor spaces can provide opportunities for observation, investigation and problem-solving and form a flexible facility often more readily adaptable to change in user requirements than the building itself. They can offer a stimulating environment suited to practical activities from which many pupils with special needs can benefit'. This idea echoes the beliefs of Long and Haigh (1992), Titman (1994), Rohde and Kendle (1994), Lucas (1996), Stoneham (1997), Moore (1999), Malone and Tranter (2003), Woolley (2003), Maller and Townsend (2005/2006), Souter-Brown (2015) and Winterbottom and Wagenfeld (2015), that outdoor environmental learning can influence children's behaviour in terms of reducing aggression and assist in their development in terms of mental health, emotional and social relationships as well as providing a stimulating sensory experience, especially being in contact with animals and plants. This notion has received further support from a teacher at one of the case-study sites who noted: 'Pupils are most likely to succeed when they are involved in "doing" activities rather than academic learning'. Multi-sensory environments are used by individuals with all kinds of disabilities in special schools where this offers them the opportunity to engage in self-stimulating activities while enhancing learning opportunities outdoors.

One way of achieving a multi-sensory environment is to have plants that are both functional and able to provide visual stimulation through the use of colours, tactile stimulation through textures and olfactory stimulation through different scents (Hussein, 2005; Cooper Marcus *et al.*, 2014; Souter-Brown, 2015; Winterbottom *et al.*, 2015). These plant qualities must be carefully considered so that they are pleasant and also stimulate experiences. It was observed in one school garden that the staff and students liked to brush their legs and hands against lavender bushes while walking on the paths. A few of them smelt their hands after touching them. In an interview I conducted with a teacher at one of the case study sites, she mentioned a particular child with poor sight who successfully navigated her way around the sensory garden using the scent of lavender and that when she (the child) smells it, it reminds her of her mother at home, who had planted it in their garden. Lynch (1960) described what he termed the *imageable* elements of the environment. These are not necessarily visual; they can be distinctive sounds, smells or tactile experiences. Encountering familiar features and recognisable landmarks may help way-finding (Lynch, 1960; Kaplan, 1976; Kaplan *et al.*, 1998). The key aspect of designing for way-finding depends on the distinctiveness of landmarks, their placement and the way they can connect between spaces. A range of different sensory experiences, which would encourage a greater understanding and exploration by users of a sensory garden, could help to increase users' enjoyment of an environment. However, if these are not met, users may feel frustrated and even threatened; thus, it will add to their fears and apprehension of getting lost. When users feel orientated, their eagerness to explore the environment is increased and their general anxieties are lessened (Kaplan *et al.*, 1998).

SPECIAL EDUCATIONAL NEEDS AND DISABILITY

The term 'special educational needs' covers an array of difficulties highlighted in the 2001 Special Educational Needs Code of Practice in the United Kingdom, which 'recognises a wide spectrum of special educational needs that are frequently inter-related, although there are also specific needs that usually relate directly to particular types of impairment'. The Pupil Level Annual Schools Census data set was amended in 2004 to include twelve categories of special educational needs: specific learning disability; moderate learning disability; severe learning disability; profound and multiple learning disability; emotional and behavioural difficulty; speech, language and communication needs; hearing impairment; visual impairment; multi-sensory impairment; physical difficulty; Autism Spectrum Disorder; other. Most of the sensory gardens visited as part of my research provided access to children with at least one, often more of the special educational needs. In this chapter, the term 'special educational needs' will be used when referring to the 'students' of the case-study sensory gardens.

Mount *et al.* (1995) and Chawla *et al.* (2002) mentioned the richness of the visual, auditory and tactile stimuli that gardens can offer and the opportunities for exploration and how they could therefore assist users to develop an understanding of the environment. However, any impairment, disability or handicap will limit a person's ability to engage with the environment to a greater or lesser extent. As garden designer Noel Farrer, of Farrer Huxley Associates (2008:17), states: 'When designing for children with disabilities, it's vital to understand that their senses are completely different. You are not dealing with the same sort of physicality, you are dealing with texture, smell and sound; motor skills are far more localised'. He added that practitioners can draw together relevant information from *Building Bulletins* 102 (2008) and 77 (1992), which provide a comprehensive framework and guidelines for designing for children with special educational needs. Case studies and illustrated examples show how these can be put into practice.

Passini and Proulx's (1988) and Jacobson's (1998) research found that it is easier for a visually impaired person to orientate and navigate outdoors when landmarks and paths are distinguishable through texture or other means to provide clues, such as surface changes. Tyson (1998:75) noted that 'the planting composition, strategic location and significant elements could orientate people with impairments around green spaces'. Kaplan *et al.* (1998:50) supported this, stating: 'The distinctiveness of such elements, where they are placed, and the number of them are all key aspects of designing for way-finding'. This was evident during one of my observation days at the case study sites. 'Eileen', who has special educational needs, was able to find her way back to her classroom after a literacy session through the use of plants. In other words, users respond in fundamentally different ways when they encounter familiar or unfamiliar features which challenge their perception and movement. Furthermore, the various garden attributes motivate them to practice their motor skills and use them for way-finding. This is important for facilitating children's educational development and social interaction.

McLinden *et al.* (2002:54) differentiate between the close (or proximal) senses (touch and taste), and the distance senses (sight, smell and hearing). They note that 'when the distance sense of vision is impaired, young children may be able to compensate to some extent by making greater use of their other distance sense – hearing'. For example, during my observation period at the case study gardens, a teacher expressed her feeling that it was a pity that the water feature was not working because her visually-impaired student loved to hear the sound of the water and when he did, he would remain at the Central Water Area of the garden for a longer period.

DESCRIPTIVE SUMMARIES OF THE CASE STUDIES

It was vital to choose sensory gardens which had been designed by landscape architects. The potential final case studies were short-listed based on a set of five criteria:

i) Completed and operational. The sensory gardens in these case studies had to have been completed and in use for the outdoor activities they were offering.
ii) The design and its recognition. The selected sensory gardens must offer a variety of attributes and had to be recognised for their good design, as evidenced by being reviewed in landscape architecture websites and magazines. In addition, they had to have been recommended by Jane Stoneham of the Sensory Trust, the key expert in this area.
iii) Accessibility. The availability of information about the chosen case studies and easy access to them were important for the practicality of the research.
iv) The spatial location. The location of the sensory garden in relation to the associated school building was considered, into in order to find out whether this aspect would influence how the area was used, whether this factor was likely to result in high levels of use and whether landscape architects took that aspect of accessibility into account during design.
v) Time and funding. Choice of site locations was also limited by what could be achieved with the funding available and the time required to conduct my research.

Of the fourteen potential sites for study across the United Kingdom, two sites were chosen, based on these key factors: Lyndale School and the Royal School for the Deaf and Communication Disorders.

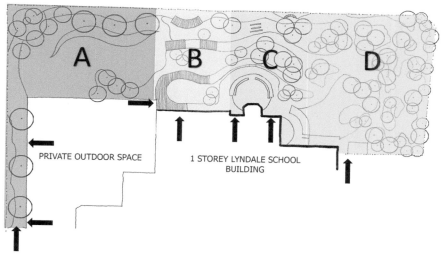

The Lyndale School, UK

FIGURE 4.1 Plan of the sensory garden, showing the themed zones at Lyndale School
Credit: University Malaya Press

Lyndale School in Liverpool is a non-residential special school for children with complex needs, and profound and multiple disabilities. It caters to children from the ages of two to eleven years. A landscape architect from Groundwork Wirral, Mark Boothroyd, designed the sensory garden, which was completed in 2005. The project's success relied on extensive local community fundraising. The garden is attached to the school building, with an open view to the residential backyard. It has a linear form with a combination of flat and undulating topography. The school relies on volunteer efforts for the garden's maintenance. The sensory garden has four themed zones: (A) Rainbow Walk, (B) Water Garden, (C) Green Space and (D) Woodland Garden (Figure 4.1).

The Royal School for the Deaf and Communication Disorders (RSDCD) in Manchester is a residential, co-educational special school and college. The students' disabilities range from severe and complex learning difficulties, autism, emotional and behavioural difficulties, multi-sensory impairment, to medical, physical and language disorders. Their age range is from two to twenty years. The sensory garden was designed in 2000 by Sue Robinson, a landscape architect from Stockport Metropolitan Borough Council. The garden, called the Multi-Sensory Millennium Maze, is situated in the middle of the school, between two buildings. It is a square form: a courtyard with flat topography. The sensory garden has six themed zones: (A) Parents' Waiting Area, (B) Exploraway, (C) Green Space One, (D) Green Space Two, (E) Asteroids Arts Garden and (F) Water Central Area (Figure 4.2).

RESEARCH STRATEGY AND METHODS

In an interview I conducted with a retired deputy head teacher at Lyndale School, she mentioned that, 'Every special school has slightly different needs. The sensory garden will reflect those needs, so no sensory garden will be the same. They might have similar elements but there will always be an emphasis upon the needs of their individual children'. Following on from that statement, the objective of this study is to observe and record how children with special needs and their adult carers responded to and engaged with the attributes in a sensory garden.

In this study, the focus of the analysis was on observation and behaviour mapping. The interview material is the secondary data of the study (see Table 4.1). While undertaking the behaviour mapping, observation notes were written up to help to interpret the results. The similarities and differences between the interviews and observation results could be used to inform landscape architects' future practice and/or educators when designing for sensory

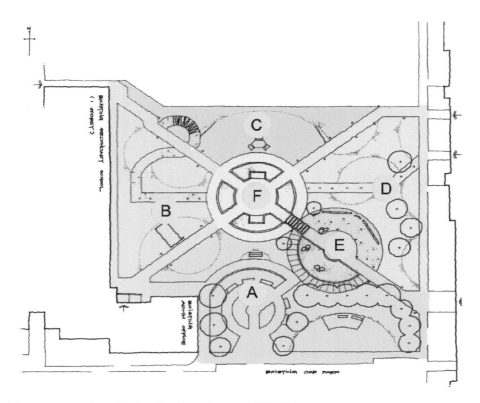

FIGURE 4.2 Plan of the sensory garden, showing the themed zones at RSDCD
Credit: University Malaya Press

TABLE 4.1 The sequential method used for data collection with the landscape architects and school staff for their respective sensory gardens

Method	Respondents	Objectives
i) Interview with the landscape architects was conducted in two sessions: • At a place of their choice • A walkthrough in the sensory garden.	Lyndale School (n=1) RSDCD (n=1)	To investigate the design process and the landscape architect's design intentions. To find out the challenges he or she had to deal with. To allow subsequent assessment of whether users utilise areas and garden attributes in the way they are meant to.
ii) Interview with the teachers and therapists at the sensory garden.	Lyndale School (n=9) RSDCD (n=6)	To enquire their experience of and benefits in having the sensory garden. To assess the garden attributes and any problems identified in the sensory garden.
iii) Observations and behaviour mapping were conducted in May and July, for seven days each month, on weekdays during the opening hours of the school during the term.	Lyndale School and RSDCD (All users)	To understand how users behave in the sensory garden and engage with the garden attributes.

gardens. For example, they should ensure that all users are offered a variety of activities to engage with the garden attributes as well as minimising barriers to allow users full access to and from the garden. When presenting the findings, these two aspects are integrated together.

THE SIMILARITIES BETWEEN THE TWO GARDENS

The most successful attributes in terms of usage recorded during the observation period at RSDCD were the mobility on pathways and pathway varieties. The landscape architect mentioned that she had seen how users utilised the pathway; directionally and criss-crossing from one end to another. This aligned with her design description to provide a strong overall framework to channel and encourage movement from one area to another. The sensory gardens in both case study sites are used as a place to conduct speech therapy. One of the standard multi-sensory curriculum items, which is used by teachers in all special schools, is PECS (Picture Exchange Communication System), which involves showing photographs and finding objects in the sensory garden using touch, hearing, smell and sight. This exercise is beneficial for wayfinding and identifying significant attributes in the sensory garden. The following observation illustrates how a speech therapist used the images on the rubber walkway at Green Space Two (see Figure 4.3):

One afternoon, a therapist and a student with speech difficulties were strolling in the sensory garden. When the therapist reached the rubber walkway, she jumped onto one of the images and said, '*Flower!*' Then she jumped from the 'flower' onto a blank space and let the student jump onto the flower image. The student copied what her therapist had done and responded very well. Seeing that the student had behaved positively, the therapist continued jumping onto a series of different images until the end of the walkway.

FIGURE 4.3 Location where a speech therapist and a student with speech difficulties were recorded using the images on the rubber-surfaced walkway to encourage verbal communication
Source: the author

The observation at Lyndale School identified that the boardwalk and path network at the Water Garden were the least used parts of the garden. Teachers said that they were concerned about the boardwalk near the pond because it was slippery and hazardous for students. As a result, they used the steps instead. In addition, students in their wheelchairs wanted to continue their exploration of the boardwalk but could not do so because the path came to an end. This corresponded with the landscape architect's interview where he said that the surface material and accessibility of the boardwalk were not constructed as he had originally envisaged. Teachers also expressed their frustration about the fact that at that time the interactive fountain was not working, because their students loved watching the water and talking about it. When the landscape architect was asked about this, he thought it was a technical problem at that particular time.

The observations at RSDCD showed the least-used themed zone to be the Exploraway. Although this is the second-largest area, users engaged with its features such as the lawn patch, lighting bollards, gravel surface and path. These elements are few compared to the other areas in the sensory garden. The Exploraway with its gravel surface was underused because the gravel surface is unsuitable for wheelchair users and mobility exercise. For example, students on a specially-adapted bicycle wanted to cycle on the Exploraway but they did could not do so because of the surface material. The school staff concurred with this view and according to the landscape architect, the Exploraway should be bumpier in order to offer a better mobility challenge, hence she also thought this area to be the least successful part of her design.

At Lyndale School, while the landscape architect predicted that the feature that would be most frequently used and popular would be the sound stimuli at the Woodland Garden, he was surprised to see that the majority of students were drawn towards this. The observation data demonstrated that this area was the most used, especially by partially-sighted students who liked to touch, feel and hold the rope railing while walking on the boardwalk. The following observation illustrates how a student runs about and listens to the sound stimuli:

> A young boy was walking hand in hand with his teaching assistant in the sensory garden. Both of them were silent – listening to the humming insects, chirping birds and the wind in the leaves. As they were strolling together, one of the sound stimuli went off by itself. The boy let go of his assistant's hands and ran towards the sound. Soon he managed to find the source of the sound, he walked towards the researcher and asked, 'Are you here to see the flowers? It's a nice garden, isn't it?' He then smiled and continued strolling with his teaching assistant.

THE DIFFERENCES BETWEEN THE TWO GARDENS

The landscape architect of RSDCD's sensory garden predicted that the Asteroids Arts Garden and the Central Water Area would be the most popular. This is because the Asteroids Arts Garden was particularly requested by school staff during the sketch design phase and the Central Water Area is located at the centre of the sensory garden, which she thought would be fairly well maintained. However, three of the school staff pointed out that although the musical instruments are located along the path, they are inaccessible to wheelchair users and do not produce much sound. At the Central Water Area, the observation results showed that students in wheelchairs wanted to feel the water but could not manage to do so because of the shrubs around it. This concurred with information provided in an interview with the teachers. The students also wanted to touch the plants in the raised beds but did not manage this either, because of the height of the wall; students who were more mobile had to step over or on the shrubs planted around the water feature before they could touch the water. Inevitably, some parts of the planting beds were sparse due to this (Figure 4.4).

School staff at RSDCD mentioned that due to the willow tunnel's location in the sensory garden, this is the least successful feature in terms of use. However, during the observation period, I found that students were fond of

FIGURE 4.4 Shrubs planted around the water feature were seen by the users as a barrier to getting closer to this feature
Source: the author

willow weaving and engaging with the artwork display in the willow tunnel. A partially-sighted student and a student in a wheelchair were also observed using the willow tunnel. The students were fearful of going into the tunnel because of the changes in the surfacing material so that teachers had to cheer them on and convince them to walk through it. The following observation illustrates how the willow tunnel at Green Space One was used:

> One morning, two teachers decided to experience the willow tunnel with one student who was in a wheelchair and one student who was partially-sighted. The two teachers went through the willow tunnel and waited for more than five minutes as both of their students had a fear of going through the tunnel due to the changes in its material on the floor surface. One of the teachers tried to convince both students by saying, 'Come on, Steve...you can do it!', while the other teacher walked through to the end of the willow tunnel and said, 'Look! I'm here'. The students looked surprised. Then she walked back through the willow tunnel and cheered on both students to join them. The partially-sighted student put one foot tentatively on the chip-bark surfaces. He then smiled and walked slowly towards his teachers. As he approached, one of the teachers held his hands and said, 'Yes! You've made it!'. The other student in his wheelchair was still on the pathway. He looked confidently at his mate and slowly wheeled his chair onto the bark surface. They continued to cheer him on. As he came closer to them, one of the teachers said, 'Well done, Steve!'. They then engaged with the willow tunnel. One teacher and student played with some of the artwork displays while the other pair spread their arms wide while feeling the willow. The four of them finally walked towards the end of the willow tunnel and returned back to the pathway. Besides experiencing the features of the willow tunnel, it also increased the students' confidence.

The sensory garden at Lyndale School is often used as an extension of the school classrooms and provides teachers a creative alternative location to conduct speech therapy. The landscape architect of Lyndale School's sensory garden predicted that the least used themed zone would be the Rainbow Walk (Figure 4.5). This, he felt, would be due to the relative poverty of features and lack of maintenance. However, the teachers preferred to use this area as an outdoor classroom in support of communication therapy.

FIGURE 4.5 Besides using the Rainbow Walk as an outdoor classroom, users also carried out tree-rubbing activities
Source: the author

The following observation illustrates how users of the sensory garden used the Rainbow Walk as an outdoor classroom:

> One morning, a group of female staff and students with various kinds of impairment were walking hand in hand through the sensory garden of the school to find the perfect tree to do some bark-rubbing. As they neared a huge shady tree, a teacher said, 'Let's feel this tree'. She placed her hands on the tree trunk. A male student moved his hands over the bark and slid his arms around the trunk until they met. His face was touching the bark and he said, 'This is the perfect tree!'. So they all got out their paper and pencils and started a bark-rubbing activity.

Another observation demonstrates how a group of teachers wheeled their students with special educational needs out from their classroom to the *Rainbow Walk*:

The morning weather was fine with sunny spells and the wind was blowing in between the leaves. 'Do you know where we are going, David?' asked a teacher. 'David' jumped in his wheelchair while his hands grasped the armrest. He was making a loud sound, showing anticipation. As the large group reached the area, they formed a circle around the conifer tree. As the teachers and students gathered in pairs around the conifer tree, with a plank as the floor surface, the teachers sang, 'Here we go 'round the mulberry bush'. As they chanted, I thought it was a perfect song to sing, as it invited many physical movements that generated sound and vibration for the students, such as stamping, jumping, skipping, clapping and cheering. The students responded positively by swinging their hands while turning their heads from one side to another. Some students opened their mouths and tried to mimic their teachers. This observation illustrates that the design of the sensory garden challenges the students' perception and motivates them to practice their literacy skills.

DISCUSSION

The findings showed that the teachers and students prefer areas with hard surface paths, allowing accessibility and easy way-finding into the sensory garden and back to the school building, as well as having the ability to move around the garden. This helps to promote educational development and social skills. They also favour zones with different functional and garden attributes placed directly next to an accessible and continuous path. This enables users to engage with it easily, thus affording them a richness of activities in the sensory garden. This concurs with Cosco's (2006) study on physical activity affordances in preschool play centres: that diverse areas comprising paths and features are likely to be the most active. This also echoed research undertaken by Moore et al. (2007) on inclusive parks, which showed that a wide pathway that gave access to the facilities that were readily accessible was a highly positive feature and the most popular among the users. Another of their findings was that a winding pathway afforded inclusion and added visual interest to the pedestrian experience. Winterbottom et al. (2015) also agreed that meandering garden paths may offer richer experiences for therapeutic relief and sensory stimulation to the users. This raised another question in my mind about the direct pathway at RSDCD compared to the curving one at Lyndale School: *Does the formation of a path play an important role in encouraging the richness of activities and behaviour?* The study looked back at the overall design framework related to the path layout of both sensory gardens.

The landscape architect intended, when designing RSDCDs' sensory garden, to improve the sense of direction, to offer paths of different widths and textures and to provide areas which offered a rich experience within a protected environment. For Lyndale School, the landscape architect intended to maximise the potential of the site with landform and to create a meandering path network that would provide a range of options and opportunities to move through spaces along the way. When the uses in both sensory gardens were recorded and compared, it seemed clear that users preferred to stroll on continuous paths, linking one zone to the next with readily accessible and functional features next to the paths. It is the layout of the path, therefore, that enables user behaviour and use of an area, rather than users seeking out corners or zones which have particular individual attributes. Thus, a higher number of users and a longer time spent there were recorded in relation to these design qualities. This is significant new knowledge, from a design point of view, indicating that path layout is more important than the particular design of features, as long as the pathways are accessible. This matched the idea of teachers of RSDCD to provide a 'sensory trail'. *How is a 'sensory trail' different from a sensory garden?* In the sensory garden, users are encouraged to maximize their enjoyment and engagement of their senses. The features in their sensory garden that the landscape architect aimed to maximise enjoyment need to be adjacent to the path. Ideally, a sensory garden should have a continuous circulation network that links all zones with easy access to the different features. Thus, what a landscape architect should be designing is a garden that is linked by a sensory trail which, in one sense, becomes the sensory garden.

The findings further suggest that a successful sensory trail comprises a combination of natural and manmade elements in a specific zone, along with a sufficient quantity of furniture such as seating, lighting and shelters. This would help to form the composition into a coherent whole within the sensory garden for easy wayfinding, generating activities and responses. Landscape architects can be given improved guidance about how spaces in the garden could be structured, offer a richness of activities and lessen the number of barriers that obstruct access. Another contribution to knowledge is the design aspect of sensory value. Users of the sensory garden thought that the features should not just be aesthetically and visually attractive, but that they should also be nice to touch, hear, smell and taste. In other words, aesthetic values should be formed from all sensory possibilities. In fact, in the context described here, what the site or features look like is much less important than how they feel, sound, smell or taste, since giving users maximum access to the features with these multi-sensory attributes is very important. The ability of users to engage directly with the sensory features is the key point when designing for a sensory garden. It is more to do with where the features are sited than what they are.

CONCLUSIONS

As the two case studies have shown, the integration of sensory garden design into the overall design of special schools, and including their use in the curriculum, could encourage the creation of an outdoor environment which could offer a wide range of multi-sensory learning experiences for students with special educational needs. The students' experiences at RSDCD and Lyndale School showed positive user functioning in three respects: sensory stimulation, physical (mobility) and social (speech and communication). For example, for students with special needs (RSDCD), getting to and around the sensory garden, then back to the school building (way-finding), was particularly important, as many, if not all, had some form of mobility impairment.

Landscape architects should ensure, firstly, that sensory garden design is integrated into the overall planning phases of the development (or re-development) of a special school. Secondly, they should recommend that students (and their carers) are involved in the design of their sensory garden. These two recommendations, if followed, would foster greater design integrity of the entire school plan.

Landscape architects should observe and record users' daily routines, to gain a better understanding of the activities and the way users perceive them. In so doing, the landscape architect, teachers and therapists could make sure the design phase and its realisation enable part of the school curriculum to be taught there, and to view the garden as an area which offers the potential *for* learning, rather than just as an outdoor area which is there to be used only in breaks *from* classroom learning.

Landscape architects should consider accessibility to, and the functionality of, the constructed surfaces and elements (including water features and artefacts), vegetation and natural elements (including animals and microclimate) and landscape furniture (for example, seating, lighting, signage and shelters). With a continuous circulatory path network, user enjoyment of and engagement with the individual elements is likely to be enhanced, so they are used as markers and trigger memories; the sensory trail is one very good way to achieve that.

Landscape architects must think about maintenance and upkeep because there is no point in having carefully designed landscapes unless they can be properly maintained (for example water features that break down are particularly disappointing). It would be useful for landscape architects to translate their design intentions effectively into a set of detailed construction drawings for the groundwork department of the school, as well as to produce a comprehensive maintenance and management schedule that would be easy to understand by the school maintenance staff or volunteers. Design consultants could also train the appointed maintenance contractors in how to look after the sensory garden.

Finally, landscape architects must also consider health and safety and risk assessment concerns when providing challenges to meet different user abilities, for example, in the Exploraway at the RSDCD. Although different surface materials should be considered, designers should bear in mind that being wheeled over a rough and bumpy terrain may not always be a pleasant experience, particularly for someone with limited mobility. Nevertheless, landscape architects should try to offer as wide a range of challenges in a garden as possible, to match the ability range and ages of the students. Where a school's intake is likely to change over time, landscape architects should consider leaving scope for further development of the garden. This would allow levels of challenge to be added later, for uptake by users whose capabilities were suited to them, or who, with the encouragement of their teachers and carers, could rise to such new challenges, for example, the willow tunnel at RSDCD or a 'wibbly-wobbly way' that is wheelchair accessible (Stoneham, 1996:50).

This chapter has illustrated the strengths and weaknesses in two sensory gardens in two special schools by evaluating their areas and attributes and how they were used by children with special educational needs and their adult carers. When I interviewed Jane Stoneham, director of the Sensory Trust in the United Kingdom, she said that landscape architects make many assumptions about how disabled people navigate and benefit from an outdoor environment. She added that detailed guidelines for sensory garden design are few, a view endorsed by designers such as Petrow (2006), Mathias (2006), Robinson (2007) and Boothroyd (2007) (in interviews with the author). My findings can support a further improvement in, and the creation of, a higher standard of sensory garden design by landscape architects. These recommendations, when integrated into detailed guidelines, as Stoneham and others recommend, would support better design of coherent garden spaces, further learning experiences and greater enjoyment, within users' physical, mental and sensory capabilities. In a talk given by Clare Cooper Marcus, an expert in healing gardens at Edinburgh College of Art (6 March, 2009), she said, 'Landscape architects should design gardens, not architects. You do not want a brain surgeon to replace your hip, do you?'

REFERENCES

Bell, J. (1993) 'Educating the multiply disabled blind child', in A. Fielder, A.B. Best and M. Bax (eds) *The management of visual impairment in childhood*, pp. 150–156, London: Mackeith Press.

Building Bulletin 102 (2008) *Designing for disabled children and children with special educational needs*, The Stationary Office, Norwich: HMSO.

Building Bulletin 77 (1992) *Designing for pupils with special educational needs: Special schools*, Department for Education, London: HMSO.

Byers, R. (1998) 'Sensory environments for pupils with profound and learning difficulties: Innovations in design and practice', *PMLD Link* **32**:28–31.

Chawla, L. and Heft, H. (2002) 'Children's competence and the ecology of communities: A functional approach to the evaluation of participation', *Journal of Environmental Psychology* **22**:201–216.

Cooper Marcus, C. and Barnes, M. (1999) *Healing gardens: Therapeutic benefits and design recommendations*, New York: John Wiley and Sons, Inc.

Cooper Marcus, C. and Sachs, N.A. (2014) *Therapeutic landscapes: An evidence-based approach to designing healing gardens and restorative outdoor spaces*, New Jersey: John Wiley and Sons, Inc.

Cosco, Nilda G. (2006) 'Motivation to move: Physical activity affordances in preschool play areas', unpublished doctoral thesis, Edinburgh College of Art.

Farrer, N. (2008) 'Golden moments', *Landscape Design: Journal of Landscape Institute* **53**:10–20.

Frank, A. (1996) 'Learning curves', *Landscape Design: Journal of Landscape Institute* **249**:22–25.

Gaskell, J. (1994) 'Sensory gardens', *Growth Point* **3**:206.

Hirstwood, R. and Gary, M. (1995) *A practical guide to the use of multi-sensory rooms*, Leicestershire, UK: Toys for the Handicapped.

Hogg, J., Cavet, J., Loretto L., and Smeddle, M. (2001) 'The use of "Snoezelen" as multisensory stimulation with people with intellectual disabilities: A review of the research', *Research in Developmental Disabilities* **22**, 5:353–372.

Hogg, J. and Sebba, J. (1986) *Profound retardation and multiple impairment*, Volume 1: *Development and learning*, London: Croom Helm.

Hulsegge, J. and Verheul, Ad. (1987) *Snoezelen: Another world – A practical book of sensory experience environments for the mentally handicapped*, trans. by R. Alink, Rompa.

Hussein, H. (2005) 'Encouraging a barrier-free built environment in a Malaysian University', *Journal of Design and Built Environment* **1**:33–40.

Hussein, H. (2009) 'Therapeutic intervention: Using sensory gardens to enhance the quality of life for children with special needs', unpublished doctoral thesis, Edinburgh College of Art.

Hussein, H. and Daud, M.N. (2015) 'Examining the methods for investigating behavioural clues of special-schooled children', *Field Methods* **27**, 1:97–112.

Jacobson, R. Dan (1998) 'Cognitive mapping without sight: Four preliminary studies of spatial learning', *Journal of Environmental Psychology* **18**:289–305.

Kaplan, S. (1976) 'Adaptation, structure, knowledge', in Moore, G.T. and Golledge, R.G. (eds) *Environmental knowing: Theories, research and methods*, pp. 32–45. Stroudsburg: Dowden, Hutchinson and Ross.

Kaplan, R., Kaplan, S. and Ryan, R.L. (1998) *With people in mind: Design and management of everyday nature,* Washington, DC: Island Press.

Lambe, L. (1995) 'Gardening: A multisensory experience', in J. Hogg and J. Cavet (eds) *Making leisure provision for people with profound and multiple learning disabilities*, pp. 113–130. London: Chapman and Hall.

Longhorn, F. (1988) *A sensory curriculum for very special people*, London: Souvenir Press.

Long, A.P. and Haigh, L. (1992) 'How do clients benefit from snoezelen? An exploratory study', *British Journal of Occupational Therapy* **55**, 3:103–106.

Lucas, B. (1996) 'A feast for the senses', *Landscape Design: Journal of Landscape Institute* **249**: 6–28.

Lynch, K. (1960) *The image of the city*, Cambridge, MA: The MIT Press.

Maller, C. and Townsend, M. (2005/2006) 'Children's mental health and wellbeing and hands-on contact with nature', *International Journal of Learning* **12**, 4:359–372.

Malone, K. and Tranter, Paul J. (2003) 'School grounds as sites for learning: Making the most of environmental opportunities', *Environmental Education Research* **9**, 3:283–303.

McLinden, M. (1997) 'Children with multiple disabilities and a visual impairment', in Mason, H. and McCall, S. (eds.) *Visual impairment: Access to education for children and young people*, pp. 313–323. London: David Fulton.

McLinden, M. and McCall, S. (2002) *Learning through touch: Supporting children with visual impairment and additional difficulties*, London: David Fulton Publishers.

Moore, R.C. (1999) 'Healing gardens for children', in Cooper Marcus, C. and Barnes, M. (eds) *Healing gardens: Therapeutic benefits and design recommendations,* pp. 323–385. New York: John Wiley and Sons, Inc.

Moore, R.C. and Cosco, N.G. (2007) 'What makes a park inclusive and universally designed? A multi-method approach', in Ward Thompson, C. and Travlou, P. (eds) *Open space: People space*, pp. 85–110. London: Taylor and Francis.

Mount, H. and Cavet, J. (1995) 'Multi-sensory environments: An exploration of their potential for young people with profound and multiple learning difficulties', *British Journal of Special Education* **22**, 2:52–55.

Nebelong, H. (2008) 'A sense of place: Improving children's quality of life through design', *Green Spaces* **45**:20–24.

Passini, R. and Proulx, G. (1988) 'Wayfinding without vision: An experiment with congenitally totally blind people', *Environment and Behaviour* **20**, 2:227–252.

Philips, C. and Butler, P. (2011). *Barwon Community Leadership Program 2011, Community Project*, Murray Howard-Brooks.

Rohde, C.L.E. and Kendle A.D. (1994) *Human well-being, natural landscapes and wildlife in urban areas*, Peterborough: English Nature.

Shoemaker, C. (2002) *Interaction by design: Bringing people and plants together for health and well-being, an international symposium*, Iowa State Press.

Special Educational Needs Code of Practice (2001) London: Department for Education and Skills.

Souter-Brown, G. (2015) *Landscape and urban design for health and well-being: Using healing, sensory and therapeutic gardens*, Abingdon: Routledge.

Stoneham, J. (1996) *Grounds for sharing: A guide to developing special school sites*, Winchester: Learning through Landscapes.

Stoneham, J. (1997) 'Health benefit', *Landscape Design: Journal of Landscape Institute* **249**:23–26.

Stoneham, J. and Thoday, P. (1994) *Landscape design for elderly and disabled people,* Chichester: Packard Publishing Ltd.

Titman, W. (1994) *Special places, special people: The hidden curriculum of school ground*, Cambridge: Learning through Landscapes/World Wide Fund for Nature UK.

Tyson, M. (1998) *The healing landscape: Therapeutic outdoor environment*, New York: McGraw Hill.

Westley, M. (2003) 'Sensory-rich education', *Landscape Design: Journal of Landscape Institute* **317**:31–35.

Winterbottom, D. and Wagenfeld, A. (2015) *Design for healing spaces: Therapeutic gardens*, London: Timber Press.

Woolley, H. (2003) *Urban open spaces*, London: Routledge.

5

CAN ACTIVE PLAY ENCOURAGE PHYSICAL LITERACY IN CHILDREN AND YOUNG PEOPLE?

Patrizio De Rossi

INTRODUCTION

The role of physical activity in the primary and secondary prevention of numerous chronic diseases is clear. There is evidence of the positive effect of physical activity in conditions such as cardiovascular disease, diabetes, cancer, osteoporosis, hypertension, depression, and obesity (Lee, 2012; Warburton et al., 2006). However, despite this evidence, in the Minority World[1] (Punch, 2000 p.60), a large part of the population is still inactive (Hallal, et al., 2012). In England, for example, according to the Health Behaviour in School-Aged Children Study (HBSC) (Inchley et al., 2016), 25% of boys and 20% of girls aged 11 years old meet the required amount of physical activity (60 min per day of moderate-vigorous intensity physical activity) but only 18% of boys and 9% of girls aged 15 are active.

The Global Matrix 2.0, a worldwide study which compares, among other indicators, physical activity levels and government strategies, investments, community, and the built environment all aimed at promoting physical activity in 38 countries on 6 continents, showed that the countries which have low scores in policy, investment, and infrastructure have high scores in young people's participation in physical activity and vice versa (Tremblay et al., 2016). These results seem clear: policies for promoting participation in physical activity are not appealing to young people and children and young people are more active when physical activity is self-fostered for its intrinsic pleasure. The prevailing utilitarian discourse around physical activity promotion that focuses on health benefits is characterizing physical activity as a duty (Kretchmar, 2005). The results of this approach are not positive, most notably for adolescents, and especially for adolescent girls (Dumith, et al., 2011; Pearson, et al., 2015). An alternative to this current approach is to place emphasis on the joy of movement, promoting the idea that movement is important for its own sake, it is a source of pleasure and enjoyment, and supports intrinsic motivation (Kretchmar, 2008).

Active play is a type of activity which has all these joy-oriented characteristics and it is carried out for its intrinsic pleasure. Active play is defined as "unstructured physical activity that takes place outdoors in the child's free time" (Veitch et al., 2008 p 870). It is self-chosen and personally directed and fun is an essential element (Else, 2014a). Active play encourages enjoyment, creativity, and autonomy in a non-judgemental environment supporting movement skills, self-esteem, resilience, problem-solving, managing stress, and social, emotional, and cognitive well-being (Brockman et al., 2010; Ginsburg et al., 2007; Kentel and Dobson, 2007; Matthews et al., 2011; NICE, 2008; Truelove et al., 2017). In addition to all these benefits, active play has the potential to foster physical literacy; during play children "know through movement, about movement, and because of movement" (Kentel and Dobson, 2007, p. 159).

In the last few years, physical literacy has become a significant concept in education, sport, and physical activity promotion, policy, and practice in different countries (Dudley et al., 2017; Edwards et al., 2017; Shearer et al., 2018). Physical literacy is defined as "the motivation, confidence, physical competence, knowledge and understanding to maintain physical activity throughout the lifecourse" (Whitehead, 2010a, pp. 11–12) and is appropriate to each individual's capacity for movement. For this reason, everyone can achieve physical literacy since it is considered a potential that everyone possesses at their own level and it is not related to a defined period of life (Whitehead, 2010a). A physically literate individual is competent in considering and critically evaluating their movement experiences.

They are also able to understand the importance of physical activity, to involve peers, promoting their participation, and to talk about these topics (Edwards et al., 2017; Whitehead, 2010b). Through positive experiences they will enhance self-esteem and self-confidence. All these attributes are interrelated and the improvement of one of these leads to the advancements of all the others. Positive self-perception, intrinsic motivation, and perceived competence, which are key predictors of lifelong participation in physical activities (Cairney et al., 2012; NICE, 2007) are also the attributes of a "physically literate" individual (De Rossi et al., 2012; Whitehead, 2010b).

In keeping with the key themes of linking active play and physical literacy with fostering joy in movement, this chapter draws on the results of a research project (De Rossi et al., 2012) that explored children's perspectives and experiences of active play.

The chapter begins with an overview of key themes and approaches pertaining to physical activity promotion. It then goes on to outline physical literacy and active play and exploring possible links between them, considering children's perspectives and direct experiences. The chapter concludes with considerations and recommendations for creating environments which support active play.

PHYSICAL ACTIVITY PROMOTION STRATEGIES

There is a general assumption, in educational curricula, academic research, and international and national policies, that physical activity can be promoted as a means to achieve diverse outcomes. These can vary from health enhancement to political or social purposes and improvement of socially accepted behaviours. The "obesity crisis" (Kirk, 2006) and the utilitarian perspective on physical activity considered as a solution for health issues have influenced academic research and school curricula, and shaped national and international policies and strategies aimed at improving physical activity participation. However, this approach has failed in involving children and particularly adolescents to become more active. Children and adolescents are not inactive because of a lack of knowledge. They know about the consequences of being inactive (Symons et al., 2013); what they want are more opportunities to be active in a way that is closer to their interests (Dollman, Norton, and Norton, 2005). Little attention has been paid to the potential of the joy-oriented approach to physical activity and to the impact that active play can have on fostering and motivating physically active behaviours throughout life.

Society and natural and human environments have been subjected to rapid and intense changes in the last 40 years. Increased urban expansion, greater volumes of traffic, digital technologies, families' lifestyle choices, and perceptions of children and young people through childcare, education and healthcare have been affecting almost every element of human life. The different lifestyle which has been shaped by these changes has had clear consequences. Some adolescents have fewer opportunities to play outdoors outside school (Gleave and Cole-Hamilton, 2012). The increasing number of children, young people, and adults in the "Minority World" (Punch, 2000 p. 60), who are overweight or obese (Swinburn et al., 2011; Wang and Lobstein, 2006; Wiklund, 2016) is another consequence of this contemporary lifestyle. Physical inactivity is considered the fourth leading risk factor for global mortality (WHO, 2010). However, the important role of physical activity goes beyond the primary prevention of excess weight, obesity, cancer, and other health issues. From a holistic perspective, physical activity plays a fundamental role in the lifelong development of the physical, cognitive, affective, and social domains, along with wellbeing and life skills (Marchetti, Bellotti, and Pesce, 2016; Whitehead, 2010a). The solution in governmental strategies, policies, and educational curricula for promoting physically active behaviour in children and adolescents has emphasized the links between health behaviours, wellbeing, and physical activity, providing more opportunities for organised sports (Else, 2014b). Yet it is the intrinsic motivation, the drive to do something because "it is inherently interesting or enjoyable" (Ryan and Deci, 2000, p.55), the involvement of young people in creating spaces and opportunities for a wide choice of different activities (structured and unstructured), and the promotion of physical activity for its own sake through active play, that may have the greatest opportunity of changing adolescents' behaviour.

Children and adolescents want to be more active (Corder et al., 2013). They need activities which are closer to their interests and physical and social environments which encourage these activities (Dollman, Norton, and Norton, 2005). A survey by the Women's Sport and Fitness Foundation (WSFF, 2012) that examined the perspectives of adolescent girls about their physical activity experiences found that in England, in 2008, while only 12% of girls aged 14–15 were physically active (NHS, 2008), 76% of the participants wanted to be more active but they were discouraged, among other perceived barriers, by high levels of competition in traditional sports and the limited choice of activities during physical education lessons. When adolescents are intrinsically motivated, they are more active (Martins et al., 2015; Symons et al., 2013). A joy-oriented approach, which highlights the pleasure of the movement for its own sake, supports the intrinsic motivation to spontaneous, competent, and creative movements (Kretchmar, 2008).

THE JOY OF MOVEMENT

The current utilitarian message which promotes physical activity as work, as an instrument to get health benefits, has not been successful in motivating children and young people in adopting a physically active lifestyle. Kretchmar outlines two weaknesses relating to this approach (2005). The first relates to the fact that physical activity for health supports extrinsic behaviour, while it is intrinsic motivation that is associated with participation in physical activity. Extrinsic motivation may produce positive results, but they often only have short-term effects. In contrast, intrinsic motivation seems a stronger facilitator for long-term effective behaviour change (Ryan and Deci, 2007). The second weakness is that the message of considering movement as work in order to be a healthier adult or as a weight-loss programme is not a convincing one for children or young people whose health is not considered at risk at the moment. Rather, the following factors – fun, intrinsic motivation, perception of competence, the impact of friends, adults (parents, physical education teachers, and sports coaches), and environment – are the facilitators of physical activity for adolescents (Martins et al., 2015). The factor which was most frequently indicated by the adolescents was fun. Podilchak's qualitative analysis of young people's (mean age of 22 years old) interviews offers one of the most cited descriptions of fun. He defined fun as "active involvement in an activity which the individual is doing" (Podilchak, 1991, p. 140) together with others. This definition considers the interactive participation of the physical, mental, cognitive, social, and emotional capacities of the individual. He also found that the same respondents considered the intrinsic aspect of the activity less important when they were considering enjoyment. Enjoyment seems to link more with emotional and internal aspects rather than external (type of activity) aspects. It seems that in order to foster the joy of movement, it is not the activity which matters, but the emotional environment which the participants (and the adult facilitator) create.

PLAY: USEFUL AND FUNCTIONAL OR UNPRODUCTIVE AND FUN?

Play has long been the subject of academic research, emphasising the important and fundamental role that play has in the life of children and young people. However, play has mostly been considered for its instrumental value, for achieving outcomes that are more adult-orientated, rather than for its intrinsic value (Lester and Russell, 2010). From this perspective, adults have the power to enhance forms of play which can be considered beneficial in later life and criticise other types of play which they consider not functional to development. This approach mostly affects adolescents' play behaviour, which is often critiqued as unproductive. While play is supported in primary schools, it is restricted in secondary schools. For example, a report from Scotland looking at the views held by secondary school students about play reported that teachers and parents pressured them into behaving "like adults" (Robinson, 2014, p. 6) including in the playgrounds during break times. This adult behaviour reflects the development perspective where young people are seen as "adults-in-becoming" (Thorne, 1987, p. 93) and they are expected to do something productive even in their "free" time. However, there are voices in physical education studies who advocate for the importance of play. Hawkins affirms that play is the most "essential meaning of physical education" (2008, p. 353) and Siedentop argued that:

Play is the proper classification for physical education, both from a logical and psychological perspective. Classifying physical education as a form of play puts it clearly in perspective alongside other primary institutionalized forms of play – art, music, and drama

(1980, quoted in Hawkins, 2008, p. 247)

Kretchmar argues that it is easier to understand play on a continuum line with shallow and deep play at the extremes. Shallow play is intrinsically motivated, it is fun but it "does not engage the imagination, … inspire … carry us away on the wings of desire" (Kretchmar, 2005, p. 150). Shallow play, however, is better than just repetitions at the gym or during physical education lessons. At the other extreme of the continuum is deep play. Deep play is personal. It becomes part of who we are and, perhaps even more importantly, who we are in the process of becoming (Kretchmar, 2005, p. 151). The joy of movement is found in deep play, the "peak moments" (Arnold, 1979) or "flow" (Csikszentmihalyi, 1990), when we experience the embodied sensations of skilful movements and when we feel at one with the activity. Deep play could be one of the objectives of programmes of promotion of physical activity through the joy of movement. Deep play has the potential to foster lifelong physically active behaviour, and shallow play can lead to deep play. Deep play supports the discovery and the development of one's own playground (Kretchmar, 2005). The playground is an activity which has evolved into a "second world" (Blankenship and Ayers, 2010, p. 172) for the player. It is an environment in constant evolution through participation and effort (Kretchmar, 2005).

There should be always a balance between perceived skills and challenge. Play is engaging and enjoyable when the tasks are not too simple or too difficult. Active play promotes the "zone of proximal development" (Vygotsky, 1978) which is the difference between the "actual development level" (where a child can perform a skill independently and with competence), and the "potential development level" (the limit to which the ability can be stretched with the assistance of a more competent peer or adult, but not beyond the capabilities and understanding of the child). According to Vygotsky (1978), a child can learn and improve her or his cognitive and socio-emotional abilities through play. Even if Vygotsky was interested in the role of play in pre-schoolers' development and the concept of "zone of proximal development", his theory can be applied both in primary and secondary school PE pedagogy and during adulthood in order to expand holistically all the areas of development: physical, cognitive, social, emotional, and creative. This approach suggests the idea of lifelong playing could become an important aspect of lifelong development.

A CASE STUDY IN THE UK

The following section outlines the result of a research study which investigated the role of active play in encouraging physical literacy from children's perspectives. The research project was designed as a case study and was set in a community primary school in a rural part of Gloucestershire, UK. The University of Gloucestershire ethical board approved the study. The aim of this study was to explore how active play could encourage physical literacy from children's perspectives and experiences of play. The seven students participating were all children in their final year of primary school (11 years old). The project involved five meetings with the students. Each of these meetings lasted approximately an hour. Play activities were used during all these meetings in order to establish an informal relationship between the children and the researcher and to facilitate discussions. In the first meeting the project and its aims were presented to the children, and the children's role within the project was discussed with them. During the second meeting, the four boys and three girls received a disposable camera to create their own "play diary" for a week. In the third meeting the children received copies of their photos to look at, and together with the researcher they decided how the photo elicitation sessions would be run. It was decided to discuss their pictures together as a group with each child taking their turn. The child interviewed would choose the first photo that they wanted to talk about and the other participants were free to take part in the discussion and to question their peers about the pictures that they had taken and what they represented. The second picture was chosen by the researcher, and after that it alternated. This procedure helped to create a relaxed environment and placed the children's perspective at the centre of the conversation. The photos, combined with the photo-elicitation discussions, created a narrative: every photo had a story behind it. The photo elicitation sessions took place in the third and fourth meetings. The last meeting involved a group discussion.

The children produced 99 photographs showing the places where they play in a normal week (all the photos in this chapter were taken by the children themselves during the research project). A majority of these photographs (89) showed outdoor spaces. It is important to consider that during the week when the children had the camera there were seven sunny and warm days and also, as one of the children pointed out while looking at another's photographs "I also play indoors but I forgot to take a photo". Among the outdoor places there was an even distribution between the school playground (30), gardens at home (31), and parks, playground, or sports grounds (28). In the spider diagrams and subsequent photo-voice discussions, three different kinds of play activities emerged as the most common: sports such as football, rugby, rounders, tennis, hockey, netball, and tennis; play activities such as trim trail, trampolining, biking, and playing with pets; traditional playground games such as 4040[2], tag, bulldog, and other activities that are in an area between unstructured play activities and traditional games, such as games that the children create such as bounce tag or balls tag played on the trampoline, that shows how difficult it is to order and separate different types of play.

Through the processes of "narrative analysis", an analysis of the data was undertaken to identify emergent themes (Riessman, 2005). The key themes explored were the characteristics of play from the players' perspectives and the role of unstructured active play activities and semi-structured (traditional playground games) active play activities in encouraging physical literacy.

Characteristics of active play from the players' perspectives

Closely related to the idea of physical activity which supports the joy of and in movement is active play. The important role of play in the physical, cognitive, emotional, and social development of children and young people is recognised (UNCRC committee, 2013). While these benefits are important, play should be valued primarily for its autotelic value and for the enjoyment and the pleasure of doing it. Bruner (1977) stated that "the main characteristic of play – child or adult – is not its content, but its mode. Play is an approach to action, not a form of activity". It is a way of behaving; we can have a playful attitude in any task, and we can play the same game playfully or not.

The role of a playful approach was confirmed by the perspectives of the children involved in the research project. In line with Buytendijk (1933), who suggested that the experts in distinguishing play from other kinds of activities are the players (in this case the children) themselves, it was important to ask the children what the characteristics of play are, and what is the difference between play and other activities. The children considered active play as a fun activity that should be new, challenging, and inclusive: "play should be with friends all having a great time". It is important for them to choose if and how they participate. They considered that the difference between play and sport lies in the way of approaching any activities. One of the main points for them was the importance of being in charge of the activity:

> **Alice**[3]: "When you do, like, sport you do in a club. You have been told what you have to do, while when you're doing your own game, you're doing whatever you wanted."
>
> **Chiara:** "If you are tired and you like a game, like really energetic, like running around, like cops and robbers or bulldog and they are usually your favourite games, and that day you had a really hard day and you feel really tired and you don't want to play."

Luca also considered that the difference between play and sport is in the rules that come from outside and are not changeable: "When you play football they have a set of rules, like you cannot pick the ball up in front of it and try to score a goal".

Matteo talked about a game that he likes to play with friends, "Bikeball", which "is a bit like football and you are on your bike and you jump around with your bike and you try to score a goal"; that he liked this game because "It's just different, not many people play it, you can make up your own rules".

Traditional playground games are a clear example of activities where the participants keep the ownership of the games, changing the rules and the conditions and creating an inclusive environment to let the game flow with a mixture of competition and cooperation:

> **Matteo:** "You can add new rules. It's like people use new rules in a different way because it's like your own game."
> **Luca:** "You could play like bulldog or cops and robbers and change the game."
> **Researcher:** "How do you feel when you play a game that has a rule you added?"
> **Chiara:** "Good. It makes you feel good because the game you invented got success."
> **Laura:** "Satisfied. That's quite a big word for me! … happy because this is something you have done and people actually like it."

Active play activities allow the participants to change rules, which will fit different elements such as the players' abilities, the environment, and the time. The possibility of changing rules will support the participants' sense of autonomy, which must accompany optimal challenges to support intrinsic motivation (Ryan and Deci, 2007). Play is perceived by the participants as linked with the possibility to determine for themselves or among peers the kind of activity, the involvement, and the possible conflicts or unexpected situations which can arise. They develop the capacity to negotiate play rules and conditions without the directions of adults who, for the majority of the time, shape their life.

Playing is a process where all the different dimensions of an individual (physical, social, cognitive, emotional, and spiritual) are actively involved in a simultaneous intra-dependent relationship. Active play supports an approach which emphasizes the value of physical activities that are "innately rewarding and self-affirming" (Whitehead, 2010b, p.39), focused on the expression of the potential of the individual. Active play with its own characteristics (pleasurable, constantly transforming, requiring active and holistic engagement from the players) has the potential to encourage physical literacy.

UNSTRUCTURED AND SEMI-STRUCTURED ACTIVE PLAY ACTIVITIES AND PHYSICAL LITERACY: THE LINK

Physical literacy has become an important concept in the past few years for its role in supporting lifelong participation in physical activities. Physical literacy encapsulates the motivation in taking part in physical activities and the desire to repeat the experience because of its rewarding and enjoyable nature. A physically literate individual will exhibit coordination and control of the body as well as an understanding of their embodiment in a variety of environments (Edwards et al., 2017; Jurbala, 2015; Whitehead, 2010b). They perceive and read stimuli from both the physical and social environments, and react to them with movements that are coordinated, controlled, intelligent, emphatic, creative, and appropriate for the individual in the different conditions.

Active play is the kind of activity where the player can explore and test all their physical capabilities in a relaxed environment. Through the child participants' narratives, general themes emerged regarding the attraction of unstructured play activities: the possibility of experimenting with new skills and the infinite alternatives that these activities provide for them. Unstructured play activities were extremely popular: trampoline, trim trail (playground equipment where the participants are involved in different activities focused on balance and hand-eye and leg-eye coordination skills), and bike tricks featured in many of their photos. The common element which attracted the participants was their malleability and the capacity of these tools to adapt to different situations, and to allow different forms of play.

FIGURE 5.1 Trim Trail: "you can do lots of things on there" – Daniele
Source: the author

FIGURE 5.2 Trampoline: "It is something both my sister and I both like and we play nearly every day" – Alice
Source: the author

For example, Daniele liked the trim trail (Figure 5.1) "because it's fun, you can do lots of things on there, you don't get bored because you can play in all different ways. You don't have to do the same each time", and Laura added "lots of different ways you can do it".

It is possible to create different courses: using the same material in different ways: "there are logs and you crawl under the logs" (Alice); making it more difficult by the intervention of the other players: "someone is in there we swing around they have to hang on and jump off" (Alice); testing your level: "a friend has a stopwatch we see how fast we can go" (Fabio); or experimenting with new skills: "when someone does it in a different way it looks quite fun and you try to copy it" (Luca).

The trampoline is another example (Figure 5.2): it allows the participant to play in standard ways (bouncing or experimenting skills), but also in alternative and creative ways such as playing bounce tag or balls tag:

FIGURE 5.3 Play companions: "I chose it because there are my favourite things I play on. First it is my goal and my football, then it is my dog, I like to play with him chasing around the climbing frame, and up there, there is a tree house. I can play football with my dog. I have the ball and he tries to take the ball from me. He is really fast at running and I try to run away from him, and he tries to tackle me. He always fouls me from behind" – Daniele
Source: the author

Alice: "It is something both my sister and I both like and we play nearly every day … it is not just you have to do one thing, you do anything; it is different, you can create things, we make up different things, different games like bounce tag. It is like normal tag, but you have to bounce and if you don't bounce you automatically do a forfeit, usually it's just me and my sister who're playing, but when my cousin came to visit, we played all together."
All: "Oh that is fun!"
Alice: "It is a fun game."
Researcher: "Do you play the same game?"
Fabio: "When my friends are over, we put the football, rugby ball, tennis balls cricket balls, and whatever and we put [them] inside in the middle of the trampoline … you have to jump and then dodge the balls coming towards you … and if you get touched by a ball you have to do a forfeit."
Researcher: "How many of you are there?"
Fabio: "Usually 2, 3, 4."

Apart from playing with peers, adults, or by themselves, a common play companion is a pet (Figure 5.3). Laura described a game with the trampoline: "I've got a friend that has a big dog and he keeps chasing us, then we had to try to open the zip to go on the trampoline before the dog came in it and sometimes he caught you, the dog was very fast and you had to do it quickly."

One of the main attractions of biking in the park is to look for and use the different natural obstacles as affordances for experimenting with tricks (Figure 5.4):

Luca: "This is a jump we do with the bike, and every time we go, we try different jumps, see if you can just run off or see if you can jump with one wheel or if you can land on the front wheel."

These quotes highlight the role that active play has in exercising and developing the children's motor competencies. Motor competencies include movement vocabulary, movement capacities, and general and specific movement patterns (Whitehead, 2010a). A perceived motor competence is positively correlated with child and adolescent

FIGURE 5.4 Jumping with the bike: "This is a jump we do with the bike, and every time we go, we try different jumps" – Luca
Source: the author

physical activity levels (Barnett et al., 2009; Lima et al., 2017; Lubans et al., 2010; Stodden, Langendorfer, and Roberton, 2009; Wrotniak et al., 2006). During active play children interact, through movement and the body, with others and the environment, in a continuous, evolving process. This form of interaction shapes their development and their relationship with others and the environment.

Some of the participants' stories about their best playtime experiences involved traditional playground games. Traditional playground games do not require equipment and they are played in any kind of place. Participants play for the intrinsic pleasure, for the joy of movement and their challenging nature.

> **Matteo:** "One day me and my friends… we usually play this game where you have a base and someone on it and no places is not allowed so we played in a big estate and you have to like trying to get back to the base without getting tagged … the people I played with, they were older and faster, so you got to really think what to do and how to get there."
>
> **Laura:** "…and when you succeeded you feel ecstatic."

Through experiences of active play, children and adolescents can interact with the affordances of the environment (Gibson, 1979). The affordances are the possibilities that result from the active interaction between the environment and the individual. Responding to affordances in the environment and reacting appropriately to them through a holistic involvement of the individual let them transform an "empty space" into a "play space". For example, when a child is creative in reading the affordances of the environment, her house's garage wall can become a play companion when she is alone (Figure 5.5).

> **Chiara:** "This is my garage wall, I kick the ball up against it if no one wants to play with me or play with a tennis ball and throw it or play with the basketball hoop. I also draw on it with chalk and use it as a target drawing circles with numbers on and get certain numbers if you hit it."

Through the act of "reading" the affordances from the environment, children and adolescents learn to react to the possibilities that the environment offers with movements that are coordinated, controlled, intelligent, emphatic, creative, and appropriate for the individual in the different conditions, the attribute of a physically literate individual.

FIGURE 5.5 Is it just a wall? "This is my garage wall I kick the ball up against it if no one wants to play with me or play with a tennis ball and throw it or play with the basketball hoop" – Chiara
Source: the author

During unstructured or semi-structured active play activities children and adolescents develop motor competencies, active interaction, the ability to read the environment, non-verbal communication and empathic relationship with others, holistic engagement of all the domains of the individual (physical, cognitive, emotional, and social), and the ability to solve motor problems through personal and individual sequences of movements, which all lead towards the development of a physically literate individual.

CONCLUSIONS

While the focus of this chapter has been on the benefits of active play for children and adolescents and its role in supporting physical literacy, active play activities are beneficial at every age. Play should be considered not just as an activity but as a form of behaviour. Play, according to his view, is not just a child's behaviour but can be considered as a "life-long" attitude. During early childhood, play is considered fundamental in the relationship that the child builds with her or his body, other children, and the environment. As soon as the child enters the school environment and from then on throughout her or his entire life, play seems to lose its importance in the adults' (parents, teachers) view, judging it as a relaxing time or a distraction from "serious" activities. During adulthood play becomes leisure, confined to limited spaces and moments.

The experiences and perceptions of the young people involved in the research project, and the literature presented earlier in the chapter show that free, unstructured, and semi-structured (traditional playground games) active play activities have the potential to encourage the development of physical literacy. During active play the participants can experience the joy and the intrinsic value of movement in a free and autonomous approach without adults or peers telling them what to do. In this way they have the opportunity of experimenting and developing their ability and coordination, expressing themselves through movement in a non-judgemental environment. They can develop a sense of competency, of ability to do something. The positive experiences that the participants enjoy during active play activities will enhance their self-esteem and self-confidence, increasing their motivation to participate in these activities.

Physical literacy is linked to approaches to physical activity and education in which the child and the young person are at the centre of the learning process. Physical literacy rejects the Cartesian body/mind dualism and asserts a monist perspective, where body and mind cannot be separated. Physical literacy marks a difference from a pedagogy of physical education and sport where the individual is seen as an aggregate of parts which are continuously dis- and re-connected in some improved form (Whitehead, 2010c). It supports active participation in a variety of movement forms, where the individual is physically, emotionally, and intellectually engaged. This approach is linked with the meaning of the word "education" itself. "Educe" means bring out (*The Concise Oxford Dictionary of English Etymology*) implying that the student should not be considered as a "sponge" – an object to fill with notions and knowledge, but an individual that can bring out their potential and capacity. This perspective challenges the current discourses on the pedagogy of PE focused on high-level performance and elitism (Brown, 2008), which is also one of the main barriers to participating in physical activities that young women reported in the WSFF (2012) report.

RECOMMENDATIONS

Active play gives players new problems that they have to solve; each individual in a different way according to their experiences and potential. In order to develop the attributes of a physically literate individual, adults should consider activities that require perception of the situation, intentional adjustments, choices, and decisions for action. Movements such as running, jumping, catching, and throwing should be used in a wide range of different environments and a variety of ways, giving the individual the possibility to enhance their movement vocabulary. This vocabulary comprises all the different movements that are possible, its breadth allows the individual to recognise patterns of conditions and respond to them appropriately. Motor problem-solving tasks that emphasize exploration and discovery are important to develop motor skills (Pesce, 2002). The ability to adapt skills and coordination according to the situation is considered the highest form of movement coordination (Meinel and Schnabel, 1984). This is the same level of ability which is indispensable in succeeding in open skills sports, such as team sports or individual sports like tennis, judo, or fencing.

The important role that traditional playground games occupy in children's lives is evident from their narratives. These activities have the potential to support the development of physical literacy. Traditional playground games are played for the intrinsic joy that playing these kinds of games can give. To an external observer they could seem repetitive, but the same activity would never be identical to previous occasions. By playing, the players develop and acquire more experience, and the game, as a consequence, becomes more complex. These games are a mixture of competitiveness and collaboration without giving too much importance to the results. If the game is too easy or too hard players are less motivated in taking part; the main goal at the end of these activities seems not to be to win, but to immediately start another round and make the experience of play last longer. Furthermore, these games do not need expensive equipment and can be played anywhere. Since they are games that were also played by parents and grandparents when they were younger, it could be a way to create stronger bonds between generations and at the same time improve the physical activity levels of all family members.

Unstructured and semi-structured active play activities that create motor problems to solve should be part of a PE curriculum aimed at improving physical literacy, which has the holistic education of every child's potential as a core objective. As has been noted earlier in the chapter, it is fundamental to create a playful and enjoyable environment which supports and respects every student's holistic potential, the timing of development and learning. Here the role of the adult (teachers, parents, sports coaches) is important in creating a non-judgemental atmosphere where a "mistake" has its own value in learning a different way to construct their own experience (Mazzoni, De Rossi, and Albanese, 2010); where the child and the adolescent are the main actors of their own motor experiences and the adult is in the background; where they can experience the joy of movement and the pleasure of involvement in deep play, create their own playground, and enjoy an active lifestyle throughout their life.

NOTES

1   "Minority World" refers to the "developed countries" or "First World" while the "Majority World" refers to the "developing countries" or "Third World".
2   4040 is a game that mixes hide and seek and tag; in tag, the person who is "it" has to run after the other people and try and touch them. If you are touched by "it", then you then become "it"; in bulldog, one person is "on" (the chaser), and you go across without that person getting you; if they do get you you're "on" with them and you get the other people that have not been tagged.
3   All names are pseudonyms, all the children involved adopted an Italian name.

REFERENCES

Arnold, P.J. (1979). *Meaning in movement, sport and physical education*. London: Heinemann.
Barnett, L.M., van Beurden, E., Morgan, P.J., Brooks, L.O., and Beard, J.R. (2009). Childhood motor skill proficiency as a predictor of adolescent physical activity. *Journal of Adolescent Health*, **44**, 252–259.
Blankenship, B.T., and Ayers, S.F. (2010). The role of PETE in developing joy-oriented physical educators. *Quest*, **62**, 171–183.
Brockman R., Jago R., and Fox K.R. (2010). The contribution of active play to the physical activity of primary school children. *Preventive Medicine*, **51** (2), 144–147.
Brown, T.D. (2008). Movement and meaning-making in physical education. *ACHPER Healthy Lifestyle Journal*, **55** (2/3), 5–9.
Bruner, J. (1977). Introduction. In B. Tizard, and D. Harvey (eds) *Biology of play*. London: Spastics International Medical Publication, pp. v–vi.
Buytendijk, F.J.J. (1933). *Wesen und sinn des spiels*. Berlin: Karl Wolff.
Cairney, J., Kwan, M.Y.W., Veldhuizen, S., Hay, J., Bray S.R., and Faught, B.E. (2012). Gender, perceived competence and the enjoyment of physical education in children: A longitudinal examination. *International Journal of Behavioral Nutrition and Physical Activity*, **9** (26), 1–8.
Corder, K., Atkin, A.J., Ekelund, U., and van Sluijs, E.M.F. (2013). What do adolescents want in order to become more active? *BMC Public Health*, **13** (1), 718–727.
Csikszentmihalyi, M. (1990). *Flow*. New York: Harper and Row.
De Rossi, P., Matthews, N., MacLean, M., and Smith, H. (2012). Building a repertoire: exploring the role of active play in encouraging physical literacy in children. *Revista Universitaria de la Educación Física y el Deporte*, **5** (5), 38–45.
Dollman, J., Norton, K., and Norton, L. (2005). Evidence for secular trends in children's physical activity behaviour. *British Journal of Sports Medicine*, **39**, 892–897
Dudley, D., Cairney, J., Wainwright, N., Kriellaars, D., and Mitchell, D. (2017). Critical considerations for physical literacy policy in public health, recreation, sport, and education agencies. *Quest*, **69**, 436–452.
Dumith, S.C., Gigante, D.P., Domingues, M.R., and Kohl H.W., III (2011). Physical activity change during adolescence: A systematic review and pooled analysis. *International Journal of Epidemiology*, **40**, 685–698.
Edwards, L.C, Bryant, A.S., Keegan, R.J., Morgan, K., and Jones, A.M. (2017). Definitions, foundations and associations of physical literacy: A systematic review. *Sports Medicine*, **47** (1), 113–126.
Else, P. (2014a). *Making sense of play: Supporting children in their play*. Maidenhead: Open University Press.
Else, P. (2014b). Teenagers and playing: Are pastimes like neknominate a usual response to adolescence? *Children*, **1** (3), 339–354.
Gibson, J. J. (1979). *The ecological approach to visual perception*. London: Houghton Mifflin.
Ginsburg, K.R. and the Committee on Communications and the Committee on Psychosocial Aspects of Child and Family Health (2007). The importance of play in promoting healthy child development and maintaining strong parent-child bonds. *Pediatrics*, **119**, 182–191.
Gleave, J. and Cole-Hamilton, I. (2012). *'A world without play'– A literature review*. Playengland.org.uk. Available online at: www.playengland.org.uk/media/371031/a-world-without-play-literature-review-2012.pdf [Accessed 10th Aug 2018]
Hallal, P.C., Andersen, L.B., Bull, F.C., Guthold, R., Haskell, W., and Ekelund, U. (2012). Global PA levels: Surveillance progress, pitfalls, and prospects. *The Lancet*, **380** (9838), 247–257.
Hawkins, A. (2008). Pragmatism, purpose, and play: Struggle for the soul of Physical Education. *Quest*, **60** (3), 345–356.

Inchley, J., Currie, D., and Young, T. (2016). *Growing up unequal: Gender and socioeconomic differences in young people's health and well-being. Health behaviour in school-aged children (HBSC) study: International report from the 2013/2014 survey.* Health Policy for Children and Adolescents, No. 7. Copenhagen, Denmark: WHO Regional Office for Europe.

Jurbala, P. (2015). What is physical literacy, really? *Quest*, **67**, 367–383.

Kentel, J. A., and Dobson, T. B. (2007). Beyond myopic visions of education: Revisiting movement literacy. *Physical Education and Sport Pedagogy*, **12** (2), 145–162.

Kirk, D. (2006). The "obesity crisis" and the school physical education. *Sport, Education and Society*, **11** (2), 121–133.

Kretchmar, R.S. (2005). *Practical philosophy of sport and physical activity* (2nd edn). Champaign, IL: Human Kinetics.

Kretchmar, R.S. (2008). The increasing utility of elementary school physical education: A mixed blessing and unique challenge. *The Elementary School Journal*, **108** (3), 161–170.

Lee, I.M., Shiroma, E.J., Lobelo, F., Puska, P., Blair, S.N., and Katzmarzyk, P. T. (2012). Effect of physical inactivity on major non-communicable diseases worldwide: An analysis of burden of disease and life expectancy. *Lancet*, **380**, 219–99.

Lester, S. and Russell, W. (2010). *Children's right to play: An examination of the importance of play in the lives of children worldwide*, Working Paper no. 57. The Hague: Bernard van Leer Foundation.

Lima, R.A., Pfeiffer, K.A., Larsen, L.R., Bugge, A., Møller, N.C., Andersen, L.B., and Stodden, D.F. (2017). Physical activity and motor competence present a positive reciprocal longitudinal relationship across childhood and early adolescence. *Journal of Physical Activity and Health*, **14**, 440–447.

Lubans, D.R., Morgan, P.J., Cliff, D.P., Barnett, L.M. and Okely, A.D. (2010). Fundamental movement skills in children and adolescents: Review of associated health benefits. *Sports Medicine*, **40** (12), 1019–1035.

Marchetti R., Bellotti P., and Pesce C. (2016). *Insegnare la vita con il movimento e con lo sport.* Perugia: Calzetti and Mariucci.

Martins, J., Marques, A., Sarmento, H., and Carreiro da Costa, F. (2015). Adolescents' perspectives on the barriers and facilitators of physical activity: A systematic review of qualitative studies. *Health Education Research*, **30** (5), 742–755.

Matthews, N., Kilgour, L., De Rossi, P., and Crone, D. (2011). *Literature review to investigate the evidence underpinning the role of play for holistic health: Final report.* Gloucester: University of Gloucestershire.

Mazzoni, A., De Rossi, P., and Albanese, M.P. (2010). *Fiabe motorie movimento, fantasia e creativita.* Roma: Armando Editore.

Meinel, K. and Schnabel, G. (1984). *Teoria del movimento.* Trans. by M. Gulinelli. Rome: Societa' Stampa Sportiva.

NHS (2008). National survey for England. Available online at: http://content.digital.nhs.uk/catalogue/PUB00430/heal-surv-phys-acti-fitn-eng-2008-rep-v2.pdf [Accessed 10th Apr 2018].

National Institute for Health and Clinical Excellence (NICE) (2007). Physical activity and children review 3: The views of children on the barriers and facilitators to participation in physical activity: a review of qualitative studies. Available online at: www.nice.org.uk/guidance/ph17/evidence/review-3-qualitative-correlates-371245645 [Accessed 10th Apr 2018].

National Institute for Health and Clinical Excellence (NICE) (2008). Promoting physical activity for children: Review 8 – Active play review of learning from practice: children and active play. Available online at: www.nice.org.uk/guidance/ph17/evidence/review-8-active-play-371252125 [Accessed 10th Aug 2018].

Pearson, N., Braithwaite, R., and Biddle, S.J. (2015). The effectiveness of interventions to increase physical activity among adolescent girls: A meta-analysis. *Academic Pediatrics*, **15** (1), 9–18.

Pesce C. (2002). Insegnamento prescrittivo o apprendimento euristico? *Sds-Scuola dello Sport*, **55**, 10–18.

Podilchak, W. (1991). Distinctions of fun, enjoyment and leisure. *Leisure Studies*, **10** (2), 133–148.

Punch, S. (2000). 'Children's strategies for creating playspaces: Negotiating independence in rural Bolivia'. In Holloway, S. and Valentine, G. (eds) *Children's geographies: Living, playing, learning and transforming everyday worlds.* London: Routledge, pp. 48–62.

Riessman, C.K. (2005). *Narrative analysis: In narrative, memory and everyday life.* Huddersfield: University of Huddersfield.

Robinson, M. (2014). 11–18 Secondary school play: Views and voices from Scottish schools. Grounds for learning. www.ltl.org.uk/ltlscotland/ [Accessed 24th April 2020].

Ryan, M.R. and Deci, E.L. (2000). Intrinsic and extrinsic motivations: Classic definitions and new directions. *Contemporary Educational Psychology*, **25**, 54–67.

Ryan, R.M. and Deci, E.L. (2007). Active human nature: Self-determination theory and the promotion and maintenance of sport, exercise, and health. In Hagger, M. and N.L.D. Chatzisarantis (eds). *Intrinsic motivation and self-determination in exercise and sport.* Champaign, IL: Human Kinetics, pp. 1–19.

Shearer, C., Goss, H.R., Edwards, L.C., Keegan, R.J., Knowles, Z.R., Boddy, L.M., Durden-Myers, E.J., and Foweather, L. (2018). How is physical literacy defined? A contemporary update. *Journal of Teaching in Physical Education,* **37** (3), 237–245.

Siedentop, D. (1980). *Physical education: Introductory analysis* (3rd edn). Dubuque, IA: Wm. C. Brown.

Stodden, D., Langendorfer, S., and Roberton, M.A. (2009). The association between motor skill competence and physical fitness in young adults. *Research Quarterly for Exercise and Sport*, **80** (2), 223–229.

Swinburn, B.A., Sacks, G., Hall, K.D., McPherson, K., Finegood, D.T., Moodie, M.L., and Gortmaker, S.L. (2011). The global obesity pandemic: Shaped by global drivers and local environments. *Lancet*, **378**, 804–14.

Symons, C., Polman, R., Moore, M., Borkoles, E., Eime, R., Harvey, J., Craike, M., Banting, L., and Payne, W. (2013). The relationship between body image, physical activity, perceived health, and behavioural regulation among Year 7 and Year 11 girls from metropolitan and rural Australia. *Annals of Leisure Research*, **16**, 115–129.

Thorne, B. (1987). Re-visioning women and social change: Where are the children? *Gender and Society*, **1** (1), 85–109.

Tremblay, M.S., Barnes, J.D., González, S.A., Katzmarzyk, P.T., Onywera, V.O., Reilly, J.J., Tomkinson, G.R., and the Global Matrix 2.0 Research Team (2016). Global Matrix 2.0: Report card grades on the physical activity of children and youth comparing 38 countries. *Journal of Physical Activity and Health*, **13** (Suppl 2), S343–S366.

Truelove, S., Vanderloo, L.M., and Tucker, P. (2017). Defining and measuring active play among young children: A systematic review. *Journal of Physical Activity and Health*, **14** (2), 155–166.

United Nations Committee on the Rights of the Child (2013). The right of the child to rest, leisure, play, recreational activities, cultural life and the arts (Article 31). Available online at: www.iccp-play.org/documents/news/UNGC17.pdf [Accessed 10th Apr 2018].

Veitch, J., Salmon, J., and Ball, K. (2008). Children's active free play in local neighborhoods: A behavioral mapping study. *Health Education Research*, **23** (5), 870–879.

Vygotsky, L. (1978). *Mind in society*. Cambridge, MA: Harvard University Press.

Wang, Y. and Lobstein, T. (2006). Worldwide trends in childhood overweight and obesity. *International Journal of Pediatric Obesity*, **1**, 11–25.

Warburton, D.E.R.; Nicol, C.W., and Bredin, S.S.D. (2006). Health benefits of physical activity: The evidence. *Canadian Medical Association Journal*, **174** (6), 801–809.

Whitehead, M. (2010a). The concept of physical literacy. In M. Whitehead (ed.) *Physical literacy throughout the life course*. Abingdon: Routledge, pp. 10–20.

Whitehead, M. (2010b). Motivation and the significance of physical literacy for every individual. In M. Whitehead (ed.) *Physical literacy throughout the life course*. Abingdon: Routledge, pp. 30–43.

Whitehead, M. (2010c). The philosophical underpinning of the concept of physical literacy. In M. Whitehead (ed.) *Physical literacy throughout the life course*. Abingdon: Routledge, pp. 21–29.

Wiklund, P. (2016). The role of physical activity and exercise in obesity and weight management: Time for critical appraisal. *Journal of Sport and Health Science*, **5**, 151–154.

Women's Sport and Fitness Foundation [WSFF] (2012). *Changing the game for girls.* London: Women's Sport and Fitness Foundation.

World Health Organization [WHO] (2010). *Global recommendation on physical activity for health.* Geneva: World Health Organization.

Wrotniak, B.H., Epstein, L.H., Dorn, J.M., Jones, K.E., and Kondilis, V.A. (2006). The relationship between motor proficiency and physical activity in children. *Pediatrics*, **118**, e1758–e1765.

Part 2
PLACE AND PEDAGOGY

6

TURNING THE CLASSROOM INSIDE OUT: LEARNING AND TEACHING EXPERIENCES IN AN EARLY CHILDHOOD SETTING

Muntazar Monsur

INTRODUCTION

Does the built-environment influence teaching and learning behaviour in an early childhood classroom? We know little about this complex science of learning environments, which is remarkably underdeveloped. For me, an architect who is interested to learn about the behavioural consequences of design in children's space, this question has always been an intriguing one. In a research study taking place in 2014–2015 in Wake County, North Carolina, I collected data from several early childhood classrooms (with three to five-year-old children) to understand the value of specific architectural elements which define the indoor–outdoor relationship of space. However, there was no single answer to this question, nor was it evident in the findings of other relevant scholarly studies. In this chapter, I will share my experience of researching children and their teachers to understand how specific architectural elements may influence their learning and teaching behaviour, and have tried to explain my findings in the light of a broad range of related literature. At the end of the chapter, I will try to draw a conclusion on how we can bring research findings into policy and design guidelines for early childhood learning environments, so that architects, landscape architects and educators can design better, and make the most out of the indoor–outdoor relation of space in early childhood classrooms.

Since the early 1970s, with the growing amount of criticism and dissatisfaction with highly praised architectural projects, the need for undertaking research into the complex relationship between human behaviour and the built environment has been evident in the field of design. Writing as far back as 1978, Irwin and Joachim described schools, including childcare environments, among the four most important environmental settings in the lives of the children alongside home, neighbourhood and nature. How the architectural design of a school influences children's, as well as teachers' behavioural outcomes, is, therefore, an emerging issue both in the fields of design and environmental behaviour research. The classroom and school have become an important area of discussion in the present contextualization and assessment of appropriate and successful contemporary educational delivery (Uduku, 2015). However, when it comes to design issues in childcare centres and early-childhood settings, it is difficult to find studies examining the impact of architectural variables on children's and teachers' learning and teaching behaviour.

With an increasing number of families with working parents, the need for quality care for children under the age of five has become an extremely important issue in many parts of the world. In the US, nearly 11 million children under age five are in some type of childcare arrangement every week, which is more than 50% of the total population of children in that age range in the country (Laughlin, 2013). On average, children of working mothers spend 35 hours a week in childcare (Laughlin, 2010). For those children, undoubtedly, childcare settings are as important as their home environments. The quality of childcare has a lasting impact. A National Institute of Child Health and Human Development (NICHD) report found that high-quality childcare leads to more positive outcomes even during the teenage years (CCAA, 2012). Higher quality care predicted higher cognitive–academic achievement at age 15, with escalating positive effects at higher levels of quality (Vandell et al., 2010). Quality childcare environments are also important for teachers and caregivers, not just for children. In the US alone, the number of teachers and caregivers who work in centre-based settings is more than one million (Brandon et al., 2011).

Educational research has focused on what is taught and how it is taught. What has received too little attention is the physical environment in which education occurs (Sanoff, 2009). Childhood, play, learning, teaching and designed environments are all interrelated concerns. Early childhood institutions are much more than just institutions for education and care. Children spend most of their waking hours in such environments (Goelman and Jacobs, 1994) and that reason should, in itself, prompt investigation into the impact the designed physical environment has on them.

WHY INDOOR–OUTDOOR SPACE?

Before trying to justify why the indoor–outdoor relation of space needs special attention to understand the role of architecture on learning outcomes, I will first attempt to come to an agreeable definition of the indoor–outdoor relation of space in the context of early childhood classrooms. Olds's well-known *Childcare Design Guide* (2001) offered specific instructions for providing strong relationships between indoor and outdoor spaces in childcare centres. Her ideas were incorporated in the *Childcare Center Design Guide* by the US General Service Administration (GSA). They also provided guidance for creating stronger bonds between indoor–outdoor spaces in childcare centres by providing well-designed transitional spaces (GSA, 2003). For Olds, indoor–outdoor relationships of space from children's and teachers' points of view were all about accessibility and continuation, and she emphasized creating direct access from each group room to an outdoor play area. She also mentioned that usable transitional space between the classroom indoor space and the outdoors should be sufficiently deep (no less than 6 ft./1.8 m) and be shaded. Olds's discussion of the indoor–outdoor connection mainly emphasizes spatial relationships. Although her definition was limited to physical access between indoors and outdoors, it pointed out key architectural elements that I decided to measure in my study. I defined the indoor–outdoor relation of space as the visual and physical connections between the indoors and the outdoors. Based on this definition, it was not challenging to identify the architectural elements that denote this relationship. Indoor–outdoor spatial relations in an early childhood classroom were defined as the combination of physical (e.g. exterior doors, transitional spaces) and visual (e.g. windows, views, skylights) access between an enclosed indoor classroom environment and the immediate surrounding outdoor environment (landscape) of that classroom. Here, all the mentioned architectural elements must connect the indoor environment to the outdoors – physically and/or visually. For example, only doors which opened directly to the outside would be considered for the definition. Interior doors or windows connecting the classroom with other interior spaces (lobby, other classrooms, etc.) were not included as indoor–outdoor elements. However, the question worth asking is: why was it important to study indoor–outdoor spaces when there are so many different aspects of the architectural design of an early childhood classroom or childcare centres in general? The indoor–outdoor relation of space needs special attention for its direct association with three important criteria: a) the amount and quality of daylight inside the classroom; b) the view towards outside from the classroom; c) attention restoration.

a) Daylight

Scientific findings on the positive consequences of daylight are well-established and ample. Appropriate daylight levels have been found to be associated with less stress and discomfort (Cuttle, 1983), productivity and improvement in job performances (Hedge, 1994; Abdou, 1997) and satisfaction (Dasgupta, 2003) in adults. The presence of natural light, which is facilitated by the presence of windows, has also been shown to aid recovery following spinal surgery (Walch et al., 2005).

Perhaps the two most significant studies in the related fields focusing on the effects of natural light on children showed that elementary school students in classrooms with larger window areas scored higher in mathematics and reading when compared with those in classrooms with smaller windows and less access to light (Aumann et al., 2004; Heschong et al., 1999). Those effects were shown even after controlling for factors such as grade level, size of the school and student absences. Heschong et al.'s study, conducted with over 8,000 third to sixth-grade students in 450 classrooms in California, found a positive relationship between elementary students' test improvement and the presence of daylight in their classrooms. The study provided empirical evidence that various window characteristics of classrooms had more explanatory power in clarifying variation in student performance, as opposed to more traditional educational metrics such as teacher characteristics, number of computers or attendance rates.

b) View

The indoor–outdoor relation of space is not just about daylight; the views through the windows (and doors, skylights, etc.) are also important aspects of the built environment. Having visual access to nature is known to be beneficial across a wide range of contexts. The seminal work by Ulrich (1984) showed that patients recovering from gall bladder surgery with window views of trees recovered from surgery significantly faster, had fewer negative interactions with nursing staff and used fewer analgesic medications when compared with those recovering in rooms with a less scenic brick wall window view. In children, two studies gave evidence that views of nature contribute to the self-discipline of adolescent girls and cognitive functioning of children (Taylor, 2002; Wells, 2000). The first study investigated the role of near-home nature in three forms of self-discipline among children (Taylor, 2002). The sample in the study was composed of 169 inner-city children randomly assigned to 12 architecturally identical high-rise buildings with varying levels of nearby nature. The results showed that the more natural a girl's view from home was, the better was her performance in the tests of self-discipline. The second study (Wells, 2000) showed that children who relocated to homes that improved the most in terms of surrounding naturalness tended to have the highest levels of cognitive functioning.

Most of these studies were conducted in different work environments such as office spaces, residences or hospitals and mostly with adults and older children, but they suggest that similar positive effects of daylight and view are also likely to motivate teachers and children in early childhood classroom environments.

c) Attention restoration by nature

Attention Restoration Theory (ART) as proposed by Kaplan (1995) claimed: "interacting with environments rich with inherently fascinating stimuli invokes involuntary attention modestly, allowing direct-attention mechanisms a chance to replenish". ART is based on past research showing separation of attention into two components: a) involuntary attention, where attention is captured by inherently intriguing stimuli; and b) directed attention, where attention is directed by cognitive-control processes (Kaplan, 1995). One study argued that nature, which is filled with intriguing stimuli, modestly grabs attention in a bottom-up fashion (Berman et al., 2008). The indoor–outdoor relation, as a mode for nature-connections, should be examined critically for its potential impact on attention restoration of children (and teachers) in early childhood classrooms.

DRAWING INSPIRATION FROM MONTESSORI: ARCHITECTURAL INTERPRETATION OF EDUCATIONAL PHILOSOPHIES

Here, I turn to Maria Montessori, who played an important role in inspiring my research with her visionary interest in connecting indoor classroom activities to the outdoors (Moore and Cosco, 2007). In attempts to define the trademark Montessori learning environment known as the *Children's House*, Dr. Maria Montessori, the legendary physician and educator, best known for her philosophy of education which now bears her name, described a garden:

> A garden which contains shelters is ideal, because the children can play or sleep under them, and can also bring tables out to work or dine. In this way, they may live almost entirely in the open air and are protected at the same time from rain and sun.

> (Montessori, 2011)

The description depicts her passion for indoor–outdoor interactions of space for young children, which can be interpreted in architectural design as more accessibility between the classroom and the immediate outdoor environments. Dr. Montessori always advocated the potential to involve the outdoors to enrich the learning experiences of the indoors. Her deliberate choice of classroom space, on the open veranda of Olcott's bungalow (within the territory of the Theosophical Society in India) expresses her inclination for rich indoor–outdoor spatial relations for a learning environment. Her vision was further supported by other eminent educators and experts (Olds, 2001; Moore and Cosco, 2007), who addressed the numerous potential benefits of indoor–outdoor relations for early childhood education.

Designs of early examples of Montessori schools bear signs of that vision for using transition spaces for special activities connecting classrooms to the outdoors. A transition space bears the spatial relationship between the indoor environment and the outdoor environment. This is, perhaps, the earliest attempt by a reformist to incorporate indoor–outdoor spatial connections as an important aspect of design for motivating play and learning among young children.

Similar inspirations were also found in the works of other pioneers of early childhood education like Friedrich Froebel (1895) and Margaret McMillan (1921). In her remarkable book titled *Bringing Reggio Emilia Home*, author Louise Cadwell described specific architectural characteristics which she found to be critical for housing the Reggio Emilia philosophy in US schools (1997). She emphasized the need for transparency in the walls so that the classroom is not separated from the rest of the school. Transparency in early childhood classrooms, in other words, is the degree of indoor–outdoor relation of space. Architectural interpretation of early childhood educational philosophies is important and such interpretations of the two most prominent philosophies indicate that we need special considerations for designing the indoor–outdoor relation of space in classrooms for young children.

BRING THE OUTDOORS IN

In eighteenth- and early nineteenth-century Europe, gardens and architecture were understood as important instruments in pedagogical theory and practice and were often deployed as primary instruments in the education of young children (Diana, 2012). In the early twentieth century, open-air schools became common in Northern Europe, designed to prevent the then widespread rise of tuberculosis that occurred in the period leading up to the Second World War (Nessy, 2016). Though short-lived, the open-air school movement became popular in parts of Europe and the US, encouraging all students to be outdoors as much as possible.

A growing body of recent research has again started to emphasize the developmental benefits of bringing nature and the outdoors into the learning process of young children. Child advocacy expert Richard Louv, in his influential work about the divide between children and nature, discussed the lack of nature in the lives of today's wired generation. He calls it "nature deficit disorder" and points to it as a cause of some of the most disturbing childhood trends, such as the rises in obesity, attention disorders and depression (Louv, 2008). The indoor–outdoor relationship is an efficient way to increase interactions with nature when children and teachers are in an enclosed classroom environment. Other research supports this potential (Lieberman et al., 2000; Malone and Tranter, 2003; Tai et al., 2006). While learning outdoors is effective and crucial, climatic constraints may restrict such activities during adverse times of the year (e.g. extreme heat, inclement winter weather). The merit of such indoor–outdoor relations, therefore, should be subjected to serious empirical research, because it is the key to increasing the amount of naturalness inside a classroom.

WHAT WE ALREADY KNOW: EXTENDED RESEARCH AND ITS FINDINGS

Most notable among the recent studies related to this topic was the finding that high-school students perform better on tests if they are in a classroom with a view of a green landscape, rather than a windowless room or a room with a view of built space (Li and Sullivan, 2016). In a randomized controlled experiment with 94 high-school students at five high schools, participants were randomly assigned to classrooms without windows or with windows that opened onto a built space or a green space. Participants engaged in typical classroom activities followed by a break in the classroom to which they were assigned. Results demonstrate that classroom views to green landscapes cause significantly better performance on tests of attention and increase students' recovery from stressful experiences.

Another study showed that for high-school students, views with greater quantities of trees and shrubs from classroom windows were associated with positive academic performance (Matsuoka, 2010). Classroom windows were found to be positively associated with standardized test scores, graduation rates, percentages of students planning to attend a four-year college and fewer occurrences of criminal behaviour. In a similar study, Tanner (2009) found that standardized test scores could be accounted for environmental ratings related to window views. More positive scores on vocabulary, language arts and mathematics were predicted by higher ratings of the types of view present (e.g. larger windows or natural views). Additional research shows that natural views are subjectively important to students and teachers. For instance, Karmel (1965) showed that high-school students in windowless classrooms, when asked to draw a picture of the school, were more likely to draw windows when compared with those in classrooms with windows. Likewise, Gulwadi (2006) found that elementary school teachers spontaneously seek out natural, restorative settings during breaks and downtime as a way of coping with stress and daily events. The study by Tanner (2009) reported that when a student needed to take a break from learning, it was easier to get back on track after taking a quick look outside at a pleasant view than after doodling on paper. A two-year study by Hathaway et al. (1992) examined the effects of different lighting systems on the performance of elementary-school children. The study of fourth-grade students concluded that full spectrum lighting, like natural lighting, produced positive effects. The students had better attendance, increased academic achievement and better growth and development than students using classrooms with conventional light. One study (Lindsten, 1992) concluded that windowless classrooms were not only associated with decreased academic performance; they also caused severe health consequences such as hormonal imbalance and lower annual body growth. A study by Benfield et al. (2013) showed that students in the natural view classrooms rated their courses more positively.

In summary, most of the literature which found an association between indoor–outdoor variables and children's learning outcomes focuses on primary and secondary schools (Hathaway, 1992; Aumann et al., 2004; Heschong et al., 1999; Tanner, 2009). Two studies investigated high-school students' academic outcomes (Matsuoka, 2010; Karmel, 1965). Some of the studies were conducted with college students (Benfield et al., 2013; Slopack, 2011). Although the information generated from these studies is valuable, it cannot be generalized to an early childhood classroom environment, where children are in critical developmental stages. Table 6.1 summarizes the complex array of background literature relevant to the study.

RESEARCHING EARLY CHILDHOOD CLASSROOMS: THE NEED FOR CREATIVITY

One obvious reason for the limited research on early childhood learning environments is the lack of measurable outcome variables. Most of the contemporary scientific studies investigating the role of school/classroom architecture relied on standardized test scores as indicators of learning outcomes. However, test scores are not practicable learning outcomes in an early childhood learning environment. Again, I borrowed creative inspirations from *Dr. Montessori's Own Handbook* (Montessori, 2011). The teacher's role in the Montessori approach is defined primarily as one of observation. Dr. Montessori's own clinical background convinced her that the best way to learn what the children are free to do is to go to their habitat (in this case, their classrooms) and attempt not to disturb them in order to see everything they do. The benefits of observational techniques include its purposeful assessment done during authentic activities in a naturalistic setting without diverting children from natural learning processes (Nilsen, 2013). Self-assessment techniques in small children have been criticized because at an early age a child does not usually obtain a correct appreciation of his or her own thoughts and actions (Perry and Winne, 2006). Systematic observational methods, on the other hand, have multiple advantages (Whitebread et al., 2008). First, such methods record what learners actually do, rather than what they recall or believe they do. Second, they allow links to be established between learners' behaviours and the context of the task. Direct observation can

TABLE 6.1 What do we know about the impact of indoor–outdoor relations of space?

Category	Subcategory	Relevant findings and/or statements	Sources	Scope
Design guidelines and principles	Design guidelines	A strong relationship is needed between the indoor and outdoor environment of an early childhood classroom.	Olds 2001 GSA 2003	Lack of empirical findings that indoor–outdoor relations can benefit children and teachers
		A variety of transitions between buildings and the outdoors for early childhood classrooms is recommended.	Moore and Goltsman 1992	
	Scholarly writings	The best learning places flow between the indoors and the outdoors.	Frost, Wortham, and Reifel, 2001	
		Where classrooms meet the outdoors are crucial areas.	Moore and Cosco 2007	
Empirical research	Impact of windows, daylight, and views in learning	High-school students perform better on tests if they are in a classroom with a view of a green landscape, rather than a windowless room or a room with a view of built space.	Li and Sullivan, 2016	Does not address early childhood age children and early childhood teachers' behaviour
		Elementary-school students in classrooms with larger window areas scored higher in math and reading.	Aumann et al. 2004, Heschong 1999	
		Classroom windows were positively associated with standardized test scores and graduation rates in high-school students.	Matsuoka, 2010	
		College students in the natural view classrooms had higher grades.	Benfield et. al, 2013	
		Unrestricted, functional and living views help elementary school children's attention restoration.	Tanner, 2009	
		Windowless classrooms decreased academic performance.	Küller and Lindsten, 1992	
Extended research	Impact of windows, views on health, wellbeing, and behaviour	Near-home nature contributes to the self-discipline of children.	Taylor, 2002; Wells, 2000	Does not address learning or teaching behaviour
		A view from the window can influence health outcomes.	Devlin and Arneill, 2003	
		Presence of natural light and green view is associated with quicker recovery from surgeries.	Ulrich, 1984; Walch et al., 2005	
		Nature views promoted residential satisfaction and overall resident well-being.	Kaplan, 2001	
		Outdoor environment influences children's behaviour.	Moore, 1996; DeBord et al., 2005; Shim et al., 2001	
	More nature = more learning	Learning outdoors in nature has health, psychological and cognitive benefits.	Hopwood-Stephens, 2013	Indirectly support the needs of indoor–outdoor spatial relations
		The students learn better when the lesson incorporates the natural/outdoor environment.	Hopwood-Stephens, 2013; Lieberman, Hoody, and Lieberman, 2000; Malone and Tranter, 2003	

simultaneously provide contextually rich data on the setting in which the activity occurs (McKenzie, 2010). Self-report measures such as questionnaires or interviews largely depend on the verbal proficiency of the subject and can be a threat to the validity of a study involving young children. Also, test scores of children have many alternative explanations, which are beyond the scope of measurement.

DATA COLLECTION

The study investigated whether variation in indoor–outdoor spatial relationships in early childhood classrooms could explain variation in learning outcomes. Therefore, the chosen sample unit was an individual classroom. Samples were selected randomly from a list of 55 centres that were affiliated with the Natural Learning Initiative (NLI) at NC State University located in Raleigh, North Carolina, USA. As a research assistant at the time of sample selection, I had access to centres which were working closely with NLI. Additionally, three qualifying criteria were imposed for selecting centres. Only licensed childcare centres, not family care homes, were considered for the study. Only centres in Wake County, NC with a minimum of three-star ratings in the NC Childcare Rating Scale were selected as samples. Ten centres were selected randomly (by assigning random numbers) from the list.

Data for this study were gathered in 22 early childhood classrooms with 26 teachers/caregivers and approximately 295 children in selected childcare centres in Wake County, North Carolina. I visited the classrooms personally and collected data primarily by systematic observations. Convinced by the appropriateness of observational techniques for my research, I developed six dependent (outcome) variables attempting to measure the teaching and learning activities and behaviours inside an early childhood classroom during regular operation days. Four variables were employed to collect learning engagement behavioural data of children and two variables were measured to rate teacher motivation. All child variables were strictly observational, while teacher motivation variables were combinations of observational and self-reported survey data:

- *Children's collective engagement* examined the collective engagement of children during classroom activities.
- *Percentage of engaged children* quantified the number of engaged children (in different activities) by looking into individual behaviour.
- *Distracted children* measured the number of distracted children by observing individual behaviour and provides a negative measure for learning engagement of children.
- *Number of behavioural guidance directives by teachers* hypothesized that more engagement of children would result in fewer behavioural guidance directives by the teachers and counting the number of behavioural guidance directives would provide the researcher a negative measure of child engagement in the classrooms.

Teaching motivation was the sum of the teacher-reported number of hands-on and innovative lessons in a typical week and the number of hands-on lessons in a classroom display. Hands-on lessons refer to activities that involved children and teachers to create something in order to teach and learn. Innovative lessons were the lessons which the teachers claimed to be entirely their own unique ideas. Both innovative and hands-on lessons were counted from teachers' answers to the questionnaire survey, while hands-on lessons on display were calculated by systematic direct observation by the researcher in the selected classrooms. In other words, teaching motivation was the sum of teachers' enthusiasm (to involve children and display their works) and innovations.

Previous studies also helped me to operationalize variables to measure the indoor–outdoor relationships in early childhood classrooms. Table 6.2 summarizes previous studies' measurement criteria, which largely guided how I decided to measure indoor–outdoor characteristics for my own research.

Based on the information provided in Table 6.2, my research defined indoor–outdoor spatial relations in terms of four architectural elements: doors, windows, views and transitional spaces. I was interested to know what learning opportunities these elements *afford* to influence behaviour. Therefore, at its operational level, the study proposes a

TABLE 6.2 Measurement of indoor–outdoor space in the relevant literature

Indoor–outdoor spatial characteristics	Criteria	Measurement Technique/Criteria	Source
Exterior door	Availability (no exterior door)	Yes/no	Aumann et al., 2004
	Number (two exterior doors)	Yes/no	Aumann et al., 2004
Window	Scale (windows are at children's eye level)	Yes/no	DeBord et al., 2005
	Operability (can be opened to allow fresh air)	Yes/no	DeBord et al., 2005
	Window orientation (five orientations of windows: primary window facing east, west, north, south, or no window)	Yes/no	Aumann et al., 2004
	Window area (two conditions: area of view window at a height between desk and door, and high window area, higher than the door)	Measured area (square feet)	Aumann et al., 2004
	Window tint	Scalar (0–2): 0=clear glass, 1= slight tint, 2= heavy tint	Aumann et al., 2004
	No blinds or curtains	Yes/no	Aumann et al., 2004
	Window amount	Children's spaces in new construction must have a total window area of at least: 8% of the floor area of the room if windows face *south* directly to the outdoors 10% for *east or west* 15% for *north.*	GSA, 2003
View	Window view	scalar (0–3): 0=no view, 1=near view (<25'), 2=mid view, 3=far view (70'+)	Tanner, 2009
	View vegetation	Yes/no	Aumann et al., 2004
	View activity	Yes/no	Aumann et al., 2004
	Views overlooking life	scalar (0–10)	Tanner, 2009
	Unrestricted views	scalar (0–10)	Tanner, 2009
	Living views (such as gardens, wildlife, fountains, mountains and the sky)	scalar (0–10)	Tanner, 2009
	Functional views	scalar (0–10)	Tanner, 2009
	View green areas	scalar (0–10)	Tanner, 2009
	View naturalness	scalar (0–4)	Matsuoka, 2010
Transitional space	Availability	Yes/no	DeBord et al., 2005
	Depth of transitional space	Measurement (feet)	Olds, 2001

systematic way to measure the learning affordances of doors, windows, views and transitional spaces of the pre-school classroom:

- *Door Affordance*: Number and availability of doors that connect the classroom directly to the outdoor environment and the visual transparency of such doorways.
- *Window Affordance*: Number of windows, window scale, window operability, visual transparency of windows, window depth, window orientation and window amount.
- *View Affordance*: View of vegetation, activity, distance and greenness.
- *Transitional Space Affordance*: Availability of transitional space, depth and usability of transitional space, activity zones and vegetation in transitional space.

To make sure that the variables stated above do not explain away the entire association between indoor–outdoor spatial relations and child engagement or teaching motivation, a total of 19 control variables were also adopted. Once the variables were all set, I started collecting data for my research.

Hierarchical Multiple Regression was chosen for the statistical analyses of the study to investigate associations between independent and dependent variables of the study. It is a variant of the basic multiple regression procedure that allows a research design to specify a fixed order of entry for variables in order to control for the effects of co-variates or to test the effects of certain predictors independent of the influence of others. Findings indicate that improved conditions of classroom indoor–outdoor relationships enhance both child engagement and teacher motivation, even after controlling for other significant environmental and demographic variables.

FINDINGS AND THEIR MEANINGS

The findings of my study suggested that specific architectural attributes of early childhood classrooms (windows and views) may support teacher motivation and child engagement in childcare settings.

More indoor–outdoor relations motivated teachers

One of the most significant findings of the research was the effect of window-view affordances on teaching motivations. The regression model showed the window-view affordances to be the only statistically significant predictor of teaching motivation with a significance of $p < .05$ level and an unstandardized coefficient value of 0.162. Due to the small sample size ($n = 22$), the study used $p \leq .10$ level for significance, instead of the traditional $p \leq .05$ level. Although window-view is the only statistically significant variable in the model, the model also included door affordances, along with teacher qualifications. These three variables were significant in a model, which predicted 63.6% variance ($R2 = .636$) in the teaching motivation value. The findings are consistent with one previous qualitative study (Slopack, 2011), which showed that windows in a classroom contributed to increased concentration, alertness and motivation for teachers and students at a large urban college. Studies that connect teaching motivation to windows and views in the early childhood environment are limited; however, we can think of a few mediators which may explain this relationship between window-view affordances and teaching motivation.

One of the contributing factors of the window-view affordance score was the number and size of windows (see Figure 6.1). The amount of window space is responsible for the amount of daylight inside a classroom. The classrooms that scored higher in the window-view affordance index were also rich in daylight quantity. Studies showing evidence of the positive influences of daylight on adults' productivity and motivation were mostly conducted in different work environments like office spaces or hospitals, but findings in this study indicated that similar positive effects of daylight are also likely to be found among teachers in early childhood classrooms in childcare settings.

Teachers' appreciation of daylight was also evident in certain observations during data collection in classrooms. In many classrooms with rich daylight, teachers tended to use fewer electric/artificial lights. Rather, a combination of table and stand lamps were used, which provided a stimulating lighting environment.

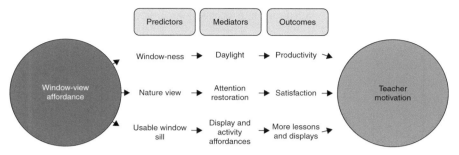

FIGURE 6.1 Mediators explaining influences of window-view affordance on teaching motivation
Source: the author

The view component of the window-view affordance measure in my research had two indicators: view naturalness and view activity. View naturalness measured the amount of nature (trees, plants, grassy area, sky, etc.) and the view activity rated how stimulating a view was. The classrooms which scored higher in window-view affordances contained more natural and stimulating views. Having visual access to nature is known to be beneficial across a wide range of contexts. Natural views were associated with increased feelings of privacy, satisfaction, patience, task enthusiasm and lower levels of frustration. The view affordance scale rated fully natural and stimulating views as the highest level. For example, views full of nature or children's play activities scored high on the scale. One of the reasons why window-view affordance was significant in predicting teacher motivation may be that teachers in those classrooms had more opportunities for attention restoration by looking at more natural or stimulating views. Teachers who needed to take a break from classroom activities may have found it easier to get back on track after taking a quick glance outside at a pleasant view of nature or children playing outdoors.

The window affordance scale rated different design characteristics of the windows (Figures 6.2 and 6.3). One such characteristic was the depth of the window sill. It was assumed that the wider depth of window sill afforded more learning activities in early childhood classrooms. Children's hands-on works displayed by their teachers were counted as an indicator of teaching motivation. Classrooms with sufficient depth of window sills allowed teachers more shelving space to display children's hands-on works. Those areas were always busy with learning activities – growing plants, drying artworks, conducting science experiments, etc. Classrooms without such design features as window sills may restrict learning activities near the windows.

The indoor–outdoor relation inspired nature-based teaching and learning

Teachers were asked how many times in a week they used a natural element to teach children. Such lessons ranged from teaching leaf patterns with real leaves to showing the sky through a window to teach diurnal variations. The researcher also counted nature-based learning activities in the classroom. These two values were added to measure nature-based learning. It was hypothesized that more indoor–outdoor relations would predict more nature-based learning in a classroom. Hierarchical multiple regression for nature-based learning showed that window-view affordance was the only significant predictor for this dependent variable. Due to the small sample size (n = 22), the study used $p \leq .10$ level for significance. Window-view was significant ($p < .01$ level) and, together with the other variables in the model, explained the 51.4% variance in nature-based learning practices in a classroom. It was likely that teachers used more nature-based teaching when the window-view index had a higher/richer value. Windows were the sources of daylight in classrooms. Daylight was essential for many nature-based experiments. For example, in one classroom, the teacher pasted some dried leaves against a window to teach children about leaf anatomy. The daylight through the window afforded the teacher opportunities to show the pattern of leaf veins clearly to children. Similarly, for many other nature-based science experiments, window-areas provided the ideal space for activities. In addition to science experiments, indoor-planting activities were also motivated by the presence of windows and window-sill depth. Indoor planting activities allowed teachers more opportunities to teach children with natural elements. More windows provided more daylight, display shelving and more opportunities for indoor planting activities, which, in turn, provided teachers more affordances to teach with natural elements. It can

FIGURE 6.2 The full width of the window sills was busy with learning activities
Source: the author

FIGURE 6.3 Lack of depth in window sills minimized shelving affordances
Source: the author

be argued whether nature-based learning is a valid indicator of teaching motivation; however, it is a measure of teaching style and designates good practice in an early childhood classroom. Numerous studies have shown that children learn better when the lessons incorporate nature and the outdoor environment (Lieberman et al., 2000; Malone and Tranter, 2003; Tai et al., 2006).

Higher indoor–outdoor relation predicted higher engagement in children

My findings also predicted that more children will engage in activities during free activity sessions when the window-view score was higher (p < .01 level). This phenomenon of children's higher engagement in self-assisted activities with more windows and views can be explained by the previously discussed Daylight Theory and Attention Restoration Theory (ART). Although no studies were found which linked child engagement with daylight, it can be assumed that the positive effects of increased daylight (as a consequence of increased windows) would be applicable for younger children as well.

Other findings

Teachers were asked to rate the most and least popular activity zones for children in their respective classrooms. While the activity of playing with blocks was a clear winner as the most popular activity, the writing desk was surely the least popular activity among children in the 22 classrooms. However, things were different in one classroom (Figure 6.4), where the writing desk was integrated with a classroom window and was a popular space.

I observed children using that zone as frequently as the other obvious popular choices like blocks, dramatic play, etc. The teachers confirmed what I observed and said that the writing desk was popular only in that particular classroom. While architectural indoor–outdoor spatial relationships are important, it is also equally important to arrange the indoor activity zones in harmony with classroom doors, windows, views and transitional spaces of the classroom. Some of the activity zones have the chance to function better when they are placed close to a window/view or in a transitional space.

CONCLUSION AND REFLECTIONS

Table 6.3 provides a summary record of the major findings (statistical and qualitative), their implications and recommendations for design policies and research.

Architecture is a neglected aspect of educational research and information is limited regarding the influence that the built environment has on academic outcomes. Considering the growing demand for childcare facilities in the US,

FIGURE 6.4 Is a writing desk more functional when integrated with a window?
Source: the author

TABLE 6.3 Summary of findings, implications, and recommendations

	Findings	Implications	Recommendations
Statistical findings	More window-view affordance = more teaching motivation (hands-on and innovative lessons) More window-view affordance = more engaged children More window-view affordance = more nature-based learning in classrooms	Teacher motivation and children's engagement may be improved in early childhood classrooms designed with high affordance scores for windows and views. Existing designs can be improved by developing the immediate surrounding landscape.	Newly designed classrooms should accommodate more windows. Windows should be designed at children's scale, and with wider sill-depth to afford window-zone learning activities. In existing classrooms, where new windows cannot be installed, the immediate surrounding landscape can be improved to afford interactive views emphasizing nature. Designing more windows with sufficient sill-depth can be an effective way to promote nature-based learning in an early childhood classroom design.
Qualitative findings	The mean values of child engagement, teacher motivation and nature-based learning are considerably higher in classrooms with transitional spaces.	Transitional space can be considered as an 'essential' classroom element rather than just an extension of space.	More research is needed to evaluate the influence of a transitional space on learning outcomes. Design guidelines and official rating systems for childcare centres and early childhood classrooms should emphasize the inclusion of transitional spaces as a required design criterion.
	The contained immediate outdoor environment encourages teachers to increase indoor–outdoor spatial accessibility.	The contained immediate outdoor environment may add to the affordances of indoor–outdoor spatial relations of a classroom.	Landscape design should accentuate classroom design intentions regarding indoor–outdoor relations.
	Indoor classroom zoning and arrangement of activities may reinforce the positive effects of indoor–outdoor spatial relations to learning engagement.	Teachers can be encouraged to become aware of the potentials of classroom arrangement/zoning in influencing learning behaviour.	Design guidelines/policies and official rating systems should inform teachers/caregivers/directors about zoning principles to emphasize indoor–outdoor spatial relations in early childhood classrooms.
	Regulations and management policies may hinder indoor–outdoor classroom accessibility.	Policies and design implications can converge to maximize the influences of indoor–outdoor spatial relations on the learning environment.	Design guidelines and childcare policies need to be reviewed to remove conflict and revised to accommodate indoor–outdoor spatial affordances for learning and teaching.

further investigation of this neglected aspect of early childhood research is timely. The findings and relevant other studies discussed in this chapter call for reforms and developments in design guidelines and policies regarding childcare centre architecture. Improving indoor–outdoor spatial relations and their consequential positive motivational outcomes cannot be entirely achieved by the architect or the landscape architect or the classroom teacher alone. Rather, achieving such outcomes demands a harmonizing effort of all parties. We need to work together to pave the way for improved practices and collaboration among architects, landscape architects and educators for enhancing indoor–outdoor spatial relations in early childhood classrooms, in order to enhance the qualities and effectiveness of the learning environment for both children and their teachers.

REFERENCES

Abdou, O. A. (1997) Effects of luminous environment on worker productivity in building spaces. *Journal of Architectural Engineering*, **3**, 124–132.

Aumann, D., Heschong, L., Wright, R., and Peet, R. (2004) Windows and classrooms: Student performance and the indoor environment. Paper presented at the American Council for an Energy-Efficient Economy (ACEEE), California.

Benfield, J. A., Rainbolt, G. N., Bell, P. A. and Donovan, G. H. (2013) Classrooms with nature views: Evidence of differing student perceptions and behaviours. *Environment and Behavior*, **47**(2), 140–157.

Berman, M. G., Jonides, J. and Kaplan, S. (2008) The cognitive benefits of interacting with nature. *Psychological Science*, **19**, 1207–1212.

Brandon, R., Stutman, T. and Maroto, M. (2011) The economic value of the US early childhood sector. In E. Weiss and R. N. Brandon (eds), *Economic analysis: The early childhood sector*, pp. 19–41. Washington, DC: Partnership for America's Economic Success.

Cadwell, L. B. (1997) *Bringing Reggio Emilia home: An innovative approach to early childhood education*. New York: Teachers College Press.

CCAA (2012) *Child care in America (2012): State fact sheets*. Arlington, VA: Child Care Aware of America.

Cuttle, K. (1983) People and windows in workplaces. Wellington, NZ: Proceedings of the People and Physical Environment Research Conference, 47–51.

Dasgupta, U. (2003) The impact of windows on mood and the performance of judgmental tasks. MSc in Lighting Thesis, Rensselaer Polytechnic Institute, New York.

Debord, K., Hestenes, L. L., Moore, R. C., Cosco, N. G., and Mcginnis, J. R. (2005) *POEMS: Early childhood outdoor environment measurement scale*. Winston-Salem, North Carolina: Kaplan, Inc.

Devlin, A. S. and Arneill, A. B. (2003) Health care environments and patient outcomes: A review of the literature. *Environment and Behavior*, **35**, 665–694.

Diana, R. J. (2012) Imagining the garden: Childhood, landscape, and architecture in early pedagogy, 1761–1850. PhD Thesis, Harvard University.

Frost, J. L., Wortham, S. and Reifel, S. (2001). *Play and child development*. New Jersey: Merrill Prentice Hall.

Fröbel, F. (1895) *Friedrich Froebel's pedagogics of the kindergarten* (Vol. 30). New York: D. Appleton and Company.

Goelman, H. and Jacobs, E. V. (1994) *Children's play in child care settings*. New York: SUNY Press.

GSA. 2003. Child care centre design guide [Online]. Available at: www.gsa.gov/cdnstatic/designguidesmall.pdf [Accessed 7 August 2019].

Gulwadi, G. B. (2006) Seeking restorative experiences: Elementary school teachers' choices for places that enable coping with stress. *Environment and Behavior*, **38**, 503–520.

Hathaway, W. E. (1992) *A study into the effects of light on children of elementary school-age: A case of daylight robbery*. Alberta Department of Education, Edmonton. Planning and Information Services.

Hedge, A. (1994) Reactions of computer users to three different lighting systems in windowed and windowless offices. *Work and Display Units*, **94**, B54–B56.

Heschong, L., Mahone, D., Kuttaiah, K., Stone, N., Chappell, C., and Mchugh, J. (1999) Daylighting in schools: An investigation into the relationship between daylighting and human performance. Summary for the Pacific Gas and Electric Company on behalf of the California Board for Energy Efficiency Third Party Program.

Hopwood-Stephens, I. (2013) *Learning on your doorstep: Stimulating writing through creative play outdoors for ages 5–9*. New York, London: Routledge.

Irwin, A. and Joachim, W. (1978) *Children and the environment*. New York: Plenum Press.

Kaplan, S. (1995) The restorative benefits of nature: Toward an integrative framework. *Journal of Environmental Psychology*, **15**, 169–182.

Kaplan, R. (2001) The nature of the view from home psychological benefits. *Environment and Behavior*, **33**, 507–542.

Karmel, L. J. (1965) Effects of windowless classroom environment on high school students. *Perceptual and Motor Skills*, **20**, 277–278.

Küller, R. and Lindsten, C. (1992) Health and behaviour of children in classrooms with and without windows. *Journal of Environmental Psychology*, **12**, 305–317.

Laughlin, L. (2010) Who's minding the kids? Child care arrangements, Spring 2005/Summer 2006. Washington, D.C.: US Department of Commerce, Bureau of the Census.

Laughlin, L. (2013) Who's minding the kids? Child care arrangements, Spring 2011. Washington, D.C.: US Department of Commerce, Bureau of the Census.

Li, D. and Sullivan, W. C. (2016) Impact of views to school landscapes on recovery from stress and mental fatigue. *Landscape and urban planning*, **148**, 149–158.

Lieberman, G. A., Hoody, L. L., and Lieberman, G. M. (2000) *California Student Assessment Project Phase One: The effects of environment-based education on student achievement*. San Diego, CA.: State Education and Environment Roundtable, California Department of Education.

Louv, R. (2008) *Last child in the woods: Saving our children from nature-deficit disorder*. Chapel Hill, N.C.: Algonquin Books.

Malone, K. and Tranter, P. (2003) Children's environmental learning and the use, design and management of schoolgrounds. *Children, Youth and Environments*, **13**(2), 87–137.

Matsuoka, R. H. (2010) Student performance and high school landscapes: Examining the links. *Landscape and Urban Planning*, **97**, 273–282.

Mckenzie, T. L. (2010) C. H. McCloy Lecture. Seeing is believing: Observing physical activity and its contexts. *Research Quarterly for Exercise and Sport*, **81**, 113–22.

McMillan, M., (1921) *The nursery schools*. New York: Dutton.

Montessori, M. (2011) *Dr. Montessori's own handbook*. New York: Schocken Books.

Moore, R. C. (1996) Outdoor setting for playing and learning: Designing school grounds to meet the needs of the whole child and whole curriculum. *The NAMTA Journal*, **21**, 97–121.

Moore, R. C. and Cosco, N. (2007) Greening Montessori school grounds by design. *The NAMTA Journal*, **32**, 128–151.

Moore, R. C. and Goltsman, S. M. (1992) *Play for all guidelines: Planning, designing and management of outdoor play settings for all children*. Berkeley, CA.: Mig Communications.

Nessy, M. (2016) Classrooms without walls: A forgotten age of open-air schools [Online]. Available at: www.messynessychic.com/2016/03/15/classrooms-without-walls-a-forgotten-age-of-open-air-schools/ [Accessed 7 April, 2020].

Nilsen, B. A. (2013) *Week by week: Plans for documenting children's development*. Cengage Learning (online).

Olds, A. (2001) *Child care design guide*. Washington D.C.: McGraw-Hill.

Perry, N. E. and Winne, P. H. (2006) Learning from learning kits: Study traces of students' self-regulated engagements with computerized content. *Educational Psychology Review*, **18**, 211–228.

Sanoff, H. (2009) Foreword. In Walden, R. (ed.), *Schools for the future: Design proposals from architectural psychology*, pp. v–viii. Hogrefe and Huber Publishers.

Shim, S. Y., Herwig, J. E. and Shelley , M. (2001) Preschoolers' play behaviors with peers in classroom and playground settings. *Journal of Research in Childhood Education*, **15**, 149–163.

Slopack, M. (2011) The impact of a window in the classroom on learning as perceived by students and teachers. Doctoral dissertation, George Brown College, George Brown College's Institutional Repository of Applied Research – Archive.

Tai, L., Haque, M. T., Mclellan, G. K., and Erin, K. J. (2006) *Designing outdoor environments for children*. New York: McGraw-Hill.

Tanner, C. K. (2009) Effects of school design on student outcomes. *Journal of Educational Administration*, **47**, 381–399.

Taylor, A. (2002) Views of nature and self-discipline: Evidence from inner city children. *Journal of Environmental Psychology*, **22**, 49–63.

Uduku, O. (2015) Spaces for 21st-century learning. In McGrath, S. and Gu, Q. (eds), *Routledge handbook of international education and development*. Abingdon: Routledge.

Ulrich, R. (1984) View through a window may influence recovery. *Science*, **224**, 224–225.

Vandell, D. L., Belsky, J., Burchinal, M., Steinberg, L., and Vandergrift, N. (2010) Do effects of early child care extend to age 15 years? Results from the NICHD study of early child care and youth development. *Child Development*, **81**, 737–756.

Walch, J. M., Rabin, B. S., Day, R., Williams, J. N., Choi, K., and Kang, J. D. (2005) The effect of sunlight on postoperative analgesic medication use: A prospective study of patients undergoing spinal surgery. *Psychosomatic Medicine*, **67**, 156–163.

Wells, N. M. (2000) At home with nature: Effects of "greenness" on children's cognitive functioning. *Environment and Behavior*, **32**, 775–795.

Whitebread, D., Coltman, P., Pasternak, D. P., Sangster, C., Grau, V., Bingham, S., Almeqdad, Q., and Demetriou, D. (2008) The development of two observational tools for assessing metacognition and self-regulated learning in young children. *Metacognition and Learning*, **4**, 63–85.

7

BECOMING NATURISH: WAYS OF COMING TO KNOW NATURE IN THE PRIMARY SCHOOL

Cathy Francis

INTRODUCTION

This chapter comprises my most recent reflections on the recursive and co-constructive processes of children's knowing and noticing of Nature. The reflections are focussed on a group of school children's embodied experiences at a local beach and their emergent ecological identities. The eight and nine-year-old children, from the north east of Scotland, visited the beach with me, their class teacher, for two hours each week for eleven weeks as part of their regular schooling. Having walked to the beach, we made art together, played games and beachcombed while we built our curricular knowledge and understanding of Learning for Sustainability (LfS) and Science, as outlined in Scottish education's Curriculum for Excellence (CfE) (Education Scotland, 2004). The children expressed their experiences in writing and art-making. I took photographs and made video and voice recordings. Quite apart from any curricular 'gains', a few weeks into the project the pupils suggested expressing their growing appreciation of their immediate natural environment and their place within it, as *becoming naturish*. The children decided upon the following definition of becoming naturish as:

> Liking the outdoors and knowing what it means. When you know a lot about nature and you're really used to it.

Furthermore, they described their embodied, experiential activities leading to naturishness as *plearning* and *flearning. Plearning* and *flearning* are portmanteaus, created from the phonetic blending of play and fun with learning respectively. Their meanings are also combined. The children described plearning as: 'Something between playing and learning' and flearning as: 'A mixture of fun and learning'. The children felt no need to define either play, fun or learning, as these terms were considered well established within our classroom culture already.

I begin this chapter with an examination of my relationship, as a primary school teacher, with Nature. I explain how this relationship came to influence the pedagogical decisions I made day to day. I then offer the reader some thoughts on the contested nature of Nature and explore the relationality of children and of education with Nature today. The relationality is described from a distinctly north western European perspective which, while I recognise it is not representative of all children's experiences of compulsory schooling, is the context from which this chapter is written.

I then explore facets of children's noticing and knowing of Nature gathered during our term's worth of beach visits. They are described within a dynamic framework of four successive quadrants. Our activities and experiences at the beach were many and varied; however, for the purposes of this text, I have focussed on the embodied interactions between seaweed and children to populate the framework explicitly. I call these experiences *seaweed vignettes.*

In conclusion, I suggest teachers could usefully refer to such a framework when embarking upon learning and teaching in Nature outside the classroom. I believe that through it, children may be given time and space to make meaningful connections with natural places and their co-inhabitants, i.e. Nature. I argue that, were teachers to become more aware of the subtle interactions occurring between children and Nature, they would become more aware of the power of Nature as a teacher, influencer and leader of learning. If teachers could build trust in Nature, as I have, they might be more inclined to allow it space to infiltrate the lives of the young learners so that alternative ways of knowing may be privileged.

MYSELF, EDUCATION AND NATURE

Inspired by a love of Nature, I have learned alongside children for over thirty years. Whenever possible I have taken learning and teaching outside of the classroom and into Nature so that we may gather authentic experiences at first hand. I have witnessed Nature invoke a range of emotional responses in young learners ranging from joy, fear, love, aversion, surprise and on occasion, even boredom. It is a context from within which I have watched young learners run, jump, climb and be still. Almost without exception, our forays have yielded awe-inspired moments of wonder which have had the capacity to quite literally stop us in our tracks!

I suspect this recognition has sprung from my early childhood experiences of playing outside, such as riding my bike alone along treelined, ancient bridleways, paddling in rivers with school friends catching dragonfly larvae or being sandblasted along the long flat beaches of Kent and Essex walking backwards, while balanced on the feet of my dad.

As a professional teacher I was aware of the effects of movement and emotion on learning. This, combined with an altruistic urge to foster a love of Nature in the children with whom I found myself working, led me to lead them outside, because this was surely where Nature is found. Predicated upon my belief and trust that Nature, in a state of perpetual change yet constancy, would inevitably lead the learner on a path of discovery I consciously allowed space, temporal and spatial, for Nature to exert her full effect on the young learners whenever I could.

I led children outdoors, pied piper-like, to discover Nature through self-led exploration, otherwise termed play. Schiller considers play to be the ultimate experience of any human individual or group:

> Our humanity depends on it, he was sure, because playfulness for Schiller is no frivolous pastime. Play is the instinct for freedom and for art, the drive that can harmonize man's two other and mutually murderous instincts, transforming the conflict between passion, the Sinnestrieb, and reason, the Formtrieb, into aesthetic pleasure. Man is mortal flesh, driven by the material instinct that enslaves him to nature through the passions and holds him back in a savage state. He is also a timeless spirit that obeys the instinct of reason, which organizes the world into abstract, pitiless principles that can reduce human life to barbarity.
>
> (Sommer 2009: 86)

Schiller's sentiment is that *play* is at the heart of human being or becoming. Likewise, the children identified *play* critical to their *being* at the beach. During a conversation in the classroom following one of our visits the children invented the portmanteau *plearning* to describe this state of being.

Despite my disposition to consider excursions into Nature valuable, as a primary school teacher I have learned it takes time, perseverance, resourcefulness and ingenuity to find space within the school day to *fit Nature in* (Christie *et al.* 2014). Therefore, rather than offer the opportunity to learn about and build connection with Nature as an additional or extra entity, deemed onerous or bonus, I have latterly attempted to layer the experience over that which a child would normally *expect* to experience at school through a subtle 'tinkering' with their educational *lifeworld*. I adopt and employ lifeworld almost literally in the spirit of Husserl's description of Earth as a place 'on which we coincidentally crawl about' (Husserl in Østergaard 2017: 563). Lifeworld is otherwise described simply as 'the world in which we live' (ibid.: 564).

I am struck by the tension inflicted upon a teacher who, while tasked with engineering the curriculum and adjusting pedagogy to best suit the needs of the child, is also expected to perform this feat within educational systems so often resistant to change. Philosophical, economic, political, social and cultural norms promulgate a rigidity to education (Cole 2010). For as long as education is measured using formal assessment tasks, checked against benchmarks or reported in attainment levels this will perhaps ever be so. When teaching and learning is situated in Nature, however, the rigid framework of compulsory education finds itself within a context characterised by diversity and flux. For example, any lesson planned with reference to the collection and identification of rockpool creatures although carefully synchronised with the tide tables may suddenly have to be curtailed because of an unexpected hailstorm. We might now learn of cloud formation or prevailing winds. Alternatively, an appearance of a school of dolphins in the bay is likely to disorient a lesson focussed on appreciating the adaptation of wading sea birds to their shellfish diet. We might now learn of team work and co-operation or how dolphins are adapted and therefore able to leap so powerfully over the waves.

Teachers and Nature might be considered powerful allies when learning and teaching is displaced outside of the classroom. Within a natural environment, a union of teachers and Nature may be able to offer children dynamic and creative opportunities to learn. Distanced from a fixed agenda of knowledge to be attained, teachers and learners might generate shared knowledge and understanding provoked and encouraged by Nature. An apparent handing over of the learning agenda to Nature will take a brave and committed community of learners situated within a global community of humans who trust and love Nature just as I did as a child.

I perceive that other tensions are lessened in intensity when learning is situated within Nature. Nature has brought me closer to learners, physically and emotionally. We have built trusting and open relationships based on our shared experiences outside. For example, as we walk together over slippery rocks, we look out for one another. It was not unusual for us to literally hold hands with one another as we explored the marine landscape together. This suggested foreshortened distancing and shift in relationality has the capacity to alter the hegemonic hierarchy of power between pupils and teachers (Uitto and Syrjala 2008); a more democratic learning community is possible. Simple evidence of this is found within my field notes where I have consistently used 'we', in place of me or they.

The democratic learning community is further diversified when Nature becomes an equal third member. For an understanding of this perspective on Nature's participation and influence, with and upon others, please see De Laet and Mol's (2000) account of the Zimbabwean bush pump.

KNOWING NATURE

Before going further, I should perhaps explain what Nature is. It is a contested and complicated term that has evaded precise definition, for many years, by scholars far more qualified than I. It is also one which, I suspect, will continue to provoke discussion for many years to come. I suggest Nature is ephemeral yet consistent, inclusive yet exclusive. It is, in the same moment, completely visible yet invisible. Furthermore, Uggla suggests humans have a 'deeply ambivalent relationship with nature, which oscillates between romantic devotion to nature and attempts to conquer it' (2010: 80).

Historically, works by Gainsborough, Constable or Turner depicted Nature as places of untamed wilderness or pristine beauty. Here Nature can be found comprising landscape (rocks, mountains and water features) or seascape. Such visions are still considered today by many to be the apices of truly natural contexts. However, I suggest the designation and maintenance of such areas, in an assumed effort to protect them, serves only to further distance humans from Nature rather than build any connection. Critics of conservation projects designed to protect or reinstate such areas of wilderness or pristine beauty further suggest there is little point in such aims as we live within a post-Nature environment where no untouched areas of wilderness exist (Sitka-Sage *et al.* 2017).

Humans have profoundly altered, and continue to alter, the composition and processes of our atmosphere and hydrosphere globally (ibid.). With growing acknowledgement that we are living in the Anthropocene, I suggest it fallacious to think we might have no impact or leave no trace on Nature anywhere on Earth. The point is that we have a trace (Loynes 2018), so let us aspire to make it a less destructive and selfish one. I posit that were humans to become a little more modest in their actions, they may then be considered just another species, among others, living unavoidably within the web of Gaia and therefore intimately a co-constituent of Nature (Lovelock, 2000).

No clear consensus was noted on human presence within, or distancing from, Nature during my conversations with the children during our weekly excursions. They contended that Nature could be found equally at the woods or the beach (where people could or could not be present) but not in a city centre or at the North Pole (one place full of people and the other without). Humans are variously present and absent in each of these contexts.

Despite the engrossing academic or philosophical discourse on the composition, concept or whereabouts of Nature, I suggest a realisation that humans and Nature are relational is of greater importance, where that relationality is founded upon one's understanding of one's physical, emotional, cognitive and spiritual relationship with self and other (Thorburn and Marshall 2014).

THIS PROJECT'S DEFINITION OF NATURE

Although man's relationship with Nature may be contested and complicated, it is useful to have a working definition of Nature for the reader of this chapter. I have chosen to use the children's definition which surfaced at the commencement of our beach visits. Nature, in its simplest form, might be considered the collection of the living and the non-living; furthermore those 'things' are not created by man (Bonnett and Williams 1998; Tillmann *et al.* 2019). I posed this statement to the children during one of our first visits to the beach while standing at the water's edge. Through our informal conversation the following was elucidated:

> leaves, wildlife, creatures, rain, sea, sun, clouds, hills, wind, sea glass, shells, stones, clothes, the burn, bridge, loch, woods, grass, crops, combining, dogs, birds/pigeons, rabbits, wild rabbits, cats, tadpoles, fish, cows, sheep, pigs, horses, ice, snow.

Apart from combining (harvesting barley for its grain and for straw), the children's understanding of Nature is consequently understood to be a list of things. Therefore, growing one's knowledge could simply be interpreted as lengthening a lexicon-like list and reciting it on demand. However within the context of curricular learning in Science, Colucci-Gray and Camino warn against such 'thingifying' views of science (and of the world itself) because it may promulgate 'a sense of alienation, if not fear, toward nature'. They continue: 'the emotional dimension of knowing nature plays an important role that, perhaps, has been underestimated in our increasingly urbanized society' (2016: 34). Such other ways of learning are expanded upon later.

KNOWING NATURE AT SCHOOL

Making acquaintance with Nature

For one to understand one's relation to another, presumably one must either meet the other or at least know of the other. The difficulty with helping children to know Nature, during school hours, has been the *disembodiment* of education (Rathunde 2008) and a gradual trend to remove education[1] from the outdoors. This shift in learning emphasis and method has largely been in response to an economic or political aspiration to use education to produce a workforce destined to fuel a consumer-driven economy (Darling 2014). The system has perhaps favoured more didactic teaching methods thought better to meet increasing curricular pressures, timetabling, league tables or national testing. Schools have become places of production, run as business enterprises rather than places of altruistic learning and human flourishing. This is in stark contrast to the personal experiences within Nature I recollected at the beginning of this chapter, which shape the pedagogical decisions I make today.

It is recognised that a relationship with Nature is very important in the lives of humans, particularly of children, and much has been published of the consequences of a loss of connection. Louv (2005) described the phenomenon of a nature deficit disorder, whereby children's developmental health and wellbeing is compromised through a lack of exposure to the natural world outdoors. This lack of exposure to Nature has been suggested to cause depression, anxiety, stress and obesity (Louv 2009).

A lack of exposure, while concerning, is perhaps of lesser importance than the nature of that exposure when or if it happens. Schools in Scotland may well boast good attendance at day or residential outdoor learning centres, but what is the nature of the young people's exposure to Nature at these places? The aims and outcomes of many centres appear rather more focussed on developing young people's leadership and survival skills than evoking any sensitive connection with Nature (Nicol and Higgins 2007). The commodification of the provision of outdoor learning opportunities is criticised by Loynes (1998) as having disassociated unique experiences offered to participants from the very community and place which inspired their creation. For example, the experience of being harnessed-up and fitted with a hardhat, as a defence to potential injury, is clearly a somewhat different experience to that of wandering almost aimlessly along a beach searching for, picking up and gently turning over in one's hand the most beautiful shell (Rautio, 2013).

Education to deliver a sustainable future

With the realisation that we are living beyond our planetary limits (World Commission on Environment and Development 1987; Scottish Government 2012; EPA 2015), society is beginning to question the economic models and associated technology thought to deliver sustainable growth and development for all effectively (United Nations 2012; Ellen Macarthur Foundation 2015). Learning, and by extension education, plays an important role within any society.

Ogbuigwe suggests that 'Education is considered the backbone of the transformation of societies and can inspire the adoption of sustainable practices' (cited in Corcoran et al. 2017: 15). Within Scotland, the government encourages schools to play their part as they translate CfE guidelines into authentic learning opportunities for children outdoors in planned progressive experiences for children from three to eighteen (Learning And Teaching Scotland 2010). Globally, Somerville and Williams (2015) report that more recently the benefits of learning outside have found a secure foothold in research communities, social movements and community initiatives.[2] I am encouraged by this and further concur with Sterling (2002), when he intimates that teachers need not necessarily wait for central guidance to act; hence this chapter, my teaching and latterly, my research.

In my experience, however, it is only truly committed or very well supported staff which are successfully and repeatedly able to negotiate barriers to learning outdoors (Christie et al. 2014). Support may come from peers, management, parents or friends. I find support and enthusiasm from the pupils very efficacious when the going gets tough. A small girl reminding me of the soggy feet she experienced the previous week while crossing the burn, or the boy who appeared to have more sand than feet in his boots on his return to school, each with broad smiles across their faces, are enough.

NATURE OF KNOWING

I hope by now the reader has developed an appreciation of our perception and interpretation of Nature. I trust it also follows that the reader might agree that it is perhaps obvious to state that if one does not meet Nature, one may never notice it, and if one does not notice it, one may never have the pleasure of its company. More importantly perhaps, if one does not know of something or some other, how can one ever care for it? Pyle comments on the relationship between humans and Nature:

> The result of the loss of contact and subsequent alienation is the Extinction of Experience: an inexorable cycle of disconnection, apathy, and progressive depletion.

> (2003: 206)

Kahn *et al.* describe a growing lack of ability or inclination to notice Nature as 'environmental generational amnesia', and is concerned that:

> by adapting gradually to the loss of actual nature and to the increase of technological nature, humans will lower the baseline across generations for what counts as a full measure of the human experience and of human flourishing.

> (2009: 37)

I argue that, if children can only be bought into Nature, then it can prove to be a rich and self-perpetuating context intrinsically in which to hone the skills of noticing. The dependable, predictable rhythm of the tides, juxtaposed with chanced-upon beachcombing treasure washed up on the shore one morning, surely cannot fail to prompt the perceptive skills of a visitor to a beach. I suggest Nature's constancy pitched against its dynamic diversity might continually serve to prick a child's subconscious Bayesian logic to make an emergent meaning of their experiences (Schulz *et al.* 2007). This logic invokes elements of memory and skills of prediction. This prompting of continual response to a changing environment is made with reference to the discussion of Nature's ephemerality yet constancy earlier.

One's capacity to notice Nature is not seated exclusively within the mind. Within the human person, a fundamental connection of body and mind to context exists wherever they find themselves (Johnson 2006). Pink develops the paradigm of 'emplacement' as an active exchange between 'bodies, minds and the materiality and sensoriality of the environment' (2015: 28). She suggests one becomes aware of one's place in the world through the sensorium where the sensorium is the full suite of human senses which work in concert: touch, smell, sight, hearing and taste. Together, they allow one to make sense of one's place in the world. I suggest this is loosely reminiscent of Steiner's philosophy of Anthroposophy (Steiner 1996) upon which Waldorf Schools were founded over one hundred years ago. Steiner (1916) posited twelve senses possessed by the human body which facilitate response to, and connection with, a material and spiritual world. He concluded the human body to possess the senses of: ego, thought, speech, hearing, warmth, sight, taste, smell, touch, balance, movement and life. This chapter is thus situated within a rich and diverse sensory matrix, privileging an organic, embodied perception.

Returning to Pink's sensorium (2015), as far as touch is concerned, it indicates the situation where the surface of the body meets the outside world. If one combines this perception with an acknowledgement of an ongoing process of affordance and agency, the environment itself could be considered a teacher as much as another human, in that it provides an opportunity to learn. Briefly, affordances are possibilities for action offered by the environment, for good or ill (Gibson in Khatibi and Sheikholeslami 2015); and agency, the consequent or subsequent enacted action. Importantly, J. J. Gibson considers 'animals needn't learn to perceive; rather, they perceive to learn' (cited in Adolph and Kretch 2015: 1). Therefore, alongside the child's parent or the school teacher, lies the environment, which Malaguzzi termed the 'third educator' (Rinaldi 2006: 60). As a human teacher might adapt teaching and learning opportunities, so does a changing environment, as is the belief of Reggio Emilia proponents (Strong-Wilson and Ellis 2007).

There is insufficient space here to describe the human ability to make meaning as an independent individual and/or as a member of a learning community. But it is important to note that although perhaps my peers are well-versed in Vygotskian (Daniels 2016) or Kolbian (Kolb 1984) learning theory, they are generally far less familiar with the mechanisms or philosophy of body and mind, knowing, noticing or simply *being* in the world through emplacement.

This project's weekly excursions into Nature were intended to gently expand upon children's lifeworlds. I argue that during these excursions, because of my increased awareness of the pedagogical choices made available by Nature, children were able to explore and connect with Nature in deeper and more meaningful ways than perhaps is normally experienced. I specifically describe embodied and emplaced interactions between seaweed[3] and children within an imagined framework. Importantly, because embodiment is a genre of learning which largely appears to have dropped out of the *modern* teacher's lexicon, a framework such as this might prove useful reference for practitioners keen to develop a more nuanced approach to teaching and learning outdoors in Nature.

To explore children's noticing and knowing of Nature I imagined a structure consisting of four quadrants, each flowing into the next. The quadrants comprise: encounter, touch, affiliation and surrender (see Figure 7.1). Some may consider them perhaps reminiscent of the John Muir Award's challenge levels (Discover, Explore, Conserve and Share),[4] particularly because we are dealing with Nature and the outdoors. However, the quadrants here are conceived in relation to a single person's embodied response to Nature and would therefore perhaps all fit into the 'Explore' section of the John Muir framework. The raison d'être of this framework is to challenge the hegemony of exploring to control, conquer or claim Nature (Uggla 2010). It offers a different connection with Nature through coming to know it in alternative ways.

There was no expectation for the amount of time to be spent in each section of the framework nor of the overall speed of circumnavigation. Indeed, one child may well circle around the complete framework while others dwell a while in one quadrant. I determined that the activities I chose were fun filled and playful as it was *flearning* and *plearning* that the children identified as crucial for their becoming naturish. As the teacher, I kept curricular aims and gains in soft focus while maintaining my gaze on the dynamic interactions of Nature and children.

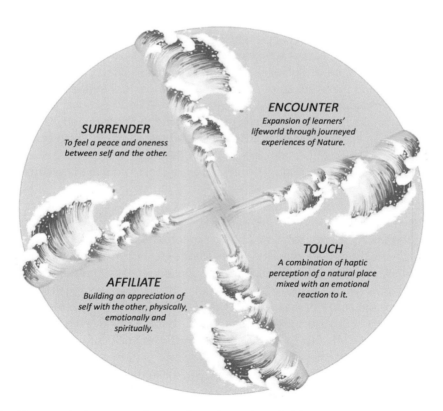

FIGURE 7.1 The imagined framework of a process of connection or becoming naturish
Source: Cathy Francis

Earlier I wrote that a human individual may be continuously embedded within Nature so that they are a contiguous part of it (Pyle 2003); likewise, one may argue a school may be similarly situated. However, doors, keypads and gates equipped with CCTV often secure the boundaries of a school, ensuring a separateness from the rest of the world. In such a scenario there is a clear division between Nature and the schoolchild. I wonder if the intention to keep children *safe* also allows Nature to be kept safe from us?

Beyond the school gates children on excursions are, for obvious reasons, typically kept under tight control. This often effectively means staying 'with your group' and certainly in close proximity to the teacher or other accompanying adult. Crossing the boundary between school and Nature is a risky business, a business which requires teachers and learners to be determined and brave. However, I encourage the reader to consider for a moment the risks to all concerned (including Nature) when teaching and learning remains within the confines of the classroom.

Vignette 1 – Seaweed and David

Having crossed the boundary from school and into Nature, David singularly chose to encounter Nature in his own way each week. He chose to encounter Nature by himself. I regularly observed him standing at the water's edge mesmerised by the waves and thrilled to be allowed to be so close to the water (see Figure 7.2).

Allowing David to stand thus allowed him space to fill his body with sensations of sounds and smells, and of distance. I hoped that such sense-able encounters would stimulate the body and mind of the individual so they might make deeper meaning of the world. When I caught up with him, in his own time, David spoke eagerly to the video camera about his feelings of wonder and how he loved the waves.

This encounter was prompted by an activity requiring seaweed to be collected and washed, but the draw of the sea took over. David was supposed to be at the water's edge to wash his seaweed free of sand and creatures so

FIGURE 7.2 David at the water's edge
Source: Cathy Francis

that he could take it back to school to weave with. However, the rhythmic ebb and flow of the waves caught his attention. Instead of calling him back to the group, from a distance I watched him standing still and alone by the water's edge for about ten minutes. Aware of the framework, I chose to let him stand alone, I knew he was safe, and I knew he wasn't dodging work, he was simply captivated. When I did catch up with him on the journey back to school he animatedly told me:

> I've enjoyed most er, picking er, up the seaweed and like erm waves, I've been like having fun playing with the waves an' I kinda got wet a little bit but that's OK.

Each week David was the child to get wet, the waves were like a magnet to him whatever the activity. However, instead of continually reprimanding him for going 'off task', leaving the group or getting wet, I watched him. After the last trip he described his most important feeling about the beach was that it made him feel like a 'wonderer' and that he was in a place which gave him space to think. I considered I had given space for Nature, to give him space to think. At the conclusion of the project David chose to depict himself as 'wonderer' in his collage, whereas the other children chose to depict themselves gregariously, as either artists, scientists, explorers or carers. David identified himself as a lone figure and was happy for it, he was plearning and flearning.

TOUCH

Touch has at least two interpretations: simple physiological or haptic touch and affective or emotional reaction in response to the other. In each case we touch others as they touch us. The mixing of rational and emotional meaning-making of touch renders the situation yet more complex. There is insufficient space here for a full description of the complexity of touch, but it is important for the reader to consider the intimate connections between body, mind and Nature. Within this chapter I urge the reader to consider the power of learning made possible through a physical connection with Nature in particular, as a challenge to the hegemony of brain/mind-centric cognitive gains prescribed by curriculum.

The children apparently found writing about the sensation of touch difficult or perhaps insufficiently important to mention. The children did not appear to notice their irresistible handling of the sandy substrate about them as we chatted, plearned and flearned at the beach. I found it significant that when I kindly commented on them 'fidgeting' with the sand they all too often brushed their hands clear of the sand and simply commented 'I don't know I'm doing it'; alternatively, they just fell silent. With their hands trailing through the sand they spoke to me freely, once their hands were still their minds were apparently rendered likewise.

Vignette 2 – Seaweed and Rosalind

Figure 7.3 shows Rosalind's pre-visit picture of herself at the beach. There is no seaweed, she has no fingers, there is no beach! There is no chance she and the seaweed are going to touch each other. However, by the end of the project she had grown to notice seaweed so intimately that she could identify several species confidently and reliably, to her friends, to me and to visitors some weeks later.

Other children's drawings (left and right) similarly showed a physical distancing of self from seaweed or the beach. Most pictures showed no seaweed, many figures had no fingers. Although initially surprised to see such drawings, I soon realised that with respect to physical touching with skin, a significantly reduced 'touching toolkit' was available to these children while visiting a beach in Scotland in December and January. Their skin, the human body's largest sense organ was almost entirely wrapped in several layers of clothing (described in the poem on p. 117) and their hands were gloved, stuffed in pockets or held buckets, nets or spades (evidenced in children's drawings and in photos). Ironically, the items I had provided to aid the children's exploration of the beach (buckets, spades, guidebooks and nets) had stifled the tools nature had bestowed upon them, namely their hands and fingers.

FIGURE 7.3 Examples of children's drawings of themselves at the beginning of the beach visits. Rosalind's is the centre picture
Source: Cathy Francis

Rosalind's seaweed encounters at the beach appear to have made a considerable impact on her embodied consciousness of the beach. Her detailed description of the texture of seaweed exclusively comprises the middle verse of her poem 'Becoming Naturish':[5]

Shiny wellies walking
Waterproof trousers crumpling
Hi-viz vest reflecting
Cosy jacket blowing

Wet kelp blowing
Slimy sugar kelp moving
Rough bladder wrack drying

Cold children running
Yucky wellies squelching
Disgusting giggler treatment hiding
Massive lorries honking

Vignette 3 – Seaweed and Maudie

Towards the end of our series of beach visits I had conceived and engineered a cascade of seaweed-based activities in direct response to a comment made by Rosalind's friend Maudie. Perhaps Rosalind's learning and change of awareness of the beach was prompted by something else or would have happened anyway, but Maudie's comment was less than sanguine:

Sea-weed? It's only a weed, what good is it? I hate it, it makes me slip and fall.

I was sensitive to these kinds of comments, especially as I had spent some time the previous week showing children some particularly slimy kelp we had chanced upon. I had considered it beautiful and tried, fairly unsuccessfully, to encourage the children to come close to it. I was only able to persuade a few children to actually touch the sugar kelp to experience its cool, slippery yet bumpy surface. The video of the children's meeting with the seaweed shows grimaced faces and physical movement of their whole bodies away from the seaweed. I combined my memory of the derogatory comment above with this recorded aversion to touch, and determined to challenge the children's reactions.

I sensitively increased the demands made of touch in the activities I devised. I hypothesised that if I could encourage them to touch, I could encourage connection, because they would be propelled onwards through the theoretical framework.

We made faces in the sand and used seaweed for hair. We collected seaweed to weave baskets to take home. Ultimately, we ate dried seaweed at the parents' 'open classroom' day. In eating the seaweed, I suggest the connection of seaweed and children was perhaps most complete; the seaweed was literally incorporated into the body. Having previously considered seaweed 'just a weed', Maudie wrote in her field diary at the end of the project:

> I know that the seaweed smells
> I notice that it can be slippey
> I think that I like to play with seaweed
> I wonder if you can get aquwa couler.

In her diary and in video footage of our trips she considered her work with seaweed as plearning. The connection between seaweed and Maudie has changed.

AFFILIATION

This quadrant of the theoretical framework equates to the inclination of human and Nature to be drawn to one another. Kellert and Wilson called this attraction 'biophilia' (1993). An important aspect of biophilia is the understanding that direct experiences in Nature during childhood, alongside significant others who demonstrate a 'love' of nature, can be hugely influential in later life, especially in respect of developing environmentally responsible behaviour (Kals, Schumacher and Montada 1999; Chawla 2006; Zylstra et al. 2014).

The next vignette draws on an activity mentioned earlier, where the previously 'revolting and useless' seaweed is now recognised as beautiful.

Vignette 4 – Seaweed, Alice, Albert and Hilary
At the beach the task had been to:

> Collect as many different sorts of seaweed as you can. Do not tear any from the rocks but collect loose pieces from the strandline. Take care to feel the difference between the different sorts, you are going to weave with it. Here is your basket to collect it in, which will become the one you weave the seaweed through. Once you have weaved with the seaweed, we will plant the baskets up with bulbs for a Mother's Day gift to take home.

Following these instructions, the children headed off excitedly in pairs or threes to collect their seaweed. As we walked along the strandline, I was able to have conversations with various groups about what would make good weaving material and what definitely would not. I asked the children to take the decision to collect or not, based on the weavability of the seaweed. It was a conscious decision to encourage the children to handle the seaweed physically in order to evaluate it. I reasoned one cannot accurately gauge strength, flexibility or slipperiness visually, one had to touch it. The children would also have to be selective as the baskets were quite small.

Here is the conversation, once back in class and at our tables, as we began to weave. During the flowing conversation all participants (including myself) were handling seaweed pieces, turning them over in our hands and bending stipes and blades[6] into shape:

Teacher: 'So how are you feeling about seaweed then?'

Alice: 'Now I feel more confident with the seaweed because it's natural. I'm getting used to the feel of it 'cos I'm working with it I'm getting more confident; I mean when you actually work with it.'

Teacher: 'Anyone else have any ideas?'

Gerald: 'I'm accustomed to it.'

Teacher: 'What does accustomed mean?'

Gerald: 'Get more accustomed means you get used to it.'

Alice: 'Make it a part of your life. This is getting horrible. This strand is very slimy, and it keeps slipping out the bottom. We're destroying nature before we realised how amazing it was.'

Naomi: 'Going to the beach has taught me it's not slimy yucky stuff. It's actually quite healthy. I didn't realise people could bath in it.'

Alice: 'I'm not scared of seaweed, I used to be. I was hardly able to walk on it. I didn't know it was so important'

There is insufficient space here to make any detailed analysis, but I suggest this short transcript is heavily laden with sentiment, realisation and shifting perspectives. All, I contend, were stimulated by the embodied exchange between seaweed and children which began at the beach and continued into the classroom. While at the beach, the seaweed was variously walked upon and slipped on. It was picked up and examined. In the classroom the seaweed was arranged on the desks where the children sat in friendship groups, to craft their woven Mother's Day seaweed basket gifts. At the beach, the fresh smell of the seaweed wafted about and was blown into our faces. Later in the classroom, the aroma was intensified and it felt as if it thickly percolated the whole space around and about us. It commanded our olfactory attention. The direct, precise and considered touching and handling of seaweed I observed as we wove in the classroom spoke for itself. The activity invited opportunity for the seaweed to touch us as we touched the seaweed. It was touched respectfully, and I felt the seaweed was almost in charge at some points because it was its inherent qualities which dictated to the children its possible incorporation into the crafting. Once again, plearning and flearning were mentioned in the children's beach diaries.

SURRENDER

Vignette 5 – Nature and Bridget

There is insufficient space in this chapter to fully discuss the concept of surrender, but perhaps Bridget's definition of *becoming naturish* is sufficient:

> Liking the outdoors and knowing what it means. When you know a lot about nature and you're really used to it.

Bridget mentions positive emotion towards Nature ('liking the outdoors') and proclaims to understand it, not control it. This is suggestive of a respectful, modest connection with Nature. Bridget's mention of becoming 'really used to it' suggests she has incorporated Nature into her lifeworld. It is part of her everyday life experience. For reasons discussed earlier, although apparently increasingly difficult to achieve during the school day, the simple series of weekly excursions to the beach of this project has afforded Bridget an expansion of experience and a connection with Nature. She values 'knowing a lot' about Nature which might echo the hegemony of teacher-directed curricular gains, but she does not mention what this 'knowing' actually means. If one looks through her diary and reflects upon the pictures of Bridget at the beach one can see a range of knowing. Furthermore, it was Bridget who led the class discussion which surfaced the terms plearning and flearning.

The individual vignettes presented afford the chance to delve into the depth of experience the children and I experienced during this project. However, I was also careful to record the children's overall feelings towards their becoming naturish in a more holistic manner.

I drew concentric circles in the sand at the beginning and end of the project. On each occasion I asked the children to place a stone in the circles to represent their naturishness. The centre circle represented a belief of the self being completely at home in nature and comfortable in nature or in a state of surrender. Each successive circle represented a state less so. The stone placing was completed in mindful silence. The children chose to place their stones in a range of circles at the beginning of the project, whereas almost all are situated in the centre circle at the conclusion of the visits (see Figures 7.4a and b).

An added detail was that I asked the children to search for and use a stone about the size of their fist. As they were searching, I realised this size would also be about the size of their heart. I told the children this. I had wanted to encourage a visceral connection with Nature and likening a piece of the beach to a body part appeared a great idea. Upon reflection I realised I had subconsciously, quite literally, silently asked the children to locate their heart within Nature.

However, I suggest extreme caution should be exercised with regard to such placement of stones. Although silently placed, I was aware that peer pressure or teacher expectation may have influenced the children's choices. Therefore, I collected opinions on how one becomes naturish as a result of the various activities experienced during the beach visits. I placed a large copy of the theoretical framework on the floor and asked the children

FIGURE 7.4A Measuring becoming naturish at the beach through placing stones within concentric circles, the centre circle most naturish, week three
Source: Cathy Francis

FIGURE 7.4B Measuring becoming naturish at the beach through placing stones within concentric circles, the centre circle most naturish, week eleven
Source: Cathy Francis

to vote by moving about and pointing their toe to the quadrant they felt had most influenced their plearning and flearning at the beach. We engaged in a free-flowing class discussion of the project while we did this, and I took the opportunity to remind the children to make up their own minds. After they had made their choices I asked them to explain their reasoning to the class. Although perhaps still subject to peer pressure or teacher expectation, this exercise required children to explain their choice explicitly to others. Figure 7.5 records the children's verbal responses to my questions.

CONCLUSION

Gray argues that:

> if we truly want young people to understand the world, to understand nature, their immediate environment and their place within it then a considerable amount of the learning that they undertake has to be situated in that very environment in a process of reciprocal interbeing and recursive enaction.
>
> (Gray 2012: 6)

I interpreted this as giving opportunity for Nature to become a part of the schoolchild's educational lifeworld. The children's growing appreciation of themselves in relation to nature, or their becoming naturish, may have simply arisen through having more time to notice (and therefore to know) than perhaps is usual. But I suggest the theoretical framework conceived and presented here encouraged me to adopt a consistent and intentional embodied approach to learning. As one becomes more aware of one's environment and of the ways to learn about it, arguably one also becomes more self-aware from a multiplicity of perspectives. The children's repertoire of learning

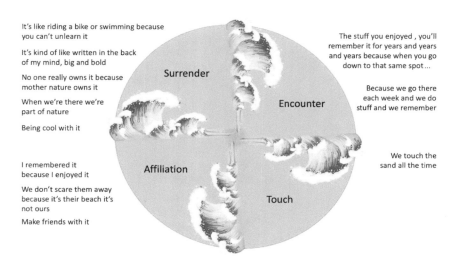

It's like riding a bike or swimming because you can't unlearn it

It's kind of like written in the back of my mind, big and bold

No one really owns it because mother nature owns it

When we're there we're part of nature

Being cool with it

I remembered it because I enjoyed it

We don't scare them away because it's their beach it's not ours

Make friends with it

Surrender

Encounter

Affiliation

Touch

The stuff you enjoyed, you'll remember it for years and years and years because when you go down to that same spot...

Because we go there each week and we do stuff and we remember

We touch the sand all the time

FIGURE 7.5 Children were asked to point their toe to the quadrant of the theoretical framework they felt most influenced their becoming naturish and were then given the opportunity to comment on its significance
Source: Cathy Francis

now includes plearning and flearning. Ontological and epistemological understandings of self and other have also entwined. This understanding makes clear our unique separateness juxtaposed with an embedded symbiosis, our becoming naturish.

NOTES

1 Schooling.
2 www.theguardian.com/education/2018/apr/02/forest-schools-grow-in-scotland-as-grasp-of-benefits-takes-root
3 There were many and varied interactions between children and the many components of the beach such as crabs, jellyfish, litter, stones and the sea itself. There is insufficient space here to tell the story of each relationship.
4 www.johnmuirtrust.org
5 The poem consists of three verses. One covers the walked journey to the beach; the centre verse reflects experiences gathered while at the beach; and the last verse encompasses the journey back to school.
6 Stipe is the stalk of kelp and blade the leaf part.

REFERENCES

Adolph, K. and Kretch, K. (2015) 'Gibson's Theory of Perceptual Learning', in Wright, J. D. (ed.), *International Encyclopedia of the Social & Behavioral Sciences*, 2nd Edition, pp. 127–134. Amsterdam: Elsevier. doi: 10.1024/0301-1526.32.1.54.

Bonnett, M. and Williams, J. (1998) 'Environmental Education and Primary Children's Attitudes towards Nature and the Environment', *Cambridge Journal of Education*, **28**(2), pp. 159–174. doi: 10.1080/0305764980280202.

Chawla, L. (2006) 'Learning to Love the Natural World Enough to Protect It', *Barn* **2**, pp. 57–78.

Christie, B. *et al.* (2014) 'Outdoor Education Provision in Scottish Schools', *Scottish Educational Review*, **46**(1), pp. 48–64.

Cole, M. (2010) 'What's Culture Got to Do With It?: Educational Research as a Necessarily Interdisciplinary Enterprise', *Educational Researcher*, **39**(6), pp. 461–470. doi: 10.3102/0013189X10380247.

Colucci-Gray, L. and Camino, E. (2016) 'Looking Back and Moving Sideways: Following the Gandhian Approach as the Underlying Thread for a Sustainable Science and Education', *Visions for Sustainability*, **6**, pp. 23–44. doi: 10.13135/2384–8677/1869.

Corcoran, P. B., Weakland, J. P. and Wals, A. E. J. (2017) *Envisioning Futures for Environmental and Sustainability Education*. Wageningen: Wageningen Academic Publishers.

Daniels, H. (2016) *Vygotsky and Pedagogy*, second edition. Abingdon: Routledge. doi: 10.4324/9781315617602.

Darling, K. (2014) 'Learning as Knowledge Creation: Learning For, and From, All', *Education in the North*, **21**(special issue), pp. 21–37.

Education Scotland (2004) Curriculum for Excellence: Sciences: Experiences and Outcomes. www.education.gov.scot/Documents/sciences-eo.pdf (accessed 24 April 2020).

Ellen Macarthur Foundation (2015) *Towards A Circular Economy: Business Rationale For An Accelerated Transition*. www.ellenmacarthurfoundation.org/publications/towards-a-circular-economy-business-rationale-for-an-accelerated-transition (accessed 8 April 2020).

EPA (2015) *Climate Change in the United States: Benefits of Global Action.* Washington D.C.: United States Environmental Protection Agency.

Gray, D. S. (2012) 'Walking in the Mindfield or the Classroom As a Cartesian Constraint: The Reunification of Body, Mind and Nature', *International Journal of Environmental Research and Public Health*, **1**(1), pp. 1–8.

Johnson, M. (2006) 'Mind Incarnate: From Dewey to Damasio', *Daedalus–Journal of the American Academy of Arts and Science*, **135**(3), pp. 46–54.

Kahn, P. H., Severson, R. L. and Ruckert, J. H. (2009) 'The Human Relation With Nature and Technological Nature', *Current Directions in Psychological Science*, **18**(1), pp. 37–42. https://depts.washington.edu/hints/publications/Human_Relation_Technological_Nature.pdf (accessed 3 April 2017).

Kals, E., Schumacher, D. and Montada, L. (1999) 'Emotional Affinity toward Nature as a Motivational Basis to Protect Nature', *Environment and Behavior*, **31**(2), pp. 178–202. doi: 10.1177/00139169921972056.

Kellert, S. R. and Wilson, E. O. (1993) *The Biophilia Hypothesis: Frontiers in Ecology and the Environment.* Washington, D.C.: Island Press. doi: https://doi.org/10.1177/027046769501500125.

Khatibi, M. and Sheikholeslami, R. (2015) 'Gibson's Ecological Theory of Development and Affordances: A Brief Review', *Journal of Indian Psychology*, **2**(4).

Kolb, D. (1984) *Experiential Learning: Experience as the Source of Learning and Development.* Englewood Cliffs, N.J.: Prentice-Hall.

De Laet, M. and Mol, A. (2000) 'The Zimbabwe Bush Pump: Mechanics of a Fluid Technology', *Social Studies of Science*, **30**(2), pp. 225–263.

Learning And Teaching Scotland (2010) Curriculum for Excellence Through Outdoor Learning. https://education.gov.scot/Documents/cfe-through-outdoor-learning.pdf (accessed 15 April 2020).

Louv, R. (2005) *Last Child in the Woods: Saving Our Children from Nature-Deficit Disorder.* Chapel Hill, NC: Algonquin Books.

Louv, R. (2009) 'Do Our Kids Have Nature-Deficit Disorder?', *Educational Leadership*, **67**(4), pp. 24–30.

Lovelock, J. (2000) *Gaia: A New Look at Life on Earth.* Oxford: Oxford University Press.

Loynes, C. (1998) 'Adventure in a Bun', *Journal of Experiential Education*, **21**(1), pp. 35–39. doi: 10.1177/105382599802100108.

Loynes, C. (2018) 'Leave More Trace', *Journal of Outdoor Recreation, Education and Leadership*, **10**(3), pp. 179–186.

Østergaard, E. (2017) 'Earth at Rest: Aesthetic Experience and Students' Grounding in Science Education', *Science and Education*, **26**(5), pp. 557–582. doi: 10.1007/s11191-017-9906-2.

Pink, S. (2015) *Doing Sensory Ethnography.* Thousand Oaks, Ca.: Sage.

Pyle, R. M. (2003) 'Nature Matrix: Reconnecting People and Nature', *Oryx*, **37**(2), pp. 206–214. doi: 10.1017/S0030605303000383.

Rathunde, K. (2008) 'Nature and Embodied Education', *Journal of Developmental Processes*, **4**(1), pp. 70–80.

Rautio, P. (2013) 'Children Who Carry Stones In Their Pockets: On Autotelic Material Practices In Everyday Life', *Children's Geographies*, **11**(4), pp. 394–408. doi: 10.1080/14733285.2013.812278.

Rinaldi, C. (2006) *In Dialogue with Reggio Emilia: Listening, Researching and Learning.* Abingdon: Routledge.

Nicol, R. and Higgins, P. (2007) *Outdoor Education in Scotland: A Summary of Recent Research.* Perth: Scottish Natural Heritage.

Schulz, L. E., Gopnik, A. and Glymour, C. (2007) 'Preschool Children Learn About Causal Structure from Conditional Interventions', *Developmental Science*, **10**(3), pp. 322–332. doi: 10.1111/j.1467-7687.2007.00587.x.

Scottish Government (2012) 'One Planet Schools'. www.gov.scot/Topics/Education/Schools/curriculum/ACE/OnePlanetSchools (Retrieved 29 December 2015).

Sitka-Sage, M. D. et al. (2017) 'Rewilding Education in Troubled Times; Or, Getting Back to the Wrong Post-Nature', *Visions for Sustainability*, **8**, pp. 20–37. doi: 10.13135/2384–8677/2334.

Somerville, M. and Williams, C. (2015) 'Sustainability Education in Early Childhood: An Updated Review of Research in the Field', *Contemporary Issues in Early Childhood*, **16**(2), pp. 102–117. doi: 10.1177/1463949115585658.

Sommer, D. (2009) 'Schiller and Company, or How Habermas Incites Us to Play', *New Literary History*, **40**(1), pp. 85–103. Available at: www.jstor.org/stable/20533136.

Steiner, R. (1916) 'Toward Imagination: Lecture 3: The Twelve Human Senses' Rudolf Steiner Archive and e.Lib. https://wn.rsarchive.org/Lectures/GA169/English/AP1990/19160620p01.html (accessed 8 April 2020).

Steiner, R. (1996) *Anthroposophy (A Fragment).* Anthroposophic Press.

Sterling, S. (2002) *Sustainable Education: Revisioning Learning and Change.* Green Books Ltd.

Strong-Wilson, T. and Ellis, J. (2007) 'Children and Place: Reggio Emilia's Environment As Third Teacher', *Theory into Practice*, **46**(1), pp. 40–47. doi: 10.1080/00405840709336547.

Thorburn, M. and Marshall, A. (2014) 'Cultivating Lived-Body Consciousness: Enhancing Cognition and Emotion through Outdoor Learning', *Journal of Pedagogy*, **5**(1), pp. 115–132. doi: 10.2478/jped-2014-0006.

Tillmann, S. et al. (2019) ' "Nature Makes People Happy, That's What It Sort Of Means:" Children's Definitions and Perceptions of Nature in Rural Northwestern Ontario', *Children's Geographies*, **17**(6), pp. 1–14. doi: 10.1080/14733285.2018.1550572.

Uggla, Y. (2010) 'What Is This Thing Called 'Natural '? The Nature-Culture Divide in Climate Change and Biodiversity Policy', *Journal of Political Ecology*, **17**, pp. 79–91.

Uitto, M. and Syrjala, L. (2008) 'Body, caring and power in teacher-pupil relationships: Encounters in former pupils' memories', *Scandinavian Journal of Educational Research*, **52**(4), pp. 355–371. doi:10.1080/00313830802184517.

United Nations (2012) 'Back to our Common Future: Sustainable Development in the 21st Century (SD21) Project'. http://sustainabledevelopment.un.org/content/documents/UN-DESA_Back_Common_Future_En.pdf (accessed 8 April 2020).

World Commission on Environment and Development (1987) *Report of the World Commission on Environment and Development: Our Common Future (The Brundtland Report).* doi: 10.1080/07488008808408783.

Zylstra, M. J. et al. (2014) 'Connectedness as a Core Conservation Concern: An Interdisciplinary Review of Theory and a Call for Practice', *Springer Science Reviews*, **2**(1–2), pp. 119–143. doi: 10.1007/s40362-014-0021-3.

8

CLOSING THE ATTAINMENT GAP IN SCOTTISH EDUCATION: THE CASE FOR OUTDOORS AS A LEARNING ENVIRONMENT IN EARLY PRIMARY SCHOOL

Jamie McKenzie Hamilton

INTRODUCTION

The attainment, or achievement, gap "refers to any significant and persistent disparity in academic performance or educational attainment between different groups of students" (The Glossary of Education Reform, 2013). In Scotland, the attainment gap between achieving and underachieving populations has long been recognised as a particular national challenge (Scottish Government, 2008). Scotland has the best educated population in Europe, but the continent's third highest proportion of people with no academic qualifications (Herald Scotland, 2014). Recent figures suggest around a third of pupils are leaving primary school without reaching expected standards in literacy and numeracy, and concerns have been expressed about impacts on the future economy (Denholm, 2018).

Underachievement varies substantially across different council areas and schools, and corresponds closely to levels of socio-economic deprivation (Audit Scotland, 2014; Denholm, 2018). In 2017, the Scottish Government announced a new National Improvement Framework and Plan, which aims to deliver excellence in education regardless of social circumstances (Scottish Government, 2018). This emphasises the need for early intervention, which has consistently delivered educational benefits up to adulthood, with the largest gains seen in disadvantaged children (Barnett, 1995). The transition from nursery to primary school is a critical policy focus for the Scottish Government, where strategies to promote pupil motivation and engagement are strongly recommended (Scottish Government, 2008; Audit Scotland, 2014). Starting school is recognised to be a significant step for children around the world, one which can determine long-term academic success or failure (Fabian and Dunlop, 2007).

Outdoor learning is on the increase in Scotland (Christie et al., 2014), where it is strongly supported by the Government's national curriculum, Curriculum for Excellence (CfE), their Learning for Sustainability agenda and a number of other public and private sector organisations. Nevertheless, the national pattern remains variable (Mannion et al., 2015) with advocates highlighting the need for a decisive national policy commitment to motivate and regulate quality provision (Higgins et al., 2013). The lack of this may be due to an assumption that outdoor learning is not a legitimate approach to improving educational attainment, currently the only national performance indicator with an explicit link to CfE. Studies have suggested the decision to take Scottish schoolchildren outdoors is often weighed against core curricular objectives (Ross et al., 2007). While a few outdoor learning studies have demonstrated impacts on attainment and cognition, these remain in the minority. Evidence pertaining to the transition between nursery and primary school, where intervention could be most far-reaching, remains largely anecdotal.

In this chapter, I will expand on the literature comparing the impacts of outdoor and classroom settings, before focusing on some developmental considerations related to experiential learning and environmental motivation. I then describe my doctoral research, and the general model of environmental motivation to which it gave rise. The model may assist in organising and explaining various impacts of outdoor and indoor classrooms relevant to the attainment gap. It highlights the importance of motivating physical environments for school starters, and opportunities and practical applications for the Scottish Government, educationalists and design practitioners in general. The question I hope it provokes is not whether the outdoors is superior to the classroom in supporting early years' attainment, but rather what environmental qualities are important for engaging all school starters in curricular learning and reducing the attainment gap. While acknowledging that knowledge is inevitably interpretative, theory-laden and influenced by perspective, I take the position that when studying the impacts of the physical environment on learning in young children, one can only assume a realist ontology. This underpins my consideration of child development and research design, where there is always emphasis on the totality and functionality of the physical interaction, or coupling, between children's cognition and environment.

IMPACTS OF CLASSROOM AND OUTDOOR SCHOOL SETTINGS

Empirical support for the impacts of the outdoors on pupil performance compared to the classroom is increasing. Studies in Bangladesh (Khan, 2017), Denmark (Nielsen et al., 2016), Germany (Dettweiler, 2015) and the USA (SEER, 2005) have all reported improved academic achievement, motivation and social interaction. Some UK studies suggest enhanced confidence and self-sufficiency to be general features of forest schooling (Waite and Davis, 2008; Waite, 2007). Other research has reported cognitive benefits which are associated with school performance, notably memory and attention (Dadvand et al., 2015), and related factors including well-being (Roe and Aspinall, 2011), teacher-child relationships (Raffan, 2000) and physical activity (Lovell, 2009). Some attribute general findings to an innate affinity for natural surroundings, which is prevalent in childhood (Kellert and Wilson, 1995; Kahn Jr. and Kellert, 2002) and may serve to motivate developmentally-significant interaction, most notably between the ages of 6 and 12 (Bateson and Martin, 2000; Cobb, 1977; Sobel, 2013). Declining opportunities for nature engagement, which some link to an increasingly indoor, technological, risk-averse culture (Guldberg, 2007; Playday, 2010; Wooley et al., 2009), have been held responsible for an escalation of problems associated with poor school performance, including disruptive behaviour (Louv, 2010), attentional disorders (Halperin and Healey, 2011) and poor physical fitness (Higgins and Nicol, 2013).

The literature also suggests classrooms may be less engaging for children by comparison with the outdoors. Teachers typically spend more time on activity and behaviour management than instruction (Jackson, 1990). Recitation – where teachers pose questions to the class, then respond to answers – could take up between ⅓ and ⅔ of lesson time, and opportunities for pupils to question or elaborate on material are a relative rarity (Gump, 1967). A major UK longitudinal study found significantly poorer linguistic interaction in classrooms than at home, and concluded that schools were not fostering language development (Wells, 2009). Contextual classroom stressors, such as noise and proximity to others, have also been linked to negative educational impacts (Evans, 1984; Glass and Singer, 1972; Klatte et al., 2013). One review concluded that the association between classroom settings and repeated denial, delay, interruption and distraction could be responsible for a steady decline in motivation over school life (Jackson, 1990). Two strong predictors of classroom engagement and attainment are pupils' perception that their context is autonomy-supportive (Deci et al., 1991; Ryan and Grolnick, 1986) and that they have a good relationship with their teacher (Hughes, 1973; Klem and Connell, 2004; Sanders, Wright and Horn, 1997).

EXPERIENTIAL LEARNING

A common theme of the developmental literature is that experiential learning provides the foundations of formal learning capacity (Piaget and Cook, 1998). Esther Thelen describes this relationship:

> Language, logic, consciousness, imagination, and symbolic reasoning are not "above" the processes of motivated perception, categorization, and action … rather they are part and parcel of these processes, seamless in time and mechanism … higher cognition is developmentally situated. It grows from and carries with the history of its origins … cognition is embodied and socially constructed.
>
> (Thelen, 1996, p.321)

Iain McGilchrist (2012) argues that this process can be thought of in terms of the specialist split-functioning of the human brain. Our 'experiencing' right hemisphere builds simulations of the world, from which our left hemisphere – the domain of language and formal learning – is then able to model, grasp and control particular conceptual or linear aspects of reality 'off-line'.

These viewpoints imply that without the prior embodied experience necessary to inform concepts or requirements introduced in a school setting, a child may find them challenging or impossible to comprehend. For example, a teacher participating in my research highlighted that a child who has never been read stories may not have the requisite knowledge of character, structure, narrative or basic themes to participate in a story-writing task. At a more basic level, E. Gibson and N. Rader speculate that the ability of a schoolchild to choose between alternative courses of action could require "prior maturation of exploratory and motor capacities for search, manipulation and locomotion, and time to try them out" (Gibson and Rader, 1979, p.18).

FUNCTIONAL ENVIRONMENTAL MOTIVATION

Some ecological theories propose that experiential learning is underpinned and driven by a functional motivational relationship with affordances (Berlyne, 1971; Csikszentmihalyi, 2000; Deci and Ryan, 2000; Kim, 2013; Kyttä, 2003; Lewin, 1946; Thelen, 1996). An 'affordance' is a specific aspect of an environment which an organism utilises to support life, the totality of which constitutes its ecological niche (Gibson, 1986). Affordances are held to be perceived directly (i.e. non-mentally) as an action possibility – building, sitting, moving, feeding, etc. – and therefore encompass both organism and environment. The affordance relationship can be viewed as a functional state of the organism moving within a setting for which it is biologically prepared, where fine-grained functional processes serve to motivate and regulate novel stimulation and challenge. When affordances and autonomy enable the organism's effort after meaning and value at optimal levels, the relationship is characterised by effortless motivation, attention and exploration, and positive emotion. When they do not, there is over- or under-stimulation, demotivation and a negative emotional response, which in humans is associated with stress, loss of confidence, aversion, social withdrawal, or boredom and distraction.

Some also argue functional environmental motivation can be a collaborative process. Csikszentmihalyi describes "group flow" where "there is no need to negotiate roles (as) participants need no self to bargain with about what should or should not be done (and) as long as the rules are respected … is a social system with no deviance" (Csikszentmihalyi, 2000, p.43). The philosopher Edward Reed envisages group motivation as:

> A collective effort after meaning and value … This need not mean that every individual in a group does the same thing, or that each individual has internalized the same motivational ideal or mechanism; on the contrary, each individually may do something that is unique in order that the group as a whole achieves its needs.
>
> (Reed, 1996, p.11)

Taking an educational perspective, group motivation bears similarities to positive interdependence, where the value of one's own unique contribution is also considered a driving force (Johnson and Johnson, 1989). "Positive interdependence" refers to task situations where individuals perceive achieving personal goals to depend on fulfilling the goals of collaborators, and is more strongly associated with attainment, recall, persistence and productivity than solitary working (Johnson and Johnson, 1989). Vygotsky's concept of a zone of proximal development (ZPD) implies that in these situations the children least equipped developmentally or experientially advance the furthest (Vygotsky, 1978). The ZPD also predicts cognitive impact to be related to the novelty and diversity of individual contributions negotiated therein, which in the context of environmental motivation is in turn enabled and sustained by meaningful affordances.

Csikszentmihalyi describes the effortless flow of activity enabled by motivating environments as the optimal experience, which he links to feelings of effectance, self-confidence and absorption with loss of ego-concerns (Csikszentmihalyi, 2000). Deci and Ryan term this emotion "eudaimonic well-being", or feeling "fully functioning" and aware of one's own "vitality, psychological flexibility and deep inner sense of wellness" (Deci and Ryan, 2002, pp.22–23). Eudaimonic well-being is viewed to have adaptive significance by forging positive associations with, and prompting return to, settings that promote effective functioning, self-development and perceived self-efficacy (Lewis et al., 1984; Preyer, 2001; Thelen, 1996). Deci and Ryan postulate that an organism which cannot manage its environmental relationships towards self-actualisation and self-regulation risks being entrained down maladaptive paths by external factors. This is why they view autonomy as a principal enabler of motivation, and a basic need which is "perhaps, the most fundamental characteristic of (all) living things" (2000, p.253).

The sustained attention and activity absorption associated with environmental motivation finds support in recent neurophysiological theory and research. This shows attention is not a clear skill or concept, as is commonly assumed by educationalists (Smith and Kosslyn, 2013). Rather, it is a cognitive bias and emergent property of multiple neural mechanisms working to resolve competition between environmental and internal stimuli for behavioural control and visual processing (Corbetta and Shulman, 2002; Desimone and Duncan, 1995). This also implies an optimal relationship between self and the world, where there is minimal competition or internal regulatory requirement and distinction between the two. It also suggests attention will be cognitively demanding to the extent that environmental affordances are incompatible with our needs and goals, personal and functional. Psychologists term this 'directed attention', which is effortful and under the will of the agent, as distinguished from 'fascination', or effortless attention controlled or supported by environmental stimuli (James, 2012). However, from the neurophysiological perspective, these two are not either/or states, but rather reflect levels of competition between environmental stimuli and our personal efforts after meaning and value.

Some developmental psychologists posit that a child's attentional ability emerges from environmental interaction, where, initially, affordances assume the mental lead or load, motivating and sustaining orientation, coordination and movement (Gibson and Rader, 1979). If a child's past or present environment lacks personally-enabling affordances, this suggests they will find it difficult to exercise, or be taught, directed attentional control and flexibility. The rapid rise in attentional disorders, generally acknowledged to be a major contributor to Scotland's attainment gap (Scottish Government, 2011) and underachievement worldwide (Hicks, 2013), has been attributed to a childhood where rich environmental interaction is increasingly displaced by indoor and screen-based activities (Palmer, 2016). Such disorders have been shown to involve a broad pattern of deficits distributed across brain regions which are relevant to embodied cognition, including motivation, directed attention, inhibitory control and functions related to cognitive energy and rewards (Halperin and Healey, 2011).

Recent research on "joint attention", or the ability to attend to an object together with another person, also suggests rich environmental interaction to underpin core facets of social cognition. These include many relevant to school success such as perspective taking, imitative learning, language comprehension and production, and environmental understanding. Infants appear to have an innate capacity to perceive the affordance relations of others as their own, by mapping them non-consciously onto their own motor repertoire (Seeman, 2012), and the literature implies this underlies a developmental programme characterised by increasing capacity for social interaction (Tomasello, 1995). This proceeds through stages of mirroring what and how others do things, through how they feel and think about and articulate doing, towards integrating their behaviours, motives and worldview, and which bear striking similarities to Parten's theory of play (Parten, 1932). Both theories concur with studies demonstrating that the majority of early years' peer interaction is facilitated by affordances (Piaget and Cook, 1998) and occurs in the context of play (Hughes, 2009). They also imply the challenges children may experience negotiating meaning face-to-face in the manner of adult conversation, without mutual affordances as a medium.

In summary, functional environmental motivation may be a fundamental, albeit implicit, driver of cognitive, social and personal development. It is argued that several aspects of child performance might be regarded as emergent properties of it, notably task motivation, positive emotion, attention and social interaction. All of these are also distinguishers of outdoor versus indoor classroom research, and strongly associated with attainment. A body of cross-cultural research worldwide does suggest a general relationship between levels of naturalness and positive emotion, effortless attention and environmental preference. Here environmental preference is held to be under-pinned by an "assessment of the environment in terms of compatibility with human needs and purposes", where settings perceived to promote effective functioning and learning are preferred (Kaplan and Kaplan, 1989, p.10). In short, it may be that the educational and cognitive benefits associated with outdoor classroom settings are under-pinned and explained by functional environmental motivation powered by natural affordance richness.

There follows an outline of my doctoral research, and the resulting model, which add support to this hypothesis. Their implications are that these basic developmental processes remain the principal engine of learning in early primary school and may be important for motivating engagement in curricular learning, particularly for pupils most relevant to the attainment gap.

FIELD EXPERIMENTS

Four field experiments were conducted with 71 pupils and 4 teachers from 3 distinctive Scottish primary schools, 2 urban and one rural. Children were mainly school starters with an average age of 5½ years, but included one older class from the rural school –termed the "experienced group" – who had taken weekly outdoor lessons for 4–5 years. Thirteen children overall were classified as "underachievers" by their teacher. The rural school task was supervised by 2 teachers with extensive outdoor experience, and the 2 urban schools by one teacher each, neither of whom had taught outdoors prior to the study.

Classes were split into groups matched for numbers of boys and girls, and able and underachieving pupils. Each performed a curriculum task outdoors in either a wood or a playground, and then the same task again in a class-room, or vice versa. The four tasks chosen were to make a toy, build a den, conduct a puppet tour and invent a story about an adventure on an alien planet (see Table 8.1).

The original aim was that all participants would perform the same task with a statistical control. This proved non-viable due to the different sizes and approaches of the schools, so it was decided to emphasise ecological over external validity. Therefore, each task was an upcoming indoor lesson, which the teacher thought might also work outdoors. Other than the requirement for precisely consistent instructions across settings, I played no part in their design or content, and they occurred as they would have done in my absence.

Nevertheless, the tasks still sought to apply a scientific approach to the extent possible in an actual school situation. They entailed matched within-groups and a repeated measures design. A significant majority of pupils completed a treatment in both conditions of the independent variable – i.e. the same task performed indoors and outdoors – and the dependent variable was compared between them – i.e. children's performance. Order effects on performance were controlled for by varying setting order for two of the three schools, and were found to have no statistical effect within or between tasks. In short, while each task featured a unique design and no statistical control, the design allowed for comparison of all four in the manner of a classical experiment, and task assessment and measures were consistent across the study. In these respects, it is argued that the design was adequate to support cross-task analytical generalisation.

The two overarching research hypotheses were that the children's performance would be better outdoors than indoors, and positively associated with levels of natural richness. Settings were categorised for natural richness using a Richness Index, which included sixteen items split into two equal categories, biodiversity and affordances,

TABLE 8.1 Schools, groups and tasks

School: Urban wood

	Children (Av Age 5yrs) Total	m	f	*UA	Teachers	Task 1: Make a Toy Setting 1	Setting 2	Task 2: Puppet Tour Setting 1	Setting 2
Early yrs group 1	13	7	6	3		Indoors	Wild	Indoors	Indoors
Early yrs group 2	16	8	8	4		Indoors	Indoors	Wild	Indoors
Totals:	29	15	14	7	1				

School: Urban playground

	Children (Av Age 5yrs) Total	m	f	*UA	Teachers	Task: Build a Den Setting 1	Setting 2
Early Yrs Group 1	10	4	5	3		Indoors	Playground
Early Yrs Group 2	9	5	5	3		Playground	Indoors
Totals:	19	9	10	6	1		

School: Rural Wood

	Children Total	m	f	*UA	Teachers	Task: Alien Adventure Setting 1	Setting 2
Early Yrs***	9	4	5	0		Indoors	Wild
Experienced**	14	6	8	1			
Totals:	23	10	13	1	2		

GRAND TOTALS:	**71**	**34**	**37**	**14**	**4**

*UA: Underachievers

**Av age 9½; ***Av age 5½

KEY:

Experiment
Control

TABLE 8.2 Richness index

RICHNESS INDEX (RI)	School: Setting:	Playground		Urban Wood		Rural Wood	
		play-g	class	wood	class	wood	class
BIODIVERSITY:							
1. Mix of Animal and Bird Life		0	0	1	0	1	0
2. Mix of Insect Life		0	0	1	0	1	0
3. Mix of Trees of Different Species and Ages		0	0	1	0	1	0
4. Mix of Shrubs or Hedges		0	0	1	0	0	0
5. Mix of Other Flowers, Plants and Fungi		0	0	1	0	1	0
6. Logs and Deadwood on the Ground		0	0	1	0	1	0
7. Areas of Meadow or Grass		1	0	1	0	1	0
8. Water features: Puddles, Ponds, Streams or Wetland		0	0	0	0	1	0
Total:		**1**	**0**	**7**	**0**	**7**	**0**
AFFORDANCES:							
1. Soil, Mud or Sand for Creative Manipulation		1	0	1	0	1	0
2. Loose Materials for Creative Manipulation or Den Building		1	1	1	1	1	1
3. Slopes and Dips for Running, Rolling or Hiding		0	0	1	0	0	0
4. Water for Paddling and Splashing		0	0	0	0	1	0
5. Upright and Fallen Trees, and Stumps		0	0	1	0	1	0
6. Other features for Climbing, Balancing, Jumping Off or Hiding		1	1	0	0	0	1
7. Pathways for Walking, Running or Hiding		0	0	1	0	1	0
8. Open Spaces/Mix of Cover/Glades for Walking or Running		1	0	1	0	1	0
Total:		**4**	**2**	**6**	**1**	**6**	**2**
GRAND TOTAL		5	2	13	1	13	2
RICHNESS CATEGORY SCORE		2	1	4	1	4	1
CATEGORY: *I=Indoors; P=Playground; SW=Semi-Wild; W=Wild*		P	I	W	I	W	I

RICHNESS CATEGORIES and CATEGORISATION CRITERIA
INDOORS ONLY: Relevant Affordances criteria
PLAYGROUND: Scoring <5/16, *including* <6 for 'Biodiversity' and <5 for 'Affordances'
SEMI-WILD: Scoring <10/16 and >5 overall
WILD: Scoring >10/16 on SITE CRITERIA, *including* >5 for 'Biodiversity' and >4 for 'Affordances'

and where each setting scored one for each of the items present (see Table 8.2). This was developed from Forestry Commission checklists for evaluating outdoor site quality for educational and funding purposes. In order of richness from least to most, the tasks featured four 'indoor' classrooms, one 'playground', and two 'wild' woodland settings (see Figure 8.1).

Methodology and analysis were structured by a holistic systems-based theoretical framework informed by the Santiago Theory of Cognition (Maturana and Varela, 1992). This viewed each task situation as a discrete system and divided phenomena into four interrelated categories: the environment, the individual child's experience, the teacher's experience and the socio-linguistic domain. The socio-linguistic domain can be thought of as representing interaction at a group level, that is between a purposeful class or workgroup composed of individual experiences and the task environment.

Researching young children is a recognised challenge (Fabian and Dunlop, 2007). Primary school spans a period of cognitive development and consolidation that has a complex relationship with formal learning. Due to their developmental stage, younger children display a wider variation in memory, language and metacognitive capacities, and may have a qualitatively different perception of the world. Attainment measures are largely precluded because many are pre-numerate and pre-literate, and particularly those underachievers of most interest to this research.

'Indoor' and 'Wild' settings for urban wood task 1 – "Make a toy"

'Indoor' and 'Wild' settings for urban wood task 1 – "Puppet tour"

'Indoor' and 'Playground' settings for urban playground task – "Build a den"

'Indoor' and 'Wild' settings for urban rural task – "Alien adventure"

FIGURE 8.1 Field experiments: Indoor and outdoor settings

Therefore, my approach sought empirical support for factors directly linked to cognitive and educational benefits. There were three stages of data gathering and analysis. The first involved task observations and outcomes. The second was a short two-part questionnaire taken 6–7 months later. This recorded free recollections, and task ratings and setting preferences for nine performance and restorativeness criteria. The restorative criteria were the Perceived Restorativeness Scale (PRS), which was devised to assess Attention Restoration Theory (ART) (Kaplan and Kaplan, 1989). I adapted this for young children by distilling each component down to one simple statement while expressing any abstract concepts in concrete active terms. The performance criteria sought to translate the inputs and dynamics of the theoretical framework into measures (see Figure 8.2). Children expressed responses to criteria statements by pointing at pictures or a 'smiley' Likert scale. The third and final stage was about a month after stage 2, and entailed focused interviews with the teachers, where they also took the children's questionnaire.

I will now set out the findings by differences, first between outdoor and indoor settings and then between specific groups within-setting, with an emphasis on underachievers. These are grouped under common themes, rather than by stages. Following this, I present a general model of environmental motivation to organise and explain the various results, and which draws on prior discussion. In advance, however, I want to address briefly the potential influence of the novelty factor. While most participants were new to outdoor learning, two findings suggest this

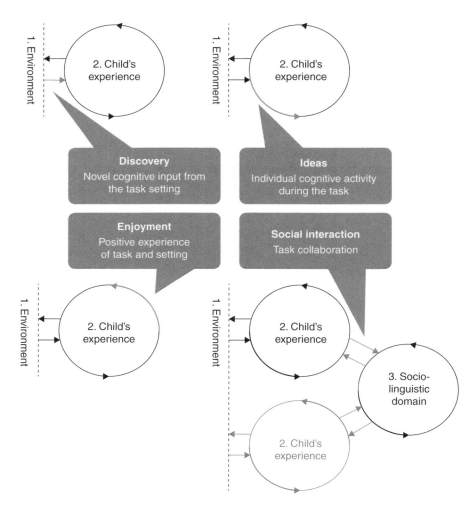

FIGURE 8.2 Performance criteria
Source: the author

might be discounted. Firstly, the strongest outdoor preferences were returned by the "experienced group", for whom forest learning was the least novel. Secondly, there were no significant differences whatsoever between early years' wild setting recollections and preferences across a variety of tasks, settings and schools, including a group who had been forest learning for over a term. That there were significant differences between playground and wild settings, strongly implies that the influence of natural richness overrode all other variables, including novelty.

BETWEEN-SETTING DIFFERENCES

Recollections. Outdoor tasks were recalled in greater detail by children than indoor tasks, and were remembered first by 74% of the children. More was recalled about wild settings than playgrounds, implying the influence of natural richness. The experienced outdoor teachers reported stronger recollections as a general characteristic of woodland lessons and spoke about how these are used to support indoor learning for underachievers:

> Some of them don't get a lot of storybooks read to them so they don't have a great bank of knowledge, but when they go out there it allows them to open up. It's giving them the experience to tell their story.
> (Rural wood teacher 2)

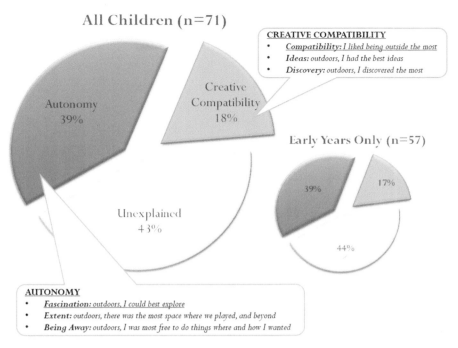

All Children (n=71)

CREATIVE COMPATIBILITY
- **Compatibility:** *I liked being outside the most*
- **Ideas:** *outdoors, I had the best ideas*
- **Discovery:** *outdoors, I discovered the most*

Autonomy
39%

Creative
Compatibility
18%

Early Years Only (n=57)

39%

17%

44%

Unexplained
43%

AUTONOMY
- **Fascination:** *outdoors, I could best explore*
- **Extent:** *outdoors, there was the most space where we played, and beyond*
- **Being Away:** *outdoors, I was most free to do things where and how I wanted*

FIGURE 8.3 Principal components analyses: % variance explained by each component
Source: the author

Pupils who took the "build a den" task demonstrated explicit problem-solving and reflective observation when responding to questions about the playground components, but not their indoor counterparts. This suggested they were able to review internally the knowledge they gained outdoors.

Preferences. Setting preferences and task ratings were significantly higher outdoors than indoors for the nine criteria statements designed to evaluate the perceived performance and restorative benefits of each setting.

Autonomy. A Principal Components Analysis (PCA) grouped children's setting preferences statistics into two components (see Figure 8.3). The foremost, and the one which most strongly distinguished the outdoor settings, was named "autonomy", because the statements for the three PRS criteria it included – "fascination", "extent" and "being away" – seemed linked by the idea of personal freedom to move and act.

It is interesting that the adaptation of the PRS scale and related findings seemed to shift its emphasis from restorative response to active autonomy. As both might be considered complementary properties of functional environmental motivation, this may imply a deeper relationship between environment and motivation underlying ART.

All teachers felt that the children's greater perceived freedom was the factor most responsible for their superior outdoor performance. They linked this to improved motivation, creativity, absorption and self-confidence, noting particularly the impacts on underachievers:

> In the classroom it might feel a bit more confined, or that there's a right or wrong … it was very clear
> to them out there that this is completely creative and open, and so they just dived in and got on with it.
> (Urban wood teacher)

Creative compatibility and natural richness. The second PCA component was named "creative compatibility", because the statements for its three performance criteria – "discovery", "ideas" and "compatibility" – implied the degree to which children felt comfortable, resourceful and stimulated by novelty in task settings (see Figure 8.3).

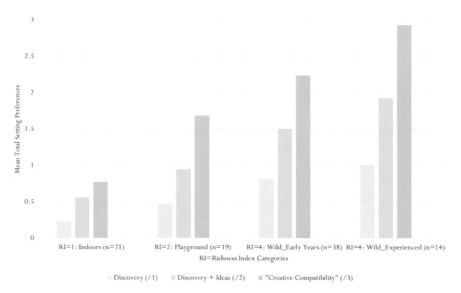

FIGURE 8.4 'Creative compatibility': Setting preference means against natural richness
Source: the author

The mean statistics for "creative compatibility" and these criteria exhibited a remarkable gradation against natural richness categories (see Figure 8.4). For "creative compatibility" and the "discovery criterion" ' the difference between indoor and playground settings, and playground and wild, was significant for both the early years and experienced groups, and stronger for the latter.

The greater diversity and creativity of outdoor activities and productions was a main task observation. For example, in the first ten minutes of the puppet tour task, 50% more categories of activity were recorded in the wild setting than indoors, where activities and productions were more conventional and prosaic. The general capacity of the outdoors to supply novel experiences and ideas was a core theme of the teacher interviews:

> (Indoors) they didn't learn that much because there wasn't anything new in their environment … there was more variety outdoors, and more change as they worked through it.
>
> (Urban wood teacher)

Collaboration. Children's preferences and task ratings for teamwork were significantly stronger for outdoors versus indoors. When asked what they enjoyed most about the 'build a den' task, 23% mentioned teamwork for the playground, while none did for the classroom. All teachers perceived outdoor collaboration to be less hierarchical and more productive, and noted children working with different peers than they typically do indoors.

> (Outdoors) they all worked together really well … they all seemed a bit more equal … it wasn't clear who was the high achiever, they were all on an even playing field, and they all worked with people they don't normally tend to work with in the class naturally.
>
> (Urban wood teacher)

Higher levels of positive interdependence were observed outdoors, particularly in the wild settings. While receiving identical instructions in both settings for "make a toy", each child worked on average with five classmates on three projects in the wood, and this was higher for underachievers, who frequently led projects. Indoors, children worked only on their own toy, though routinely incorporated concepts from neighbours. This was not so for underachievers, whose productions were always standalone and often confused. During the "puppet tour", a completely open-ended task, pupils tended to move from individual activity to group projects in the wild setting, but exhibited the opposite trend indoors. On "alien adventure", children's wild setting stories – co-presented by pairings of early years and "experienced" pupils – were richer, and more coherent in terms of theme and individual contributions, than indoors. These findings imply the capacity of the wild settings to enable individual contributions, which in turn provided attractors, motivation and sustenance for effective creative collaboration.

The idea that early years' collaboration centres on mutual affordances and joint attention might explain the trend from individual activity towards collaborative projects, and the untypical pattern of peer interaction, also a finding of other forest learning studies (Mygind, 2009; Waite and Davis, 2008). This would view children as trialling shared experiences before settling on the one most personally suitable, where experiential value outweighed the collaborator in determining choices. The eudaimonic wellbeing and loss of ego-concerns associated with activity absorption may also have helped to regulate cooperation and more level and fluid hierarchies. Conversely, the disintegrative pattern of social interaction indoors might be accounted for by an absence of mutual affordances sufficient to sustain collaboration. This might be seen as a regression from cooperation, into increasing parallel and solitary play (Parten, 1932), and consciousness of self and group (Lewin, 1946). Notably, primary school research does reveal a strong correlation between levels of social competence and play (Uren and Stagnitti, 2009), and between social withdrawal and underachievement (Perkins, 1965). In light of their rich outdoor collaboration, the underachievers' isolated concepts on "make a toy" may indicate the difficulties they experience integrating new ideas in social situations without motivating mutual affordances.

UNDERACHIEVERS

Of most significant and particular relevance to the attainment gap were the impacts on the underachievers. These children remembered significantly more about wild setting tasks than their peers, and returned the most extensive recollections of these and the playground tasks. They rated the outdoor tasks higher for PRS criteria, implying that they may have perceived the indoor tasks as more stressful relative to the outdoors than their classmates. The inexperienced outdoor teachers noticed qualities, competencies and learning potential in underachievers they had not seen before:

> You know, I saw them as new characters and I really do think you see their potential to see them do so well at something and enjoying it and being confident.
>
> (Urban wood teacher)

Underachievers showed no evidence outdoors of typical classroom issues such as shyness, misbehaviour and most notably, poor attention, which was a characteristic of all of them. That their attention levels outdoors seemed indistinguishable from their peers is an extraordinary finding.

Improved attention, wellbeing, confidence and collaboration, those outdoor impacts most conspicuous for the underachievers, are all emergent properties of functional environmental motivation. Taken together, these findings could indicate the benefits of a functionally and socially enabling task setting for children less prepared for the classroom, experientially or developmentally. Their significantly stronger wild setting recollections, another extraordinary statistic, might then reflect the greater cognitive change they underwent on these tasks, compared to peers with more social or activity-relevant experience. This interpretation supports the idea proposed earlier that the ZPD is not a purely socio-cultural phenomenon, but also contingent on affordance richness.

OTHER GROUP DIFFERENCES

"Experienced group" children returned task ratings and setting preferences that were significantly stronger for the outdoor setting, but weaker for the indoors, than early years' children, suggesting performance benefits which endure throughout primary school.

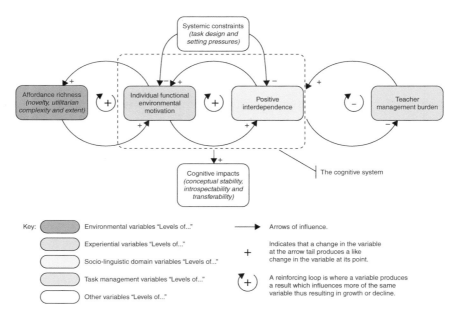

FIGURE 8.5 General model of environmental motivation
Source: the author

Teachers returned significantly stronger outdoor recollections, task ratings and setting preferences. Their PRS ratings for the indoor task were lower than the children's. In the classroom they perceived a larger burden when managing tasks and displayed a more conventional, teacher-led approach. They enjoyed the outdoor tasks more and perceived a better, more authentic, relationship with the pupils. They all agreed children's performances were better outdoors than indoors, and that "natural" changes to their own mood and approach had contributed to this:

> (Outdoors) I'm less controlling … that sounds terrible (but) I think it happens naturally … I feel that we're giving the children much more freedom to express themselves. I genuinely had never thought about that but yeah I think we let go a bit.

> (Rural wood teacher 2)

GENERAL MODEL OF ENVIRONMENTAL MOTIVATION

The general model of environmental motivation in Figure 8.5 seeks to summarise all findings linking setting to performance across the four tasks. The model is presented in the form of a causal loop diagram (CLD), a practical tool for thinking about complex situations from the systems dynamics methodology (Forrester, 1971). CLD enables themes to be expressed as variables, and then represented within a whole system of hypothetical reinforcing (+) or balancing (–) relations and loops. There follows an explanation of the variables, which arose from systematic data analyses structured by the categories of the theoretical framework.

Environment. Analysis of data pertaining only to the physical settings implicated three perceived qualities associated with natural richness were relevant to performance benefits.

The first was **utilitarian complexity**, or the number of perceived uses the setting and its affordances were able to support (Zamani and Moore, 2013). Utilitarian complexity is related to the abundance of natural objects and materials – trees, sticks, leaves, mud and stones – and the range of different uses and interpretations to which these could be put, which provided a rich workshop for children's imagination and activities:

Outdoors the thing was never going to look realistic so it begs for your imagination more. Whereas indoors they became concerned with making it look "right", outdoors it's unlikely to ever really look right … you can have something, actually quite a basic shape, but they're pretending it's a castle, or a car, or whatever, and they're enjoying using it.

(Urban wood teacher)

In cognitive terms, utilitarian complexity signifies the potential for immediate personally-meaningful thought and action. The ideal setting is complex and organised, qualities also statistically associated with environmental preference (Kaplan and Kaplan, 1989).

The second quality was **novelty**, or the capacity of natural richness to continually offer up new ideas, experiences and challenges. In the context of a task, levels of novelty and utilitarian complexity seem directly related, as is also implied by the Theory of Loose Parts' premise that "in any environment, both the degree of inventiveness and creativity, and the possibility of discovery, are directly proportional to the number and kind of variables" (Nicholson, 1971). However, novelty also pertained to other aspects of natural richness, including multisensory discoveries and unexpected encounters with living things and their by-products. Novelty and challenge are fundamental drivers in theories of functional environmental motivation (Berlyne, 1971; Csikszentmihalyi, 2008; Kim, 2013; Kyttä, 2003; Thelen, 1996).

If we had a classroom in the woods or we lived in the woods for me there would be something new every day.

(Rural wood girl (early years))

The outdoors is better for learning because you learn new things.

(Rural wood boy (early years))

The final quality is **extent**, or a form of active space which helped to immerse the child in their task setting. Whereas space in the indoor and playground settings was something children occupied or passed through during the task, in the wild settings it seemed an integral part of their creative processes and constructions:

They had the space to spread out to use different open areas of the school … but when we went outdoors, they had a space which was part of the story.

(Rural wood teacher 2)

Extent is considered equivalent to the similarly-named construct in ART, defined as the sense of the scale and connectedness of elements in an environment, and the experience of it as "a whole little world' … captured in a small space" (Kaplan and Kaplan, 1989, pp.191–192). ART proposes 'extent' is constructed through fascination-driven exploration involving both perception and imagination, and thus it might be considered an intangible affordance.

The individual child's experience. It is argued that levels of the three environmental qualities in an open-ended task setting are directly related to the capacity of individual children to contribute in ways which are personally meaningful and challenging. The functional environmental motivation enabled by these qualities is what gives rise to various study findings including enhanced task attention, resourcefulness, perceived autonomy and self-efficacy, and eudaimonic wellbeing. This interpretation supports the hypothesis that children between the ages of six and twelve are predisposed towards exploring naturally-rich environments as a basis for personal development.

Aside from natural richness, it is also postulated that extrinsic systemic constraints may have also impacted on individuals' perceived autonomy and competence, and therefore also on these functional processes (Deci and Ryan,

2002). These constraints included the specific task design, the freedom this allowed for peer interaction and implicit pressures of the school behaviour setting and related past experiences.

The socio-linguistic domain. It is further argued that the three qualities also enabled and sustained group motivation. This was facilitated by rich mutual affordances, regulated by absorption in activity and eudaimonic well-being, and reinforced by positive interdependence, entailing rich individual contributions, ideas exchange and productive controversy. The ZPD relates the cognitive impact of the domain to the richness of its content, where the most disadvantaged pupils advance farthest.

Teacher management burden. Functional environmental motivation involving the three qualities is also proposed to underlie outdoor findings for the teachers, including their enhanced enjoyment, perceived autonomy and child-led interaction. A reinforcing factor could be the capacity for natural richness to sustain pupils' self-sufficiency, thereby alleviating the teachers' management burden. Conversely, the greater burden they perceived indoors, and indeed findings on classroom behaviour management in general, could indicate a systemic need for teachers to compensate for affordances less able to support general task activity:

> In the classroom you're trying to get ideas from them, but at the same time you're trying to help them all … in the woods I felt a lot freer and more relaxed … when it's happening (indoors) it's more of a challenge, whereas (outdoors) it's more the preparation, and then it's kind of fine once you're there.
>
> (Urban wood teacher)

Cognitive impacts. It is argued that the enduring stability of children's outdoor task recollections, and their capacity to reflectively observe knowledge gained on the playground tasks, reflects the greater cognitive change they underwent as a result of a richer environmental and social experience. Levels of all variables associated with deep memory processing were likely to be higher outdoors than indoors, including attention, environmental compatibility, sensory input, personal meaning and group negotiation (Craik and Lockhart, 1972).

CONCLUSIONS

The study found the natural richness of the outdoor settings promoted task performance, including impacts on motivation, memory, attention and positive interdependence. Performance variations between the settings are argued to be attributable mainly to their capacity to sustain personally-meaningful activity, which in turn was underpinned by three qualities which fuelled functional environmental motivation. In this respect, the wild settings might be viewed as a workshop which allowed children to determine their own learning goals and pathways across a variety of school task situations. Strongly implied is the importance of generally-motivating environments and affordances for delivering high-quality educational experiences and outcomes.

The improved engagement and performance of the children, particularly the underachievers, highlight the potential for outdoor learning to improve attainment, while reducing the gap. The richer recollections indicate the capacity of natural environments to produce stable and transferable task-related knowledge, the bedrock of academic learning. The rural schoolteachers' use of outdoor memories as a classroom resource explicitly illustrates this strategy in action. Sustained motivation, attention and positive interdependence were general characteristics of all the outdoor tasks, and are all predictors of academic achievement. That these seemed enhanced for children and teachers with extensive experience of outdoor learning, suggests enduring curricular benefits. Another implication is that outdoor teaching may include more child-led interaction and opportunities to spend time with pupils with support needs, both associated with improved attainment.

All this suggests outdoor learning is an effective approach to engaging children in formal learning at transition and throughout primary school. Most notable are the particular benefits for underachievers. Functionally-motivating affordances have the potential to enable those children most pertinent to the attainment gap to participate and collaborate in schoolwork, while simultaneously providing them with developmentally-significant experiences. A decisive Scottish Government policy commitment in support of outdoor learning would therefore seem advantageous in terms of national educational objectives.

Richness Indices could help inform the design of effective learning spaces for young children for architects and practitioners. A key implication here is that "un-designed" natural affordances may better enable and sustain meaning, imagination and resourcefulness than the artificial prescriptive affordances of a typical school playground or classroom. The findings may indicate the value of "rewilding" school grounds. Richness Indices might also help providers pre-assess the capacity of task affordances and settings to fuel individual and group performance, particularly on open-ended tasks or those involving creative collaboration. Evidently, more research is needed to clarify and validate relationships between functional environmental motivation and attainment, and to better understand how tasks, settings and practice can best be configured to deliver curricular aims.

To conclude, the relationship between affordance richness and school performance might be considered to entail two perspectives. The first sees an organism coupled to an ecological niche where functional processes motivate and regulate interaction consistent with developmental needs and goals. The second sees a child performing in a specific task context, towards curricular ends. In the four field experiments, the two perspectives cannot reasonably be considered separately. Performance seems underpinned by the capacity of affordances to motivate basic integral processes of perception, categorisation and action within task parameters. In this respect, the wild settings seemed like the Room of Requirement: a sentient room from the Harry Potter books which "transforms itself into whatever the witch or wizard needs it to be at that moment in time" (Fandom, 2015).

A related implication has been that impoverished environments, past and present, may constitute a barrier to a child's learning which cannot be overcome by classroom instruction alone. If they lack relevant experience or personally-meaningful affordances, a child executing a task cannot simply be taught attention, motivation, inhibitory control, persistence or social competence. Considering this, it is an extraordinary study finding that outdoors, children with attention deficit showed engagement and persistence, the shy and withdrawn exhibited proactive teamwork and leadership, and problem types behaved well and respectfully to others. The implication of this is that the "problem child" could be more attributable to the poor quality of classroom settings, than their innate disposition or socioeconomic background.

McGilchrist argues that, while the advantages of our left-brain culture are huge, the downside is that the right-brain's holistic world of environment and experience "ceases to exist as far as the speaking hemisphere is concerned" (McGilchrist, 2012, p.115). Could this left-brain blind spot explain why, typically, we give so little weight to the role of the physical environment in early years' development and learning, and even less so when there is an attainment problem? If this is true, then I hope this chapter goes some way to indicate the educational opportunity and benefits of acknowledging and addressing our environmental blind spot. In terms of primary schoolchildren, the implication is that natural task settings could not only help reduce the attainment gap, but also promote resilience, persistence, self-confidence, creativity, interpersonal skills, physical fitness and care for the natural world. One must ask if there is an approach for education in Scotland, and in general, better able to deliver both core curricular objectives, and a generation equipped to face and resolve the socioeconomic challenges of an uncertain future.

REFERENCES

Audit Scotland (2014). *School Education*. Edinburgh: Audit Scotland.
Barnett, W. S. (1995). Long-term effects of early childhood programs on cognitive and school outcomes. *The Future of Children*, **5**(3), 25–50.
Bateson, P. and Martin, P. (2000). *Design for a Life: How Behaviour Develops* (new edition). London: Vintage.
Berlyne, D. E. (1971). *Aesthetics and Psychobiology*. New York: Appleton-Century-Crofts.

Christie, B., Beames, S., Higgins, P., Nicol, R. and Ross, H. (2014). Outdoor learning provision in Scottish Schools. *Scottish Educational Review*, **46**(1), 48–64.

Cobb, E. (1977). *The Ecology of the Imagination in Childhood*. New York: Columbia University Press.

Corbetta, M. and Shulman, G. L. (2002). Control of goal-directed and stimulus-driven attention in the brain. *Nature Reviews Neuroscience*, **3**(3), 201–215.

Craik, F. I. M. and Lockhart, R. S. (1972). Levels of processing: A framework for memory research. *Journal of Verbal Learning and Verbal Behavior*, **11**(6), 671–684.

Csikszentmihalyi, M. (2000). *Beyond Boredom and Anxiety: Experiencing Flow in Work and Play* (Anniversary edition). San Francisco, CA: Jossey-Bass.

Csikszentmihalyi, M. (2008). *Flow: The Psychology of Optimal Experience*. New York: Harper Perennial Modern Classics.

Dadvand, P., Nieuwenhuijsen, M. J., Esnaola, M., Forns, J., Basagaña, X., Alvarez-Pedrerol, M. and Sunyer, J. (2015). Green spaces and cognitive development in primary schoolchildren. *Proceedings of the National Academy of Sciences*, **112**(26), 7937–7942.

Deci, E. L. and Ryan, R. M. (2000). The 'what' and 'why' of goal pursuits: Human needs and the self-determination of behaviour. *Psychological Inquiry*, **11**(4), 227–268.

Deci, E. L. and Ryan, R. M. (2002). Overview of self-determination theory: An organismic dialectical perspective. In Deci, E. L., and R. M. Ryan (eds), *Handbook of Self-determination Research*, pp. 3–33. New York: Rochester University Press.

Deci, E. L., Vallerand, R. J., Pelletier, L. G. and Ryan, R. M. (1991). Motivation and education: The self-determination perspective. *Educational Psychologist*, **26**(3–4), 325–346.

Denholm, A. (2018). Poor pupils lagging behind richer classmates in literacy and numeracy. *The Herald*, 11 December. www.heraldscotland.com/news/17290589.poor-pupils-lagging-behind-richer-classmates-in-literacy-and-numeracy/ (accessed 8 April 2020).

Desimone, R. and Duncan, J. (1995). Neural mechanisms of selective visual attention. *Annual Review of Neuroscience*, **18**(1), 193–222.

Dettweiler, U. (2015). Designing Mixed Methods Research: Fitting the statistical to the empirical model. Paper presented at the PhD Course "Udeskole and outdoor learning", 28–30 April, at Skovskolen, University of Copenhagen.

Evans, G. W. (1984). *Environmental Stress* (new edition). Cambridge: Cambridge University Press.

Fabian, H. and Dunlop, A.-W. (2007). Outcomes of good practice in transition processes for children entering primary school. *Working Papers in Early Childhood Development*, **42**, 1–34. The Hague.

Fandom (2015). Room of Requirement. Available from: https://harrypotter.fandom.com/wiki/Room_of_Requirement (accessed 20 April 2020).

Forrester, J. W. (1971). Counterintuitive behaviour of social systems. *Technology Review*, **73**(3), 52–68.

Gibson, E. and Rader, N. (1979). Attention: The perceiver as performer. In G. A. Hale and M. Lewis (Eds), *Attention and Cognitive Development*, pp. 1–21. Boston: Springer.

Gibson, J. J. (1986). *The Ecological Approach to Visual Perception*. Hillsdale, NJ: Psychology Press.

Glass, D. C. and Singer, J. E. (1972). *Urban Stress: Experiments on Noise and Social Stressors*. New York: Academic Press.

Guldberg, H. (2007). Are children being held hostage by parental fears? Spiked Online www.spiked-online.com/index.php?/site/article/3465/ (accessed 10 October 2010).

Gump, P. V. (1967). The classroom behaviour setting: Its nature and relation to student behaviour. US Office of Education Cooperative Research Branch, Project NO. 5-0334. Final report. Mimeo.

Halperin, J. M. and Healey, D. M. (2011). The influences of environmental enrichment, cognitive enhancement, and physical exercise on brain development: Can we alter the developmental trajectory of ADHD? *Neuroscience and Biobehavioural Reviews*, **35**(3), 621–634.

Herald Scotland. (2014). UK statisticians: Scotland is the most highly-educated country in Europe. *The Herald*, 5 June. www.heraldscotland.com/news/13163915.UK_statisticians__Scotland_is_the_most_highly_educated_country_in_Europe/ (accessed 8 April 2020).

Hicks, M. R. (2013). Why the increase in ADHD? *Psychology Today*, 5 August. www.psychologytoday.com/blog/digital-pandemic/201308/why-the-increase-in-adhd (accessed 8 April 2020).

Higgins, P. and Nicol, R. (2013). Outdoor education. In T. G. K. Bryce, W. M. Humes, D. Gillies, A. Kennedy, D. Gillies and A. Kennedy (eds), *Scottish Education: Referendum*, Vol. 68 (4th Revised edition), pp. 620–627. Edinburgh: Edinburgh University Press.

Higgins, P., Nicol, R., Beames, S., Christie, B. and Scrutton, R. (2013). Education and Culture Committee: Outdoor Learning Submission from Professor Peter Higgins. www.scottish.parliament.uk/s4_educationandculturecommittee/inquiries/prof_higgins_submission.pdf (accessed 18 April 2020).

Hughes, D. C. (1973). An experimental investigation of the effects of pupil responding and teacher reacting on pupil achievement. *American Educational Research Journal*, **10**(1), 21–37.

Hughes, F. P. (2009). *Children, Play, and Development* (4th Edition). Los Angeles: SAGE Publications, Inc.

Jackson, P. W. (1990). *Life in Classrooms*. New York and London: Teachers College Press.

James, W. (2012). *Psychology: The Briefer Course*. New York: Dover Publications.

Johnson, D. W. and Johnson, R. T. (1989). *Cooperation and Competition: Theory and Research*. New York: Interaction Book Company.

Kahn Jr., P. H. and Kellert, S. R. (eds) (2002). *Children and Nature: Psychological, Sociocultural and Evolutionary Investigations*. Cambridge, MA: MIT Press.

Kaplan, R. and Kaplan, S. (1989). *The Experience of Nature: A Psychological Perspective*. Cambridge: Cambridge University Press.

Kellert, S. R. and Wilson, E. O. (1995). *The Biophilia Hypothesis*. Washington, DC : Island Press.

Khan, M. (2017). Environment, engagement and education: Investigating the relationship between primary school grounds and children's learning: a case study from Bangladesh. PhD Thesis, University of Edinburgh.

Kim, S. (2013). Neuroscientific model of motivational process. *Frontiers in Psychology*, **4**(98), 1–12.

Klatte, M., Bergström, K. and Lachmann, T. (2013). Does noise affect learning? A short review on noise effects on cognitive performance in children. *Frontiers in Psychology*, **4**. https://doi.org/10.3389/fpsyg.2013.00578.

Klem, A. M. and Connell, J. P. (2004). Relationships matter: Linking teacher support to student engagement and achievement. *Journal of School Health*, **74**(7), 262–273.

Kyttä, M. (2003). *Children in Outdoor Contexts: Affordances and Independent Mobility in the Assessment of Environmental Child Friendliness*. Espoo: Helsinki University of Technology, Centre for Urban and Regional Studies.

Lewin, K. (1946). Behaviour and development as a function of the total situation. In L. Carmichael (Ed.), *Manual of Child Psychology*, pp. 791–844. Hoboken, NJ: John Wiley and Sons Inc.

Lewis, M., Sullivan, M. W. and Michaelson, L. (1984). The cognitive-emotional fugue. In C. E. Izard, J. Kagan and R. B. Zajonc (eds), *Emotions, Cognition, and Behaviour*, pp. 264–288. Cambridge: Cambridge University Press.

Louv, R. (2010). *Last Child in the Woods: Saving Our Children from Nature-Deficit Disorder*. London: Atlantic Books.

Lovell, R. (2009). An evaluation of physical activity at Forest School. PhD Thesis, University of Edinburgh.

Mannion, G., Mattu, L. and Wilson, M. (2015). Teaching, learning, and play in the outdoors: A survey of school and pre-school provision in Scotland. Scottish Natural Heritage Commissioned Report, 779. Scottish Natural Heritage. https://dspace.stir.ac.uk/handle/1893/21623 (accessed 8 April 2020)

Maturana, H. R. and Varela, F. J. (1992). *The Tree of Knowledge: The Biological Roots of Human Understanding* (3rd revised edition). Boston: Shambhala Publications Inc.

McGilchrist, I. (2012). *The Master and His Emissary: The Divided Brain and the Making of the Western World* (2nd edition). New Haven, CT; London: Yale University Press.

Mygind, E. (2009). A comparison of children's statements about social relations and teaching in the classroom and in the outdoor environment. *Journal of Adventure Education and Outdoor Learning*, **9**(2), 151–169.

Nicholson, S. (1971). How NOT to cheat children: The theory of loose parts. *Landscape Architecture*, **62**, 30–34.

Nielsen, G., Mygind, E., Bølling, M., Otte, C. R., Schneller, M. B., Schipperijn, J. and Bentsen, P. (2016). A quasi-experimental cross-disciplinary evaluation of the impacts of education outside the classroom on pupils' physical activity, well-being and learning: The TEACHOUT study protocol. *BMC Public Health*, **16**, 1117.

Palmer, S. (2016). Why the iPad is a far bigger threat to our children than anyone realises. *Daily Mail*, 28 January www.dailymail.co.uk/femail/article-3420064/Why-iPad-far-bigger-threat-children-realises-Ten-years-ago-psychologist-SUE-PALMER-predicted-toxic-effects-social-media-sees-worrying-new-danger.html

Parten, M. B. (1932). Social participation among pre-school children. *The Journal of Abnormal and Social Psychology*, **27**(3), 243–269.

Perkins, H. V. (1965). Classroom behavior and underachievement. *American Educational Research Journal*, **2**(1), 1–12.

Piaget, J. and Cook, M. (1998). *The Origins of Intelligence in Children*. Madison, CT: International Universities Press.

Playday (2010). Playday Opinion Poll Summary. www.playday.org.uk/campaigns-3/previous-campaigns/2010-our-place/2010-opinion-poll (accessed 18 April 2020).

Preyer, W. T. (2001). *The Mind of the Child: Part 1. The Senses and the Will*. New York: Adamant Media Corporation.

Raffan, J. (2000). *Nature Nurtures*. Toronto, Canada: Evergreen Association.

Reed, E. S. (1996). *Encountering the World: Toward an Ecological Psychology*. Oxford: Oxford University Press.

Roe, J. and Aspinall, P. A. (2011). The restorative outcomes of forest versus indoor settings in young people with varying behaviour states. *Urban Forestry and Urban Greening*, **10**(3), 205–212.

Ross, H., Higgins, P. and Nicol, R. (2007). Outdoor study of nature: Teachers' motivations and contexts. *Scottish Educational Review*, **39**(2), 160–172.

Ryan, R. M. and Grolnick, W. S. (1986). Origins and pawns in the classroom: Self-report and projective assessments of individual differences in children's perceptions. *Journal of Personality and Social Psychology*, **50**(3), 550–558.

Sanders, W. L., Wright, S. P. and Horn, S. P. (1997). Teacher and classroom context effects on student achievement: Implications for teacher evaluation. *Journal of Personnel Evaluation in Education*, **11**(1), 57–67.

Scottish Government (2008). *The Early Years Framework*. Edinburgh: Scottish Government.

Scottish Government (2011). Improve Levels of Educational Attainment [Info Page, 9 December]. www.gov.scot/About/Performance/scotPerforms/indicator/attainment (accessed 12 January 2016).

Scottish Government (2018). National Improvement Framework. https://beta.gov.scot/policies/schools/national-improvement-framework/ (accessed 8 April 2020).

Seeman, A. (Ed.) (2012). *Joint Attention: New Developments in Psychology, Philosophy of Mind, and Social Neuroscience*. Cambridge, MA: MIT Press.

Smith, E. E., and Kosslyn, S. M. (2013). *Cognitive Psychology: Mind and Brain*. London: Pearson.

Sobel, D. (2013). *Beyond Ecophobia: Reclaiming the Heart in Nature Education* (2nd edition). Great Barrington, MA: Orion Society.

State Education and Environment Roundtable (2005). *The Effects of Environment-Based Education on Student Achievement*. Phase 2. SEER (online).

The Glossary of Education Reform (2013). Achievement Gap Definition. www.edglossary.org/achievement-gap/ (accessed 8 April 2020).

Thelen, E. (1996). *A Dynamic Systems Approach to the Development of Cognition and Action* (New edition). Cambridge, MA: MIT Press.

Tomasello, M. (1995). Joint attention as social cognition. In C. Moore, P. J. Dunham and P. Dunham (eds), *Joint Attention: Its Origins and Role in Development*, pp. 103–130. Psychology Press.

Uren, N. and Stagnitti, K. (2009). Pretend play, social competence and involvement in children aged 5–7 years: The concurrent validity of the Child-Initiated Pretend Play Assessment. *Australian Occupational Therapy Journal*, **56**(1), 33–40.

Vygotsky, L. (1978). *Mind in Society: Development of Higher Psychological Processes* (New edition). Cambridge, MA: Harvard University Press.

Waite, S. and Davis, B. (2008). The contribution of free play and structured activities in Forest School to learning beyond cognition: An English case. In Kryger, N. and Ravn, B. (eds), *Learning beyond Cognition*, pp. 257–274. Copenhagen: the Danish University of Education.

Waite, S. (2007). 'Memories are made of this': Some reflections on outdoor learning and recall. *Education 3–13*, **35**(4), 333–347.

Wells, G. (2009). *The Meaning Makers: Learning to Talk and Talking to Learn* (2nd edition). Bristol, New York, Ontario: Multilingual Matters.

Wooley, H., Pattacini, L. and Somerset-Ward, A. (2009). Children and the natural environment: Experiences, influences and interventions – Summary. *Natural England Research Reports*, **040**. http://publications.naturalengland.org.uk/publication/37005 (accessed 8 April 2020).

Zamani, Z. and Moore, R. C. (2013). The comparison of cognitive play affordances within natural and manufactured preschool settings. In Wells, J., Pavlides, E. and Davis, J. C. (eds), *Proceedings of the 44th Annual Conference of the Environmental Design Research Association*. McLean, VA: Environmental Design Research Association.

9

SCHOOL GROUND INTERVENTIONS FOR PEDAGOGY AND PLAY: HOW CAN WE EVALUATE THE DESIGN?

Matluba Khan, Simon Bell and Sarah McGeown

INTRODUCTION

Whenever Matluba Khan, the lead author of this chapter, presents her research project about co-design, development and evaluation of a school ground intervention in Bangladesh, she is asked, 'Oh, you mean the school playground?' School grounds are often considered as places for play and not seen as having any role or value as places for teaching and learning. Although it is difficult to differentiate between learning and play as far as children are concerned, the common view is that play is not generally considered to be learning. Those who research children's places, however, often view school grounds as potential outdoor learning environments, recognising that a well-designed outdoor learning environment can be valuable for the whole development of the child. Landscape architects also bring their unique perspectives to the design of school grounds where the spatial arrangement and functionality of different elements, combined with an appreciation of the role of sensory stimulation and aesthetics, can together create exciting and versatile spaces. Consultation with children when designing specific school grounds is becoming more common. However, the extent to which children's perspectives are fully taken into account in the development of the design largely depends on adults' (design professionals' and relevant authorities') perception of children's competence to be able to express themselves and to conceptualise spatial ideas (Khan, 2018).

Once a design is completed, constructed and handed over to the clients, landscape architects usually move on to their next project. Few return to their designed spaces to find out whether the project fulfilled its original design intentions. In addition to the affordances the designers intended, a well-designed school ground can create new opportunities that are only discovered by children when they start using it, while some elements might not work or be used the way they were originally intended. In most cases, opportunities are missed when the designers fail to take what can be learnt from evaluation of their projects to their next designs. Post-occupancy evaluation (POE) is an increasingly important activity in some sectors, such as hospitals and care settings (Cervinka, et al., 2014; Davies, 2001) and to some extent school buildings (Wheeler and Malekzadeh, 2015), and is spreading to other sectors, but its implementation in playgrounds and/or school grounds is rare. POE of the school environment generally focuses on the accessibility and safety of different spaces in the school building and outdoors. Rarely does it offer any information on whether the designed outdoor spaces actually offer children the intended range of affordances or whether there are enough opportunities available for children's physical, social and cognitive development or for teaching and learning.

Evaluation research on school ground interventions has so far investigated whether they had an impact on children's physical activity, reduction of stress, BMI levels, academic performance and well-being (Dyment et al., 2009; Kelz et al., 2013; Kelz, 2010; Kweon et al., 2017; Li and Sullivan, 2016). While these studies provide the evidence for positive impacts of school ground design on those specific aspects, they do not evaluate the efficacy of the design itself. Very little research has explored these two aspects together – linking the design of the space with the impact on children. This again shows that school grounds are not seriously considered as places for pedagogy; the published research, to our knowledge, rarely investigates their efficacy as places for teaching and learning, let alone the important role of play in cognitive development.

This chapter attempts to fill the identified research gap to some extent, especially in terms of the methods that can be applied, presenting and discussing a comprehensive approach for the evaluation of a school ground intervention for both pedagogy and play. We first illustrate the theoretical framework that underpins the approach and go on to discuss the pros and cons of using different methods by referring to several case studies. In particular, we focus on a realised design project at a school in Bangladesh, where there was a unique opportunity to follow and monitor the design development, implementation and post-implementation use and outcomes, applying several methods.

SCHOOL GROUND INTERVENTIONS FOR PEDAGOGY AND PLAY

Historically, as school grounds have been used mainly for purposes of physical education (Adams, 1993) this also guided their design – although at break times these spaces were also used for spontaneous play of limited varieties (owing to the lack of facilities). More recently, the use of school grounds has extended beyond physical education to encompass a wide range of educational activities – at least in some places – and for demonstration purposes, even if the practice has not become universal. The outdoor environment of primary schools can be a valuable place for the development of cognitive and socio-emotional skills in young children (Khan, 2012) when designed specifically to accommodate children's learning. Rich and diverse outdoor environments afford more opportunities for play and learning (Moore and Wong, 1997; Cosco, 2006), whereas barren school grounds discourage children from diverse play, social interaction, environmental experience and learning, which often leads to boredom and aggressive behaviour (Samborski, 2010). Asphalt- or tarmac-surfaced playgrounds provide little or no opportunity for connection with nature compared with greener school grounds (Bell and Dyment, 2008). Therefore, poorly designed outdoor environments can be just as limiting as dull indoor spaces.

How school grounds perform will depend on the purposes for which they are designed. The school grounds designed principally for physical activity might not create opportunities for cognitive and social play. Therefore, an evaluation which focuses only on a school ground's affordances for physical activity would not tell us whether the same design would also support pedagogy. For a school ground to be effective as a place for the 'whole development' of children it should be designed with their holistic development in mind. The evaluation should also focus on how the design supports all of these aspects. Only a comprehensive evaluation, looking into the effectiveness of school ground design for children's learning, play and well-being can test the impact in its totality and provide useful feedback for practitioners.

It is important to engage children in research concerning them and also in the design and planning of the places that they will use and which will affect their development. Researchers and designers are now, quite rightly, attempting to incorporate children's voices in their work by following the principles contained in the UN Convention on the Rights of the Child (UNICEF, 1989). Thus, comprehensive evaluation should also incorporate explorations of children's views and preferences on the design and use of school grounds.

THEORETICAL FOUNDATIONS

Theories of child development

In order to design with the 'whole' development of the child in mind, and to evaluate that post-occupancy, it is important that designers of children's environments have a basic understanding of how children undergo the cognitive, socio-emotional and physical development process.

Children from 6 to 11 years old – the age of most primary or elementary school education systems – learn most effectively when their learning is associated with doing. This stage is termed the 'Concrete Operational Stage' by Piaget, who placed an emphasis on children as intellectual explorers, constructing their knowledge through the exploration of their surroundings (Piaget, 1964). Children explore the surrounding environment, make their own discoveries and construct knowledge according to their personal experiences (Wood, 1998; Biehler and Snowman, 1982; Turner, 1984).

Vygotsky, known for his theory of social constructivism, believed that learning depends on the Zone of Proximal Development (ZPD), when children are active in the context of both socialization and education. Children internalise the experiences gathered from their contact with the social environment on an interpersonal level. The earlier knowledge base developed in the child's schema and new experiences that they come across in their immediate surroundings influence the child, who then constructs new ideas (Vygotsky et al., 1978). Vygotsky puts more emphasis on the roles that adults and more mature peers play in influencing children's cognitive development. Piaget believes that a constructivist environment must provide a variety of activities to challenge the children to accept individual differences, to increase their readiness to learn, to discover new ideas and to construct their own knowledge (Inhelder and Piaget, 1969). A well-designed school ground would be one where children would have more opportunities to explore, experience and work co-operatively with their peers.

The socio-emotional development of children between the ages of infant and adolescent includes the development of their self-concept and self-esteem, motivation, personality, moral development and use of social comparison to evaluate and judge their own capabilities (Biehler and Snowman, 1982). Self-concept is often considered to be the cognitive or thinking aspect of self (belief or opinion about one's personal existence) whereas self-esteem refers to the emotional or affective aspect of self (how one feels about or values oneself) (Huitt, 2011). According to Erikson (1995), at this age, children try to prove themselves 'grown up' through independent action, in co-operation with groups and by performing in socially acceptable ways. Children who have difficulty in school tend to develop poorer self-concepts, which might result in poor performance in upper grades (Biehler and Snowman, 1982). If a child can make and do things well, his or her self-concept develops, which often confers positive benefits on motivation to learn. In well-designed and facilitated outdoor classes, children are provided with the opportunities to form groups, to reach consensus and to develop critical thinking and problem-solving skills with their peers.

Children experience many physical changes between the ages of 6 and 12, for example the development of physical or gross motor skills used in different activities such as running and jumping, and fine motor skills, used in activities such as different art, science or craft projects (Biehler and Snowman, 1982). The capacity of the outdoors to contribute to this overall development of children has been largely ignored (Dudek and Baumann, 2007) as a result of an adherence to the 'surplus energy theory' (Spencer, 1855). The 'surplus energy theory', very dominant in play theory, was first proposed by the nineteenth-century psychologist Herbert Spencer. It has had a great influence in the design of the outdoor environment of children ever since and is still found to be deeply embedded in school-culture (Malone and Tranter, 2003). Spencer believed that the main reason children play is to get rid of their excess energy and this belief has been profoundly debated by many researchers and developmental theorists. People have generally considered the outdoor as a place for play, games and sports and not for formal learning or educational purposes. However, the character and form of the outdoors, holding two different types of activity – physical education or sports-based activity, and learning through environmental interaction, exploration and play – can be easily distinguished (Malone and Tranter, 2003) (see Figure 9.1a and b). It is the responsibility of the designer to design school grounds in a way that can provide opportunities for both.

Affordance theory

The affordances of an environment (a term already used earlier in this chapter) are those possibilities it offers or provides for the user, depending on what the user wants or needs (Gibson, 1979; Heft, 2010). For example, a simple object such as a wooden box can offer the opportunity for the child to climb up on, jump off, sit on, hide behind, use as a table or game board, etc.; many more could be thought of and all are beyond the original purpose of the box (as a container). This concept of affordance has substantially contributed to the development of research in landscape architecture, environmental preference and environment–behaviour interactions (Ward Thompson, 2013). The concept of affordance is important in developing the framework for design evaluation as it helps to identify the environmental attributes that are associated with specific behavioural responses (Gibson and Pick, 2000). Affordance

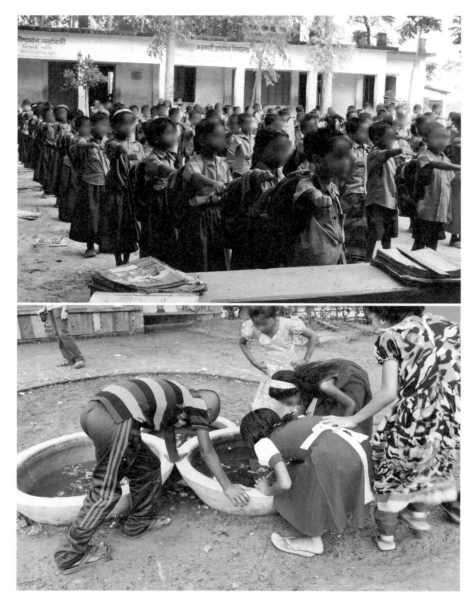

FIGURE 9.1 Contrast in the design of children's environments in elementary schools in Bangladesh, supporting different activities: a) shows that the grounds lack opportunities for exploration, unlike the setting in b, but can afford ball games and running, while b) contains opportunities for exploration and discovery
Source: Matluba Khan

theory stresses the possibility or potential for action in an environment; it may therefore help the designer in formulating design features with specific user needs in mind or with a range of potential uses.

In the field of design, affordances are generally regarded as the functional property of the environment relative to an individual (affordances of grasping, twisting, throwing, etc.) (Heft, 2010). Heft (1988) formulated a functional taxonomy for children's environments based on the physical properties, for example of a flat surface to walk on, relatively smooth slope to roll down, etc. But the concept of affordances has the 'potential to be extended to comprise even emotional, social, and cultural opportunities that the individual perceives in the environment' (Kyttä, 2004, p181). Kyttä's affordances for sociality include possibilities to play rule games and role play, playing home or war, being noisy and the possibility of sharing or following adults' business (Kyttä, 2002). Subsequently, Roe (2008) explored 'emotional affordances' in forest settings and defined them in terms of how the attributes of the environment make a person feel. Additionally, Gaver (1996) used the concept of affordance to study how different properties of indoor and outdoor environments might influence social interaction among people in the field of architecture and landscape architecture. Matluba Khan introduced 'cognitive affordance' in her PhD thesis, which was helpful to understand the relationship between environment and cognition in the school ground in Bangladesh that forms the case study discussed in this chapter (Khan, 2017).

Theory of behaviour settings

Closely related to the concept of affordances is the theory of behaviour settings. These are 'ecological units' (or specific parts of a site) where the physical environment and behaviour are linked together in time and space (Barker, 1968; 1976). Barker (1976) described the concept based on his observation of children's behaviour over many years. Behaviour settings are composed of two sets of identifying characteristics: 1) a specific set of time, place and object props (such as tree logs, sand, rocks) and 2) a specific set of attached standing behaviours or behaviour episodes (climbing, sitting, walking, reading a book) (Barker, 1968; Scott, 2005). Both of these clusters together form a behaviour setting (Scott, 2005). This concept can be applied within design research for analysing human behaviour in different type of spaces or settings. It can help identify specific behaviour settings in the landscape of schools and their association with pedagogy and play, which is essential for understanding the impact of different elements of nature on children's learning and play. Behaviour settings thus act as a medium for the identification of potential affordances of different types of spaces and associated materials and equipment.

Behaviour settings can therefore be rich with many interconnected elements and they regulate the behaviour episodes occurring within them (Barker, 1976). They are objective, occurring naturally in a specified time–space locus and independently of any individual's perception of it (Barker, 1976; Scott, 2005). The variables of behaviour settings have a stronger influence than individual difference variables, i.e. children's behaviour varies less across different children within a given setting than within the same child across different settings (Barker, 1976; Ward Thompson, 2013). Certain environments or settings elicit particular kinds of behaviour and different sets of people and objects exhibit the same patterns of behaviour within the same behaviour setting. These attributes of the ecological environment are important in order to understand how much an environment can influence children's behaviour.

TOWARDS A THEORETICAL FRAMEWORK FOR EVALUATION OF SCHOOL GROUND DESIGN

No single theory can therefore guide the framework for evaluation of a design. Since the nature of such an evaluation is multidisciplinary and comprehensive, different theories should be considered together in order to obtain a better understanding of the multidirectional relationship between the environment and learning. To understand how the physical environment influences the teaching and learning process, it is necessary to understand how children construct their knowledge. The theories of Piaget and Vygotsky can provide the basis for this understanding, stating that children construct knowledge through exploration of their surrounding environment and interaction with their peers. Therefore, the physical environment of the school should be designed in ways that offer opportunities for such exploration and interaction. In order to investigate whether the designed outdoor environment supports both pedagogy and play, theories of ecological psychology (i.e. the concept of affordance and the theory of behaviour settings) are crucial.

RESEARCH METHODS

A wide variety of approaches and methods have been used in research with and for children. No single method can obtain a holistic picture of children's use of school grounds and their impact on learning and behaviour. In an evaluation of a design different methods can help to answer different questions, taking into account the particular needs

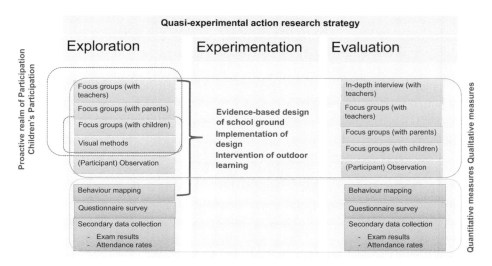

FIGURE 9.2 Methodological framework for the quasi-experimental action evaluation strategy
Source: Matluba Khan

and characteristics of the participants, ethical issues, the cultural and physical context of the study and limitations of time and resources, as recommended by Punch (2002) and Christensen and James (2008). Thus, a range of strategies and methods that have been applied in different research contexts and have been developed in different disciplines can be adapted for application in a specific context. The strategy for a holistic evaluation of a school ground design that we are proposing can be termed a *quasi-experimental action evaluation strategy*.

This particular strategy involves three phases: exploration, experimentation and evaluation, with data collection taking place during the exploration and evaluation phases. The *exploration* phase may include seeking the preferences and desires of teachers and children about the design and use of the outdoor environment. This is also the period for collecting any pre-test (pre-experiment) data (e.g. attainment scores, surveys using standardised tools and behaviour mapping and observational data of the school ground before any design work). The second phase is the *implementation* of the design (in the case of a POE this is a real design to be evaluated) and intervention (could be an experimental design for a research), i.e. use of the designed outdoor environment for teaching and learning by teachers and school students. In the *evaluation* phase, post-test data is collected and analysed to find out the effective settings for learning and also the criteria for the design of those settings. Figure 9.2 presents a schema for this quasi-experiment action evaluation strategy, where the design is considered as an experiment as noted above.

We applied the above-mentioned strategy in a research study conducted in Bangladesh which included co-design and development of a primary school ground with children, teachers and the community, bearing in mind the educational needs and evaluation of the school ground for pedagogy and play (see Figure 9.3a and b). We compared the data collected from this school through a questionnaire survey, attainment scores, observation and behaviour mapping, focus groups and semi-structured interviews with a control school which did not undergo any change in the environment. We also examined the impact on the experimental school through before-and-after evaluation of the school ground design. We will refer to this study in our discussion of methods for application in different phases of an evaluation study.

METHODS FOR ENGAGING CHILDREN AND TEACHERS

Different methods have been used in research studies to engage children and adults in the design process. Clark and Moss (2005) introduced the mosaic approach for effective participation of young children in the design of spaces. Methodological elements of the mosaic approach include observation, interviews with children, informal

FIGURE 9.3 The case-study primary school ground in Bangladesh before (a) and after (b) an experimental intervention
Source: Matluba Khan

interviews with parents and practitioners, book-making, photography, child-led tours and 'magic carpet' (slide show of familiar and different places). A combination of methods is useful for engaging children at different developmental stages. We believe the selection of methods depends on many aspects, and the pieces of the mosaic might vary for children of different ages in different contexts. We will cover focus group discussions, children's drawings and a model-making exercise that we used in our research project.

Focus group discussion

We used focus group discussions in order to gain insight into the participants' experiences, attitudes and perceptions regarding the design and use of the outdoor school environment for learning. Focus groups are considered a better method than interviews for gathering qualitative data from children (Greene and Hogan, 2005). Children are more comfortable sharing ideas and discussing in groups rather than being asked as individuals (Darbyshire et al., 2005), which has led to an increased use of this method in research with children. Children are willing to share their opinions when they find their friends doing so; some children's opinions can also trigger others' memories. The duration of focus groups with children under 10 years should be less than 45 minutes (Greene and Hogan, 2005). The ideal size is five to eight participants, but small focus groups comprising four to six participants are more popular since they are easy to administer and participants feel more comfortable (Krueger and Casey, 2009). A wide range of techniques can be used during focus groups to make the experience more fun and to promote and prompt discussion among the participants (Fargas-Malet et al., 2010). The use of visual stimuli can liberate participants' ideas about the design of the environment and also make the experience enjoyable (Greene and Hogan, 2005; Fargas-Malet et al., 2010).

We found focus group discussion to be a useful tool to obtain qualitative information about the use of the outdoor environment. The purpose of focus group discussion in quasi-experimental action evaluation research can be two-fold: 1) to learn about the existing use of the school ground; and 2) to generate ideas for the design of the school ground that would be conducive to pedagogy and play.

Focus group discussion is also very effective as an exploratory tool after the intervention in order to gather data on children's use of the different designed settings for pedagogy and play and the underlying reasons for any expected (or unexpected) changes in behaviour. It is also a useful tool to use with adults; we used it as a brain-storming tool with teachers in order to generate ideas on how the school ground could be designed as a place for teaching and learning. Separate focus group discussions should be held with children, teachers and parents.

Children's drawing

Visual methods have been increasingly used in research as they can help in improving the degree of participation by children and even adults (Hart, 1997; Greene and Hogan, 2005; Monsoureh and Ismail, 2012). The visual method that is often considered first in research with children is drawing. However, Hart (1997) discouraged the use of *individual* drawing as the primary method to listen to children's voices because children may come up with stereotyped images they have learned to draw. In a small study in Bangladesh in 2009 with children of a primary school, Matluba asked the children to draw their dream school. The children came out with drawings of the school exactly as it looked at that time! However, drawings can be an effective warm-up exercise for pre-adolescent children to stimulate further discussion or activities (Hart, 1997).

In our study, we found the combination of focus groups with drawings to be very useful. At the end of each focus group the children were asked, when still in groups of five or six, to make a *combined* drawing, on a 50x75cm sheet of paper, of their school ground as they wanted it to be, including different elements they would like to see and activities they would like to do either with their peers or alone (Figure 9.4). While drawing, the children interacted with each other, discussed what they wanted and also conveyed their desires to us. After they had finished, the children were asked to explain their drawings of their dream school ground. They were also asked whether any of the elements they wanted in the school ground had any implications for what they learnt from their textbooks or were taught in classrooms. There might be debate on whether children can provide useful information or to what extent they can contribute to the design of a place for pedagogy; however, we found the children's contributions useful (for more information on the detail of co-design and development of the school ground see Khan et al., 2020). We found the combination of focus group discussion and drawings useful, as they did not leave any scope for ambiguity in their interpretation, since they themselves explained them during the discussion.

Model-making

Model-making, according to Hart, is a 'highly effective strategy for involving children of all ages from 5 years and older in the design of school grounds and playgrounds' (Hart, 1997, p109). In everyday play, children communicate with each other using toys, which can also be used as a medium for engaging them in activities that help us to discover their desires. Even very young children can express their design preference through manipulation of their toys. However, children's individual spontaneous statements might not be sufficient for ascertaining their true desires for activities in the school ground. Hart (1997) referred to the use of visuals, e.g. video clips or images,

FIGURE 9.4 Combined drawing exercise as part of focus group discussion at the study school in Bangladesh
Source: Matluba Khan

to trigger children's thoughts and ideas. Sometimes our actions are based on pre-conscious factors of which we are unaware (Eiser, 1986). Visuals of children engaging in such activities, i.e. building or making something, might stimulate individual responses in focus groups, and model-making exercises (for both children and adults) can draw out aspects of place experience, activities and artefacts that the participants identify in a positive way. Later on, this may help in generating newer themes through the modelling of the school ground to give a visual form to the preferences of children.

Model making can be designed as a child-led activity. Children should be the main performers in such an activity, although participation of teachers in leading children can also create an environment where children can learn how to negotiate. We conducted the first – to our knowledge – model-making workshop with children and teachers in Bangladesh as part of the project (Figure 9.5). Adults often think children are not competent enough to be engaged in a model-making exercise; many do not think highly of children from a developing country. We found child-led model-making very useful for discovering how children viewed their dream school ground. Two teachers also participated in the model-making exercise led by five children. Though the principal performers were the children, there were some negotiations between children and teachers.

We found children were more attentive to the details of each element they wanted in their school ground rather than considering the whole layout as a single scheme. They seemed to view the school ground as a place for performing different activities and cared less about how the school ground would look as a whole. Thus, it is the role of the landscape architect to make a school ground a functional and aesthetically satisfying whole, incorporating all the elements that children wished to have in their school ground as far as is practically possible.

METHODS FOR EVALUATING THE EFFICACY OF THE ENVIRONMENT FOR PEDAGOGY AND PLAY

One objective of a quasi-experiment study is to find connections between two or more variables (Groat and Wang, 2002). The use of quantitative measures, such as questionnaires and/or standardised tools, objective measures

FIGURE 9.5 a) Model making activity and b) the resulting model
Source: Matluba Khan

through an instrument (e.g. accelerometer or pedometer) or standardised test scores can help to measure objectively to what extent a school ground design can contribute to an outcome, for example academic attainment, motivation to learn or Body Mass Index (BMI).

Questionnaires

Questionnaires are considered to be instruments for a deductive approach in empirical measurement and data analysis (Neuman, 2003). The main purpose of using a questionnaire is 'to discover regularities among groups of people by comparing answers to the same set of questions asked of a large number of people' (Zeisel, 1984, p157). In an evaluation research design, rather than using a single primary data collection method, a mix of different instruments can be adopted to collect data, according to their suitability for the type of study. A form of questionnaire (there are many varieties) can provide useful data when there is a well-defined problem and the major concepts are already clear to the researchers when they begin the study (Zeisel, 1984). The ability of children to provide reliable responses is often undervalued (Matthews, 1985); however, Christensen and James (2008) argue that children can provide reliable answers if they find the questions meaningful to their lives. Again, with age, children become better able to assess their competences realistically (Harter, 1982).

Self-reported questionnaires have been used in research with children to compare their opinions and experiences in different contexts. Mygind (2009) used questionnaires to compare children's statements about social relations and teaching in the classroom and in a forest setting. In our study in Bangladesh we used questionnaires to compare the responses of children related to their experiences in the classroom and outdoors both before and after the intervention (the school ground design). Two sets of questionnaires were administered at the same time, one in the intervention school and one in the control school, asking about their experiences in the classroom and their perceptions related to taking classes outdoors. The responses of children in the experiment school were compared to that of the control school in order to measure the impact of intervention.

Standardised instruments

In order to find the link between the design of the school ground and outcome measures, it is important to test the impact on children objectively. The design and use of a school ground can have an impact on children's academic attainment (Khan et al., 2019a; Kweon et al., 2017), their perceived motivation to learn (Khan, 2017), recovery from stress (Kelz et al., 2013) and well-being (Kelz, 2010; Khan, 2017). Rather than preparing a new instrument for measuring certain outcomes, already established and validated ones should be used. For example, Kelz et al. (2013) used the Basler Well-Being Questionnaire, a standardised German instrument, to measure well-being, the Perceived Restorativeness Scale (Hartig, 1996) to determine the subjective restorative qualities of the school ground and the Attention Network Test (ANT) to determine the change in executive functioning among children.

Standardised tests

The use of standardised tests as outcome measures is not new in this research field; however, they have not often been applied in the field of environment behaviour research in order to find the relationship between attributes of the primary school landscape and children's academic outcomes. In 2010, Matsuoka investigated the association between the degree of naturalness in high-school grounds and students' academic performance (Matsuoka, 2010). The influence of the overall school architecture on student outcomes in the USA was investigated by Tanner using standardised tests as the outcome measures (Tanner, 2000, 2009). In an absence of standardised tests, we used exam scores in key subject areas as a measure of children's academic attainment in our study. Most Government primary schools in Bangladesh do not use standardised tests. However, three exams are taken at four month intervals in April, August and December, called the first terminal, second terminal and annual examinations respectively. The questions for different subjects like mathematics or science for these examinations are the same across all the schools within a single sub-district. Since there can be issues related to the reliability of tests which are not standardised but might be marked in a subjective or imperative manner, we only used mathematics and science exam scores as outcome measures since the questions and scoring of these subjects are more objective (there are right and wrong answers). These were also the subjects that were taught in the outdoor environment after the intervention design was implemented.

An instrument like an accelerometer can be used to measure children's physical activity objectively. Such measures can be a reliable tool for obtaining more accurate information on physical activity levels but they also present some limitations. For example, children would need to wear a device which might fall off or the child might forget to put it back on after taking a shower. Physical activity is also the measure that has been examined most in studies related to children. We could say that there is enough evidence already about what kind of landscape elements can lead to increased physical activity. However, in a holistic evaluation it is worth exploring how and whether elements designed to enable pedagogical processes stimulate more physical activity or what kind of physical activity – sedentary, moderate or vigorous – takes place in different behaviour settings.

METHODS USED FOR FINDING THE LINKS BETWEEN DESIGN AND PEDAGOGY AND PLAY

Participant observation

For an in-depth understanding of the influence of the outdoor environment, especially the relationship of affordances to behaviour settings as well as social processes, participant observation is considered to be suitable (Humberstone and Stan, 2011). The term 'participant observation' refers to the role of the researcher as observer in a group or setting, observing behaviour and listening to conversations with each other and also with the observer (Bryman, 2012). However, observers in environment–behaviour research also look at whether behaviour in the physical environment is supported or deterred by its characteristics (Zeisel, 1984). Participant observation has been widely used in research with children as it is regarded as being able to obtain the most authentic impression of human behaviour (Christidou et al., 2013, p63). With this method, researchers not only observe what is happening in a place but also try to identify what is not there. They can try to uncover the silent voices of children (Greig et al., 2007). Participant observation can be particularly useful for landscape architects to test the extent to which their design enabled or deterred different kinds of activities (planned for as well as spontaneous) in the school ground. In a quasi-experiment action evaluation study such as ours, participant observation was used to examine children's behaviour in the outdoor environment, and to find out what activities children were engaged in before and after the intervention.

Exploration of what the school ground can offer for teaching the curriculum requires careful observation of the actions in order to understand the meanings. Therefore, participant observation can be used to understand the educational context in order to find the underlying reasons behind teachers' use of the outdoors for teaching, children's response to the tasks and to ascertain how the environment helped or deterred the process of teaching and learning. In our study, Matluba recorded observations in the form of blog posts in order to interact with her co-authors (https://matlubafrombangladesh.blogspot.co.uk/) and also kept a field journal and took photographs that complemented it. The field journal contained a reflexive account of thoughts for the day, reasons behind children's reactions to certain situations or to the presence of the researcher, the interactions of the children with the environment and the dialogue between Matluba and the teachers and visitors to the school (mostly parents and community people). The dialogue between Matluba and her research assistant (an architecture and urban design graduate who helped with data collection) reflecting upon the data was also recorded in the field journal. Reflexivity is considered a valuable feature of social research, as researchers participate in the social world and eventually reflect on the products of that participation (Humberstone and Stan, 2012). The field journal, accompanied by photographs taken during the whole period, gave useful information about the pattern of use of the school ground throughout the time.

Behaviour mapping

The observation of children can also be carried out by mapping their activities in different settings within the school ground, using the behaviour mapping approach, which is characterised as an objective method to measure how spaces are used (Moore and Cosco, 2010). It can be used to record simultaneously both the location of the participants in the space and their activity. It can provide useful information about the relationship between environment and behaviour and can guide design interventions (Cosco et al., 2010) (see also Chapter 3). Behaviour mapping has been used as the primary investigation tool in many research projects involving children (Cosco, 2006;

Hussein, 2009). The theory of behaviour settings and concept of affordances are the basis for this observational tool. Behaviour mapping can be used to determine which settings and components are used to what degree by children and to identify the physical components that most support learning, social interaction and exploration of the environment in the school ground.

There are established behaviour mapping protocols (Moore and Cosco, 2007, 2010) that can be used to observe children's activities during play and recess. SOPLAY (System for Observing Play and Leisure Activity in Youth) is one technique that has been widely used to investigate children's play and recess activities in school grounds and playgrounds (Anthamatten et al., 2011; Colabianchi et al., 2009; Janssen et al., 2013; Willenberg et al., 2010). Since children are engaged in diverse play activities in different cultures and spaces, the behaviour mapping coding protocols need to be adjusted and adapted to specific contexts. We used behaviour mapping in our study for the first time in Bangladesh. We studied children's play behaviour in order to develop a coding protocol suitable for the context. Matluba's upbringing in a rural area in Bangladesh contributed to an in-depth understanding of the nature of play behaviours of primary school children there.

Though there are established behaviour mapping protocols for observing children's behaviour during play and leisure, there was nothing for observing children during their outdoor learning activities as part of the curricular teaching and learning. We therefore developed a specific protocol and coding system for observing pedagogical activities during outdoor classes. Environment behaviour researchers suggest recording answers to specific questions during the behaviour mapping procedure. For example Goličnik (2005, p66) suggested thinking about 'Who is doing what, where and with whom?' or 'Where and for how long is what taking place?' to make the behaviour maps condensed and inclusive. However, while recording children's outdoor activities during their outdoor lessons, more questions should be considered to make those maps meaningful, for example: *'What is being taught in the outdoor classes?'*, *'How did the teacher integrate different settings of the environment with the contents she was teaching?'* and *'How did the children respond to those tasks through the use of different elements?'* The procedures and the categories of behaviour maps were standardised for this specific location in order to make the maps useful (Zeisel, 1984; for more about behaviour mapping protocols during outdoor lessons see Khan, 2017).

QUALITATIVE METHODS (EXPLORATORY)

While quantitative measures are useful to measure the impact of the design and observation and behaviour mapping give information on how different settings in the school grounds are used, qualitative methods after the intervention are also necessary to learn the underlying reasons for any impact that the change in the school ground has had on children. Focus groups with children can be used to learn about their experiences of place and their preferences, their feelings about learning in the school ground, whether they themselves perceive any change in their behaviour and attitude and their views on methods of teaching used in the school ground. In-depth interviews and/or focus group discussions with teachers can provide useful information on these aspects from the teachers' perspective. The teachers can also provide additional information on the benefits and challenges they encountered when teaching in the school ground and how different settings helped or hindered them in their teaching practice. It is important that landscape architects know of this information to improve the design of their next projects or to rectify the problems which emerged in the existing design. Furthermore, focus groups with parents can provide useful information on the extent to which they have seen attitudinal changes in their children because of the change in the environment.

Semi-structured interviews

In-depth interviews with teachers can be used as a follow-up to the other data collection methods in order to achieve a fuller picture. While structured interviews are used to ensure consistency and to keep interview-related error to a minimum, semi-structured interviews provide the flexibility to follow the respondents' replies (Bryman, 2012). Interviewing in person can also offer the opportunity to note the expressions of the individuals while recording the answers to the questions. We interviewed the teachers who were engaged in teaching outdoors in our study. Two teachers who were involved in teaching science and mathematics to children in the outdoors were interviewed after the intervention in order to gain an in-depth insight into the influence of the designed outdoor environment. While we developed a structured questionnaire, Matluba also used the freedom to ask follow-up questions in response to any interesting or unexpected points made by the teachers.

For an evaluation of a design, the location of focus group discussion or in-depth interviews is important. Conducting the interviews within the environment under consideration is a useful tool to explore different dimensions of place and examine participants' experiences, interpretations and practices (Khan, 2012; 2017). Often 'go-along interviews' are conducted by researchers with the same purpose – to observe participants' experiences and interpretations at the same time (Kusenbach, 2003; Carpiano, 2009). Go-along interviews are useful for a large site when the whole school ground cannot be seen from any suitable location for a sit-down interview.

A framework for analysis to link children's behaviour with design elements

The analysis of data gathered from all these methods can yield a holistic picture of how a school ground design can influence the everyday lives of children in their primary schools. A school ground designed as a combination of different behaviour settings offering multiple affordances (cognitive, physical, social and emotional) can influence pedagogy and play (Khan, 2017). However, as already described, the design of the school ground should be guided by: 1) the views and preferences of children, teachers and parents; 2) evidence from relevant research; and 3) the intuitions and judgments of the designers involved in interpreting the perceived affordances of different behaviour settings in physical forms. The same behaviour settings could take different physical forms in the hands of different designers. Therefore, we do not propose to evaluate the quality of physical forms of the various elements in terms of landscape architecture design quality, but rather to focus on the affordances that the newly designed school ground provides. Unlike adults who see the forms in the environment, children usually look for their functional properties (Heft, 2010). Instead of an artefact or an element which offers little or no activity potential, children are more likely to be attracted to those which afford any or many functions, like the opportunity to sit on or to step into them (Ward Thompson, 1995).

Therefore, the framework for analysis in an evaluation of a school ground design should include: 1) looking into the intention of the designers (perceived as potential affordances[1] of the settings); 2) the affordances actualised as per designers' perceptions; 3) new affordances discovered by the users beyond designers' expectations; and 4) the perceived affordances that are not actualised. An example summary of the framework is given in Table 9.1.

An inclusive picture of potential, intended actualised, unintended actualised and intended but not actualised affordances of different behaviour settings can help researchers and designers look into what elements of design are successful and what can be modified, rectified or improved to match intentions. The actualisation of the affordance of a design element can depend on the ability of the perceiver, in this case a child, yet if the affordance of a design element intended by the designer is not actualised the way it was intended, then this can refer to a problem within the design rather than a child's inability to recognise the affordance. If these can be pointed out to the designer, then they can revisit the design and rectify the problem in the existing design or avoid the same mistake in future.

In our project we designed an area with loose materials in the school ground which we found was not used to the extent it was intended or expected. After consultation with teachers and children we found out that the way it was designed was not suitable for the context: the area with recyclable waste materials (considered as 'loose parts') was perceived to be messy and dirty to the villagers (the school had no boundary walls and was therefore accessible to everyone after school hours), who had taken the responsibility to clean up the place. As these same loose materials were found useful by teachers for pedagogical purposes and were used frequently, we figured out that we should have designed a mechanism for easy transport of loose materials between a storage space and the place for their use in the design.

TABLE 9.1 Potential (perceived by designers) and actualised affordances of different behaviour settings during formal learning in outdoor classes

Behaviour settings	Design intentions (potential affordances as perceived by designers)	Actualised affordances	Unintended actualised affordances	Intended not actualised
Natural learning area	• Collecting leaves for counting • Learning about the interdependence of plants and animals • Building knowledge of plants and trees	• Learning the interdependence of plants and animals • Building knowledge of plants and trees • Counting	• Digging, collecting leaves for compost bin • Working in groups	
Gardens	• Growing plants • Building knowledge on how plants grow from seed, flower and fruit and reproduce • Knowledge of different types of plants • Learning about interdependence of plants and animals	• Growing plants • Taking care of plants • Building knowledge on how plants grow from seed, flower and fruit and reproduce • Knowledge of different types of plants • Learning about the interdependence of plants and animals	• Counting • Working in groups	
Amphitheatre	Context for learning through interaction with peers and more mature adults in any area of curriculum	Learning through interaction with peers and more mature adults in any area of curriculum	• Observing built and natural environment • Working with loose materials • Measuring • Drawing • Working in groups	
Water area	• Learning the water cycle • Learning the life cycle of aquatic plants and animals • Learning pressure and flow • Measuring • Experimenting with water and sand	Learning from close connection with nature: water cycle, life cycle of aquatic plants and animals	Working in groups	Measuring Experimenting with water and sand

UNDERSTANDING OF THE COMPLEX DYNAMICS OF THE SCHOOL GROUND

Our Bangladesh research study confirmed our initial hypothesis that a well-designed outdoor learning environment (designed as a combination of different behaviour settings involving children, teachers and parents) can positively influence children's formal (academic performance) and informal (cognitive, social and physical activities during playtime) learning, and their motivation to learn. However, the relationship between the design of the environment and children's learning is more complex. Research that explores only one aspect of the impact of a school ground might miss out the complex dynamics that exist in the school environment. Landscape architects in their designs, if the users are not involved, often focus on the use of new materials and technology, boldness of forms and the overall aesthetics of the environment. In this whole picture the child itself is often missing and their perceptions are often not considered as reliable for evaluation of the environment that is designed *for* them, and it is rare that it is designed *with* them.

CAN WE BRIDGE THE GAP BETWEEN RESEARCH AND PRACTICE?

Existing studies of school ground evaluation yielded useful information on the benefits of the outdoor environment and the positive impact of school ground design, but offered very little information on the quality of the design itself that could be useful for architects, landscape architects and planners in their practices. Nor did the studies link impact to the quality of design elements. In school ground settings, research studies have investigated the relationship of environmental features with children's play (referred to as environmental learning in some research) comparing 'good' vs 'bad' (Lindholm, 1995) or 'traditional' vs 'contemporary' (Susa and Benedict, 1994) playgrounds. Later research studies investigated the association between the availability of 'greenness' and children's play and academic outcomes (Kuo et al., 2018; Mårtensson et al., 2014; Matsuoka, 2010), but do not define 'greenness' in a way that designers might find useful.

Conversely, studies that focus on developing design recommendations rarely describe the design in terms of what it offers for children. Adams (1990) investigated the potential of school grounds as a context for teaching and learning and also reported on the design, management and use of school grounds in three counties in the UK. In order to come up with some design recommendations for school grounds, Adams and colleagues conducted a thorough literature search and investigated some school grounds, focusing on the qualities of the physical environment: layout, sensory qualities, sense of place, differentiation of spaces, micro-climate and pollution, access and circulation, landforms and soils, hard surfaces and site furniture, planting and security and safety. These investigations relied on the researchers' perception of the quality of the environment and did not include an empirical account of affordances provided by the school ground based on children's interaction with the environment during formal and informal learning.

In order to make the research findings useful for practitioners, these two aspects of research should come together and look at the picture holistically in order to provide more useful recommendations for landscape architects. Landscape architects also need to look at the school grounds not only as a combination of different landforms, hard elements, site furniture, plants and safety and security, but also as a place offering numerous opportunities for children to explore, interact, create, modify and manipulate.

School ground design as a combination of different behaviour settings was found conducive to pedagogy and play (Khan, 2017; Khan and Bell, 2015). There are large and small school grounds, some in urban areas in the middle of chaos and some in rural areas amidst the bounties of nature. Children in Bangladesh play 'patapata'; British children grow up playing hopscotch. Thus, school ground design should reflect the differences in culture and context. The implementation of this kind of research strategy can help to create recommendations on what kind of design features and behaviour settings might be useful for children in different parts of the world.

In an ideal world we would recommend that researchers and practitioners work together on every project, evaluating it as a whole rather than dividing it into separate parts which do not offer useful application. The quasi-experiment action evaluation research design can be helpful for understanding the whole picture and also for giving useful recommendations to landscape architects. We have been able to implement the research design in one study, but a wide-scale implementation could lead to much stronger evidence of the benefits of school ground design and more useful recommendation to landscape architects.

NOTE

1   Potential affordances are those that the designers intend to offer in the design, whereas actualised ones are those with which the users engage themselves.

REFERENCES

Adams, E. (1990). *Learning through landscapes: A report on the use, design, management and development of school grounds.* Winchester: Learning Through Landscapes Trust, 1990.

Adams, E. (1993). School's out!: New initiatives for British school grounds. *Children's Environments*, **10**(2), 180–191.

Anthamatten, P., Brink, L., Lampe, S., Greenwood, E., Kingston, B., and Nigg, C. (2011). An assessment of schoolyard renovation strategies to encourage children's physical activity. *International Journal of Behavioral Nutrition and Physical Activity*, **8**(1), 1–9.

Barker, R. G. (1968). *Ecological psychology: Concepts and methods for studying the environment of human behavior.* Stanford, Calif.: Stanford University Press.

Barker, R. G. (1976). On the nature of the environment. In H. M. Proshansky, W. H. Ittelson, and R. G. Rivlin (eds), *Environmental psychology: People and their physical settings* (pp. 12–26). New York: Holt, Rinehart and Winston.

Bell, A. C., and Dyment, J. E. (2008) Grounds for health: the intersection of green school grounds and health-promoting schools. *Environmental Education Research*, **14**(1), 77–90.

Biehler, R. F., and Snowman, J. (1982). *Psychology applied to teaching.* Boston: Houghton Mifflin Co.

Carpiano, R. M. (2009). Come take a walk with me: The "go-along" interview as a novel method for studying the implications of place for health and well-being. *Health and Place*, **15**(1), 263–272.

Cervinka, R., Röderer, K., and Hämmerle, I. (2014). Evaluation of hospital gardens and implications for design: Benefits from environmental psychology for architecture and landscape planning. *Journal of Architectural and Planning Research*, **31**(1), 43–56.

Christensen, P., and James, A. (2008). *Research with children: Perspectives and practices.* New York, London: Routledge.

Christidou, V., et al. (2013). Exploring primary children's views and experiences of the school ground: The case of a Greek school. *International Journal of Environmental and Science Education*, **8**(1), 59–83.

Clark, A., and Moss, P. (2005). *Spaces to play: More listening to young children using the mosaic approach.* London: National Children's Bureau.

Colabianchi, N., Kinsella, A. E., Coulton, C. J., and Moore, S. M. (2009). Utilization and physical activity levels at renovated and unrenovated school playgrounds. *Preventive Medicine*, **48**(2), 140–143.

Cosco, N. G. (2006). Motivation to move: Physical activity affordances in preschool play areas. PhD Thesis. University of Edinburgh.

Cosco, N. G. et al. (2010). Behavior mapping: a method for linking preschool physical activity and outdoor design. *Medicine and Science in Sports and Exercise*, **42**(3), 513–519.

Darbyshire, P. et al. (2005). Multiple methods in qualitative research with children: more insight or just more? *Qualitative Research*, **5**(4), 417–436.

Davis, B. E. (2001). Healing the whole person: A post occupancy evaluation of the rooftop therapy park at Fort Sanders Regional Medical Center, Knoxville, Tennessee. Master Thesis. Louisiana State University and Agricultural and Mechanical College.

Dudek, M., and Baumann, D. (2007). *Schools and kindergartens: A design manual* [electronic resource]. Basel, Boston: Birkhäuser.

Dyment, J. E., and Bell, A. C. (2007). Grounds for movement: Green school grounds as sites for promoting physical activity. *Health Education Research*, **23**(6), 952–962.

Dyment, J. E., Bell, A. C., and Lucas, A. J. (2009). The relationship between school ground design and intensity of physical activity. *Children's Geographies*, **7**(3), 261–276.

Eiser, J. R. (1986). *Social psychology: Attitudes, cognition and social behaviour.* Cambridge: Cambridge University Press.

Erikson, E. H. (1995). *Childhood and society,* revised edition. London: Vintage.

Fargas-Malet, M., McSherry, D., Larkin, E., and Robinson, C. (2010). Research with children: Methodological issues and innovative techniques. *Journal of Early Childhood Research*, **8**(2), 175–192.

Gaver, W. W. (1996). Situating action II: Affordances for interaction: The social is material for design. *Ecological Psychology*, **8**(2), 111–129.

Gibson, E. J., and Pick, A. D. (2000). *An ecological approach to perceptual learning and development.* Oxford: Oxford University Press.

Gibson, J. J. (1979). *The ecological approach to visual perception.* Boston: Houghton Mifflin.

Goličnik, B. (2005). People in place: A configuration of physical form and the dynamic patterns of spatial occupancy in urban open public space. PhD Thesis. Heriot-Watt University.

Greene, S., and Hogan, D. (2005). *Researching children's experience: Methods and approaches.* London, California, New Delhi: Sage Publications.

Greig, A., et al. (2007). *Doing research with children,* 2nd edition. Los Angeles; London: Sage.

Groat, L. N., and Wang, D. (2002). *Architectural research methods.* New York: John Wiley and Sons.

Hart, R. A. (1997). *Children's participation: The theory and practice of involving young citizens in community development and environmental care.* London: Earthscan.

Harter, S. (1982). The Perceived Competence Scale for Children. *Child Development*, **53**(1), 87–97.

Hartig, T. (1996). Validation of a measure of perceived environmental restorativeness. *Göteborg Psychological Reports*, **26**(7), 1–64.

Heft, H. (1988) Affordances of children's environments: A functional approach to environmental description. *Children's Environments Quarterly*, **5**(3), 29–37.

Heft, H. (2010). Affordances in the perception of landscape: an enquiry into environmental perception and aesthetics. In C. Ward Thompson, P. Aspinall and S. Bell (eds), *Innovative approaches to researching landscape and health: Open space: People space 2* (pp. 9–32). Abingdon: Routledge.

Huitt, W. (2011). *Self and self-views: Educational psychology interactive*. Valdosta, GA: Valdosta State University.

Humberstone, B. and Stan, I. (2011). Outdoor learning: primary pupils' experiences and teachers' interaction in outdoor learning. *Education 3-13*, **39**(5), 529–540.

Humberstone, B., and Stan, I. (2012). Nature and well-being in outdoor learning: authenticity or performativity. *Journal of Adventure Education and Outdoor Learning*, **12**(3), 183–197.

Hussein, H. (2009). Therapeutic intervention: Using sensory gardens to enhance the quality of life for children with special needs. PhD Thesis. University of Edinburgh.

Inhelder, B. and Piaget, J. (1969). *The psychology of the child*. New York: Basic Books.

Janssen, M., Toussaint, H. M., van Mechelen, W., and Verhagen, E. A. L. M. (2013). Translating the PLAYgrounds program into practice: A process evaluation using the RE-AIM framework. *Journal of Science and Medicine in Sport*, **16**(3), 211–216.

Kelz, C. (2010). Effects of a new schoolyard design on pupils' well-being, restoration, physical fitness and cognitive functioning. PhD Thesis. Cornell University.

Kelz, C., Evans, G. W., and Roderer, K. (2013). The restorative effects of redesigning the schoolyard: A multi-methodological, quasi-experimental study in rural Austrian middle schools. *Environment and Behavior*, **20**(10), 1–21.

Khan, M. (2012). Outdoor as learning environment for children at a government primary school in Bangladesh. B.Arch. Thesis. Bangladesh University of Engineering and Technology.

Khan, M. (2017). Environment, engagement and education: Investigating the relationship between primary school grounds and children's learning: A case study from Bangladesh. PhD Thesis. University of Edinburgh.

Khan, M., and Bell, S. (2015). Improving children's outdoor learning by design: A case study from Bangladesh. In *Proceedings of the ECLAS Conference 2015: Landscape in flux* (pp. 503–509).

Khan, M., McGeown, S. P., and Islam, M. Z. (2019a). 'There is no better way to study science than to collect and analyse data in your own yard': Outdoor classrooms and primary school children in Bangladesh. *Children's Geographies*, **17**(2), 217–230.

Khan, M., Mcgeown, S., et al. (2019b). Can an outdoor learning environment improve children's academic attainment? A quasi-experimental mixed methods study in Bangladesh. *Environment and Behavior*, 1–31. Available from https://doi.org/10.1177/0013916519860868.

Khan, M., Bell, S. McGeown, S., and Silveirinha de Oliveira, E. (2020). Designing an outdoor learning environment for and with a primary school community: A case study in Bangladesh. *Landscape Research*, **45**(1), 95–110.

Krueger, R., and Casey, M. (2009). *Focus groups: A practical guide for applied research*. Beverly Hills, Calif.: Sage.

Kuo, M., et al. (2018). Might school performance grow on trees? Examining the link between 'greenness' and academic achievement in urban, high-poverty schools. *Frontiers in Psychology,* **1** [online]. Available from: www.frontiersin.org (Accessed 7 October 2018).

Kusenbach, M. (2003). Street phenomenology: The go-along as ethnographic research tool. *Ethnography*, **4**(3), 455–485.

Kweon, B.-S., Ellis, C. D., Lee, J., and Jacobs, K. (2017). The link between school environments and student academic performance. *Urban Forestry and Urban Greening*, **23**, 35–43.

Kyttä, M. (2002). Affordances of children's environments in the context of cities, small towns, suburbs and rural villages in Finland and Belarus. *Journal of Environmental Psychology*, **22**(1), 109–123.

Kyttä, M. (2004). The extent of children's independent mobility and the number of actualized affordances as criteria for child-friendly environments. *Journal of Environmental Psychology*, **24**(2), 179–198.

Li, D., and Sullivan, W. C. (2016). Impact of views to school landscapes on recovery from stress and mental fatigue. *Landscape and Urban Planning*, **148**, 149–158.

Lindholm, G. (1995). Schoolyards: The significance of place properties to outdoor activities in schools. *Environment and Behavior*, **27**(3), 259–293.

Malone, K., and Tranter, P. J. (2003). School grounds as sites for learning: Making the most of environmental opportunities. *Environmental Education Research*, **9**(3), 283–303.

Mårtensson, F., et al. (2014). The role of greenery for physical activity play at school grounds. *Urban Forestry and Urban Greening*, **13**(1), 103–113.

Matsuoka, R. H. (2010). Student performance and high school landscapes: Examining the links. *Landscape and Urban Planning*, **97**(4), 273–282.

Matthews, M. H. (1985). Young children's representations of the environment: A comparison of techniques. *Journal of Environmental Psychology*, **5**(3), 261–278.

Monsoureh, R., and Ismail, S. (2012). Methods for evaluating responses of children with outdoor environments. *Procedia – Social and Behavioral Sciences*, 4939–46 [online].

Moore, R. C., and Wong, H. H. (1997). *Natural learning: The life history of an environmental schoolyard: Creating environments for rediscovering nature's way of teaching*. Berkeley, Calif.: MIG Communications.

Moore, R., and Cosco, N. (2007). Greening Montessori school grounds by design. *The NAMTA Journal*, **32**(1), 129–151.

Moore, R. C., and Cosco, N. G. (2010). Using behaviour mapping to investigate healthy outdoor environments for children and families: conceptual framework, procedures and applications. In C. Ward Thompson et al. (eds) *Innovative approaches to researching landscape and health: Open space: People space 2* (pp. 33–73). New York: Routledge.

Mygind, E. (2009). A comparison of children's' statements about social relations and teaching in the classroom and in the outdoor environment. *Journal of Adventure Education and Outdoor Learning*, **9**(2), 151–169.

Neuman, W. L. (2003). *Social research methods: Qualitative and quantitative approaches*. Boston, Mass.; London: Allyn and Bacon.

Piaget, J. (1964). Development and learning. In R. E. Ripple and V. N. Rockcastle (eds.), *Piaget rediscovered* (pp. 7–20). New York: Cornell University Press.

Punch, S. (2002). Research with children: The same or different from research with adults? *Childhood*, **9**(3), 321–341.

Roe, J. (2008). The restorative power of natural and built environments. PhD Thesis, Heriot-Watt University.

Samborski, S. (2010). Biodiverse or barren school grounds: Their effects on children. *Children, Youth and Environments*, **20**(2), 67–115.

Scott, M. M. (2005). A powerful theory and a paradox: Ecological psychologists after Barker. *Environment and Behavior*, **37**(3), 295–329.

Spencer , H. (1855). *The principles of psychology.* London: Longman, Brown, Green and Longmans.

Susa, A. M. and Benedict, J. O. (1994). The effects of playground design on pretend play and divergent thinking. *Environment and Behavior*, **26**(4), 560–579.

Tanner, C. K. (2000). The influence of school architecture on academic achievement. *Journal of Educational Administration*, **38**(4), 309–330.

Tanner, C. K. (2009). Effects of school design on student outcomes. *Journal of Educational Administration*, **47**, 381–399.

Turner, J. (1984). *Cognitive development and education.* London; New York: Methuen.

UNICEF (1989). *Convention on the rights of the child.* United Nations.

Vygotsky, L.S., Cole, M., John-Steiner, V., Scribner, S., et al. (1978). *Mind in society.* Cambridge, Mass.: Harvard University Press.

Ward Thompson, C. (1995). School playground design: a projective approach with pupils and staff. *Landscape Research*, **20**(3), 124–140.

Ward Thompson, C. (2013). Activity, exercise and the planning and design of outdoor spaces. *Journal of Environmental Psychology,* **34**, 79–96.

Wheeler, A., and Malekzadeh, M. (2015). Exploring the use of new school buildings through post-occupancy evaluation and partici- patory action research. *Architectural Engineering and Design Management*, **11**(6), 440–456.

Willenberg, L. J. et al. (2010). Increasing school playground physical activity: A mixed methods study combining environmental measures and children's perspectives. *Journal of Science and Medicine in Sport / Sports Medicine Australia,* **13**(2), 210–216.

Wood, D. (1998). *How children think and learn: The social contexts of cognitive development,* second edition. Oxford: Blackwell.

Zeisel, J. (1984). *Inquiry by design: Tools for environment-behaviour research.* Cambridge: Cambridge University Press.

Part 3

PLACE AND PARTICIPATION

10

CHILDREN AS HETEROTOPIANS: TOWN PLANNING WITH AND FOR CHILDREN

Jenny Wood

INTRODUCTION

Children interact with their environments in a variety of ways, and while sometimes their place-based experiences may be similar to (some) adults, we cannot accurately make that assumption. Research in environmental psychology, sociology, and geography increasingly takes a child-focus, showing that children are particularly sensitive to their local neighbourhoods, cannot drive like their adult peers, and so are more dependent on active travel or the help of others and value the social connections and opportunities in their immediate surroundings. Yet, while childhood researchers frequently cite the concept of affordances as offering a starting point to understand children's environmental needs, it lacks a theoretical and practical application in the field of town planning. Considering the procedural and politicised nature of the planning profession, furthering this cause requires a nuanced understanding of power dynamics and their effect on spatial form.

Development of a child-centric understanding of place is timely given the almost universal international ratification of the UN Convention on the Rights of the Child (UNCRC) (UN 1989). This declares all children have a right to freedom of association and assembly (Article 15), and to play, rest, leisure, and access to cultural life (Article 31), along with a right to participate in the matters that affect them (Article 12). While the term 'participation' is usually used to describe only active influence in the decision-making process, as Gillespie concludes:

> the true test of children's inclusion and the development of adult capacities to genuinely engage children may rest more on children's [re]integration into the informal aspects of public space, rather than their formal participation in planning processes.
>
> (2013, p. 76)

The dearth of child-friendly urban forms and the above view shows the fundamental need to conceptualise children's participation as stated in all three of Articles 12, 15, and 31 when it comes to the environment. Along with the UN's New Urban Agenda (United Nations 2016), this gives children and young people a right to the city that demands a planning response.

In this chapter, I take the above international precedents, the views of children collected in fieldwork, and reflection on research and practice, to propose a theory of children's spatial participation that counters the current doctrine of separating child and adult land uses. It recognises children as active participants in places, whether or not they engage in formal processes, by using Foucault's theories of governmentality and heterotopia. I illustrate how space affects children, and children affect space in ways that adults cannot fully understand – *but that planners can appreciate*. I begin by exploring governmentality and heterotopia, and relate this to existing research on children and place, before elaborating this conception through participatory research with primary-school children. I end by drawing together the threads to show heterotopia as a useful conception that challenges adults' preconceived notions of what children need from place, so that we can better plan for and with their participation.

Power differentials in society are an important lift-off point for this discussion. Through conducting historical genealogy, Foucault theorised power not as something to possess, but as something to exert. This stretches from institutions to individuals, through complex networks and relations. We can thus understand it better through analysing the networks that exert it in what he terms governmentality (Foucault 2008). This shows how practices of government play out in everyday situations between individuals (Mckee 2009), and Foucault likens these structures to the form of a chain (Foucault 1980). Those that can exert the most power are those that have access to the top of the chain, in the form of resources, technologies, or networks of power, such as decision-making processes.

Foucault (1988a) identifies four features of governmentality of which two are relevant here: technologies of power and technologies of the self. These are intricately intertwined, but the former are concerned with governing others, while the latter are concerned with the way we govern ourselves. For instance, Foucault (1977) provides the overlapping examples of normalisation, surveillance, classification, hierarchisation, distribution of rank, individualisation, and examination as technologies of the self in the prison system. Institutions embody and enforce these regulations, but in so doing, infiltrate into the subjectivities of inmates – who, even in their limited freedom, self-regulate. Such analysis has been transposed to schools which regulate children's behaviour through a mix of voluntary and coercive tactics that help shape individuals into the adults demanded by society (or societal elites) (Gallagher 2004). What results is governable subjects who have been encouraged to govern themselves, and with the governing source remaining faceless. These actions can transform individuals into an order where they can attain happiness, purity and wisdom (Foucault 1988), but both prisoners and school children remain free to resist the power exerted on them through various tactics. Thus, power relations do not render children powerless (Gallagher 2008a, 2008b).

Extending governmentality to the built environment, various exertions of power from many faceless sources have contributed to the complex systems of infrastructure, architecture, and urban design we experience today. These amalgamations of many instances of power over time lead to a relatively fixed structure that influences the decisions that *can* be made in the present. Viewing space through governmentality allows an understanding of how space itself is a technology of power that unconsciously produces a variety of wider effects. For instance, playgrounds began as an adult construct of how children should play and behave, and where they should be (Cunningham and Jones 1999, Gagen 2000, Hart 2002, Davey and Lundy 2011). However, over time both planners and non-planners have come to see them as the primary place of play. Concomitantly, streets have become places for transport – not for play – and parents may be reluctant for children to travel alone in areas with high volumes of traffic (Valentine and McKendrick 1998, Barker 2003, Mitchell et al. 2007).

HETEROTOPIA

To transpose governmentality from social relations to spatial form requires a spatial perspective that can situate children as political actors in their everyday lives (Philo and Smith 2003, Kallio 2007, Skelton 2010). I therefore frame children's participation in place in Foucault's (1986) heterotopia. The word Heterotopia can be broken down to its constituent parts – 'Hetero' meaning 'other', and 'topia' meaning space – to see that a heterotopia refers literally to a space of difference. This theory explains how features of place have come to be and how they can become 'other'. I extend it to include how children understand and transform space through their actions as competent social agents (Hart 1979, Ward 1990).

Johnson (2006) explains that heterotopia 'contains a sense of both space and place that is not conveyed by the word "site"'. These places are spaces between the private and public sphere where culture and leisure occur. Heterotopias can exist anywhere, completely hidden from others or deliberately cultivated for a shared experience. Dehaene and Cauter (2008) describe them as the places of play, where fantasy exists alongside reality. They use the example of a theatre, which is a building with a stage and seating, but once a performance begins actors reimagine it into whatever space they require to tell a story. An alternative frame is a boat: this is both static and moving, with the physical space constant, but the environment changing. It is therefore 'a place without a place' (Foucault 1986, p. 26).

Heterotopia contends that there is more to place than the physical infrastructure. This leads Foucault to talk of heterotopia as 'actually existing utopia' (Johnson 2006), distinguishing his ideas from Marxist spatial theorists who place a great emphasis on revolutionising space (c.f. Lefebvre 2011). Heterotopia is about understanding how people live in the present, realising that a single place simultaneously contains 'several sites that are in themselves incompatible' (Foucault 1986, p. 25). Varying interpretations have criticised the scarce development of the theory, its loose nature (Genocchio 1995, Soja 1996, Johnson 2013), or its synergies with Lefebvre's theories (Soja 1996). On the other hand, its looseness allows existing sites to be both the topic of analysis, and aid in the analysis (Johnson 2013). Sohn explains:

> Treating all spaces and human groups that deviate from the established order as potentially subversive, challenging and resistant formations, and hence reading into them all sorts of positive, utopian transformative powers endowed by their liminality, is to miss an essential point of Foucault's heterotopia: as an ambivalent formulation meant to destabilize discourse and language, as a rather obscure conception endowed with negativity, defying clarity, logic and order.

> (2008, p. 48)

I thus use heterotopia to explore the playful (rather than confrontational) position that children in middle childhood have with their environments.

CHILDREN, POWER, AND HETEROTOPIA

If heterotopias are the spaces of play, where the inner workings of the mind meet an existing place, then children have a unique predisposition to access them. Children's play often includes a complex mix of real and imagined, and the play space can reflect and contest this simultaneously (Russell 2013). Through play, children can break from the networks of power that govern their everyday lives, and heterotopias (knowingly or not) become sites of resistance for children to the established adult order (McNamee 2000). For instance, both Ward (1990) and Lester (2014) emphasise the anarchic nature of childhood play. However, taking this back to the logic of governmentality, dominant ideas about children and planning can lead to places that eclipse potential heterotopias. Emphasis on childhood spaces being only structured and segregated is problematic, as many studies show that while parks and playgrounds are often important in children's lives, they are rarely their most important or favourite spaces to play, and children frequently report preferring less structured activities (Valentine and McKendrick 1998, Aitken 2000, Jones and Barker 2000, Valentine 2004, McKendrick 2007, Castonguay and Jutras 2009).

Without recognition that children have environmental needs beyond playgrounds, parks, and schools, they cannot participate equally in public space (Dickerson 2013); vice versa, with children in public space symbolising disorderly conduct, they cannot be taken seriously in public and political debate (Kulynych 2001). A range of social and physical issues hamper the freedom children are given to play outside, particularly by themselves. The most prominent is motor traffic which has led to a dramatic decline in children's independent mobility in the UK across the last two generations (Shaw et al. 2015). Parents mediate this most directly, but the structure of the built environment interacts with social issues and pressure to determine where parents allow children to go. As children become less visible in the public sphere and cultural norms emphasise structure and education over freedom and participation, it becomes ever-easier to dismiss children's environmental needs. This relationship between children's independence and the licenses granted them by adults lead Mikkelsen and Christensen (2009) and Nansen et al. (2015) to view children's mobility as interdependent; a complex assemblage of social, environmental, and economic issues.

To extend heterotopia, Dehaene and Cauter consider how it relates to the management of space:

> We could venture a hypothesis that many heterotopias were translated from event into building, from time to space, from transient moment to the permanence of a place, and that this translation occurred in some cases as a structural reaction to a crisis.
>
> (2008, p. 92)

For example, the UK planning system evolved from a need to manage increasingly complex demands on space in towns and cities. Rapid urbanisation birthed a modern economy that, to continue growing, required a structured land-use approach. With increasing density came a crisis in the spread of disease and poor living conditions at the end of the nineteenth century, and further crises post First and Second World Wars led to a further need for state intervention in spatial organisation. One concern for planners was idle children hanging around on city streets, and with schooling becoming compulsory, they needed to allocate more schools and find ways to organise children outside of school hours (Gillespie 2013). The result of an evolving, ever more complex society is that planners have increasingly moved to designate land use for specific purposes, and this can limit the adaptability of space to a range of other uses and users. Combining governmentality with heterotopia to explore the evolution of planning and place thus helps explain why children's movements have been particularly limited since the 1990s (Shaw et al. 2013).

To link children's use of space with land use planning, Kyttä's (2004) Field of Action Theory is helpful. In this model, the outdoor environment provides a range of potential affordances for children, in which lie three 'fields of action'. On one side, the 'field of promoted action' contains environmental exploration encouraged by adults. On the other side, the 'field of constrained action' contains explorations adults limit. For adults, these lie at opposite ends of what a child should and should not do. In the middle lies the 'field of free action', in which a child freely chooses their activities. This overlaps with the other fields, but also sits within its own sphere of 'other' activities they undertake without adult intervention. The child seeks to increase the time they spend in the field of free action, and here they experience the actualised affordances of a given environment. The challenge in practice is to increase the size of the 'field of free action' (without inadvertently turning it into a 'field of promoted action'), and reduce the 'field of constrained action'. Similarly, Wood (2017) provides a framework that shows child friendly environments lie at the intersection of supportive time, space, and attitudes from all actors involved in mediating space and access to it.

Delving further into heterotopia, Dehaene and Cauter describe a type of person that is

> hated and adored, expelled and embraced by the polis; always ambiguously hosted as representatives of otherness, of 'the rest'. That is: the sacred, the taboo, the eccentric, the abnormal, the monstrous, the secret, the extraordinary, the grandiose, the genius, the irrational, the transgressive, the frivolous or simply the aimless.
>
> (2008, p. 96)

These people seek heterotopia in all space, and are described by the authors as artists, wandering philosophers, religious leaders, and other kinds of eccentric 'others'. While they do not mention children, the description strongly parallels their ambivalent treatment in wider society (c.f. Cahill 1990), and their propensity to seek playful experiences in any place (Lester 2014, Ward 1990). This corresponds with Russell and Lester's (2013) theory that children do not 'play' in a discrete, definable way, but 'wayfare' through space. Arguably, the decline in children playing in the street was motivated by children's ability to reimagine organised space into their own imagination, and this became inconsistent with modern demands for formal organisation. It is now time for a crisis in the interdependent mobility of children to spur a more inclusive land use planning. To begin elucidating what is required, I now turn to a case study of children's participation in place.

The case study is a section of a Scottish city which covers 14km² and includes 93% of the homes of primary-school children who took part in the participatory element of this project. This mostly residential area is 3km from the city centre and includes a wide range of land uses – most notably a zoo, two sports stadiums, a prison, a golf course, and a large local park which was facing restoration at the start of the project. It contains a range of architectural styles and building types, built across a range of periods. For instance, traditional Scottish tenements make up much of the housing stock in the southern areas, but 1930s council houses make up a significant portion of the homes further west, with larger houses in the northern neighbourhoods. The area is socio-economically mixed and more ethnically diverse than the city average. Importantly, it also contains three A-roads that experience heavy traffic volumes and connect the case study with another major population centre.

The empirical evidence I present here was gathered as part of a wider research project on children's rights and the Scottish town planning system (Wood 2016). I employed a Critical Ethnographic Participatory Action Research approach consisting of a range of classroom sessions conducted in a city location with primary school children between the ages of 9 and 11 (n=60). This methodology allowed me to explore the ethics of the built environment, instances of power exertion and domination entailed by a largely static environment, and the actors that impose, negotiate, and instigate incremental change upon it (c.f. Wood 2016).

The title and basis of each data collection session with child participants is as follows:

1. *Your Local Area*
   Finding key locations on an Ordnance Survey map and individually annotating their own maps with thoughts about the area.

2. *Journey to School*
   Describing their routes to school through writing or drawing and letting me know the mode of transport they take. Some pupils also drew or wrote about their ideal route to school.

3. *What do you think of the park?*
   Completing sheets about what they like, dislike, want to stay the same, and want to change about the park (a child-friendly SWOT analysis), and then writing or drawing about improvements to make.

4. *The Park Proposals*
   Working in groups to comment on working proposals for the park, and what they would add or change, before producing a list of events they would like to see happen in the park.

5. *The Park Masterplan*
   Individually annotating a copy of the Masterplan with stickers and post-it notes to explain their views on it.

6. *Submission of the park funding bid and Interdependent Mobility*
   Discussing the process after this point in terms of the park and my research.
   Completing a worksheet about Interdependent Mobility.

Sessions took place from September 2014 to November 2015 and each began with feedback and discussion of the previous exercise and progress on the park restoration design and funding status. I was deliberately as flexible as possible in allowing the participants to write or draw their views, with ideas developing through an iterative approach with heavy child involvement. Along with outputs produced directly by the children, I kept a research diary and made notes of class discussions throughout.

In the discussion that follows, I use textual and spatial theoretical analysis conducted by myself (a trained planner) using the outputs of the children's work, photography, and lived experience as a local resident of five years. All names ascribed to children in this chapter are pseudonyms. The exploration is further peppered by insights from qualitative interviews conducted with three professionals related to the area, two third sector organisations focusing on children's play in Scotland and Wales, and two UK academics who study children's play in the environment. Finally, I attended a 'Friends Group' of the park throughout the research both as an interested member of the local community and to enhance links between the children's views and the restoration process.

The case study area has been built at various times and contains many former industrial sites. It was not planned with a coherent masterplan, and the range of decisions made by different people that impact on the built environment have come to form it, leading to instances of unintentionally unwelcome design. Industrial sites surrounded by high fences, narrow pavements, and busy roads allow cars to drive fast and dominate the streetscape which has a clear effect, most prominently around the local park. All pedestrians may feel unwelcome in this environment, but children may feel further dominated by a fence that narrows the pavement and allows only occasional access points to the park. This fence blocks access to the 'community woodland', advertised by a sign placed directly behind the fence, and Figure 10.1 shows how one of the child participants suggests replacing fences around the park with more welcoming versions that fulfil the same purpose. These subtle planning and non-planning decisions that influence the built environment can combine to create places that are unfriendly to children.

Further analysing the area from a planner's perspective, the allocation of space for certain uses and buildings may dominate other interests. For instance, some restrictions for children's use of space come to light by examining the case study through GIS maps. It includes a large park, but also a golf course which is double the size (0.4x0.2km²). The area contains 16 public parks in total that together account for slightly more space than the golf course (3.91% compared with 3.71%). However, out of eight playing fields, only two are publicly accessible (City Council 2009,

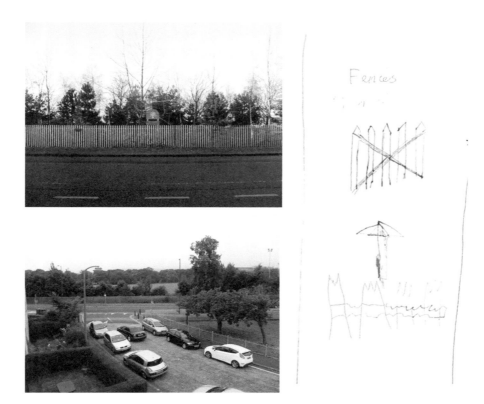

FIGURE 10.1 The local park surrounded by a high fence, and fences are common around green areas in this area of the city. On the right Hassan shows his dislike of the fences and suggests a lower alternative
Source: the author

Sandison 2012). It is also well-provided with formal sports facilities and areas for watching professional sport, but these are not free to use. Many boys in this study complained on multiple occasions of the entrance fees for the AstroTurf at the local sports complex. This fits with narratives of the privatisation of childhood space, which is separating the experience of children from more and less affluent families (McKendrick et al. 2000, Holloway 2014, Holloway and Pimlott-Wilson 2014). This broad, stylistic, adult-centred view sets the stage for the case study but only hints at the level of child-friendliness. I now move to explore some of the children's views of the area and relate this to the conception of space expounded in Heterotopia.

THE JOURNEY TO SCHOOL

Most interesting about children's experiences of the journey to school is that those driven were most likely to draw their route as a map, with landmarks picked out along the way. Conversely, the most common approach overall was

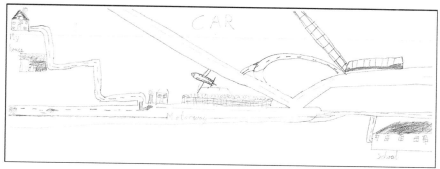

Hassan gets driven around 12.5km to school

Dylan runs the whole 1km to school and does not notice anything

Isabel walks about 1.1km to school and draws a very detailed explanation of what she sees

FIGURE 10.2 Different ways children represented their journeys to school
Source: the author

for the children to either write a passage about their journey (with or without illustrations) or to produce a labelled illustration of where they go, and what they see, hear and smell. Figure 10.2 shows this range of approaches and suggests car travel can divorce children from environmental experiences and, like the metaphor of the boat in Foucault's (1986) heterotopia, the car becomes its own 'place without a place', constantly moving but never stable. Thus, children remember well-established landmarks along the way, or the names of roads, but do not develop the experiential relationship of children who walk (Cele 2006). In contrast, Joshi et al. (1999) suggest that mode of travel to school has little effect on children's spatial perceptions, but the act of accompaniment by an adult can increase their knowledge of landmarks, and predispose them to a more technical (or adult) understanding of place.

The children who walked were better able to describe the sights and smells they noticed along the way. As the children live at varying distances, and had different opinions, some provided more detail than others. Figure 10.2 shows how Isabel demonstrated a close connection with her walking environment, remembering the details of a friend's home she passes, the relationship she has with the School Crossing Patrol Officer, and details such as a sign for a missing pet on the lamppost. On the other hand, Dylan had little to say about his route. Interestingly, participants that scooted to school on most days appeared to have a similar attachment to place as the children who walk. The way the children expressed themselves in this exercise suggests many features of the built environment, travel mode, and individual personality that affect how a walking or scooting child represents their journey. These came through less strongly for children that were driven.

Differences in perception based on travel mode are important in understanding children's relationship with place. However, a commonality across all the children was a general dislike of cars and their effects. In discussions, they were mostly negative about being driven to school. While some studies suggest this routine is a positive way for parents to spend time with their children (Granville et al. 2002), for these pupils, being driven meant getting up earlier, long, boring waits in traffic, and a lack of interaction with friends. For children who walk, scoot, or get the bus to school, traffic and the associated noise, smells, and inconvenience were the most commented on negative aspect of their journeys. This suggests both being in a car and being close to cars affects the cultivation of children's heterotopias – disrupting their ability to perceive the environment in ways that suit their needs and preferences; those within are deprived of sensory experiences and social connections, while those outside smell, see and navigate the impact of cars on their environment. This breaks the connection between internal enjoyment of space, and external pressures such as keeping safe. Moreover, adults driving children to school increases the number of cars on the road, with UK government estimates suggesting one in five cars at rush hour is transporting a child/children (House of Commons Education and Skills Select and Committee 2004).

INTERDEPENDENT MOBILITY

Table 10.1 shows the most common places the children reported being permitted to go by themselves. These show all places, broadly grouped into types, that more than three children included in their interdependent mobility exercise. Though most children can go to nearby shops by themselves, there is limited consensus on the number of places they can go without accompaniment of an adult. This means some children have significantly more freedom than others. Indeed, the worksheet asked where they could go outside with adults, and the most common answer was 'anywhere' or 'everywhere'. This suggests the children's mobility was very adult-dependent.

In several of the worksheets, the theme of safety was strongly evident:

- Alex talked of the dangers of getting lost, even when accompanied by an adult;
- Max detailed that he could cross quiet streets alone or use traffic lights, but only cross busy roads with an adult;
- Ryan detailed how his independence was dependent on whether an adult could see him from a window. He also reported some independence to walk around the district where he lives and stressed that he could go anywhere with a '<u>trusted</u>' adult (Ryan's emphasis).

TABLE 10.1 Proportion of children who were able to go to different places by themselves (Source: the author)

In/Interdependent Mobility Exercise – Where can you go by yourself?					
	School	A friend or relative's house	Close by places (such as the street or very local green space)	Close by shops	Local parks
% of children	56%	36%	32%	68%	22%

An increase in safety concerns fits with trends in previous research about parental fears and children's own concerns (Valentine 1997, Valentine and McKendrick 1998, Harden 2000, Backett-Milburn 2004, Veitch et al. 2006). Indeed, some members of the local park's Friends Group expressed concern over the safety of younger children alone in the park, citing risks such as paedophilia as a reason to ensure good surveillance.

If children's permission to walk around the local area is restricted, then other transport may provide them greater freedom. However, only a few children reported they were allowed to use public transport by themselves or with friends. Indeed, for those who could, the permission was largely conditional, such as visiting a relative, or accessing a shopping centre. This fits the trend identified by Shaw et al. (2015) that only by age 14 were the majority of children across their international comparison allowed (by their parents) to use local buses. Combining the work of Hillman et al. (1990) and O'Brien et al. (2000) shows the percentage of children age 10–11 allowed to use buses alone saw the most dramatic decline in the period from 1971 to 2000. This reluctance, along with the potential costs for some parents, is one of the greatest limitations for children to access the range of facilities they might wish to use. The technologies of power used to exert control over children's movements become embedded in social and spatial practice. In turn, children begin to internalise the logic of their experience to create technologies of the self that enable them to navigate societal expectations by governing their own behaviours.

THE LOCAL PARK AS A HETEROTOPIA OF COMPENSATION

Building on his initial conjecture of heterotopia, Foucault (1986) categorised some heterotopias as particular land uses. Heterotopias of Compensation are his term for land uses that attempt to fix a problem in society by simplifying and rendering it manageable (Johnson 2006). They provide a compensatory space for 'abnormal' things that cannot be contained within dominant structures. Playgrounds are a good example – compensating for the non-child focus of planning by assigning a space where children can safely be children. They provide the 'perfect' place for play, creating segregation from the non-child-friendly environment, and solving the 'problem' children represent.

Though playgrounds play some role in children's lives, most important for the planning system to recognise is that, when asked, children often do not cite playgrounds among their favourite places (Cunningham and Jones 1999). Indeed:

> just because there's a state of the art playground, you might find the children prefer to play in the old run-down one because dogs are allowed in and they can get in with their bikes. Yes, it might be covered in glass and needles, but that's where they'll go and hang out, and not where they are 'supposed' to play, or sign-posted to play.
>
> (Officer, play organisation)

Drawing on children's own views of the local playground, while many expressed a liking for aspects of it, most had mixed views and suggested improvements often related to an opinion that it only suits younger children. The local authority considers it to be 'very good' in their 'Play Area Action Plan', and suitable for 'Toddlers/Juniors/Seniors'.

This is an example of disconnect between how children view and use space, and what professional adults wish or expect.

Playgrounds provide for a very specific form of heterotopia of compensation and 'field of promoted action' (Kyttä 2004), but parks in general also serve this purpose by offering a break in urban form. Initially developed as spaces for the wealthy to enjoy nature, parks transformed over time into places for the working classes to find relief from the stresses of everyday life (Certoma 2015). Today, parks are targeted at all types of people, with the local park here classed as a 'premier park' by the local authority, and therefore a potential destination from across the city. An officer involved in the park restoration commented in interview:

> People got expectations of how other people should act in a park, and what's acceptable and what's not … but people can come into the park and pretty much do what they like… [This makes them] wonderful spaces actually.

The children agreed with this notion, with 33 out of 35 children who mentioned it on their maps listing it a 'liked' space, and displayed enthusiasm in expressing how it should change in the future. The park, along with the river, was described by the children as an important place to experience nature, which suggests the great value parks can have for children's play, and general health and wellbeing (Bird 2007, Hiscock and Mitchell 2011, Parkes et al. 2012).

Conversely, in Foucault's logic, parks can be places of social control (Certoma 2015), and the officer working on the park restoration ties up the idea that people can do what they want in a park, with the idea that parks are self-regulating. This can be positive as it makes a space for a variety of activities. However, one child – Harvey – reported instances where gardeners did not welcome his presence, and asked him to leave. Additionally, the park displays a sign that attempts to establish the rules of children's play. It states:

> Parks provide large open spaces for everyone to enjoy but some popular activities can cause problems.
> - Ball games: if there is no damage to the grass, no threat of damage to neighbouring properties and no threat of damage or injury to other people, then there's no problem.
> - Flying kites and operating model aeroplanes and boats: if there is no disturbance to wildlife and no threat of nuisance or injury to other people, then there's no problem.
> Do your bit by following the Park Management Rules.

These rules are arguably impossible to follow as there is always a risk that play could damage other people's property or cause subjective nuisance, yet similar risks apply to most human activity. Such instructions may lead to tighter restrictions on what adults permit children to do and constrain their 'field of free action' (Kyttä, 2004). In doing this, children may learn over time that their actions are not acceptable. Alternatively, they may resist rules, and face being labelled as disobedient and problematic.

When talking about the things they would like to see in the park, many children mentioned removing graffiti, making things more colourful, and introducing more plants and flowers. However, the needs that children have for public space, including both the park and wider area, can be at odds with not only how adults use it, but also how teenagers use it. Many children were concerned with anti-social behaviour, and this can both encourage children to mediate their own access to outdoor space, and adults to restrict their mobility (Harden 2000, Thomas et al. 2004, Prezza et al. 2005, Barclay and Tawil 2015). For instance, class discussions often turned to the 'bad things' the children have seen other people doing (such as being drunk on the street, drinking outside, and seeing or hearing about people committing crimes), and how graffiti, dog fouling, and litter affect them. Their perceptions confirm the reported fear children have of teenagers and adults who break social rules (Thomas et al. 2004). They frequently reported how they felt teenagers colonised areas such as the skatepark and expressed their disapproval of them acting in ways they deem morally wrong.

This tension between how some members of the community view the park and what others wish for it to be was also evident throughout Friends of Local Park meetings. Here, members of the local community often talked about how the behaviour of teenagers (particularly vandalism) has been a historic problem. This anti-social behaviour led to lengthy discussions and increasing involvement from the police in monitoring park activity. In fact, the local authority at the time of research was considering a youth dispersal order, which would mean youths in groups (two or more) would be required to disperse, or receive an antisocial behavioural order (Scotland and Scottish Executive 2004). This extreme step arguably stems from a lack of attention to teenagers' needs in public spaces, and the general lack of understanding and tolerance of how they act (Matthews et al. 1998, Elsley 2004). This suggests that parks, even in their aims towards inclusivity, are still subject to the norms and trends of wider society. In a similar way to playgrounds, they provide fertile ground for children to play, but the wishes of certain people can dominate in the shape of hidden social conventions (Kallio and Häkli 2011). As with the controls on children's mobility described in the preceding section, the discourses of social control found in the park encourage children to develop technologies of the self so that they act in ways adults see as most acceptable. It gives them freedom to participate in place, but not on their own terms.

The local park as a heterotopia of compensation highlights the difficulty of planning for the simultaneous needs of different groups. Perhaps seeing the park as a single and homogeneous heterotopia limits children and teenagers' ability to actualise 'fields of free action' (Kyttä, 2004). A multitude of heterotopias (both planned and unplanned) are sought by different users, and this leads to contestations of public space and the exertion of technologies of power such as signs and fences.

HETEROTOPIAS OF DEVIATION

Many of the children expressed intrigue for what Foucault (1986) terms 'Heterotopias of Deviation'. These are places that have been constructed to deal with a particular form of 'otherness' and are examples of where a social crisis has required a spatial response. This could be retirement homes or hospitals, but the places that captured the imagination of the children, were the asylum that used to exist in the local park and the local prison. These non-everyday spaces that the children frequently see, but cannot access, suggest a crossing of the real and the imaginary. As Johnson explains:

> The prison and asylum are open-ended, ambivalent and contradictory places, enclosures for both punishing and generating criminals, for both liberating and morally imprisoning the mad. They are the ideals full of fantasy, mirroring and at the same time inverting what is outside. Separate the moral intentions, the prison and the asylum become a source of fascination, a forbidden place of secret pleasures.

> (2006, p. 85)

The fascination with the prison could be an attempt by children to transcend some of the restrictions on their everyday lives, finding a 'field of free action' within a 'field of constrained action' (Kyttä, 2004). While they mostly have little direct contact with it, the prison holds symbolic meaning.

Cele (2006) found children to be intrigued by fear and 'otherness', and the forbidden element of a prison can evoke an air of mystery that may excite passers-by. The children talked about liking to walk near the prison, and one boy told me a story about how his sister had once climbed over the prison wall. To the children, a prison could be a good place, for they allow the more harmonious functioning of society by keeping bad people away, but they can also be bad spaces for the same reason. It represented intriguing possibilities for Harvey, who stated, 'I put a heart on the prison because I want to see someone being tasered', but to Kyle, the prison spurred negative emotions as 'my dad has been there before and I didnae get to see him only at the weekends' [sic]. This also shows that while the prison exists to maintain the proper functioning of society, it has its own impact on its surroundings and creates a multitude of other heterotopias for those on the outside. No matter the individual reasons for the fascination, the prison sparked wild discussions among the children and was mentioned by ten participants (six liked it, three disliked it, and one thought it was OK) on their maps.

The planning system considers prisons a bad neighbourhood development, with planners assuming people do not want to live near them. Reflecting this, the large site around the prison lay undeveloped until very recently. However, in some of the children's views it *can* be positive to live nearby. In a similar vein, Foucault views cemeteries as particularly interesting 'heterochronias' (Johnson 2006), or a discontinuity in time, because they are a place straddling the living and the dead. The children frequently flagged cemeteries as liked or disliked, often liked because they are peaceful places where they could visit relatives. However, for Joshua, they were a scary place due to a recent death in the family, and this sense of loss dominated his map.

The children's accounts of their walk to school provide further evidence of their propensity for mystery and the unknown. For instance, Callum detailed how his walk to school involved passing an area where he sees people sleeping rough. Having lived close to this area for years, I was unaware that rough sleepers used this grassy bank between an industrial site and cycle path. Indeed, I do not know if this is common knowledge to the people living by the path. This is one of the places forgotten by adults, but often flagged by the children; like land around the prison, an area disregarded by developers or public investment and therefore left unregulated. If these areas are too neglected or impenetrable, children may not be able to use them for their play and recreation, or to cross by foot to access other spaces. Yet, they may also pose a range of scary or interesting possibilities to expand children's 'field of free action', by forming private and intriguing heterotopias. In the case of the abandoned grassy bank, it contrasts with the adjacent site to the west of well-maintained and exclusive bowling greens that are a 'field of constrained action' for children (Kyttä, 2004).

PLANNING FOR HETEROTOPIA

Adults (planners in particular) seek to designate heterotopia to fix it temporally and spatially so it can be categorised and managed. This leads to the allocation of parks and playgrounds, but not to playful, engaging, and pedestrian-friendly environments (Dehaene and Cauter 2008). However, if adults view children as heterotopians, and play as a natural element of their pursuit, then the value of child-friendly environments and how adults can help cultivate them becomes clearer. Additionally, cognisance that undesignated spaces are key for children's 'field of free action' (Kyttä, 2004) must be borne in mind to avoid the pitfall of further explicit designation of play space. In other words:

> It's this dilemma about thinking that adults can provide play. They can't. You know, even putting in a playground doesn't necessarily mean kids will play there.
>
> (Play Academic)

What planners can do is ensure space is available and welcoming for children to create their own heterotopias. This would require a planning approach that understands the variety of play affordances that any given environment can provide, without seeking simply to widen the 'field of promoted action' (Kyttä 2004). For instance, when a child is presented with a doll to play with, the most likely form their play will take is to treat the doll like a baby or a small child. However, when a child is presented with a rock, they may imagine that object into any variety of potential play objects. In a similar vein, the built environment can provide standardised play equipment that a child can use for a limited number of purposes. However, open space, or the built environment as a whole can also provide a wide range of potential play experiences that cannot be envisaged by adults beforehand (Ward 1990, Lester 2014). Attention to the idea of heterotopia and the child-friendly city can help illuminate the potential of urban environments for children, but this is currently incompatible with the formalised approach of planning. One key way to do this is to combine direct participation of children with existing knowledge and theory of how to plan with children in mind. Planners can find solace in the inherent capabilities of children to develop their own play and recreation opportunities, provided that space is left for more informal practices, and that there are no undue restrictions to children's access. In planning for children's participation in place, it is about facilitation and not dictation.

CONCLUSION

This chapter has reviewed evidence of how a group of primary-school children view their local area. Using Foucault's theory of heterotopia, it has helped to position the playful demeanour of children within the built environment and elucidated how planning has often worked to establish spatially and temporally fixed heterotopias that appeal to a more ordered, adult understanding of play and leisure. Conversely, children have less need for an ordered and fixed environment and seek to create 'fields of free action' (Kyttä, 2004) within a planned and ordered social and spatial structure. Yet, without attention to the restrictions children face, the prevailing way of doing planning dominates their interests and encourages children to form technologies of self so they either restrict their own participation in place, or resist and face punitive responses. Heterotopia suggests planners should find ways to allow for a variety of experiences and perceptions of space, at any given time.

Of note is that heterotopia shows how much of space afforded to children is to compensate for environments that are otherwise relatively hostile. Yet, in so doing planners and other environmental professionals are pre-determining the abilities of children and allowing the perpetuation of unhelpful practices in the remaining space. This continues to contribute to a lack of representation of children in the public sphere. Interestingly, the concept of Heterotopias of Deviation also highlights the curiosity that children have for their environments and wish to pursue playful opportunities within 'field of constrained action' (Kyttä, 2004). While adult standards have determined what is and is not a good land use in a specific area, children often have different, more fluid views that could be channelled in planning to present an alternative opinion.

Ultimately, this exploration brings to light that children's participation in place is not only direct participation in the data-gathering and decisions planners and other built environment professionals make, but also in having a right to use the public sphere in their own playful way (Articles 15 and 31 of the UNCRC). Excessive structure and adherence to demands to make adults' lives ever more convenient are eroding children's rights in the environment, but can be reversed if we learn to appreciate how children use space and weave this into wider planning strategies and design work. The findings and recommendations of this article set out a conception for a more child-friendly practice.

REFERENCES

Aitken, S. (2000) 'Play, rights and borders: Gender-bound parents and the social construction of childhood', in Valentine, G. and Holloway, S. L. (eds) *Children's geographies: Playing, living, learning*. London; New York: Routledge, pp. 119–138.
Backett-Milburn, K. (2004) 'How children and their families construct and negotiate risk, safety and danger', *Childhood*, **11**(4), pp. 429–447.
Barclay, M. and Tawil, B. (2015) 'Assessing play sufficiency in Wrexham, Wales', *Journal of Playwork Practice*, **2**(2), pp. 191–199.
Barker, J. (2003) 'Passengers or political actors? Children's participation in transport policy and the micro political geographies of the family', *Space and Polity*, **7**(2), pp. 135–151.
Bird, W. (2007) Natural thinking: Investigating the links between the natural environment, biodiversity and mental health. The RSPB. Available at: www.rspb.org.uk/Images/naturalthinking_tcm9-161856.pdf.
Bryman, A. (2012) *Social research methods*. 4th ed. Oxford; New York: Oxford University Press.
Cahill, S. (1990). 'Childhood and public life: Reaffirming biographical divisions', *Social Problems*, **37**(3), pp. 390–402.
Castonguay, G. and Jutras, S. (2009) 'Children's appreciation of outdoor places in a poor neighborhood', *Journal of Environmental Psychology*, **29**, pp. 101–109.
Cele, S. (2006) Communicating place: Methods for understanding children's experience of place. PhD Thesis, Stockholm University.
Certoma, C. (2015) 'Expanding the "dark side of planning": Governmentality and biopolitics in urban garden planning', *Planning Theory*, **14**(1), pp. 23–43.
City Council (2009) *Open space audit*. [city anonymised]
Cunningham, C. and Jones, M. (1999) 'The playground: A confession of failure?', *Built Environment*, **25**(1), pp. 11–17.

Davey, C. and Lundy, L. (2011) 'Towards greater recognition of the right to play: An analysis of Article 31 of the UNCRC', *Children and Society*, **25**(1), pp. 3–14.

Dehaene, M. and Cauter, L. de (2008) 'The space of play: Towards a general theory of heterotopia', in Dehaene, M. and Cauter, L. de (eds) *Heterotopia and the city: Public space in a postcivil society*. London; New York: Routledge, pp. 87–102.

Dickerson, M. (2013) 'Solvitur ambulando: It is solved by walking', *Journal of Applied Research on Children: Informing Policy for Children at Risk*, **4**(2), pp. 1–9.

Elsley, S. (2004) 'Children's experience of public space', *Children and Society*, **18**(2), pp. 155–164.

Foucault, M. (1977) *Discipline and punish: The birth of the prison*. London: Allen Lane.

Foucault, M. (1980) *Power/knowledge: Selected interviews and other writings, 1972–1977* edited by C. Gordon. Brighton: Harvester.

Foucault, M. (1986) '"Des espaces autres" (Of other spaces: Utopias and heterotopias)', translated by J. Miskowiec, *Diacritics*, **16**(1), pp. 22–27.

Foucault, M. (1988) 'Technologies of the self', in Martin, L. H., Gutman, H., and Hutton, P. H. (eds) *Technologies of the self: A seminar with Michel Foucault*. Amherst: University of Massachusetts Press.

Foucault, M. (2008) *The birth of biopolitics: Lectures at the Collège de France, 1978–79*, translated by G. Burchell. Basingstoke [England]; New York: Palgrave Macmillan.

Gagen, E. A. (2000) 'An example to us all: child development and identity construction in early 20th-century playgrounds', *Environment and Planning A*, **32**(4), pp. 599–616.

Gallagher, M. (2004) Producing the schooled subject: Techniques of power in a primary school classroom. PhD Thesis, University of Edinburgh.

Gallagher, M. (2008a) 'Foucault, power and participation', *The International Journal of Children's Rights*, **16**(3), pp. 395–406.

Gallagher, M. (2008b) '"Power is not an evil": Rethinking power in participatory methods', *Children's Geographies*, **6**(2), pp. 137–150.

Genocchio, B. (1995) 'Discourse, discontinuity, difference: The question of other spaces', in Watson, S. and Gibson, K. (eds) *Postmodern cities and spaces*. Oxford, UK; Cambridge, Mass.: Blackwell, pp. 35–46.

Gillespie, J. (2013) 'Being and becoming: Writing children into planning theory', *Planning Theory*, **12**(1), pp. 64–80.

Granville, S. et al. (2002) *Why do parents drive their children to school?* Edinburgh: Scottish Executive.

Harden, J. (2000) 'There's no place like home: The public/private distinction in children's theorizing of risk and safety', *Childhood*, **7**(1), pp. 43–59.

Hart, R. (1979) *Children's experience of place*. New York: Irvington Publishers.

Hart, R. (2002) 'Containing children: Some lessons on planning for play from New York City', *Environment and Urbanization*, **14**(2), pp. 135–148.

Hillman, M., Adams, J. and Whitelegg, J. (1990) *One false move…: A study of children's independent mobility*. London: PSI.

Hiscock, R. and Mitchell, R. (2011) 'What is needed to deliver places that provide good health to children?' Review for EDPHIS. www.edphis.org.uk/Report_on_Place_and_Children.pdf (Accessed 19 January 2016).

Holloway, S. L. (2014) 'Changing children's geographies', *Children's Geographies*, **12**(4), pp. 377–392.

Holloway, S. L. and Pimlott-Wilson, H. (2014) 'Enriching children, institutionalizing Childhood? Geographies of play, extracurricular activities, and parenting in England', *Annals of the Association of American Geographers*, **104**(3), pp. 613–627.

House of Commons Education and Skills Select and Committee (2004) *The Draft School Transport Bill. This Report of Session 2003–4*. London: UK Parliament.

Johnson, P. (2006) 'Unravelling Foucault's "different spaces"', *History of the Human Sciences*, **19**(4), pp. 75–90.

Johnson, P. (2013) 'The geographies of heterotopia', *Geography Compass*, **7**(11), pp. 790–803.

Jones, O. and Barker, J. (2000) 'Melting geography: Purity, disorder, childhood and space', in Valentine, G. and Holloway, S. L. (eds) *Children's geographies: Playing, living, learning*. London; New York: Routledge, pp. 28–47.

Joshi, M. S., Maclean, M. and Carter, W. (1999) 'Children's journey to school: Spatial skills, knowledge and perceptions of the environment', *British Journal of Developmental Psychology*, **17**(1), pp. 125–139.

Kallio, K. P. (2007) 'Performative bodies, tactical agents and political selves: Rethinking the political geographies of childhood', *Space and Polity*, **11**(2), pp. 121–136.

Kallio, K. P. and Häkli, J. (2011) 'Young people's voiceless politics in the struggle over urban space', *GeoJournal*, **76**(1), pp. 63–75.

Kulynych, J. (2001) 'No playing in the public sphere: Democratic theory and the exclusion of children', *Social Theory and Practice*, **27**(2), pp. 231–264.

Kyttä, M. (2003) Children in outdoor contexts: Affordances and independent mobility in the assessment of environmental child friendliness. PhD Thesis, Helsinki University of Technology, Centre for Urban and Regional Studies.

Kyttä, M. (2004) 'The extent of children's independent mobility and the number of actualized affordances as criteria for child-friendly environments', *Journal of Environmental Psychology*, **24**(2), pp. 179–198.

Lefebvre, H. (2011) *The production of space*. Malden, Mass.: Blackwell.

Lester, S. (2014) 'Play as protest: Clandestine moments of disturbance and hope', in Burke, C. and Jones, K. (eds) *Education, childhood and anarchism: Talking Colin Ward*. London: Routledge, pp. 198–209.

Matthews, H., Limb, M. and Percy-Smith, B. (1998) 'Changing worlds: The microgeographies of young teenagers', *Tijdschrift voor Economische en Sociale Geografie*, **89**(2), pp. 193–202.

Mckee, K. (2009) 'Post-Foucauldian governmentality: What does it offer critical social policy analysis?', *Critical Social Policy*, **29**(3), pp. 465–486.

McKendrick, J. (2007) 'Making space for play in European cities', in *Expert Address to Working Group 2 (Housing and Outdoor Activities) of the European City Network. Cities for Children Founding Forum*, 25 June, Stuttgart City Hall. Available at: www.citiesforchildren.de/fileadmin/media/PDF/WG2/McKendrick_WG2-1.pdf.

McKendrick, J., Bradford, M. and Fielder, A. (2000) 'Kid customer?: Commercialization of playspace and the commodification of childhood', *Childhood*, **7**(3), pp. 295–314.

McNamee, S. (2000) 'Foucault's heterotopia and children's everyday lives', *Childhood*, **7**(4), pp. 479–492.

Mikkelsen, M.R. and Christensen, P. (2009). 'Is children's independent mobility really independent? A study of children's mobility combining ethnography and GPS/mobile phone technologies, *Mobilities*, **4**(1), pp. 37–58.

Mitchell, H., Kearns, R. A. and Collins, D. C. A. (2007) 'Nuances of neighbourhood: Children's perceptions of the space between home and school in Auckland, New Zealand', *Geoforum*, **38**(4), pp. 614–627.

Nansen, B., Gibbs, L., MacDougall, C., Vetere, F., Ross, N.J., and McKendrick, J., (2015) 'Children's interdependent mobility: Compositions, collaborations and compromises', *Children's Geographies*, **13**(4), pp. 467–481.

O'Brien, M. *et al.* (2000) 'Children's independent spatial mobility in the urban public realm', *Childhood*, **7**(3), pp. 257–277.

Parkes, A. *et al.* (2012) 'Growing up in Scotland overweight, obesity and activity'. Edinburgh: Scottish Government. Available at: www.nls.uk/scotgov/2012/9781780457437.pdf (Accessed: 9 June 2016).

Philo, C. and Smith, F. M. (2003) 'Guest editorial: Political geographies of children and young people', *Space and Polity*, **7**(2), pp. 99–115.

Prezza, M. *et al.* (2005) 'Parental perception of social risk and of positive potentiality of outdoor autonomy for children: The development of two instruments', *Journal of Environmental Psychology*, **25**(4), pp. 437–453.

Russell, W. (2013) 'Towards a spatial theory of playwork: What can Lefebvre offer as a response to playwork's inherent contradictions?', in Ryall, E., Russell, W., and MacLean, M. (eds) *The philosophy of play*. London: Routledge.

Russell, W. and Lester, S. (2013) *Leopard skin wellies, a top hat and a vacuum cleaner hose: An analysis of Wales' Play Sufficiency Assessment duty*. Cardiff: University of Gloucestershire and Play Wales.

Sandison, E. (2012) 'Edin Open Spaces ArcGIS'. online: ArcGIS. Available at: www.arcgis.com/home/item.html?id=96da899aeb2c4f6fa2d00fd003e6add7 (Accessed: 20 October 2014).

Scotland and Scottish Executive (2004) *Guidance on dispersal of groups: Antisocial Behaviour etc. (Scotland) Act 2004*. Edinburgh: Scottish Executive.

Shaw, B., Watson, B. , Frauendienst, B. , Redecker, A., and Jones, T. (2013) *Children's independent mobility: A comparative study in England and Germany (1971–2010)*. London: Policy Studies Institute.

Shaw, B. *et al.* (2015) *Children's independent mobility: An international comparison and recommendations for action*. London: Policy Studies Institute.

Skelton, T. (2010) 'Taking young people as political actors seriously: Opening the borders of political geography', *Area*, **42**(2), pp. 145–151.

Sohn, H. (2008) 'Heterotopia: anamnesis of a medical term', in Dehaene, M. and Cauter, L. de (eds) *Heterotopia and the city: Public space in a postcivil society*. London; New York: Routledge, pp. 43–49.

Soja, E. W. (1996) *Thirdspace: Journeys to Los Angeles and other real-and-imagined places*. Cambridge, Mass.: Blackwell.

Thomas, G. *et al.* (2004) *A child's place: Why environment matters to children: A Green Alliance*. London: Green Alliance.

UN (1989). *UN Convention on the Rights of the Child*. Geneva: United Nations.

UN (2016) *The new urban agenda. A/RES/71/256**. Quito: United Nations. Available at: http://habitat3.org/wp-content/uploads/NUA-English.pdf.

Valentine, G. (1997) ' "Oh yes I can." "Oh no you can't": Children and parents' understandings of kids' competence to negotiate public space safely', *Antipode*, **29**(1), pp. 65–89.

Valentine, G. (2004) *Public space and the culture of childhood*. Aldershot, Hants, England; Burlington, VT: Ashgate.

Valentine, G. and McKendrick, J. (1998) 'Critical review: Children's outdoor play: Exploring parental concerns about children's safety and the changing nature of childhood', *Geoforum*, **28**, pp. 219–235.

Veitch, J. *et al.* (2006) 'Where do children usually play? A qualitative study of parents' perceptions of influences on children's active free-play', *Health and Place*, **12**(4), pp. 383–393.

Ward, C. (1990) *The child in the city*. London: Bedford Square.

Wood, J. (2016). Space to participate: Children's rights and the Scottish town planning system. PhD Thesis. Heriot-Watt University, Edinburgh.

Wood, J., (2017). 'Planning for children's play: Exploring the "forgotten" right in Welsh and Scottish policy'. *Town Planning Review*, **88**(5), pp. 579–602.

11

THE CHAIR PROJECT: CO-CREATION THROUGH MATERIAL PLAY

Simon Beeson

In 1999, while teaching architecture at Edinburgh College of Art and the University of Dundee, I was invited by Dundee Public Arts Projects to participate in Art Links, a community-based engagement project coinciding with the opening of the new Dundee Contemporary Arts building. The ten artists selected were asked to work with local schools to introduce children to our studio practice. The project concluded with the 'Artery' exhibition at the McManus Galleries (24 October–12 December 1999), presenting work by all ten participating artists.

My studio practice is materially based, using a tactile, playful creative process of assembly, construction, and bricolage of found and made elements, to propose in scale models places of social gathering. As an architect and educator, my creative practice has always grounded abstract notions in material experience. In considering how to engage a wider, younger audience in this studio practice I focused on this idea of material configuration, but decided to limit the elements to address more directly different possibilities for places of social interaction.

The Chair Project narrows the selection of material forms to allow certain conversations and concepts to emerge, while encouraging creative interpretation and configuration (see Figure 11.1). The wooden chair form represents to us both the physical, material chair as equipment for sitting on, and the conceptual notion of the individual at rest. By congregating small-scale chairs together, ideas of gathering and social encounters can be considered. To emphasise this relationship of ideas to things the project was introduced with a short quotation from *Walden*, Henry David Thoreau's account of retreating to the woods of New Hampshire in 1845 (first published in 1854):

> I had three chairs in my house; one for solitude, two for friendship, three for society.
>
> (Thoreau 2006: 151)

Even in his humble minimal cabin he required three chairs to accommodate three different configurations of living. This statement grounds the construction of social situations in the physical location of chairs. This concept is easily grasped by all ages, with simple examples helping to illustrate the concept. For instance, the arrangement of pupils in a classroom into groups around a table immediately offers up an example of inclusion and exclusion within groups. Reconfiguring two chairs to face each other or turn their backs allows children to sit and experience the difference between face-to-face and back-to-back relative locations to each other. This idea of artefacts and placement opens up a wealth of possibilities to explore in the game-like chair and board project. The small-scale chairs were originally sized for small hands and convenient construction, using 12x12x12mm cubes and a 12x24x3mm back piece (approximately 1:35). Through the playful manipulation of these small chair-shaped wooden blocks on a 300x300x6mm MDF board, children were invited to explore the spatial relationship of the chairs and observe how these arrangements might open up a discussion of ideas of place and community.

The intention of the project was to introduce to the participants something of my own thinking and making practice. This playful methodology was additionally proposed as a tangible demonstration of the common exploratory nature of all creativity, whatever the medium or creative mode of practice.

FIGURE 11.1 The Chair Project, Dundee, 1999
Source: the author

In many ways this creative practice is not unlike kindergarten block play, and I have had a long fascination with the 'Froebel's Gifts'. In the 1830s Friedrich Froebel (1782–1852) first proposed his building block 'gifts' as part of the pre-school, pre-literate, structured educational system, an innovation that has transformed early years education ever since. Froebel's teaching practices followed his experience as a young teacher and time spent teaching with the Swiss pedagogue Johann Heinrich Pestalozzi (1746–1827). Pestalozzi had developed a teaching method structured primarily around observation and hands-on activities named *Anschauung* or 'object lessons', and through the medium of drawing, in part inspired by the protagonist of Jean-Jacques Rousseau's 1762 novel, *Émile*. Rousseau (1712–1778) proposed that children should be motivated to use their innate inquisitiveness and play-instinct to learn, rather than derive knowledge second-hand through books:

> Our first teachers of philosophy are our feet, our hands, and our eyes.
>
> (Rousseau 1892: 90 quoted by Brosterman 1997: 19)

After two years of working with Pestalozzi, Froebel returned to Germany, eventually publishing *Education of Man* in 1826 and then developing his theories through teaching. While Pestalozzi drew heavily on Rousseau, he and Froebel were also familiar with the ideas of play proposed by Friedrich Schiller (1759–1805) in his *Letters on the Aesthetic Education of Man* (Schiller 1793/2015). For Schiller, we live in a constant tension between a state of mind and matter, between the 'sensual instinct' of the material world and the 'formal instinct' of a rational mind (Schiller 1793/2015 Letter XII: 57). The 'instinct to play' seeks to reconcile these opposites and hold us in balance:

> For, to speak out once and for all, man only plays when in the full meaning of the word he is a man, and he is only completely a man when he plays.
>
> (Schiller 1793/2015 Letter XV: 73)

Schiller's sister-in-law, Karoline von Wolzogen, took her son to study at Pestalozzi's school in Yverdon, and she studied his methods herself (Silber 1960: 216). Although not explicitly referenced by Froebel (Brehony 2013: 61–62), the thoughts of Rousseau and Schiller suggest an education through a *playful* exploration of the world.

Froebel's most significant contribution to education was to introduce a series of tactical exercises, the Gifts and Occupations, designed during the 1830s as a playful, structured, constructive method of education, which could be introduced to children starting at the age of just two years. The activities encouraged a pre-literate method of engaging pupils in learning conceptual thinking through play, a method now firmly established (and debated) in early years education. In developing his Gifts, Froebel carefully considered the knowledge base he wished the child to gain. Play with the Gifts was to be guided by the teacher, usually with a grid engraved table or tablet to help organise the compositions. Alongside these activities, children engaged in physical exercises, song, nature observation, and gardening. In 1840 Froebel finally established his first Kindergarten, a name that reflects the notion of a child-centred garden of learning. (For a full account of the founding of Froebel's Kindergarten see Brosterman 1997, Brehony 2013).

It is with the Froebel Gifts, particularly the play blocks, that I wish to contextualise my own practice and the Chair Project. The first gift is simply crochet woollen balls of different colours, soft enough for a young child. Then Gift Two has three wooden geometrical forms; sphere, cube, and cylinder. These are introduced through a series of exercises of handling and observation. Gifts Three to Six develop from the one-inch cube to include rectangular and triangular prism blocks. This method of education led in turn to the wood block becoming an integral part of childhood education, including my own. Over the nineteenth century, play blocks developed from simple forms to include increasingly architectural blocks, such as arches and columns. As well as wood, other systems were developed, such as the Richter's *Ankor* blocks of compressed sand, which were specifically aimed at encouraging architectural and engineering learning, both compositionally and structurally.

In the twentieth century, even more specialised construction toys followed, introducing children to very particular methods of construction and re-configuration. Some derivatives of the Gifts retain the primary role as 'toys that teach', such as stereometric, mathematical, engineering, or scientific sets (Lewis 1992). Others accentuate their playful possibilities, such as Lego or Meccano, often grouped under the category of construction toys, and sometimes specifically architectural in design (Brosterman 1991, Salter 2011, Zinguer 2015). Increasingly, play blocks have also been introduced as part of a 'free play' environment, allowing the innate qualities of each carefully designed set to guide the student towards their phenomenal qualities and practical application, while allowing for creative innovation.

The influence of Pestalozzi and Froebel on education led to other innovators, most importantly Maria Montessori (1870–1952). The Montessori method of education broadened the educational play environment to include many more teaching aids and broader free play environments, but was again founded on simple geometrical solids.

EDUCATION AND ART

This educational method of play bocks is conjectured to have either consciously or subliminally influenced generations of creative thinkers. It has been particularly cited as a factor in the works of many early-twentieth-century artists and art movements, including Cubism, the Constructivists in revolutionary Soviet Russia, the Weimar Bauhaus, and the Dutch *De Stijl* movement (Lupton and Miller 1993, Brosterman 1997, Hall 1999). In this context, block play is usually referenced as an influence on the formal properties of these artists' works. Via such influences it might be proposed that much of what we consider the minimal geometrical formalism of twentieth-century design has been influenced by Froebel, particularly via the significant influence of the Bauhaus and its educational legacy. An often-quoted example of this is the work of Frank Lloyd Wright (1867–1959). He spoke about his mother's interest in raising her son by the Froebel method:

> I sat at the little kindergarten table-top ruled by lines about four inches apart making four-inch square; and among other things played upon these unit-lines with the square (cube), the circle (sphere) and the triangle (tetrahedron or tripod)...
>
> (Wright 1957: 19–20).

The re-configuration of simple block forms is easily related to the formal qualities of Wright's early work (Brosterman 1997: 140–144). As Fern Lerner has observed: 'Horizontal arrangement made with rectangular blocks of the Sixth Gift look remarkably like Wright's later Prairie Style houses' (Lerner 2005: 213). Indeed, there is a Froebel-inspired set of wooden blocks that are designed to create Wright's Robbie House (1910) available commercially. The Swiss-born architect Le Corbusier (1887–1965) spent his childhood close to Yverdon on Lake Neuchâtel and started his education in a Froebel School in 1891 (Vogt 1998: 286). Both the regular grid in plan and the stark geometry of his and other modernists' buildings suggest a strong formal link to block play (Vogt 1998: 286–305, Brosterman 1997: 146–151).

More fundamentally than geometric forms, the Froebel system explores a pedagogical and experiential creative play methodology that encourages re-configuration through tactile play to reveal emergent phenomena of material, artefacts, and space. The Froebel Gifts systematically accumulate their elements, from the soft spheres of wool, to wooden ball, cube, and cylinder and then in the familiar cubes, prisms, and blocks. This progression is founded on some key concepts that the pre-linguistic child can encounter through tactile play, concepts that emerge from the structured play and introduce abstract thinking. Knowledge was grouped into Froebel's conception of three realms:

> In short sessions of directed play, the gifts were used to create pictures or structures that fit loosely into three categories – forms of nature (or life), forms of knowledge (or science), and forms of beauty (or art).
>
> (Brosterman 1997: 37)

All three realms give rise to concepts in relationship and transferable into conceptual thought and language. The first concept, introduced in the spherical ball of wool in Gift One and the wooden sphere in Gift Two is that of *unity*; a singular form of a single surface, complete, indivisible, whole. In the context of Froebel's monotheistic beliefs this forms an essential point of departure. The assembly and division of the cube introduce notions of part and whole; eight small cubes creating a single larger one. Likeness and difference in each component part of the Gifts allows the experience and observation of an increasingly complex association of concepts. This expands even more after the first six Gifts when planar and linear elements are introduced, allowing more complex images and structures to be assembled. This educational methodology of 'learning-by-doing' is not simply training for manual skills or formal composition. The tactile play allows relationships and meaning to emerge through experimentation and observation, as this 1890 American text describes:

> Looking at the gifts as a whole we see at once that their basis is mathematical, and we notice that they illustrate successively the solid, the plane, and the line. We perceive, too, that they progress from undivided to divided wholes, and from these separate and independent elements. Finally, we observe that there is a suggestiveness in the earlier gifts which the later ones lack, while on the other hand the range of the latter far exceeds that of the former. The meaning of these distinctions and connections will grow clear to us as we study the common objects of the varied gifts. The objects are:
>
> I.   To aid the mind to abstract the essential qualities of objects by presentation of striking contrasts.
> II. To lead to the classification of external objects by the presentation of typical forms.
> III. To illustrate fundamental truths through simple applications.
> IV. To stimulate creative activity.
>
> (Blow 1890: 601)

Beyond simply a language of shape and form, Froebel's Gifts are intended to enlighten the child to abstract thinking, taxonomy, creativity, and truths. That the playfully tactile learning is inherently creative is a critical aspect in understanding the influence of Froebel on art education beyond kindergarten. As noted, several authors have linked Froebel to the Bauhaus. As early as 1950, Frederick Logan cited the quote above and explicitly linked the Bauhaus, Wright, Kandinsky and Mondrian to kindergarten methodologies of 'sensory education' and 'abstract forms' (Logan 1950: 40–42). This association might not be surprising when one considers that Froebel was born in and founded the Kindergarten movement in Thuringia, the German Province of Weimar, where the Bauhaus was founded in 1919. But the influence was more than geographical. One of the major proponents for a new pedagogy of playful experimentation with materials at the Bauhaus was the founder of the 'Vorkus', or preliminary course, established in 1920 by Johannes Itten. His own experience as a teacher in Switzerland (Itten 1964: 8–9) exposed him to the legacy of the radical kindergarten educators (Wick 2000: 114) 'incorporating ideas from Cizek, Pestalozzi, Montessori, and Froebel' (Lerner 2005: 215). Franz Cizek (1865–1946) was an artist and art teacher in Vienna who pioneered the exhibition of children's drawings and the notion of 'de-schooling', said to have been a major influence on Itten's teaching at the Bauhaus (Wick 2000: 97). Unlike the other three educationalists, Cizek was primarily concerned with art education, not early years education – an important distinction – but also placing art education at as the basis of early years education:

> For both Froebel and Itten, students learned by doing, experimentation for its own sake was encouraged and 'play' was considered key in imparting important theoretical discoveries.
>
> (Lerner 2005: 216)

After Itten resigned from the Bauhaus in 1923, this pedagogy was continued by Lazlo Moholy-Nagy (1895–1946) and then Josef Albers (1888–1976), who had been a student on Itten's course (Wick 2000: 34–49). While Itten was prone to stress the individual personality of the artist, Albers saw the creative process more as one of experimentation and observation of the material at hand. Albers summarised some of his ideas about teaching in a Bauhaus publication of 1928: 'The results [of students' experiments] is the student's own experience and possession, because it has been learned rather than taught' (Albers 1928, translated by F. Amrine, N. Horowitz, and F. Horowitz in Horowitz and Danilowitz 2006: 85).[1] Albers had trained first as a teacher and was familiar with the progressive theories of education, and as an artist he was primarily interested in drawing. Both of these factors led to an influence of Pestallozzi in his educational methods (Horowitz and Danilowitz 2006: 85, Füssl 2006: 90–91), but in the Vorkus and later at Black Mountain the material investigations, especially natural material studies, or *matière*, tactile material play, recalls Froebel. One of Albers' students, architect Howard Dearstyne (1903–1979), recalled Albers instructed them to 'just play around' with materials to 'discover something about them' (Lerner 2005: 218). Walter Gropius, founder of the Bauhaus, arriving in the USA in 1937, published his first article, 'Education Towards Creative Design' (*American Architect and Architecture*), encouraging a revision of school education based on the Bauhaus pedagogy, thereby bringing the Froebel's ideas full circle (Lerner 2005: 219–221). Just such an approach can be found in the late 1950s, when in Kassel, Germany, Ernst Röttger began to publish his Creative Play Series of books aimed at teachers and students. The first volume was on Creative Paper Design, one of Froebel's 'occupations', later developed and applied by Albers at Black Mountain College. In his introduction, *Creative Play*, Röttger notes:

> The child's natural urge to play takes two distinct forms: aimless play, which leads merely to tears and quarrels; and serious play, which always follows a pattern of some kind even though the child may not be aware of it … The term 'play' is not used in the visual arts. And yet, the methods of leading artists of our time show that 'play' also has its justification in sculpture and painting.
>
> (Röttger 1961: 7)

It is this 'serious play' methodology of Froebel rather than elemental form-making with which I wish to consider the Chair Project.

WHAT THEY MADE

Working with two schools, and children of between eight and fourteen years old, 44 different configurations emerged through playful exploration by the participants (Fig 11.2). The project was introduced as an exploration of how people gather together in social situations, as represented by the arrangement of chairs. Although formed to represent a chair, children had no problem with re-configuring the chair-blocks based on their repetition of form and geometry

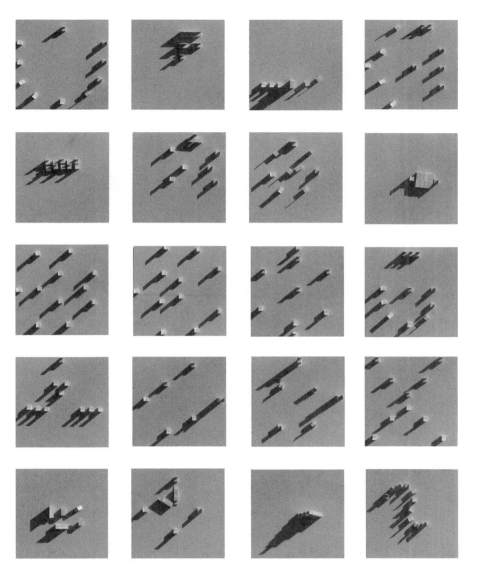

FIGURE 11.2 Examples of The Chair Project configurations
Source: the author

to create a more divergent collection of outcomes, such as pattern making and tower building, for example by interlocking two chairs to make a single block. As such, the results might be seen to belong to categories similar to Froebel's notions of forms of life, forms of knowledge, and forms of beauty. Children often began with assembling the chairs into an unstable tower, quickly learning the challenge of gravity and balance, but soon engaged in the pursuit of individual ideas (Fig 11.3). The potential of the exercise emerged through active engagement, allowing the pupils to configure and re-configure, testing ideas, watching other participants, and discovering possibilities in the form and arrangement of the blocks. Three examples exemplify the type of solutions proposed by the children. One is a simple circle of twelve chairs, representing a small group gathering in an elegant, circular manner, where all chairs are equal (Fig 11.4). A second group of twelve chairs places a central group of four in a square, surrounded by the other eight (Fig 11.5). Again, the geometry of the arrangement is carefully resolved, suggesting both a possible eccentric seating arrangement, but also an attempt at more complex pattern making. A third group of nine chairs similarly makes a ring of eight, but this time facing out, and places a single chair, isolated in the centre (Fig 11.6). It is an evocative configuration, where the high back chairs appear to wall in a single, lonely figure. These three examples demonstrate the outcome from a half-hour or so of free-play with the chairs, experimenting and evaluating their potential to construct both different arrangements and meanings.

FIGURE 11.3 Children's pursuit of individual ideas
Source: the author

FIGURE 11.4 A simple circle of twelve chairs
Source: the author

Other examples took a variety of approaches, forming either social gathering or pattern making, or a combination of the two. Some of the familiar representations included three pairs of chairs with a table (made by turning the chairs over) representing a cafe, a living room with dining table and three-piece suite, and a bedroom with bed (two chairs, one turned over), a desk and chair, a chest of drawers and a wardrobe (represented simply by two chairs interlocked in a block). Two pupils suggested chairs representing football playing configurations of 2:4:4 and 4:3:3, plus a 'goal-keeping' chair each, and then placed the boards together to represent the beginning of a game. This certainly helped to emphasise that the chair block was as much a representation of an individual as an artefact to sit on. One arrangement we titled 'tumbling chair' positioned ten chairs lined up, each revolving forty-five degrees to its neighbour and returning

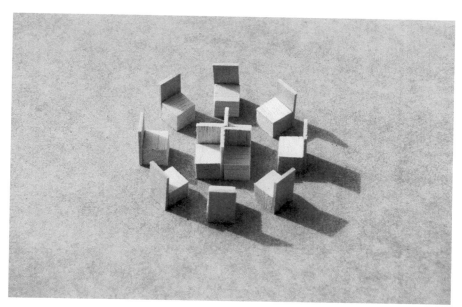

FIGURE 11.5 A more complex configuration
Source: the author

FIGURE 11.6 An evocative configuration
Source: the author

to the original location of lying on its back (Fig 11.7). In discussing how each child might propose something different there were a series of conversations about where they had seen chairs representing the relationship between people. Drawing on personal experience, two configurations that were proposed were, firstly, a wedding, and secondly, a divorce court. As pattern making, one proposal was a star, another a chessboard. Seating for cars and buses was also suggested, as was a rather evocative curve of paired seats suggesting a train snaking along its track.

The outcomes did not vary greatly between the two schools, a primary and a secondary, but the younger children certainly engaged more enthusiastically and were more careful in gluing the chairs at the end of the class. Although

FIGURE 11.7 The 'tumbling chair'
Source: the author

each arrangement was photographed, the decision to glue the arrangements down was in anticipation of a possible, yet to be realised, exhibition or artwork using them, and has allowed me to archive them. The resulting works briefly appeared in the newly opened Dundee Contemporary Arts building (by Richard Murphy Architects), as a temporary installation, but there was not enough space to show them all in the 'Artery' exhibition. One image was reproduced as a postcard, along with images from each of the other nine projects issued as part of 'Artery' (see Figure 11.1, p. 181).

PUBLIC ART AND PLACEMAKING

The Chair Project was never intended as a part of any larger project. However, while working on the Artlink's project I won a commission from The Tyrebagger Trust and Art in Partnership for a site at 'Sculpture at Tyrebagger', a woodland sculpture trail in the forests near Aberdeen Airport. The resulting proposal, 'Stepping Stones', was a series of platforms placed *ad hoc* across and between two streams to accommodate an assemblage of two bridges and a picnic table: part Forth Rail Bridge (Edinburgh), part park bench (Figure 11.8). The first model followed a similar methodology to the Chair Project, deliberately linking my studio practice and these schools' workshops. I even worked on one of the remaining MDF boards. However, in this case, I did have a specific site to respond to, which was modelled in air-dry clay, rather than the neutral flat surface used in the workshops (Figure 11.9). The model method was continued into the actual production process, using a 1:20 scale model to discuss construction with the client, steel fabricator, and timber supplier (Figure 11.10).

As part of the Tyrebagger process I continued to use the Chair Project to introduce the design process and proposal to local primary schools, both very close to the Tyrebagger site, with the addition of a full-scale chair mock-up in one school hall and site visits to the completed project. Each school produced twenty more examples of arrangements.

In 2002 I held a weekend workshop at the Henry Moore Institute, Leeds, as part of a Research Fellowship, engaging with a variety of individuals and groups, using the Chair Project to introduce and discuss my practice and the role of public art. The residency was entitled 'Play/Ground', during which I explored the medium of horizontal relief in twentieth-century art. For the first time I used some 1:20 chairs (22.5x22.5x45mm), cut from oak left over from the

FIGURE 11.8 Tyrebagger 'Stepping Stones', Simon Beeson, 2000
Source: the author

Tyrebagger project, alongside a set of Froebel Kindergarten Blocks, making an explicit link between the chair project and Kindergarten for the first time. The intention was to relate the chairs to more general block play, whereby the table's surface was transformed into a representation of the ground, and hence the chairs as a situation of living in the world.

In 2005 I returned to Aberdeenshire, this time to the town of Ellon, to develop another public art project in the riverside improvements and Heritage Walk, as part of a residency at the Scottish Sculpture Workshop, Lumsden,

FIGURE 11.9 Tyrebagger 'Stepping Stones', 1:100 model, Simon Beeson, 1999
Source: the author

FIGURE 11.10 Tyrebagger 'Stepping Stones', 1:20 model, Simon Beeson, 1999
Source: the author

working with the director Chris Freemantle. Again, the workshop engaged children in what had now become a co-creative extension of my own studio practice, discussing possible arrangements of chairs for their social and aesthetic meaning (Figure 11.11). Workshops were held with Ellon, Auchterellon, and Lumsden schools. The project concluded with a writing workshop on the site of a new gathering table on the riverside, led by poet Ken Cockburn. (I should note that both the projects in Dundee and Lumsden also engaged in a workshop for elderly residents, which similarly created chair configurations).

FIGURE 11.11 Ellon Riverside seating, Simon Beeson, 2005
Source: the author

The project continues to be applied in workshops for prospective or current students of architecture in my role at Arts University Bournemouth. However, the chairs are now reused and not stuck down in permanent arrangements. As well as photography, drawing is often introduced to capture their arrangements before they are disassembled (Beeson and Holness 2008).

What significance might the Chair Project have in the context of 'research with and for children'? In the same way as Froebel anticipates the emergence of ideas of beauty and knowledge alongside patterns of life, the 'serious play' of the Chair Project uses playful reconfiguration to both represent existing patterns of gathering and allow innovative proposals to emerge. The elements selected for play suggest just enough of human presence to represent a social context of human habitation but are ambiguous enough to allow pattern making and unusual scenarios. As a 'design' exercise it lacked any intention of realisation but explored possibilities. The further interpretation of these into public seating was informed by both the obviousness of seating and the playful outcomes of the workshops. Albers spoke of his exercises as not being art, and of his intention as 'search' not 're-search' (Albers 1969, Zender 2016). Similarly, a century after its foundation, the formalist interpretation of the Bauhaus legacy is being questioned, while being recognised as a significant experiment in creative education and an example of play as an alternative to the mystical creative 'muse' (Prager 2014).

As architectural design the project also emphasises situation over form. As such, 'architectural space' is defined by placement of materials in spatial relationships establishing situations we inhabit. By limiting the play-element to a single fixed form, the act of locating each piece relative to another is the only method of constructing meaning. But, much like chess, the combinations are endless. Familiar, unfamiliar, and strange possibilities emerge through the act of configuration.

As a methodology the intent is that the process reveals concepts through material means, a pedagogical method theorised and practiced by Pestalozzi and Froebel, and applied in subsequent educational practice, especially arts education, and in recent discussions of active learning and object-based learning. Both Pestalozzi and Froebel observed this methodology in the unstructured educational development of children through their observation and participation in the activities of life with their parents and grandparents, and alongside their peers. In the organisation and structuring of formal educational methodologies these simple observations are often forgotten in the 'fog of theory'. While modest in scope, the project attempted to give an example for practice of a generative, co-creative methodology for integrating conceptual and material thinking to challenge the bifurcation of intellect and body; the split between the conceptual and corporeal. As a collective activity, the enquiry by the group provides far more insight than any singular enquiry. Unlike the pursuit of singular truths that often characterises the STEM-based approach to contemporary education and problem solving, this co-creative, studio practice introduces the participants to the exploratory, open-ended, divergent nature of creative research and practice developed in arts-based education, where conjecture and uncertainty are explored and developed through configuration and re-configuration. I suggest that the Chair Project, which began as an example of creative practice, was developed into a pedagogical method and was applied as a research methodology.

In particular, I would stress that the spatial–material practice of the Chair Project engaged students in a thoughtful enquiry of spatial design and of how the way we arrange our lives materially constructs concepts and narratives that establish ideas of 'ways of living'. The project is an example of engaging children in research; a *search* for creative methodologies that might enrich our understanding of the places we create for living. The realised public seating projects reflect upon and apply some understanding gained through the creative and pedagogical practice of the Chair Project. Both constructed examples develop, through playful configuration, an *ad hoc* response to site and a desire to engage the users in an encounter with place.

In conclusion, I now regard this project that began as a demonstration workshop as an expansion of my architecture, art, and education practice into a co-creative practice. The simple act of arranging small scale chairs on a wooden board continues to expand my own and the participants' understanding of spatial practice, architecture, and landscape architecture, and the notion that things we make embody ideas of how we live or wish to live. Through material play we can engage in a creative *search* with and for children. Even the limited application of block play explored here seems to me to be an excellent vehicle for exploring creative practice and material thinking in an increasingly virtual and abstracted visual world.

NOTE

1   The translators give the title as 'manual', 'hands-on', or 'practical' (Weklicher) 'instruction in form' (Formunterricht); see Horowitz and Danilowitz (2006): 85; note 83: 263.

REFERENCES

Albers, J. (1928) 'Weklicher Formunterricht'. *Bauhaus* **2**(3): 3–7.

Albers, J. (1969) *Search Versus Re-Search: Three Lectures by Josef Albers at Trinity College, April 1965*. Hartford, CT: Trinity College Press.

Beeson, S. and Holness, A. (2008) 'Introducing Design Studio'. In *Designing Design Education: Designtrain Congress Trailer II, Proceedings*. Vol.1: 87–98. Amsterdam: ELIA.

Blow, S.E. (1890) 'Some Aspects of the Kindergarten'. In Barnard, H. (ed), *Kindergarten and Child Culture Papers*. Hartford: American Journal of Education: 595–616. https://ia802604.us.archive.org/17/items/kindergartenand00barngoog/kindergartenand00barngoog.pdf (accessed 3 March 2019).

Brehony, Kevin J. (2013) 'Play, Work and Education: Situating a Froebelian Debate'. *Bordón. Revista De Pedagogía*, **65**(1): 59–78.

Brosterman, N. (1991) *Potential Architecture*. Montreal: Canadian Centre for Architecture.

Brosterman, N. (1997) *Inventing Kindergarten*. New York: Harry N. Abrams.

Füssl, K-H. (2006) 'Pestalozzi in Dewey's Realm? Bauhaus Master Josef Albers among the German-speaking Emigrés' Colony at Black Mountain College (1933–1949)' in *Paedagogica Historica* **42**(1–2): 77–92.

Hall, J. (1999) *The World as Sculpture*. London: Chatto and Windus.

Horowitz, F.A. and Danilowitz, B. (2006) *Josef Albers: To Open Eyes*. London: Phaidon.

Itten, J. (1964) *Design and Form: The Basic Course at the Bauhaus*. New York: Reinhold.

Lerner, F. (2005) 'Foundations for Design Education: Continuing the Bauhaus Vorkus Vision'. *Studies in Art Education*, **46**(3): 211–226.

Lewis, M.J. (1992) *Toys That Teach*. Montreal: Canadian Centre for Architecture.

Logan, F. (1950) 'Kindergarten and Bauhaus'. *College Art Journal*, **10**(1): 36–43.

Lupton, E. and Miller, J.Abbot (eds) (1993) *The ABC's of Triangle, Square, Circle: The Bauhaus and Design Theory*. London: Thames and Hudson.

Prager, P. (2014) 'Making Sense of the Modernist Muse: Creative Cognition and Play at the Bauhaus'. *American Journal of Play*, **7**(1): 27–49.

Röttger, E. (1961) *Creative Paper Craft* (Creative Play Series no.1). New York: Reinhold.

Rousseau, J.-J. (1892) *Émile* (translated by W.H. Payne). New York: D. Appleton.

Salter, B. (2011) *Building Toys*. Oxford: Shire Publications.

Thoreau, H.D. (2006) *Walden*. New Haven: Yale University Press.

Schiller, F. (1793/2015) *On the Aesthetic Education of Man, in a Series of Letters* (translated by Reginald Schell). Classic Thought Series. Grindl Press.

Silber, K. (1960) *Pestalozzi: The man and his Work*. London: Routledge and Kegan Paul.

Vogt, A.M. (1998) *Le Corbusier, the Noble Savage* (translated by Radka Donnell). Cambridge, MA: MIT Press.

Wick, R.K. (2000) *Teaching at the Bauhaus*. Ostfildern-Ruit: Hatje Cantz.

Wright, F.L. (1957). *A Testament*. New York: Horizon Press.

Zinguer, T. (2015) *Architecture in Play*. Charlottesville: University of Virginia Press.

Zender, M. (2016) 'Design Research Pioneer Josef Albers: A Case for Design Research'. *Visible Language*, **50**(1): 48–77.

12

CHILDREN'S PERSPECTIVES ON GREEN SPACE MANAGEMENT IN SWEDEN AND DENMARK

Märit Jansson and Inger Lerstrup

The work of green space managers – local authority department staff, external contractors, or caretakers employed by institutions or companies – can be expected to have a great effect on child-friendliness by affecting mainly physical, but also socio-environmental determinants. The Scandinavian countries have a history of being world-leading in work to improve the *child-friendliness of environments*, with much awareness of this issue during the early and mid-twentieth century. Children's levels of independent mobility are generally high, but diminishing, probably due to urban densification and increased car traffic (Björklid and Gummesson, 2013). The UN Convention on the Rights of the Child has been ratified and promoted, but less attention has been given to later international movements, and planning in Scandinavia has been criticised for not taking a child-friendly direction (Björklid and Nordström, 2007), with a focus on densification, urban character and new public management solutions.

Much of the literature on child-friendly environments focuses on participatory approaches to development of the physical environment (Alarasi et al., 2016; Cushing, 2016). Children's participation in planning can be highly valuable, but is not the only way to approach child-friendly environments, since these also depend on other practices, as well as on basic physical and social environmental factors. These can be developed both with and without children's direct participation. In this chapter, we examine the specific role of green space management in developing child-friendly environments, focusing on children's perspectives. We argue the importance of green space management to children, and suggest how managers can understand and strive towards child-friendliness in their approach to management of the urban environment. We argue that this work has huge potential, which is yet to be fully acknowledged and realised.

ELEMENTS OF CHILD-FRIENDLINESS

According to Gibson (1979), what humans directly perceive as opportunities in their surroundings are affordances, here defined as *the meaningful action possibilities of the environment* (Lerstrup and Konijnendijk van den Bosch, 2017). These are situated in time and space, and depend on many variables, such as the characteristics of the individual, where age, size, ability, former experiences and company exert an influence. Richness of affordances in local environments is an important factor in itself and can also support children's independent mobility, as interesting settings can encourage children to go outdoors, providing an "outward pull" (Chatterjee, 2005:19). For planners, designers and managers, the perceptions of affordances by various user groups and individual users should be of interest and might point to new and interesting ways to develop the environment.

Child-friendly environments can have various properties, but generally have some qualities in common, such as moderate building density (Broberg et al., 2013) and limited access for car traffic (Björklid and Gummesson, 2013; Carstensen, 2006). Horelli (2007:283) defines environmental child-friendliness as: "settings and environmental structures that provide support to individual children and groups who take an interest in children's issues so that children can construct and implement their goals or projects". In other words, such environments include elements and structures providing the two components *rich affordances* and support for *independent mobility* (Kyttä, 2004; Jansson et al., 2016). They allow children to perform meaningful actions, such as constructing, affecting and creating their own places, and they often include green elements providing rich sensuous experiences, loose parts and change (Chawla, 2015; Jansson, 2015; Lerstrup, 2016; Rasmussen, 2004).

Children are often among the most frequent green space users near their homes (Florgård and Forsberg, 2006). Green spaces are important for child-friendliness (Jansson et al., 2016; Kyttä, 2004; Riggio, 2002) and several positive aspects of children's contact with such spaces have been found (Chawla, 2015). For example, they support children's physical activity, which for 11–13 year-olds can depend on the amount of space with trees and shrubs near their homes (Janssen and Rosu, 2015). Furthermore, spacious preschool yards with much vegetation and a mix of spaces that are open and spaces with natural and fabricated content are associated with children that have healthier body mass, sleep better and are only exposed to balanced amounts of solar radiation, as compared with children attending schools with other kinds of yards (Boldemann et al., 2011; Söderström et al., 2013). Thus, the access, amount and quality of green spaces are important aspects, which set a focus on the contribution of landscape practices.

The development of environments through landscape architecture is commonly divided into three phases: planning, design and management (van den Brink et al., 2016). Planning and design mainly concern the development of new elements and structures, while management deals with maintaining and developing existing elements and structures over time. These three phases can all affect environmental child-friendliness (Horelli, 2007), but management is particularly underexplored in this regard, despite being about providing qualities for people or *users*. In the context of green spaces and landscapes, management has been defined as "the activities performed by a management organization to maintain and develop existing urban green space for users" (Jansson and Lindgren, 2012:142) or as "maintaining and enhancing [a place and] its quality to maximize the benefits for users" (Dempsey et al., 2014:24). Green space managers are a range of professionals who work with management of public open spaces, but also institutions, cemeteries and housing areas that are both semi-public and private. Three management levels are generally distinguished, most clearly in local authorities: policy (politicians), tactical (civil servants) and operational (park workers) (Jansson and Lindgren, 2012; Randrup and Persson, 2009). On the policy and tactical levels, management is clearly more than operational upkeep and maintenance, and is even intertwined with planning (Jansson and Lindgren, 2012). Management processes could include users on local, informal, hands-on and 'everyday' levels, potentially facilitating inclusion of children's perspectives (Clark and Percy-Smith, 2006; Jansson, 2015). This requires approaches which give insights into children's perspectives in a way that is relevant for management.

A few previous studies have examined the child-friendliness of urban green space management. In school grounds, Malone and Tranter (2003) found management activities to be of value for promoting children's learning and play, while Jansson, Mårtensson and Gunnarsson (2018) found that children's participation in the management phase was positive for their attitude to school ground development. In other green spaces, Bell et al.,(2003) concluded that managers lack sufficient insight into the uses and perspectives of children and young people. Moreover, Roe (2006) reported that children did not feel that the management of their local environments was adapted to them and their preferences. Jansson et al., (2016) found that children can take an interest in green space management and prefer variation in management levels. In the empirical studies we detail in this chapter, we investigated how green space management and its results are actually perceived by children in Denmark and Sweden, and how management in various forms can affect and contribute to the child-friendliness of urban environments.

STUDYING GREEN SPACES WITH CHILDREN AS USERS

We collected data for the studies based on the concept of *children's perspectives* as a methodological driver for child-friendliness and child-centred methods. The concept, introduced in the 1990s (Tiller, 1991), has gained attention in the literature during recent years, including in research on children's local environments, where child-centred methodologies and children's own views are at the core (Bourke, 2014; Cele, 2005; Elsley, 2004; Jansson et al., 2016; Kylin and Lieberg, 2001; Lerstrup and Refshauge, 2016; Prellwitz and Skär, 2007; Rasmussen, 2004; Roe, 2006; Simkins and Thwaites, 2008). The approach aims at understanding children as individuals, but their perspectives also depend on a variety of factors such as age group. In our studies, we invited children in school year 4, aged 10–11, to participate through collaboration with local municipal schools. Children in this age group have previously been included in similar studies (Bourke, 2014; Cele, 2005; Kylin and Lieberg, 2001), since they generally have some independent mobility, are interested in their local environments and are able to communicate their perspectives, while still being engaged in play (Jansson et al., 2016).

Case study methodology is based on an interest in exploring context-bound cases through various methods (Stake, 1995) and is therefore valuable for studying uses related to environments. We used multiple cases in order to broaden our view and permit comparisons of children's perspectives, as previously done by e.g. Carstensen (2006) and Haikkola et al., (2007). The case study included four urban areas with similar, rather high, socio-economic status, but with variations in building density and the amount and character of green space available for users. These were two case areas in southern Sweden and two in eastern Denmark, with one urban village, representing smaller built-up areas with an urban lifestyle, and one city district, representing part of a larger and denser city, in each country. Among the cases, the Swedish urban village had the lowest density, the most green space and the most limited car traffic, while the Danish city district had the highest density, the least green spaces and much car traffic. We selected the cases to allow for comparison and generalisation of the results (Flyvbjerg, 2006).

USING CHILD-CENTRED METHODS

In our field studies, we arranged walking interviews with five to six groups of three children, with a total of 15–18 participating local children in each case area. We thus aimed to combine our former experiences of semi-structured interviews with observations of places and children's activities on-site. Methods that are child-centred and conducted outdoors (Cele, 2005) or in groups (Hill, 2006) have often been found to be valuable. These can be combined in so-called *child-led walks* where children take the lead in showing and describing their environments, supplemented by semi-structured interviews on the go. Child-led walks are increasingly being used and recommended for gathering data on children's perspectives on their environments (Cele, 2005; Jansson et al., 2016; Kylin and Lieberg, 2001; Loebach and Gilliland, 2010; Moore, 1986).

In collaboration with local schools, we obtained written consent from parents for their children's participation in the study. The teachers formed the children into groups, each containing children from the same class who knew each other well and lived close to each other. Some groups contained only boys, some only girls and some both boys and girls. Throughout the study, the children were informed about the aim to learn from them and the voluntary nature of their participation.

Before the child-led walks, we introduced the children to the research topic either during a short preparatory indoor interview or during a drawing and writing task, both with the focus on local outdoor environments. The task was given some structure by asking the children to draw or describe local outdoor areas and by posing four questions: What do you do there? What do you think of the way it is being cared for and organised? What do you think is good there? What do you think is bad there?

The walks lasted 1.5–2 hours each and were held when the weather was comfortable, during May in the Swedish urban village and in September–October in the other cases. On starting the walks, we instructed the children in each group jointly to decide which local places to visit. While walking, we had group conversations about places, activities, preferences and suggestions, supported by semi-structured questions about the environment and their use of it, places suitable or unsuitable for them, the arrangement of the outdoor environment and the management work there, what was allowed and the need for improvements. We observed how the children acted and interacted with the environment during the walks. On the go, we made digital audio-recordings and took some photographs. Immediately after each walk, we wrote down what we could recall, including observations of actions, surprising observations and reflections. After finishing each case study, we summarised the general impressions of important activities, environmental elements and general advantages and problems of the area.

When all the walks were complete, we listened to the audio-recorded interviews, transcribed sequences illuminating the research questions, went through the notes and looked at the photos taken to support memories of places and activities. We also reviewed the drawings and written statements made by the children to get an idea about how they related to their local outdoor environments, the management of outdoor areas and the affordances in the case areas for this age group. Through the content in these various data types, we formed themes related to our aim and condensed the results to facilitate comparisons between the case areas.

CHILD-FRIENDLY ENVIRONMENTS

In the following paragraphs, we describe our findings about 10–11-year-old children's use of open spaces, characteristics of child-friendly environments and the role of green space management. In all four cases, children expressed that they were connected to and liked their local environment. Many findings were general for the four sites, while some differed between them (Table 12.1). After analysing our material, the findings could be structured into four themes on how green space management can affect child-friendliness: development, maintenance, urban planning and approach to children (Figure 12.1). Within each theme, three aspects are distinguished, varying in importance from case to case.

TABLE 12.1 Differences in types of settings shown, relation to green space management and children's independent mobility in the four case areas

	Sweden	Denmark
Urban village	Playgrounds, variety of green spaces, ponds, unmanaged places (overgrown gardens and railway), streets, paved paths. Some interest in green space management. Weak feeling of influence on management. Overall much independent mobility.	Schoolyards, sport facilities, playgrounds, private gardens, low-managed places (beach, forest, hedges, grass slopes), paved paths. Low interest in green space management. No feeling of influence on management. Variation in independent mobility. Boys generally less restricted.
City district	Varied green spaces, playgrounds, low-managed places (river banks, woodlands), pavements, paved paths. Low interest in green space management. Weak feeling of influence on management. Much independent mobility, a few exceptions among both boys and girls.	Schoolyards, private courtyards, private gardens, playgrounds, squares, parks, few low-managed places. Low interest in green space management. No feeling of influence on management. Overall low independent mobility with variation between children. Boys generally less restricted.

Development of settings is one of the main tasks of green space managers. In this aspect, we identified three aspects of increasing child-friendliness for the age group investigated: to develop a variety of places for children's actions, to manage for change and to add sensory plants (Figure 12.1).

Develop variety for action

Children in all case areas used the environment for actions: to meet, play, move, construct, explore and observe, in green spaces as well as in shops and public areas. Playgrounds were used as places to *meet* and for activities with peers and siblings, and meeting a cat or a dog was interesting for most children. Apart from socialising, several enjoyed *moving around* on play equipment: climbing, jumping on trampolines, swinging, swaying and spinning when possible. Open spaces were used for group games such as tag and all kinds of moving, such as cycling, skating, running, etc., and vegetated areas for group games such as hide and seek, role play, climbing, balancing and jumping.

Generally, children valued *variation* in content and management level. They enjoyed all kinds of landscapes and wanted open spaces as well as enclosures, evenly paved ground as well as grassy slopes, short grass for ball games as well as tall grass for hiding and supporting animal life, cultivated plants such as fruit trees and berries as well as flowers and wild herbs. Children were fond of play equipment as well as natural elements such as vegetation and boulders. These preferences were evident both in their drawings, which often contained elements such as trees, grass, water and play equipment, and during the walks, where they used both green and built elements in multiple ways. A number of children wished for more smooth surfaces for skating and cycling, more challenging play equipment such as climbing structures and several large trampolines, and more interesting areas to explore with loose objects to arrange and thus leave their mark.

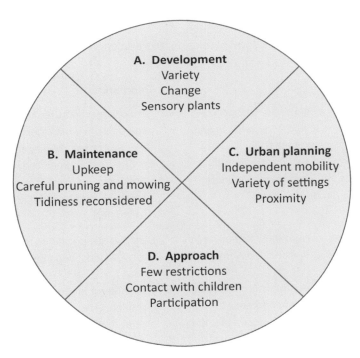

FIGURE 12.1 Four themes describing ways (A–D) for managers to affect the child-friendliness of outdoor environments
Source: the authors

Manage for change

The wish to construct, explore, observe and talk underlined children's curiosity and appetite for something new to happen, something new to experience, explore and reflect on. This is why it is important to manage for change, either by replacing elements and structures regularly or by including much vegetation, since vegetation changes naturally through the seasons and attracts wildlife.

Vegetated areas were used as resources for loose objects such as leaves, fruit, flowers and sticks for *construction*. Vegetated areas, un-managed areas and settings with water were used for *exploration*. Overall, children highly enjoyed water that they found in ponds, fountains, streams or at the beach, particularly when they had loose objects such as stones or flowers to throw in. A specific feature of the Swedish city district was the water present in streams and canals, which fascinated the children. A specific feature used by those who lived in the urban village in Denmark was strolling by the sea, finding treasures and bathing. In all study areas, *observing* peers in action or adult activities such as house and road construction, walking a dog or skinning a fish was interesting. Observing was often accompanied by *talking* and reflecting. A specific feature of the city district in Denmark mentioned as attractive was events arranged by the local chamber of commerce.

Add sensory plants

The curiosity of children was not restricted to viewing and listening, but also included senses of touch, smell and taste. They showed an interest in how to use plant material in their local environments. This was most clearly shown in the focus on growing and particularly in edible plants. During the walks, several tasted and chewed things such as leaves, fruits etc. Many children were aware of edible plants in their surroundings. They pointed out fruit trees, berry bushes, herbs, even shops giving out sweets or buns for free or very cheap. Some children participated in cultivating flowers and vegetables in their gardens and courtyards (Figure 12.2). Others, mainly in the Swedish case areas, talked a lot about fruit trees and picking fruits and berries from trees, which were seen as beautiful and useful for both play and food.

FIGURE 12.2 Tasting and eating fruit, berries and herbs was an attractive activity, particularly in the Swedish and Danish city districts
Source: Inger Lerstrup

Another main task for green space managers is maintenance and upkeep on the operational level. Connected to maintenance, we found three aspects of importance for the children: upkeep of play structures and other facilities, pruning and cutting of vegetation and the level of tidiness (see Figure 12.1, p. 198).

Take care of play structures

Common complaints among the children were that the upkeep of play equipment was poor. Swings, climbing frames, football goals and basketball hoops were not taken care of, repaired or painted, something that the children often pointed out during the walks. Between the lines, children expressed the feeling that their age group was not considered as important as younger children or adults. Settings that they preferred were often not well-kept or were even removed. Children complained about old play equipment being replaced with something less interesting and intended for smaller children, or not being replaced at all.

Prune and cut vegetation sensitively

Some complaints concerned the lack of consideration of children in management, particularly in residential courtyards, but also in some public areas. Some of this referred to 'insensitive maintenance' of vegetation, e.g. that shrubs used for hiding were pruned back too hard (Figure 12.3), grass was cut too short and interesting vegetation structures taken down. In several cases, children reported felling of beloved trees used for climbing, swinging or sitting in the shade reflecting and listening to the birds. In many places there was clearly a lack of both knowledge and child perspective in the vegetation maintenance. It appeared more focused on practical aspects and a will to demonstrate a high maintenance level than on the vegetation quality or usefulness for children. On the other hand, we observed that not all children interacted with vegetation even when this was possible.

Reconsider tidiness

Children expressed complexity in their views on tidiness and aesthetics, with a clear focus on possibilities for action. They admired beautifully coloured flowers and picked up the colourful petals from the ground and all kinds

FIGURE 12.3 Danish city district. Before maintenance, this had been an attractive place for playing hide and seek
Source: Inger Lerstrup

of sticks, stones, shells, fruits and leaves. They also enjoyed bunches of fallen leaves on the streets, soon to be removed by maintenance staff. Overall, the children showed interest in the physical environment and its loose parts and in any variations, changes or irregularities there, including broken items and litter. In the Swedish city district, children complained about lack of pavement in the streets after ground work, but at the same time played with the road gravel there.

Litter was not always considered a problem and some children in the Swedish urban village even thought it was fun to find litter items, while dumped waste, dog waste and cigarette butts, waste associated with adults, were generally disliked. The opinions on graffiti varied in the Danish case areas; many children found it amusing, but some made a distinction between 'ugly graffiti' such as tags and 'nice graffiti' with colourful images. One group expressed a wish for a wall for graffiti, so that they could contribute without breaking the rules.

C. URBAN PLANNING

Physical planning has a huge influence on children's action possibilities in environments. Planning practice is largely conducted by actors other than green space managers, but it is related to management both directly and indirectly. It sets the frames for children's possibilities and for the work of managers, but can also be dynamically related to management. In our case studies, we found three main aspects of planning that relate to management and are important for children: support for children's independent mobility, provision of various settings and proximity (see Figure 12.1, p. 197).

Support children's independent mobility
The qualities of green spaces can support children in experiencing and moving independently in their local area. The range of independent mobility varied widely between individual children in the case areas (see Table 12.1, p. 197), as revealed both in the drawings and texts and during the walks. Some did not move on their own at all and were accompanied to school and home by their parents. At the other end of the spectrum, some children were allowed to go wherever they liked on their own. Some children used the outdoors much and moved between various spaces. Others mainly reported using the outdoor environment for transport between home and school, otherwise playing computer games, watching videos and following Youtubers, or attending organised after-school activities. A few children in the Danish city district did not relate to any outdoor places and some could only draw outdoor places from locations associated with holidays, such as their summer cottage.

An important finding is that independent mobility was not only individual, but also varied much between the four case areas. The children in the Swedish case areas, particularly in the urban village, had much independent mobility. Within the village, the children were generally not restricted and freely used the path system and the streets where car traffic was low. Some even moved outside the village, going jogging or taking the train to the nearby city. In the Swedish city district, most children moved freely on foot or bike at least to school and in large areas around their homes. A clear exception was a boy who lived slightly outside the urban area and whose house had a road on one side and farmland on the other. He was not allowed outside his garden on his own and found this very limiting. In the Danish case areas, there were some children with much independent mobility, for instance some children in the urban village could go to the beach and even paddle if they liked. The children in the dense Danish city district demonstrated the most restricted independent mobility of all case areas, with a few children hardly having any places to show and being unable to find their way to known places.

Independent mobility is affected by physical environments, but relates to social factors. The areas used by the children had mostly been introduced to them by parents, older siblings or peers, but also by teachers during field trips arranged by the school. Mobility was restricted in dense areas with much car traffic, but also in relation to, for example, what parents allowed. This appeared to affect cycling more than walking. Very few children, and only boys, were allowed to cycle on their own in the Danish city district because of the traffic. On the other hand, scooters

FIGURE 12.4 A Danish courtyard in the city district, where there was formerly an opening in the fence giving children direct access to the neighbouring courtyard
Source: Inger Lerstrup

(kick bikes) were sometimes used for trips there, unlike in the other case areas. Most girls there appeared to be allowed less independent mobility than most boys, having to follow stricter routes from school to home and call their parents to ask for permission if they were invited to a friend's house, whereas many boys could wander as they pleased or just leave a message when visiting a friend.

The children wanted a large number of places to access and the possibility to move in between them, with few hindering fences and borders. Many said that they enjoyed the child-led walks and seeing the places used by other children in the group, sometimes discovering shared affection for a place, at other times being introduced to new places. Some children asked to be invited to revisit peers' private gardens or yards. This underlines the importance of friends and the places to which they provide access. The borders to use and mobility were often physical, such as car traffic and fencing. In some places, residential yards had been renovated and merged to increase the access for residents. In another case, the children had formerly enjoyed access to the next residential yard through a hole in the fence, but then the fence had been replaced (Figure 12.4), much to the displeasure of a child who had a friend in the other yard.

Provide various settings
Both planning and development can contribute to a variety of settings. The sites used by children varied naturally with the character of the case areas and the possibilities afforded by elements and structures there. These variations were prominent and reflected in the sites that the children knew and used (see Table 12.1, p. 197). The variety of settings available clearly had an impact on children's use, and thereby also on their mobility.

In the Swedish urban village, the children showed us a multitude of places. These included playgrounds, among which they had a few favourites that suited their preferences for socialising around large swings or playing in green surroundings. They also used various green spaces for ball games, exploring and moving around. Ponds and other water bodies and a few abandoned and overgrown lots were objects of much interest. Children in the Swedish city district also reported large variation in the outdoor areas they used, including playgrounds, woodlands and parks of various types and some areas clearly not intended for their use. For example, a group of girls showed a steep track through a broken fence to a beautiful view of a pond and a golf course. The Danish urban village had a network of paved paths, smaller green patches and some less intensively managed lots, but the children quite often showed their private gardens or courtyards and less often other areas. The village was surrounded by arable land, forest and the sea, which attracted some interest. The Danish city district was adjacent to quite a large park and included several small parks and a few playgrounds, but there were almost no vacant lots and un-managed places. Apart from certain areas in the park, only one unmanaged place was presented by the children, a vegetated railway embankment accessible through a hole in the fence. The children instead used many private courtyards.

Provide proximity to settings

Areas close to the children's homes were of the greatest importance for their use. Management of settings to be inviting, varied and different is also therefore particularly valuable to provide proximity. In the Swedish urban village, most children knew more or less the entire urban area, but they were much more familiar with spaces close to home. Children in the Swedish city district lived spread over a large area and mostly at some distance from the school. They rarely related to the forested areas close to their school, but frequently to their nearest neighbourhoods. In the Danish urban village district, children living in one neighbourhood mainly used the school facilities and their private gardens, but in another neighbourhood the courtyards and playgrounds were of higher importance. Likewise, in the Danish city district, some children mainly used the school facilities and private courtyards, while those living in another part of the district used a large public park and those in yet another part used squares and a shopping centre.

D. APPROACH TO CHILDREN

The affordances for children in the case areas were influenced by the mindset of the managers and their attitudes and approaches to children as actors and users. This included restrictions of children's activities, managers' contact with children, or lack thereof, and children's participation in management, or lack thereof (see Figure 12.1, p. 197).

Minimise restrictions

The children were heavily affected by local restrictions, which were more prominent in residential courtyards and thereby more influential for children in the Danish city district than in the other case areas. Certain activities were also prohibited, for instance climbing on the roof of sheds and playhouses, swinging on the gates, picking flowers, throwing apples, picking up sticks, climbing in trees, playing in shrubs or making fires. These bans were most often enforced by courtyard caretakers or green space managers, but parents of smaller children also scolded other children and restricted their actions in playgrounds. Many children also pointed out that visiting certain places was not permitted. The railway embankment was fenced off, some institutional playgrounds were not open for all children or only open within certain hours, gardens and courtyards were closed to non-residents and so on. These observations from the children chime with Wood's chapter in this volume, where even the places intended for children contain restrictions that reduce their enjoyment.

Make contact with children

Children's uses of their local outdoor environments and their views on green space management varied, but they seldom perceived management as something they could affect or even give their opinion on. The drawings and texts generally expressed little about green space management. During walks in all case areas except the Swedish urban village, we met with or saw green space managers in action. We observed that some children followed their work with interest, but others did not seem to see the managers at all and referred to them as "somebody from the local authority" when asked.

In the Swedish urban village, some children had talked to local green space managers, had some ideas about their work and said that they liked to see people take care of the environment. Some were upset about major changes to the environment, but understood that this was due to decision-makers rather than to maintenance staff. They

FIGURE 12.5 Swedish urban village. Children showed engagement in the quality and care of the green spaces, looking at a damaged tree
Source: Märit Jansson

also showed that they cared for the environment and the quality of green space (Figure 12.5). In the other areas, children did not consider it possible to talk to managers they met during the walk. When passing a playground reconstruction in a school yard in the Danish city district, children were interested, but not informed about what was being done. When passing a playground under reconstruction in the Swedish city district, the children only looked at it until the researcher encouraged them to talk to the staff. However, a few children had been in contact with managers, for example when a large grass surface was mown by horse-drawn machinery, which the children liked. Only a couple of times did we observe a dialogue between children and managers, but it was not concerning management or maintenance.

Consider dialogue and participation

In the Swedish city district and the Danish case areas, very few children had any notion of their own possible influence over green space management. In a few groups, they knew the caretakers, but it did not strike them that they could express their opinions or that they might be of interest to the staff. On the contrary, many children mentioned that trees were felled, play equipment removed, bushes and grass cut and activities forbidden, as if these were unalterable aspects of life. They had no idea whom they could inform about their wishes and thought that neither they nor their parents could have any influence with local caretakers, even in their own residential courtyards. We did not hear about direct participation by children at any level of the management process.

METHODOLOGICAL REFLECTIONS

The methods we used gave new insights into the relationship between children and the urban environment, adding to findings from previous studies. The drawings and written statements made in the classrooms provided a basis for getting an overall view of the children's use of their outdoor surroundings, but this method was more challenging in analysis and interpretation and did not reveal as rich information as when the children were outdoors.

Walking and talking with children on child-led walks gave the opportunity not only to ask questions and listen to answers, but actually to see the sites in use and to observe how children related to them. Being present at the sites, the children revealed their detailed place knowledge and place attachment. The observations made during the walks, for instance how fallen leaves were kicked, flower petals picked and admired and fruit tasted by the children, were of course season-bound, but the children also mentioned activities performed at the sites in other seasons.

The main research method used, child-led walks with open and semi-structured interviews, proved to be especially suitable for studying how children's perspectives on environments and management differ from those of adults. Actually, it was a challenge to address children directly on green space management, as they knew little about the subject. The combined method delivered much information about the children's attitudes to green space management, but most of it was indirectly shown or described.

The small groups of three children who lived quite close to each other, knew each other and were eager to go out with us were very informative about each area. This selection might be seen as a weakness of the study, since the children might not be representative for the age group, but it was a deliberate choice to gather children's place-based knowledge and encourage children's interaction in the study.

Our child-led walks showed that this method may be time consuming, but not very complicated. For local managers, it can be adjusted according to time available and, as we show, even a small attempt to make contact and listen to this user group can yield useful information. Children can show and describe their local environments very well, how they use them and can express their wishes, if adults in different roles take an interest in developing collaborative and inclusive approaches to children. An issue for the future is how green space managers can involve children practically in their work. We need to develop methods, based on child-led walks and other child-friendly approaches, whereby managers can be informed by children's views and experiences.

UNDERSTANDING CHILD-FRIENDLY GREEN SPACE MANAGEMENT

Overall, the results from our empirical studies show the importance of green space management for the child-friendliness of environments. The study confirms that children's perception of affordances and perspectives on environments and management differ from those of adults (Francis, 1988; Bell et al., 2003; Kylin, 2003). At the same time, the study shows a surprising lack of constructive contact between children and green space managers. Children's views on and interest in green space management varied, but in any case, they did not know where to express their opinions about management. This is surprising, since the UN Convention on the Rights of the Child, stating children's rights to express themselves in matters that affect them, has long been promoted in both Sweden and Denmark.

It is not easy to isolate the role of green space management, while other aspects of the physical and social environment and children's individual preferences and personalities also affect how they use their local environments. Children's individual uses are also affected by social and individual factors including parents, siblings, friends, teachers and their state of mind. However, we argue that green space management can generally contribute to child-friendliness by offering *varied, rich, allowing and changing environments, sensory plants included*. These attractive outdoor environments should be *close to children's dwellings and institutions* and *safely accessible for children*.

Participation by children can occur on many levels, from more or less decisive participation in decision-making processes to direct inclusion in operational maintenance. If green space managers want to manage with children in mind, they would benefit from knowledge on children's perspectives as green space users. This knowledge may be entirely theoretical, or may be influenced by observations of children or by wear and tear in the setting. More direct contact and dialogue between children and managers can be a way of bridging the gap between the perspectives of children and managers and of creating understanding for use on a local level. By *involving local children in management and practical green space maintenance*, green space managers have the opportunity to understand and make use of local children's place-based experiences, knowledge and visions. If green space managers are more flexible and allow children to interact, for instance providing some extra tools in small sizes, informative chats may take place and good ideas for child-friendly management may turn up. This kind of informal work and chat might fit many children well (Jansson, 2015), even better than more formal participation in indoor meetings and workshops, such as is sometimes done in planning. Drawing on more hands-on participatory methods in everyday spaces, as proposed by Clark and Percy-Smith (2006), green space managers can meet the needs of the different individuals and groups within children's communities.

All else being equal, it must be more manageable to involve children in areas where the staffing is good and the green space managers themselves know each setting well and have time to observe the use, wear and tear. The current new public management trends with use of external contractors make it less easy to observe and relate to children, unless the task 'involving children' becomes a goal in future contracts. However, our results show that long-term involved managers of more private housing areas might also fail to include children's perspectives. With the current changes towards more multifunctionality of green spaces and inclusion of several perspectives, comes a shift into a more complex task, which most green space managers have not been trained to handle (Molin and van den Bosch, 2014).

In the future we would like to learn more about child-friendly green space management in other parts of the world as well as about the views, opinions, working situations and tasks of green space managers relative to children as users and identify potential areas of conflict.

CONCLUSIONS

Environmental child-friendliness has several dimensions and is affected by individual, social and physical environmental factors. Although it varies from child to child, the local environment, including structures, elements and social environmental aspects, has a large impact.

While focus has been put on trying to include children and their perspectives in planning and design, management appears a neglected and particularly promising arena for this. In our studies, we learned that child-friendly environments for children aged 10–11 can be greatly supported by green space management approaches and we specifically identified the following management-related characteristics (see Figure 12:1, p. 198): presence of a number of varied sites, attractive places for a wide range of actions, support for change, incorporation of sensory plants, upkeep of structures, thoughtful pruning and cutting of vegetation and a reflected attitude to tidiness. Child-friendliness is also influenced by attempts to increase the possibilities for children's independent mobility and proximity of various settings. Children benefit from as few restrictions in their use of local environments as possible, and managers in various roles and levels may gain new insights into the challenges and possibilities for development of local open spaces through acquaintance with local children. This leads to the obvious conclusion that practical participation by children and their involvement in decision-making as well as in operational management can facilitate constructive communication and increase the child-friendliness of environments. While children's participation on city planning level can still be of importance, it is within management that children can clearly incorporate their local knowledge and engagement.

Child-friendliness is a complex matter involving many stakeholders, such as urban planners, green space managers, private landlords, teachers and parents. Among these, green space managers at different organisational levels might have a larger role to play than realised previously. Our data shows that, on the one hand, children are highly dependent on the management of their local environment, as their relation to place is directly affected by green space management, such as the availability of space, trees, water, playground equipment and loose items. On the other hand, children rarely see the work of managers as related to them or within their influence.

We consider children's perspectives to be a rich resource for green space managers and an important aspect of environmental child-friendliness. If the political and practical will to prioritise children is present, knowledge about children's experiences may lead to more child-friendly urban environments. In this chapter, we showed that child-led walks in children's everyday contexts constitute a promising method to gain information about children's use and knowledge of their immediate surroundings, and we suggest dialogue and children's participation in operational management as a promising way to get ideas for increasingly child-friendly management of urban green spaces.

ACKNOWLEDGEMENT

This chapter is based on research project 225-2014-1552 funded by the Swedish Research Council for Environment, Agricultural Sciences and Spatial Planning, FORMAS.

REFERENCES

Alarasi, H., Martinez, J. and Amer, S. (2016) 'Children's perception of their city centre: A qualitative GIS methodological investigation in a Dutch city', *Children's Geographies* **14**, 4: 437–452.

Bell, S., Thompson, C. W. and Travlou, P. (2003) 'Contested views of freedom and control: Children, teenagers and urban fringe woodlands in Central Scotland', *Urban Forestry and Urban Greening* **2**, 2: 87–100.

Björklid, P. and Gummesson, M. (2013) *Children's Independent Mobility in Sweden*. Stockholm: Trafikverket.

Björklid, P. and Nordström, M. (2007) 'Environmental child-friendliness: Collaboration and future research', *Children, Youth and Environments* **17**, 4: 388–401.

Boldemann, C., Dal, H., Mårtensson, F., Cosco, N., Moore, R., Bieber, B., Blennow, M., Pagels, P., Raustorp, A. and Wester, U. (2011) 'Preschool outdoor play environment may combine promotion of children's physical activity and sun protection: Further evidence from Southern Sweden and North Carolina', *Science and Sports* **26**, 2: 72–82.

Bourke, B. (2014) 'Positionality: Reflecting on the research process', *The Qualitative Report* **19**, 33: 1–9.

Broberg, A., Kyttä, M. and Fagerholm, N. (2013) 'Child-friendly urban structures: Bullerby revisited', *Journal of Environmental Psychology* **35**: 110–120.

Carstensen, T. A. (2006) 'Byrum og ruter: På tur med børn i fire danske kvarterer', in K. Rasmussen (ed.) *Børns Steder: Om Børns Egne Steder Og Voksnes Steder Til Børn*. Billesøe og Baltzer.

Cele, S. (2005) *Communicating Place: Methods for Understanding Children's Experience of the Physical Environment*. PhD Thesis, Stockholm University.

Chatterjee, S. (2005) 'Children's friendship with place: A conceptual inquiry', *Children, Youth and Environments* **15**, 1: 1–26.

Chawla, L. (2015) 'Benefits of nature contact for children', *Journal of Planning Literature* **30**, 4: 433–452.

Clark, A., and Percy-Smith, B. (2006) 'Beyond consultation: Participatory practices in everyday spaces', *Children, Youth and Environments* **16**, 2: 1–9.

Cushing, D. F. (2016) 'Youth master plans as potential roadmaps to creating child- and youth-friendly cities', *Planning Practice and Research* **31**, 2: 154–173.

Dempsey, N., Smith, H., and Burton, M. (2014) *Place-Keeping: Open Space Management in Practice*. Abingdon: Routledge.

Elsley, S. (2004) 'Children's experience of public space', *Children and Society* **18**, 2: 155–164.

Florgård, C. and Forsberg, O. (2006) 'Residents' use of remnant natural vegetation in the residential area of Järvafältet, Stockholm', *Urban Forestry and Urban Greening* **5**, 2: 83–92.

Flyvbjerg, B. (2006) 'Five misunderstandings about case-study research', *Qualitative Inquiry* **12**, 2: 219–245.

Francis, M. (1988) 'Negotiating between child and adult design values', *Design Studies* **9**, 2: 67–75.

Gibson, J. J. (1979) *The Ecological Approach to Visual Perception*. Houghton Mifflin.

Haikkola, L., Pacilli, M. G., Horelli, L. and Prezza, M. (2007) 'Interpretations of urban child-friendliness: A comparative study of two neighborhoods in Helsinki and Rome', *Children, Youth and Environments* **17**, 4: 319–351.

Hill, M. (2006) 'Children's voices on ways of having a voice: Children's and young people's perspectives on methods used in research and consultation', *Childhood* **13**, 1: 69–89.

Horelli, L. (2007) 'Constructing a theoretical framework for environmental child-friendliness', *Children, Youth and Environments* **17**, 4: 267–292.

Janssen, I. and Rosu, A. (2015) 'Undeveloped green space and free-time physical activity in 11 to 13-year-old children', *International Journal of Behavioral Nutrition and Physical Activity* **12**, 1 (online).

Jansson, M. (2015) 'Children's perspectives on playground use as basis for children's participation in local play space management', *Local Environment* **20**, 2: 165–179.

Jansson, M., Mårtensson, F. and Gunnarsson, A. (2018) 'The meaning of participation in school ground greening: a study from project to everyday setting', *Landscape Research* **43**, 1: 163–179.

Jansson, M. and Lindgren, T. (2012) 'A review of the concept "management" in relation to urban landscapes and green spaces: Toward a holistic understanding', *Urban Forestry and Urban Greening* **11**, 2: 139–145.

Jansson, M., Sundevall, E. and Wales, M. (2016), 'The role of green spaces and their management in a child-friendly urban village', *Urban Forestry and Urban Greening* **18**: 228–236.

Kylin, M. (2003) 'Children's dens', *Children, Youth and Environments* **13**, 1: 30–55.

Kylin, M. and Lieberg, M. (2001) 'Barnperspektiv på utemiljön', *Nordic Journal of Architectural Research* **1**: 63–77.

Kyttä, M. (2004) 'The extent of children's independent mobility and the number of actualized affordances as criteria for child-friendly environments', *Journal of Environmental Psychology* **24**, 2: 179–198.

Lerstrup, I. (2016) Green Settings for Children in Preschools: Affordance-Based Considerations for Design and Management. PhD Thesis, University of Copenhagen.

Lerstrup, I. and Konijnendijk van den Bosch, C. (2017) 'Affordances of outdoor settings for children in preschool: Revisiting Heft's functional taxonomy', *Landscape Research* **42**, 1: 47–62.

Lerstrup, I. and Refshauge, A. D. (2016) 'Characteristics of forest sites used by a Danish forest preschool', *Urban Forestry and Urban Greening* **20**, 387–396.

Loebach, J. and Gilliland, J. (2010)' Child-led tours to uncover children's perceptions and use of neighborhood environments', *Children, Youth and Environments* **20**, 1: 52–90.

Malone, K. and Tranter, P. (2003) 'Children's environmental learning and the use, design and management of schoolgrounds', *Children, Youth and Environments* **13**, 2: 87–137.

Molin, J. F. and van den Bosch, C. C. K. (2014) 'Between big ideas and daily realities: The roles and perspectives of Danish municipal green space managers on public involvement in green space maintenance', *Urban Forestry and Urban Greening* **13**: 553–561.

Moore, R. C. (1986) 'The power of nature: Orientations of girls and boys toward biotic and abiotic play settings on a reconstructed schoolyard', *Children's Environments Quarterly* **3**, 3: 52–69.

Prellwitz, M. and Skär, L. (2007) 'Usability of playgrounds for children with different abilities', *Occupational Therapy International* **14**, 3: 144–155.

Randrup, T. B. and Persson, B. (2009) 'Public green spaces in the Nordic countries: Development of a new strategic management regime', *Urban Forestry and Urban Greening* **8**, 1: 31–40.

Rasmussen, K. (2004)' Places for children – children's places', *Childhood* **11**, 2: 155–173.

Riggio, E. (2002) 'Child friendly cities: Good governance in the best interests of the child', *Environment and Urbanization* **14**, 2: 45–58.

Roe, M. (2006) ' "Making a wish": Children and the local landscape', *Local Environment* **11**, 2: 163–182.

Simkins, I. and Thwaites, K. (2008) 'Revealing the hidden spatial dimensions of place experience in primary school-age children', *Landscape Research* **33**, 5: 531–546.

Söderström, M., Boldemann, C., Sahlin, U., Mårtensson, F., Raustorp, A. and Blennow, M. (2013) 'The quality of the outdoor environment influences children's health – a cross-sectional study of preschools', *Acta Paediatrica* **102**, 1: 83–91.

Stake, R. E. (1995) *The Art of Case Study Research*. London: Sage.

Tiller, P.O. (1991) 'Barneperspektivet - om å se og bli sett: Vårt perspektiv på barn - eller omvendt?', *Barn - Nyt Fra Forskning om Barn i Norge*, **1**: 72–77. Trondheim: Norsk senter for barneforskning.

van den Brink, A., Bruns, D., Tobi, H. and Bell, S. (eds) (2016) *Research in Landscape Architecture: Methods and Methodology*. Abingdon: Routledge.

13

A VIEW FROM CHINA: REFLECTING ON THE PARTICIPATION OF CHILDREN AND YOUNG PEOPLE IN URBAN PLANNING

Yupeng Ren

INTRODUCTION

Creating appropriate institutional arrangements for youth participation in urban planning is increasingly acknowledged as essential for fostering young people's 'agency' in their own communities and as vital for good governance (Riggio, 2002). More specifically, the field of urban planning has for some time, and to some extent, recognised the importance of working with and for young people, reflecting a widespread commitment within planning to public participation (Rydin and Pennington, 2000, Innes and Booher, 2004), as well as recognition of the requirements of the United Nations Convention on the Rights of the Child (UNCRC), adopted in 1989. Article 12 of UNCRC has explicitly stipulated children and young people a right to participate in the matters that affect them. Nonetheless, although promoting children and young people's participatory rights is regarded as important by policy makers, there remains a relative absence of clarity in terms of how to operationalise participation effectively across all nation states, and how to incorporate the UNCRC across all policy areas that affect children and young people.

The dynamics and diversity of the way people interact with place and space is central to the practice of planning (Healey, 1997). In addition to its physicality, planning is considered as an arena with different competing actors and interest groups (Tewdwr-Jones and Williams, 2001). In order to improve understanding of planning processes and the different actors engaged in the various aspects of urban development, it is important to appreciate that power dynamics structure planning processes, affect different interests and potentially lead to status inequalities (Habermas, 1984; Innes, 1998; Healey, 1996). Thinking about this dynamic of power in planning helps to identify children and young people as particular actors in planning practice and with specific long-term interests in urban development projects. In line with Wood's approach to power (discussed in Chapter 10 of this volume), I understand power to be embedded in social practice in many forms, scales and relationships. As Foucault (1977) pointed out, power is arguably understood as a dispersed phenomenon that is present in all personal and public relationships. The distribution of power is clearly evident in urban planning and development. Power can be regarded as distributed throughout the entire planning system and exercised by means of different sets of practices at different scales in the construction and dissemination of particular bodies of knowledge (Gallagher, 2008). Therefore, I contend that adopting a social constructionist perspective not only offers an understanding of the power relations that work on young people's status in planning processes, but also reveals the structures that potentially shape people's mindsets on youth participation in planning. Following Giddens (1984) and Healey and Barrett (1990), for example, a structuralist perspective illuminates the ways of viewing and understanding youth participation in the context of China.

Children and young people in industrialised nations are increasingly provided with some opportunities to exercise their rights in certain aspects of decision-making, including the recognition of youth as stakeholders in planning processes and the institutionalisation of youth participation within formal education (Frank, 2006). In Scotland, for instance, Planning Aid for Scotland (PAS) runs programmes, such as In My Back Yard (IMBY), Youth Engagement in Planning (YEP!) and Young Placemaker, specifically for involving children and young people in place-making. With this and similar movements, a new planning bill currently making its way through the Scottish parliament at the time of writing suggests greater recognition in future. Despite increasing interest and a long-standing requirement for public participation in the UK planning system (since the 1960s), it is revealing that only in 2019 are young people being specifically recognised as planning stakeholders.

The role of young people in shaping their immediate environment becomes more problematic, however, in contexts where ideas of public participation are relatively new and under-researched, such as China. Whereas youth participation in industrialised economies is viewed as a driving force for progressive change and a means to promote citizenship and social inclusion (Kirby et al., 2003), much less is known about how these concepts play out in the Chinese context despite growing interest in the field. In China, it is maintained that planning policy and practices have to react to high-speed processes of urbanisation and regeneration, as well as their environmental impact, such as energy scarcity, air and water aggravation, noise pollution and loss of arable and natural land (Yu, 2014; Wei and Ye, 2014). Since these issues concern future generations, I argue that the voices of children and young people should be taken into account during processes of urban decision-making. Despite research in the realm of participatory planning in the context of China, the focus of these studies has rarely centred on children or young people.

The aim of this chapter is to contribute to the new body of understanding about youth participation and identify both opportunities and challenges that face Chinese children and young people with regard to participation in planning decision-making. For ease, I use 'young people' to focus on the transition between child and adult, rather than referring to children or young people in isolation. I draw on my original PhD research carried out with university students: '"Can I influence urban change?": A study of university students' participation in an age of urban transformation'. This chapter reflects critically on the opportunities and challenges presented by the socio-political contexts that informed my study, prior to engaging directly with participants.

I firstly review the socio-political context for youth participation in planning in China. Then, drawing on the theory of structuration (Giddens, 1984), I discuss the ways in which structural influences and young people agency enable or constrain youth participation in planning decision-making. I then explore how Chinese young people's urban experiences have been shaped. Finally, I will draw conclusions on the extent to which young people's participation in urban planning has been enabled or constrained by the immediate social-cultural environment and the broader politico-economic context within which their urban lives unfold and put forward some thoughts for future research.

SOCIO-POLITICAL CONTEXT

With respect to globally established rules and regulations, young people's participatory rights have been endorsed by a wide range of international policies in the past 30 years. As Gibson (2014) suggested, however, the UNCRC is the seminal statutory response to the idea of engaging youth in decision-making, providing a policy framework for considering the participatory rights of young people and offering insights to understanding young people's roles in shaping and changing their living environments.

Although the UNCRC does not directly refer to urban planning and development, it is an important framework within which nation-states and international organisations operate. The challenge for governments around the world is to implement the spirit of the UNCRC through legislation and institutionalisation. What is more, adult agencies are urged to revise their traditional ways of thinking. For instance, sustainable development should not be adult-centred with adults exercising their power as stewards on behalf of young people. It is about acknowledging young people's capacity to act as real agents and authentic participants in planning and development processes (Malone, 2001). In this sense, youth participation in environmental planning could be regarded as a catalyst for achieving sustainable urban development.

In terms of the Chinese context, after 1949, the year of the establishment of the People's Republic of China (PRC), the Chinese government held absolute power to drive urban development by dominating state ownership. Until 1978, the Chinese planning system was regarded as one of the Government's principal instruments to achieve the

FIGURE 13.1 A view of Pudong, Shanghai
Source: Weiying Wang

socialist ideology in terms of spatial development and facilitating the implementation of industrial projects drawn up under centralised planning arrangements (Abramson, 2006). Over time, the Government's role has gradually changed towards a market-oriented economy and the Chinese Government no longer has total control to mobilise social resources (Yeh and Wu, 1999).

After the market reform in 1979, the Chinese urban population grew rapidly. Figure 13.1 demonstrates the dramatic urban transformation that has taken place in Pudong, Shanghai. Figure 13.2 shows that the urban population rose from 18 percent of the total population in 1978 to more than 56 percent in 2015. The urban youth population has also increased accordingly. Over this period, the pace and impact of market reform were reflected through the growth of cities and the increase of public interest in the environment. Those interested were mainly young people. Lu (2003) has pointed out that, in China, members of Environmental Non-Governmental Organisations (ENGOs) are mostly young people. Chinese students have also played an active role in a series of protests against some major urban development projects (Liu, 2008). In this sense, Chinese young people were not merely acting as passive policy recipients to decisions of urban environmental planning in contemporary China; they were active players offering resistance. This view reflects a body of work, such as Duan (2005), Cen and Li (2006) and Kim (2008), that regards youth participation in China as responding to the authoritarian tendencies of a centralised state. However, it would appear that, despite China being a signatory of the UNCRC, existing channels and opportunities for youth participation in planning policy are still limited by structural barriers. If the principles of the UNCRC are to be followed, efforts need to be made in order to understand those barriers in process of urban planning and development.

INSTITUTIONAL ARRANGEMENTS FOR YOUNG PEOPLE'S PARTICIPATION IN CHINA

With respect to the prominent social influences on public participation in China, Chinese values and norms (informal arrangements) have defined state–society–individual relationships in terms of youth participation in decision-making. Confucianism has been central in how Chinese society functions (Waldmann, 2000). Derived from the

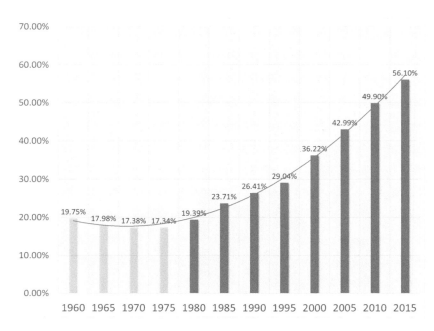

FIGURE 13.2 Urban population in China (% of total)
Source: The World Bank

teachings of the philosopher Confucius (551–479BC; his original name in Chinese was Kong Qiu) recorded in the collection called *Lunyu* or *The Analects* (Waley, 1995), the individual is regarded as a component of various social institutions and networks, within which highly defined rights and responsibilities are bound to them (Fei, 1992). The 'five virtues', which are kindness, righteousness, propriety, wisdom and trustworthiness, underpin Confucian thinking. They form the basis for state–society–individual relationships, such as the relationship of monarch and subjects, fathers and sons, husband and wife, the elder and the young, teacher and students, and others. These relationships differ, but all demand respect for the five virtues.

Confucianism sets out the five virtues as a normative framework to guide how one should act in different social relations. Nevertheless, Hofstede and Bond (1988), for example, argued that the five virtues can only function in unequal social relationships between individuals. For example, subjects of the sovereign are supposed to honour the sovereign's will; children are supposed to have unquestioned obedience to their parents; younger brothers or sisters follow the older ones; a wife submits herself to her husband; and juniors listen to their seniors in the relationship of friends (Xing, 1995). Gao and Handley-Schachler (2003) also suggested that, from a Confucian perspective, virtuous behaviours would be achieved through education, diligence, perseverance and moderation in all things. In order to achieve the five virtues, young people in China are taught to honour their parents and elders, express filial piety and respect for seniority and social position.

Confucianism has been acknowledged as the dominating ideology in China, and it is distinguished from the ways of thinking and behaving in Western countries (Figure 13.3), which pursue human liberty, development of individual personality, material enjoyment and the joy of life rather than Confucian ethics disciplines. China has forged its own path towards modernisation, which is different from Western democracy's values and norms. While seeking this path, Confucianism has been regarded as the essential tradition that might produce political and social cohesion and bolster modern-day Chinese governance.

The doctrine of Confucianism has been deeply rooted in Chinese culture for thousands of years (Hu, 2007). It prioritises the overall interests of the country and a good sense of discipline. The actualisation of Confucianism has

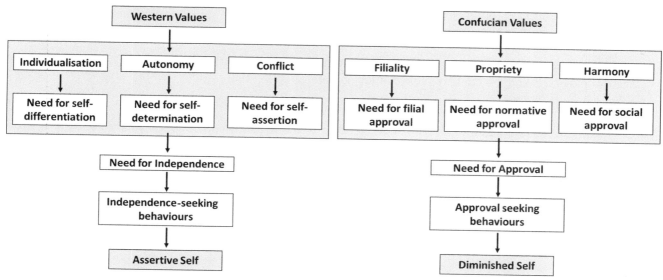

FIGURE 13.3 A comparison between Western and Confucian values
Source: derived from Lu et al., 2001

meant that young people pay a great deal of attention to self-control and they have respect for social institutions. On this basis, Confucianism may result in a different understanding of participation in public affairs, as well as in urban planning and governance, than is articulated in the West. In short, young people in China may engage in different types of behaviour with regard to urban transformation than those considered as typical from a Western democratic perspective.

Ngai et al. (2001) noted that the Communist Party of China continues to remind young people that the interests of an individual must be subordinated to the interests of the collective. Ping et al. (2004) indicated that in the syllabus for primary and secondary schools, traditional moral and ideological content is pointedly described as compulsory. At the university level, attitudes to Confucianism move closer to the cultivation of ideology and morality (Ping et al., 2004). It can thus be seen at a glance that traditional values are seen as highly important to society, as well as the connections drawn between social, interpersonal and political values. Young people are taught at school and university to have respect for others, which may potentially hinder young people participating in public affairs and becoming active citizens in accordance with Western values. In this sense, to claim and preserve young people's participatory rights should be viewed differently in the specific social, ideological and political context of China.

Human rights are often framed around western values, but as China has ratified the UNCRC it is important to understand what these ideals can and should look like in non-western countries. In spite of overlapping normative frameworks at play in the Chinese context (e.g. Confucianism and Communism) that privilege the 'collective' over the 'individual', what has not been considered is whether, within the existing social structures, there are possibilities for young people to take on the role of active agents and to gain access to knowledge of planning.

YOUNG PEOPLE'S AGENCY

A social–constructionist view of planning and the theory of structuration can help illuminate the ways in which young people around the world are constrained by structural factors in shaping urban development agendas. This line of thinking also suggests the possibility that young people can break down barriers through their own agency.

Considering young people's autonomy as active social agents has been influential in terms of facilitating young people's agency in youth research (Holland et al., 2010). As Feldman and Elliott made clear:

> Too often adolescents are portrayed as passive recipients of circumstances … In reality they play an active role in shaping the context in which they operate.
>
> (1990: 495)

This perspective suggests a more complex understanding of the relationships between young people and social structures necessary in contrast to the assumption of young people as passive recipients of structural influences. As Hil and Bessant argued:

> Most young people have less power than the adults they interact with. Yet while some people have more power than others, everyone possesses some power to influence to the course of their own lives, even in the most adverse and disadvantageous of circumstances.
>
> (1999: 45)

This argument suggests young people around the world are frequently made to comply with and internalise social structures and institutional arrangements. It also indicates young people's capacity to challenge social structures to which they are subject. In this sense, young people's agency represents their capacity to act positively in relation to surrounding structures. Therefore, the relationship between young people and social structures cannot be explained simply through a structural functionalist perspective. Structures (e.g. Socialism, Confucianism) are the products of individual agents' social interactions through which they create, negotiate, sustain and modify the social structures. Accordingly, young people's agency is not totally determined by forces external to youth agents. As Hil and Bessant argued:

> young people, like older people, are neither entirely free and autonomous nor entirely constrained by 'external forces'. Young people are linked through relationships of mutual dependence and independence, the nature of which changes as people change.
>
> (1999: 45)

Following this argument, young people's agency can be considered as shaped by society, just as they have the capacity to shape some of their own perceptions and behaviours. In the field of urban planning, the agency of young people is infused with particular structural meanings that shape the ways in which young people perceive and experience urban transformation in China. Young people's agency in this sense is not merely the product of structural forces in planning (culture, norms and legislations, etc.). Young people's agency means young people can attribute new meanings and give new interpretations to those social relationships and institutional arrangements. On the basis of young people's agency, it is held that their participation in planning is essential to ensure that the urban environment is developed in accordance with young people's specific needs (Checkoway et al., 1995). This is likely to improve the delivery of planning and design projects in terms of offering a supplementary perspective to adults and planners.

Chai (2003) and Chan and Fang (2007) have argued that Chinese young people are becoming centrally involved in, and influenced by, globalisation, social-economic reform, the spread of the Internet and social media. Perhaps one of the inevitable consequences of young people's assertion to structural changes is the combination of opportunities for developing their agency. Wilkins et al. state that young people:

> do so not through simply imitating past practices but by developing reinvigorated reactionary practices.
>
> (2000: 250)

In this sense, young people's agency may be partially culturally and historically produced and is increasingly implicated in contemporary structural changes. At the same time, young people are considered to hold perpetual agency to change social structures. This way of conceptualising young people's agency offers insights to consider institutional arrangements as opportunities and challenges for young people's participation in planning.

CIVIL ENGAGEMENT AND YOUTH PARTICIPATION IN CHINA

The centralised nature of socialist institutions in China is closely linked to the inadequate practice of public participation in urban planning. This draws my attention to the institutional arrangements for civil engagement in China. From 1949, when the socialist model of urban planning was adopted, decision-making included hardly any formal methods for public participation. However, over time, laws and policies were introduced which promoted, conferred and formalised the rights of individuals to participate in planning and managing issues arising from urban development. Today, public participation has become a guiding principle for the formulation of laws and regulations in urban environmental planning.

For instance, China's National Constitution (1954) states that people are conferred the rights of participating in the governance of the State in terms of socio-economic, cultural and political affairs. Socialist values held that state power belongs to the public, and people's participation in administrating state affairs is one of their constitutional rights and therefore should be protected by law (Zheng, 1994). As Cheng (1994) pointed out, part of the socialist ideology in China was 'serving the people'. Involving the public in decision-making could potentially address public concern and maximise their interests through empowerment (Li et al., 2012). Therefore, it may be argued that public participation in socialist China not only met the constitutional requirement, but also endorsed the socialist ideology in terms of making accountable decisions for the people.

The rights of Chinese people to participate were also stipulated in government legislation, such as the Law of the PRC on Urban and Rural Planning (2008) and Environmental Protection Law of the PRC (2015). In the Law of the PRC on Urban and Rural Planning (2008), public participation in urban planning was stipulated in explicit terms. Measures for formulating development plans emphasise public participation and ensure that the public should be able to be involved in planning processes.

In addition to legal provision, public participation is also endorsed by the institutional arrangements of the Chinese government. According to He and Thøgersen (2010), under the current institutional setting, the public can express their opinions through their representative and defend public interests in the Chinese People's Congress and Chinese People's Political Consultative Conference. Zhao (2014) added that outside of the formal channels, the public may also exert their influences through using mass media, sending complaint letters, visiting government offices and even protesting in the streets.

While formal and informal channels can help the public articulate their voices and influence decisions, however, it is widely agreed that practices of public participation largely fail to serve their purpose in the Chinese context (Johnson, 2010; Boland and Zhu, 2012; Li et al., 2012; Zhang, 2015). Wang (2003) has argued participation might serve as a tool to justify pre-decided planning decisions and in this sense, participation reinforces tendencies of 'centralisation' rather than 'decentralisation'. Tang et al. (2008) noted that legislation does not include detailed provisions identifying who should be involved in decision-making, how to involve the public at the local level, or how to deliver sufficient instruction, supervision and evaluation of the participatory processes. What has also been overlooked, and is actually very crucial, is the fact that the public's knowledge about public participation in planning is weak, merely including opportunities such as acknowledgement, hearing, consulting and seeking comments from the public (Zhang, 2015). A systematic understanding of public participation theories and practices may thus be seen as absent.

Finally, with respect to children and young people, although the Chinese government ratified the UNCRC in 1989, there are still barriers hindering the exercise of young people's participatory rights in making planning decisions. For example, in the Law of the PRC on the Protection of Minors (2006), Article 3 has legalised children and young people's participatory rights as basic rights, and Article 14 states that their voices shall be respected and listened to. These legal provisions fail to elaborate on the operational and procedural details. In terms of urban planning, there is no explicit government regulation on young people's participatory rights and no written laws to define young people's status within urban planning systems. Indeed, Wong et al. (2006) once noted that many local governments drive their development policy towards promoting administrative expediency. Elsewhere, Liu (2011) pointed out that young people are still assumed as inadequate, in terms of capability and knowledge, to engage in policy-making, while Gibson (2014) attributed the unsound implementation of the UNCRC to the resistance of the prevailing socio-political culture and the unfulfilled responsibility of the Government. This evidence suggests that when decisions are being taken by the Government, there are few opportunities for young people to articulate differing views or opinions, and even if this does occur, the participation tends to be a procedural formality. Decisions on development projects may be customarily taken by adult agencies and are rarely influenced by the genuine interests of young people. Arguably, the task facing Chinese urban planning is to identify the gaps in rhetoric and reality in relation to participation, and to consider institutional changes in order to cultivate young people as active citizens. There is a critical need to review attitudes towards young people, their capacities and values, as well as their roles in the processes of urban transformation.

CHINESE YOUNG PEOPLE IN AN AGE OF URBAN TRANSFORMATION

Having reviewed the civil society and youth participation in China, this section gives particular attention to young people's experiences and interactions with the transforming urban environments. Structural changes resulting from the move to a market economy have had effects not only on urbanisation generally but also on young people as individuals. As Nelson and Chen (2007) discussed, western individualistic values and ideologies, such as liberty and individual freedom, have been introduced and accepted by Chinese young people. In contrast, socialist ideologies and traditional Chinese culture emphasise solidarity, concern for others and integration with other people (Oyserman et al., 2002). Structural changes in China as a result of economic reform potentially create a cultural orientation on the self for young people. For example, as Chen et al. (2005) argued, a competitive society may require young people to assume qualities, such as expression of personal opinions, self-direction and self-confidence. Economy (2004) pointed out that young environmentalists are often open and aggressive, and they possess the full complement of skills necessary to organise effectively.

The use of media, such as the Internet, may also mean young people gain access to information on values and ideologies in other parts of the world (Nelson and Chen, 2007). Evidence suggests that structural changes can potentially have an impact on young people's social perceptions and behaviours. For instance, Chen et al. (1992) indicated that introverted and conservative youth behaviours were linked to certain 'positive' outcomes (e.g. social acceptance). Lau (1996) explained that those behaviours reflected group dependence and social restraint, which were valued in traditional Chinese culture. However, Chen et al. (2005) have pointed out that, in the past two decades, introverted and conservative youth behaviours have not been considered positive by Chinese youth. This suggests that social changes have raised young people's awareness of both individualism and more participatory behaviour in decision-making. This phenomenon can be witnessed through young people's dynamic attitudes to urban planning and development in recent years.

The rapid urbanisation since the 1980s has also brought a series of problems, in particular urban environmental pollution. Young people's awareness of and participation in activities regarding urban environmental protection has increased accordingly. For example, Stalley and Yang (2006) identified rapid urbanisation as the incubator for Chinese youth, and university students in particular, to develop their awareness of participation and to confront

FIGURE 13.4 The number of university environmental associations in China
Source: derived from Lu, 2003 and Ren, 2016

urban environmental degradation. Similarly, Lu (2003) and Ren (2016) reported that the number of environmental groups in Chinese universities has increased significantly since the 1990s.

Figure 13.4 shows the growth of university student environment associations from 1965 to 2010. In 1997, there were only 22 student-led environment groups, but those student-led environmental NGOs took off in the mid-1990s and accelerated within two decades. By 2010, there was at least one student environmental association in every Chinese top 100 university. This evidence shows that a growing number of university students in China have concerns about their living environment. In the immediate aftermath of the Tiananmen Square protest in 1989, many university students stopped joining political protests on the streets (Kim, 2008). Nevertheless, university students in China have shown an increasing level of urban environmental awareness.

Protests regarding urban development issues have become another arena for students' informal participation. In 2006, 10,000 university students' signatures on a petition against a series of power plant projects played a critical part in the success of the campaign (Stalley and Yang, 2006). Liu (2008) also identified that students have played an active role in a series of protests against some major urban environment projects, notably p-Xylene (PX) projects. Cheng's (2013) study of young citizens' protests against PX chemical plants in China is often cited as one of the most dramatic displays of the growing tension between young people and local governments over urban development.

Political and socio-economic dynamics influence the opportunities and initiatives for individuals' participation (Chai, 2003). Yang (2003) identified that the rise of the internet has signalled a gradual change in citizens' relationships to state politics. Chan and Fang (2007) suggest that the internet has offered Chinese young people a new way to acquire knowledge, share information and participate in discussion. Kemp (2015) claims almost ten percent of the total population are active Weibo users (Weibo is the Chinese equivalent of Twitter), and half its active users were born after 1990. Based on the evidence above, it may be argued that young people have the potential to gain access to information and develop new ways to participate in urban development and governance as a result of the internet and social media.

TABLE 13.1 Challenges for youth participation in planning in China

Evidence	Likely Implications
1) Chinese people's environmental knowledge, willingness to act and actual engagement in decision making were rather low (Chan, 1999). 2) Young people's participation was often ineffective, with adult agencies consulting young people but not acting upon their interests (Duan, 2005). 3) Due to censorship, university students appeared neither inclined to query the Government's accountability nor participate in potentially sanctioned activities (Stalley and Yang, 2006). 4) Value, overburdened academic pressure and socio-political attitudes have impeded the development of Chinese university students' knowledge, concern and action over urban planning and development (Johnson et al., 2007).	• 'NIMBYism' • Young people are assumed as inadequate, in terms of capability and knowledge, to engage in policy-making. • Decisions on development projects may customarily be taken by adult agencies and are rarely influenced by the genuine interests of young people. • When decisions are being taken by the Government, there are few opportunities for young people to articulate differing views or opinions. • Achieving a good academic grade and pursuing opportunities to enter a good university may be the priority perceived by students; • Participation in planning decision-making may be considered as less important by students.

Social changes also create opportunities for young people's participation in urban planning. Nevertheless, these opportunities should be considered in the broader cultural context which still emphasises the needs and interests of the Party State. It has been argued, for example, that social and economic modernisation may not necessarily weaken the centralised culture in group-oriented societies (Nelson and Chen, 2007). Some scholars also discuss the implications that social changes may potentially bring about to the practice of Chinese young people's participation in planning. Table 13.1 is a summary of representative literature highlighting both the evidence and likely implications of social changes in China.

Based on both the evidence and likely implications presented in Table 13.1, it may thus be argued that the age of social reform and urban transformation offers opportunities for Chinese young people's participation in planning decision-making, but there is still a gap in rhetoric and reality in relation to considering institutional changes in order to cultivate young people as active citizens. Questions remain on the visibility of children and young people in public space. To what extent can children and young people have a space in the public realm in China? Does this link with youth agency to participate in the decision-making process? What kind of processes would need to be in place for young people to have a say? Would young people's participation be viewed as a threat as young people become more and more exposed to Western views? These issues are worth discussing but have not yet received sufficient attention in academic literature. As a final comment regarding the visibility of children and young people and all the attention they have received from Chinese society, I would put the onus firmly on adults to overcome their stereotypes, considering the call for a more genuine appreciation of Chinese children and young people's characteristics, their perceptions and their needs.

CONCLUSION

China is experiencing rapid urban transformation with evidence of environmental degradation. The effects on society are dramatic, with some evidence of social unrest. As a signatory to the UNCRC, China has asserted its commitment to enhancing young people's rights. Young people are shaped by the context within which discussions will be brought about and decisions will be made. However, it does not necessarily mean young people are powerless or unable to succeed in achieving their own agendas for urban development. As Foucault (1977) contended, power embeds in social practices at different forms, scales and relationships. Young people can exercise influence and challenge power structures through shifting cultural orientation, by developing new ideas, giving new interpretations to social structure and mobilising resources for action in new ways. In a similar vein to the understanding of 'communicative rationality' (Healey, 1996), young people are the best people to define and transform their own perceptions of, and experiences in, participation in planning.

Some evidence suggests that social change may be the catalyst for deepening the implementation of the UNCRC in China. For example, it is argued that family decision-making is becoming more inclusive of young people and that modernisation of local governance systems at the neighbourhood level also provides greater potential for youth participation (Flurry and Veeck, 2009). Participation of young people in formulating legislation to protect youth welfare at different levels has served as an instrument to absorb young people's opinions and provide an outlet for youth grievance (Ngai et al., 2001). There is also some evidence that young people are engaged in national level policy-making, local level decision-making and the governance of civil institutions in China, but such practices are not widespread (Ngai et al., 2001).

Further research about Chinese young people's perceptions of their urban environment and participation in urban planning and development is needed, however, given their future roles as long-term stakeholders, active citizens in planning decision-making and potential leaders in urban change. Institutional arrangements that incorporate young people's ideas and expectations can arguably improve their experiences of engagement and allow for the development of communicative planning practices which reflect young people's needs and desires. This chapter has provided some conceptual insights into the opportunities and challenges for young people to participate in shaping future change in China.

REFERENCES

Abramson, D. B. (2006). 'Urban planning in China: Continuity and change'. *Journal of the American Planning Association.* **72** (2). pp.197–215.

Boland, A. and Zhu, J. (2012). 'Public participation in China's green communities: Mobilizing memories and structuring incentives'. *Geoforum.* **43** (1). pp.147–157.

Cen, G. and Li, D. (2006). 'Social transformation and values conflicts among youth in contemporary China'. In: Daiute, C., Beykont, Z. F., Higson-Smith, C. and Nucci, L. (eds). *International Perspectives on Youth, Conflict and Development.* Oxford: Oxford University Press, pp. 156–170.

Chai, W. (2003). 'The ideological paradigm shifts of China's world views: From Marxism-Leninism-Maoism to the pragmatism-multilateralism of the Deng-Jiang-Hu Era'. *Asian Affairs: An American Review.* **30** (3). pp.163–175.

Chan, K. and Fang, W. (2007). 'Use of the Internet and traditional media among young people'. *Young Consumers.* **8** (4). pp.244–256.

Chan, R. Y. K. (1999). 'Environmental attitudes and behaviour of consumers in China: Survey findings and implications'. *Journal of International Consumer Marketing.* **11** (4). pp.25–52.

Checkoway, B., Pothukuchi, K. and Finn, J. (1995). 'Youth participation in community planning: What are the benefits?' *Journal of Planning Education and Research.* **14** (2). pp.134–139.

Chen, X., Cen, G., Li, D. and He, Y. (2005). 'Social functioning and adjustment in Chinese children: The imprint of historical time'. *Child Development.* **76** (1). pp.182–195.

Chen, X., Rubin, K. H. and Sun, Y. (1992). 'Social reputation and peer relationships in Chinese and Canadian children: A cross-cultural study'. *Child Development.* **63** (6). pp.1336–1343.

Cheng, K. (1994). 'Young adults in a changing socialist society: Post-compulsory education in China'. *Comparative Education.* **30** (1). pp.63–73.

Cheng, Y. (2013). 'Collaborative planning in the network: Consensus seeking in urban planning issues on the Internet – the case of China'. *Planning Theory.* **12** (4). pp.351–368.

China's National Constitution (1954), Available (in Chinese) at: www.npc.gov.cn/wxzl/wxzl/2000-12/26/content_4264.htm [Accessed 4 April 2020].

Duan, G. (2005). On the participation in politics of the youth in contemporary Chinese cities [Online]. Available at: http://netx.u-paris10.fr/actuelmarx/m4duang.htm [Accessed 23 Aug 2015].

Economy, E. C. (2004). *The River Runs Black: The Environmental Challenge to China's Future.* London: Cornell University Press.

Environmental Protection Law of the PRC (2015). Available (in Chinese) at: www.gov.cn/zhengce/2014-04/25/content_2666434.htm [Accessed 4 April 2020].

Fei, X. (1992). *From the Soil: The Foundations of Chinese Society.* London: University of California Press.

Feldman, S. S. and Elliott, G. R (1990). *At the Threshold: The Developing Adolescent.* London: Harvard University Press.

Flurry, L. A. and Veeck, A. (2009). 'Children's relative influence in family decision making in urban China'. *Journal of Macromarketing.* **29** (2). pp.145–159.

Foucault, M. (1977). *Discipline and Punishment*. New York: Pantheon.

Frank, K. I. (2006). 'The potential of youth participation in planning'. *Journal of Planning Literature*. **20** (4). pp.351–371.

Gallagher, M. (2008). 'Foucault, power and participation'. *The International Journal of Children's Rights*. **16** (3). pp.395–406.

Gao, S. and Handley-Schachler, M. (2003). 'The influences of Confucianism, Feng Shui and Buddhism in Chinese accounting history'. *Accounting, Business and Financial History*. **13** (1). pp.41–68.

Gibson, C. (2014). Building up the future: The implementation of the UNCRC in China [Online]. Available at: http://scholarship.shu.edu/cgi/viewcontent.cgi?article=1133andcontext=student_scholarship [Accessed 28 Aug 2017].

Giddens, A. (1984). *The Constitution of Society*. Cambridge: Polity Press.

Habermas, J. (1984). *The Theory of Communicative Action*. Boston: Beacon.

He, B. and Thøgersen, S. (2010). 'Giving the people a voice? Experiments with consultative authoritarian institutions in China'. *Journal of Contemporary China*. **19** (66). pp.675–692.

Healey, P. (1996). 'The communicative turn in planning theory and its implications for spatial strategy formation'. *Environment and Planning B: Urban Analytics and City Science*. **23** (2). pp.217–234.

Healey, P. (1997). *Collaborative Planning: Shaping Places in Fragmented Societies*. London: Macmillan.

Healey, P. and Barrett, S. M. (1990). 'Structure and agency in land and property development processes: Some ideas for research'. *Urban Studies*. **27** (1). pp.89–103.

Hil, R. and Bessant, J. (1999). 'Spaced-out? Young people's agency, resistance and public space'. *Urban Policy and Research*. **17** (1). pp.41–49.

Hofstede, G. and Bond, M. H. (1988). 'The Confucius connection: From cultural roots to economic growth'. *Organizational Dynamics*. **16** (4). pp.5–21.

Holland, S., Renold, E., Ross, N. J. and Hillman, A. (2010). 'Power, agency and participatory agendas: A critical exploration of young people's engagement in participative qualitative research'. *Childhood*. **17** (3). pp.360–375.

Hu, S. (2007). 'Confucianism and contemporary Chinese politics'. *Politics and Policy*. **35** (1). pp.136–153.

Innes, J. E. (1998). 'Information in communicative planning'. *Journal of the American Planning Association*. **64** (1). pp.52–63.

Innes, J. E. and Booher, D. E. (2004). 'Reframing public participation: Strategies for the 21st century'. *Planning Theory and Practice*. **5** (4). pp.419–436.

Johnson, L. R., Johnson-Pynn, J. S. and Pynn, T. M. (2007). 'Youth civic engagement in China: Results from a program promoting environmental activism'. *Journal of Adolescent Research*. **22** (4). pp.355–386.

Johnson, T. (2010). 'Environmentalism and NIMBYism in China: Promoting a rules-based approach to public participation'. *Environmental Politics*. **19** (3). pp.430–448.

Kemp, S. (2015). Digital, social and mobile in China in 2015 [Online]. Available at: http://wearesocial.com/sg/special-reports/digital-social-mobile-china-2015 [Accessed 10 Feb 2017].

Kim, P. (2008). 'Chinese student protests: Explaining the student movements of the 1980s and the lack of protests Since 1989'. *Berkeley Undergraduate Journal*. **21** (2). pp.1–42.

Kirby, P., Lanyon, C., Cronin, K. and Sinclair, R. (2003). Building a culture of participation: Involving children and young people in policy, service planning, delivery and evaluation [Online]. Available at: www.gyerekesely.hu/childpoverty/docs/involving_children_report.pdf [Accessed 28 Aug 2017].

Lau, S. (ed.) (1996). *Growing Up the Chinese Way: Chinese Child and Adolescent Development*. Hong Kong: The Chinese University Press.

Law of the PRC on the Protection of Minors (2006). Available (in Chinese) at: www.gov.cn/flfg/2006-12/29/content_554397.htm [Accessed 4 April 2020].

Law of the PRC on Urban and Rural Planning (2008), Available (in Chinese) at: www.gov.cn/flfg/2007-10/28/content_788494.htm [Accessed 4 April 2020].

Li, W., Liu, J. and Li, D. (2012). 'Getting their voices heard: Three cases of public participation in environmental protection in China'. *Journal of Environmental Management*. **98** (2012). pp.65–72.

Liu, F. (2008). 'Constructing the autonomous middle-class self in today's China: The case of young-adult only-children university students'. *Journal of Youth Studies*. **11** (2). pp.193–212.

Liu, F. (2011). *Urban Youth in China: Modernity, the Internet and the Self*. London: Routledge.

Lu, H. (2003). Bamboo sprouts after the rain: The history of university student environmental associations in China [Online]. Available at: www.wilsoncenter.org/sites/default/files/CES 6 Feature Article, pp. 55–66.pdf [Accessed 25 Aug 2017].

Lu, L., Gilmour, R. and Kao, S. (2001). 'Cultural values and happiness: An East-West dialogue'. *The Journal of Social Psychology*. **141** (4). pp.477–493.

Malone, K. (2001). 'Children, youth and sustainable cities'. *Local Environment*. **6** (1). pp.5–12.

Nelson, L. J. and Chen, X. (2007). 'Emerging adulthood in China: The role of social and cultural factors'. *Child Development Perspectives*. **1** (2). pp.86–91.

Ngai, N. P., Cheung, C. K. and Li, C. K. (2001). 'China's youth policy formulation and youth participation'. *Children and Youth Services Review*. **23** (8). pp.651–669.

Oyserman, D., Coon, H. M. and Kemmelmeier, M. (2002). 'Rethinking individualism and collectivism: Evaluation of theoretical assumptions and meta-analyses'. *Psychological Bulletin*. **128** (1). pp.3–72.

Ping, L., Minghua, Z., Bin, L. and Hongjuan, Z. (2004). 'Deyu as moral education in modern China: Ideological functions and transformations'. *Journal of Moral Education*. **33** (4). pp.449–464.

Ren, Y. (2016). 'Understanding university students' perceptions of, and engagement with, processes of planning urban development projects'. *UK-Ireland Planning Research Conference*. Cardiff: Cardiff University.

Riggio, E. (2002). 'Child friendly cities: Good governance in the best interests of the child'. *Environment and Urbanization*. **14** (2). pp.45–58.

Rydin, Y. and Pennington, M. (2000). 'Public participation and local environmental planning: The collective action problem and the potential of social capital'. *Local Environment.* **5** (2). pp.153–169.

Stalley, P. and Yang, D. (2006). 'An emerging environmental movement in China?' *The China Quarterly.* **186.** pp.333–356.

Tang, B., Wong, S. and Lau, M. C. (2008). 'Social impact assessment and public participation in China: A case study of land requisition in Guangzhou'. *Environmental Impact Assessment Review.* **28** (1). pp.57–72.

Tewdwr-Jones, M. and Williams, R. H. (2001). *The European Dimension of British Planning.* London: Spon Press.

Waldmann, E. (2000). 'Teaching ethics in accounting: A discussion of cross-cultural factors with a focus on Confucian and Western philosophy'. *Accounting Education.* **9** (1). pp.23–35.

Waley, A. (trans.) (1995). *The Analects: Confucius.* New York: Dover Publications.

Wang, X. J. (2003). 'Using a participatory GIS method in land use planning process'. *Forestry and Society.* **2**, pp.21–24 (in Chinese).

Wei, Y. D. and Ye, X. (2014). 'Urbanization, urban land expansion and environmental change in China'. *Stochastic Environmental Research and Risk Assessment.* **28** (4). pp.757–765.

Wilkins, J. L., Bowdish, E. and Sobal, J. (2000). 'University student perceptions of seasonal and local foods'. *Journal of Nutrition Education.* **32** (5). pp.261–268.

Wong, S. W., Tang, B. S. and Van Horen, B. (2006). 'Strategic urban management in China: A case study of Guangzhou development district'. *Habitat International.* **30** (3). pp.645–667.

Xing, F. (1995). 'The Chinese cultural system: Implications for cross-cultural management. *S.A.M. Advanced Management Journal.* **60** (1). pp.14–14.

Yang, G. (2003). 'Weaving a green web: The internet and environmental activism in China'. *China Environment Series.* **2003** (6). pp.89–93.

Yeh, G. O. and Wu, F. (1999). 'The transformation of the urban planning system in China from a centrally-planned to transitional economy'. *Progress in Planning.* **51** (3). pp.167–252.

Yu, L. (2014). 'Low carbon eco-city: New approach for Chinese urbanisation'. *Habitat International.* **44** (2014). pp.102–110.

Zhang, Y. (2015). Public participation approaches for urban planning in China [Online]. Available at: https://dpla.wisc.edu/sites/dpla.wisc.edu/files/inline-files/15-05-Zhang%2CYining_0.pdf [Accessed 13 Jan 2017].

Zhao, Y. (2014). Policy Process and Citizen Participation in Chinese Local Government. PhD thesis, University of Pittsburgh.

Zheng, Y. (1994). 'Development and democracy: Are they compatible in China?' *Political Science Quarterly.* **109** (2). pp.235–259.

CONCLUSIONS

Matluba Khan, Jenny Wood and Simon Bell

In this final short chapter, we discuss and offer some concluding thoughts on the implications for research and practice emerging from the contributions presented in this volume. Of course, we do not pretend that it is wholly comprehensive in terms of the range of important aspects which could be considered in relation to children; however, it does reflect at least a sample of the work being done at the present time.

Although it was not planned this way, the work presented and discussed in the book focuses on younger children – pre-school to primary/elementary ages – and does not go into teenage years. This happened in part because the majority of the chapters are derived from the conference held in Edinburgh in 2017, and although a number of papers were unsuitable for the book's theme, or the authors did not wish to contribute, it was also noticeable that younger children were the focus then too. This is perhaps rather appropriate, since in many ways these are the kind and age of children who present the greatest challenges for research – communicating with younger children and ethical issues about working with them being two particular factors – but these also represent the key age groups when introducing children to nature, providing sufficient opportunities for free play and a good start to their education, which are vital aspects (among many).

The objective of the book was twofold: first, to present current and up-to-date findings to address three main areas of research in relation to children's connections to place, ensuring opportunities for them to play in the best ways possible, providing more effective early-years pedagogy and finding out how best to engage their participation in creating their own environments. The second objective was to reflect on the opportunities and challenges for conducting research with children, especially, in the light of the focus on younger age groups, the best ways to engage with them and obtain robust data – whether quantitative or qualitative – for use in research. The following sections represent our joint reflections on some of what we believe has emerged from this work.

ALL PLAY AND NO WORK?

Play is frequently seen very narrowly, even as a frivolous activity that can therefore be considered optional, to be reduced or removed from significance in children's lives. This is often in order to make time for achieving more concrete things, such as exam results and skills that may smooth access into certain schools or institutions in later life. This attitude can cause difficulties in making the case for play as an activity integral to the child's experience – in fact, as a fundamental human right. It also makes it difficult to convince parents or teachers of the wider benefits play has for pedagogy and engaging with place. This issue is discussed by Tang and Woolley situated in the context of Beijing (Chapter 2); however, it is true for many countries of the Global South and not uncommon in western societies either. The lack of time and space for play in many urban settings reflects how play is perceived by the majority of the population and their attitude towards it.

Creation of well-designed places for play is a complex task made more difficult if the multifaceted importance of play for children and the necessity of creating places for play is not perceived by the public at large or by policymakers.

In England, local authorities have closed a total of 347 playgrounds since 2014 to make space for new housing and sport facilities. Fifty-nine percent of the 172 local authorities across the UK had cut their spend (£15 million in total) on parks and green spaces between 2016–17 and 2018–19. Warwickshire County Council made the highest cut by 87% in one year, reducing spending from £108,268 in 2016–17 to £14,184 in 2017–18 (Unison 2018). English local councils planned to decrease their spending on play areas by 44 percent by 2020 (API, 2018). The situation is similar but worse in the Global South. In Bangladesh, only 2 percent of children have access to playgrounds in urban Dhaka. Apart from government schools, themselves poorly equipped, 98 percent of the private schools do not have any playgrounds either (BSS, 2017).

All the chapters in Part 1 illustrate the importance of play for fostering creativity, physical literacy and learning and the therapeutic benefits for children with special educational needs. These chapters further outline how places can be designed to create play opportunities transcending geographical boundaries and which can contribute to achieving these benefits. Mozaffar (Chapter 1) shows the importance of loose materials in the design of Scottish outdoor learning environments for early years for fostering creativity, while this is strengthened by the findings from the research conducted by Mishra et al. in the Baltic state of Estonia (Chapter 3). Both Mishra et al. and De Rossi (Chapter 5) highlight in their chapters the importance of free play afforded by natural elements and loose materials. The value of natural elements and gardens for play and pedagogy for all children is further highlighted by Hussein (Chapter 4). De Rossi focuses on physical literacy achieved through playable environments containing key features.

In many contexts, play is perceived to be happening in areas with manufactured play equipment and the importance of free and unstructured play is often disregarded. Hence the discussion is also often limited to the design of playgrounds and not extended to the design and use of the range of other places, e.g. streets, school grounds or neighbourhood open spaces, used by children on a daily basis. The challenges highlighted and recommendations for design features outlined in the chapters in the 'place and play' section can show some directions for the design of more inclusive play spaces for children.

THE LEARNING ENVIRONMENT: THE THIRD TEACHER

Philosophies of education have evolved over time from teacher-centred to more student-focused approaches, with the world-wide practice of different schools of thought including those founded by people such as Loris Malaguzzi, Maria Montessori, Margaret McMillan and Friedrich Froebel. The learning environment, often termed the 'third teacher', plays a key role in the learning and development of children. One may wonder what meanings educational approaches hold for designers of pedagogical spaces. An educator may define their individual epistemological position based on the philosophies, aims and objectives of the individual institution/society/nation they are part of; needless to say, teacher-focused approaches are still the most popular and widely practiced in most of the world. This is reflected in the still-popular design of the teacher-facing classroom setting, in which students are perceived to be the receiver of education. Design and research studies guided by educational philosophies (see Chapters 6, 8 and 9) can direct architects and landscape architects to design learning environments that can support teachers in practicing child-centred teaching philosophies.

The outdoor learning environment as a place for pedagogy has the potential to break that mono-directional teaching/learning practice by fostering child-centred educational approaches that were called 'plearning' (play+learning) and 'flearning' (fun+learning) by Francis in Chapter 7. Outdoor environments and especially natural environments can offer more opportunities for experiential or hands-on and playful learning that can help children learn faster, and could be particularly beneficial for children deemed to be underachievers. Hence, teaching and learning in outdoor environments can reduce the attainment gap, a concern for governments both in the west and the Global South. Yet, still, outdoor environments are not considered as a place for pedagogy. Taking children outdoors for teaching and learning is often perceived as 'extra' and burdensome, even though research findings indicate otherwise.

Teachers who take children outdoors regularly find teaching outdoors 'fun' 'relaxing' and 'engaging' as opposed to 'risky' 'burdensome' and 'tense'.

Interestingly the role of teachers in the design and use of school buildings and landscaping is often missing in the architecture and landscape discourse in the same way that the importance of the environment as the 'third teacher' is missing in educational discourses. The environment and the teachers must be considered as powerful 'allies', as appropriately highlighted by Francis in her chapter, where she further discusses a framework that teachers can use while teaching and learning outside the classroom. This framework is undoubtedly also useful for architects and landscape architects while designing spaces beyond the boundaries of traditional classrooms. Future research on teacher motivation is needed in this area, as well as on the design of the intersections between indoors and outdoors, a rarely researched architectural aspect. Recommendations given by Monsur (Chapter 6), supported by his empirical research, indicate how the careful design of simple architectural elements can exponentially improve children's learning experiences, and can be further enhanced by well-informed teachers.

An outdoor learning environment can bring teachers closer to learners; however, this is only possible when teachers are aware of the pedagogical opportunities offered by the environment (defined as 'cognitive affordance' by Khan et al. in Chapter 9). A teacher informed about the role of the built and natural environment can create an appropriate learning space where children can explore more and connect with their surroundings in deeper and more meaningful ways. Appropriate teacher training on the role of the school building and its surroundings can help them to build their confidence and also identify the strengths and opportunities found there.

In addition to a lack of confidence and training, lack of time and resources are also considered to be barriers to taking children outdoors. Planning and design of learning environments involving both teachers and children are considered crucial for building confidence among teachers for outdoor teaching and learning. Outdoor learning, if integrated with the national curriculum (as in the Scottish Government's Curriculum for Excellence), can pave the way for building teachers' capacity and a further improvement of the school landscape as a pedagogical place. The involvement of parents and the community in the design and development of school buildings and landscapes can be further supported by good management of designed landscapes, ensuring their sustainability.

MEANINGFUL PARTICIPATION

When looking at the tools generally used in participatory processes, we can see that there are not enough with which to engage children effectively and meaningfully, and where tools are available they are often not very child-friendly. This can result in engagement being only tokenistic – as if talking and obtaining views from children is just box-ticking, or reinforcing the legitimacy of adult-held views. There is still an assumption that children are hard to reach, when in fact it is generally very predictable where children will be. It could thus be argued instead that policymakers are hard for children to reach, and children are instead 'seldom heard'. A lack of accessible evidence can lead to practitioners seeking to engage children on place-based matters either starting from scratch, or conflating participation and education. This can mean they construct exercises that inform children rather than bring their views on board in a meaningful sense.

All the chapters in Part 3, Place and Participation, show an appetite among children to be engaged and that they hold valuable views showing a different perspective to adults on the built environment. Power relations are often poorly understood, and assumptions prevail that children's views will be unhelpful or tend towards the fanciful or absurd, such as making unrealistic demands or having over-ambitious ideas. This came through strongly in the chapters by Wood (10), Jansson and Lerstrup (12), and Ren (13). Equally, because younger children especially may not be very articulate, there may be a tendency to minimise the effort needed to engage with them.

Issues such as anti-social behaviour can be used as reasons not to provide children what they ask for – an 'it's just going to get ruined anyway' attitude, which misses the point that places designed with the input of local children and teenagers are much less likely to be vandalised than if their views are ignored. Anti-social behaviour is often proof that children do not feel ownership or inclusion in a scheme (and therefore may resent it) rather than evidence not to listen to them. However, it is notable in Wood's chapter that anti-social behaviour of older children and teenagers leads to conflict and disappointment from younger age groups. Therefore, planning for and with children must take account of the varying needs of different age groups and interests.

Beeson (Chapter 11) shows how participation can be a very valuable area of professional practice, while Wood and Jansson and Lerstrup show that planning and management decisions would be more equitable with children's involvement. Ren shows how rapid urban transformation in China is moving at such a pace that it is vital that children do not get pushed out of the picture. Unfortunately, educational demands and wider societal structures place children's participation very low on the agenda. In this sense, Tang and Wooley's chapter in 'Place and Play' serves as a contextual accompaniment to Ren's chapter in 'Place and Participation'.

THE CONNECTION BETWEEN PLAY, PEDAGOGY AND PARTICIPATION IN DESIGN OF PLACES

Research has so far tended to address the three aspects of play, pedagogy and participation in separate silos, in part because the researchers interested in them tend to be based in very different disciplines and rarely come together. In this volume, we have looked into how places are designed for play and pedagogy in the context of place and participation. This has spanned different research contexts and separate research projects. Very little research has brought these aspects together explicitly, for example examining place for play and pedagogy created through meaningful participation within the scope of a single unified project. Thus, we have limited knowledge of how a landscape offers opportunities for all activities and for fulfilling the needs for the holistic development of a child. A comprehensive methodological framework is needed to address this. Khan, Bell and McGeown (Chapter 9) have provided one such framework for investigating the effectiveness of a school ground designed for both pedagogy and play that could be useful for architects, landscape architects, planners, educationalists, sociologists and researchers. Built environment professionals could use the framework and associated methods and techniques to evaluate their own planning approaches and designed environments and learn from their own or others' works for improvement of their future projects.

At the time of writing the Scottish Government has commissioned the development of a children and young people's version of the Place Standard Tool. This is their flagship community engagement tool in planning and design. Rights-based Scottish charities Play Scotland and A Place in Childhood are producing this tool, with all major themes of this book included in some form. This, along with recent changes to planning law in Scotland, gives children and young people rights to be consulted which are very promising. The UN Sustainable Development Goals have also been pushing for more universal language about how place affects people, including children. Our experience suggests these are starting to have some traction in certain places, with Scotland and Wales examples of where these are being integrated formally into wider governmental goals. It is therefore clear that moving beyond disciplinary silos at a policy level is starting to happen in some places.

CHILD-APPROPRIATE RESEARCH METHODS

All the chapters of the book have some methodological lessons to take away. Given that the case studies reported here deal with younger children – from pre-schoolers to almost-teenagers – there have been a number of issues faced by each researcher when engaging with children as research subjects. For some of the work, direct engagement is either unnecessary or practically or ethically difficult. If the use of spaces is a subject for the research, then behaviour observation is an excellent method and requires no direct interaction with the children – in fact it is to be avoided as it may change the use patterns. The chapters by Mozaffar, Mishra et al., Hussein and Khan et al. all apply observational techniques of various sorts.

It is important to engage directly with children when wishing to develop an experimental setting such as an outdoor classroom or play space, as this is also an aspect of participatory research. Beeson's Chair Project is a good example of one method, while drawing or model-making is another, as exemplified by Khan et al. Wood and Jansson and Lerstrup use participatory research to explore the wider built environment. For Wood, this involved a range of map-based and discussion exercises, and for Jansson and Lerstrup this involved child-led walks. Indeed, the diary-based work in Tang and Wooley's chapter and diaries, photography and focus groups in De Rossi's chapters were used to great effect, yielding subjective insights that may not be garnered clearly through other approaches.

Interviews or discussions can also be useful, as long as the children are old enough to be able to express themselves adequately, which is an issue with the youngest groups. However, Hamilton's survey methods can be used with very young children and proved highly effective within his research on cognition and memory. Ethical issues play a greater role in research in this instance, as well as how to ask questions or prompt discussions with children who think there is a right answer or who want to impress figures they see as being in authority.

DISCIPLINARY SILOS: IS INTERDISCIPLINARY RESEARCH THE ANSWER TO THE QUESTION? WHAT ARE THE CHALLENGES FOR INTERDISCIPLINARY RESEARCH?

Over the last decade, interdisciplinary/transdisciplinary research has been suggested as the solution for reducing the lack of connection between disciplinary silos in all research fields. Thus, combining perspectives should produce better and more useful research results which in turn can be used to provide more meaningful recommendations for professionals and policy makers. In many instances, research undertaken with a narrow focus in one discipline might make little sense to researchers even in a related discipline. A typical example might be design-based research from architectural disciplines, compared with social science research emerging from town planners or human geographers. While the fields are interconnected in practice, there is more limited crossover in language, research design and communication style than an outsider might expect.

It is easier to undertake simpler and more clearly defined research projects on a narrow topic where the data obtained can effectively answer a limited research question. However, the world is complex and it is not always easy to implement such research findings without there being implications and consequences in other, often unforeseen directions. Another issue is the question of what constitutes 'evidence'. The kind of results from different disciplinary traditions may be seen as strong in one field but weak in another. There is always an ongoing debate about qualitative versus quantitative research and the validity or robustness of the latter over the former.

As an example, some research in landscape architecture, primarily a design discipline, might come across to some other disciplines as not being 'proper research' because the methods used to capture spatial qualities are too graphical or descriptive. For instance, in their chapter, Bhavna Mishra and her co-authors reported on how different settings in Estonian kindergartens offer opportunities for different kinds of play activities for children, findings valuable for a landscape architect but perhaps inadequate for an environmental health researcher who might not consider it 'empirical enough'. Indeed, the language used by designers may carry conceptual and abstract meanings that confuse or alienate other professionals.

Conversely, professional landscape architects might not find the epidemiology and public health research investigating the relationship between 'greenness' and health through, for example, the impact on children's play, particularly useful. This could be because the variable 'green' is rather imprecisely defined either quantitatively (such as how much green space is needed for a play area for all age groups?) or qualitatively (what kind of green spaces are best to provide the most affordances for children's play?). They might then ask, 'so how does this evidence help me design a better park for children to play?'.

In real life, landscape is not a homogenous concept and consists of many different elements and settings that offer diverse experiences to users. However, combining the perspectives and approaches applied by landscape architects with those of epidemiology or environmental psychology can potentially achieve much better and comprehensive results for use by policy makers, planners and designers, since the implications of the evidence can be translated into principles for action much more readily. This is more challenging for the researchers – in theoretical terms, in research strategy development, in methodological interactions and in terminology – but arguably achieves much better results. It also requires a willingness for individual researchers to leave their comfort zones, to be open-minded and maybe to reduce their need to be published in certain journals that are not open to interdisciplinary research.

Furthermore, the intentions of interdisciplinary research and working across boundaries are laudable and well-meaning but the reality of attempting to understand the dynamics of a different research area or profession is often difficult in practice. In fact, people can feel threatened when someone with less specialist knowledge attempts to explore an issue in a new way. For instance, a public health researcher or professional may espouse evidence as to how a place could be changed to foster better physical and mental health. While a planner may agree in principle, they may be frustrated by real or perceived assumptions or a simplistic understanding of how planning and space works. This may lead to resentment and stress that makes such partnerships difficult on a personal level, unless sufficient time and resourcing allows them to work to understand each other's terms before moving forward.

Does all this mean interdisciplinary research should become a new discipline? How can the challenges be overcome in relation to place, pedagogy and play? It can be argued that landscape architects are particularly well-placed to work in an interdisciplinary mode, since the discipline (or disciplinary field) consists of many facets from natural and social sciences as well as planning and humanities. Teaching programmes tend to be built up from disciplinary courses (such as plants, construction, drawing, ecology, etc.), but integrated through studio project teaching (learning by doing). This approach is not common outside the design disciplines.

Interdisciplinary teaching could help. For example, urban planning at Heriot-Watt University is part of a school that largely teaches engineering. Architects and landscape architects train at the University of Edinburgh (Edinburgh College of Art), but only get to interact with planners in a limited way (mainly in relation to town planning legislation). The professional world is full of resentment between people of these different disciplines, but they have to work together. Moreover, courses on children, health, and education are absent from most planning programmes and CPD (Continuing Professional Development) requirements.

One approach to integrate different disciplines could be to teach them together at postgraduate levels through a Master's programme or postgraduate diploma. One example of such an approach is the relatively new one-year Master's programme on Landscape and Well-being run in the University of Edinburgh (directed by Catharine Ward Thompson and Simon Bell). This is aimed at and attracts students from a range of disciplines – landscape architecture, architecture, horticulture, environmental psychology geography, ecology and others – who work together and exchange disciplinary backgrounds as well as learning from each other. There could easily be other similar initiatives linking other constellations of disciplines to achieve similar goals.

THE GAP BETWEEN RESEARCH AND PRACTICE

Conversion of research findings into practice remains an issue in many fields. In the design professions the application of research findings into design is weak – even though 'evidence-based design' is now an accepted concept. Post-occupancy evaluation of design projects, another route for ensuring that research findings have been implemented, remains limited in application – mainly to hospitals, for example, and landscape architecture tends only to look at the health and safety aspects.

How people use a particular space, whether the space is used in the way intended by the designers, whether the application of research findings is having an impact or whether the users have invented new uses for the designed space, are criteria suggested by Khan et al. in this volume. However, in practice these are not usually the criteria used for evaluation of a place, in part because the concept of affordances is familiar to researchers but may not be understood by practitioners. Thus, affordances might not be the central tenet for designing a child's space, so that identifying and evaluating them may appear to measure the wrong variables. Many of the authors in this volume apply the concept of affordances in their research, including Khan et al., Mishra et al., Rossi, Hamilton and Monsur. Research and practice have not often worked hand in hand in the design and evaluation of spaces but there is enormous scope to do so.

A lot of research in these areas lacks a practical edge. While worthy from the standpoint of knowledge creation, the findings need robust dissemination and appropriate explanation to professionals. Researchers should avoid being seen to be swooping in and criticising practice without understanding the realities within which professionals are working. This means researchers need to be better at communicating their research results in ways that are understandable by their target audiences. If the research is interdisciplinary, it is likely that the audience may also be from different professions. Thus, communicating guiding principles on, for example, how to design a kindergarten or nursery play area to maximise creativity may need to be presented to a playground designer in a different way from a teacher, focusing on different aspects according to their roles and responsibilities.

Politics is also key here. A lot of what we are talking about in this book has political implications, for example in educational policy, urban planning or local government spending priorities. Yet, when economic development is involved, powerful interests have to be persuaded that changing practices is good, and people have strong feelings about many aspects of policy that push against established evidence in academia. If we look at the example of China in the chapters by Tang and Woolley and Ren, we see the disconnection between understanding place as an arena for children's play, participation and pedagogy, and the high educational demands that are government priorities. There is limited traction for research that pushes against very strongly held beliefs.

Some professions are more open to change based on clearly presented new evidence than others. Health is a key area where research is held in high regard, and education seems somewhat more receptive than many. In some cases, there is also an appetite for and greater belief in quantitative than qualitative evidence – a prejudice found in health. This can exclude vast amounts of useful results that are more difficult to generalise and to work out how to apply.

FUTURE DIRECTIONS?

From the thoughts and observations of the foregoing sections, and recognising the limited sample of issues covered by the book, we nevertheless feel that there are several directions in practice and research which can briefly be summarised:

1. More work is needed on methodological development suitable for research with and for children (and to remove any use of the term 'on children'). A number of effective methods are still in development, besides those featured here. More work is needed on methods for (participatory) evaluation of children's spaces for pedagogy and play and for further development of existing evaluation frameworks. Such evaluation is a key way to learn from existing designs for better future design. Without this work the potential of such an important subject cannot be maximised.

2. The huge importance of the role of play in the development of children from an early age into all life stages still needs more emphasis. Further research to demonstrate this is necessary to support the campaigns already started by key advocates such as Richard Louv. This is particularly salient to persuade the powers-that-be about incorporating play into urban planning, without inadvertently leading to the proliferation of fixed-equipment playgrounds.

3. With children living increasingly sedentary, indoor and screen-dominated lives, the design of outdoor spaces that are attractive enough to lure them away from their virtual world are required. Such design needs children's input because they know what would attract them and they need to 'own' the spaces. This needs to happen across geographic locations, because all children have a right to be included in public space and design.

4. In a future when the majority of the world's children are likely to grow up in densely built urban areas with poor access to open spaces or play facilities, research is urgently needed on creative and effective solutions for designing the whole city as a place for pedagogy and play.

Finally, more needs to be done to uphold the UN Convention on the Rights of the Child in the areas covered by this book and pointed out in the introduction. We hope that what we have provided here goes a small way in that direction.

REFERENCES

API (2018). *Nowhere to play*. London: Association of Play Industries.
BSS – Bangladesh Sangbad Sangstha (2017). Only 2pc of Dhaka children have access to playgrounds: Survey (Accessed 9 April 2020).
Unison (2018). Budget cuts put parks in need of urgent attention. www.unison.org.uk/news/2018/06/budget-cuts-put-parks-need-urgent-attention/ (Accessed 23 April 2020).

INDEX

Note: Page numbers in *italic* denote figures and in **bold** denote tables.

academic pressures, China 32–33

active play and physical literacy 77–88; case study methods 80–81; children's perspectives of active play 81–82; joy of movement 77, 79, 80, 81, 87; physical activity promotion strategies 77, 78–79; recommendations 87–88; traditional playground games 85, 87; unstructured and semi-structured active play 82–87, *83*, *84*, *85*, *86*

Adams, E. 158

adventure playgrounds 15

affordances 43, 44, 60, 84, 85, 101, 113, 126, 127, **130**, 135, 138–139, 143, 145–147, 155, 156, **157**, 165, 168, 194–195, 228

after-school classes, China 32–33, 35, 36–37

Albers, Josef 184

Amabile, T. M. 12

Anschauung 181

Anthroposophy 113

anti-social behaviour 174, 175, 225

architecture *see* indoor–outdoor spatial relationships in early childhood classrooms

Arneill, A. B. **98**

Association for Childhood Education International (ACEI) 11

attainment gap 124; *see also* outdoor learning and natural richness

attention: directed 95, 127; involuntary 95; joint 127, 135

Attention Network Test (ANT) 153

Attention Restoration Theory (ART) 95, 104, **130**, 133, 137

attentional disorders 127

Aumann, D. **98**, **100**

Bangladesh: lack of playgrounds 223; school ground intervention study 143, *146*, 148, 149–158, *149*, *151*, *152*, **157**

Barker, R. G. 147

Barrett, S. M. 209

Basler Well-Being Questionnaire 153

Bauhaus 182, 183–184

behaviour mapping 43–45, **45**, 64, 67, 148, 154–155

behaviour settings theory 147, 155

Beijing, China *see* summer holiday activities in Beijing

Bell, J. 64

Bell, S. 195

Benfield, J. A. 97, **98**

Bessant, J. 214

bike tricks 82, 84, *85*

biophilia 118

Blow, S.E. 183

Boldermann, C. 54

Bond, M. H. 212

Bradley, R. H. 55

Brosterman, N. 183

Bruner, J. 81

built environment *see* indoor–outdoor spatial relationships in early childhood classrooms

Buytendijk, F.J.J. 81

Cadwell, Louise 96

Camino, E. 111

Campbell, S. 54

Carstensen, T. A. 196

Carter, M. 55

Cauter, L. de 166–167, 168

Cele, S. 175

Cen, G. 211

Chai, W. 214

Chair Project 180–192, *181*; children's configurations 184–188, *185*, *186*, *187*, *188*; Froebel's Gifts 181–184; public art and placemaking 188–191, *189*, *190*, *191*

Chan, K. 214, 217

Charter for Children's Play, Play England 2

Chawla, L. 65–66

Chen, X. 216

Cheng, K. 215

Cheng, Y. 217

child development theories 144–145

child-friendliness of green space management 194–207; attitudes and approaches to children *198*, 203–204; case study methods and site 195–197, **197**, 204–205; children's independent mobility and 194–195, **197**, 201–202, *202*, 206; development of settings 198–199, *198*, *199*; elements of child-friendliness 194–195; maintenance of settings *198*, 200–201, *200*; urban planning *198*, 201–203

child-led walks 196–197, 202, 204–205, 206–207

children's drawings 150, *151*

children's participation in place 165–177, 224–225; case study methods and site 169–171, *170*; heterotopias of deviation 175–176; interdependent mobility 167, 172–173, **173**; journey to school experiences 171–172, *171*, 176; local parks as heterotopias of compensation 173–175; planning for heterotopia 176–177; *see also* Chair Project; child-friendliness of green space management; youth participation in Chinese urban planning

children's perspectives approach 195–196

China *see* summer holiday activities in Beijing; youth participation in Chinese urban planning

Christensen, P. 153, 167
Cizek, Franz 184
Clark, A. 148, 206
Clark, S. 60
Clements, R. 11
Cockburn, Ken 190
cognitive impacts, of outdoor learning environment 138
collaboration, outdoor learning and 134–135
Colucci-Gray, L. 111
Confucianism 211–213, *213*
constructive play 15
convergent thinking 12, 13
Cosco, Nilda G. 73, **98**
creative play 11–28; case study methods and site 16–18, *17*, **18**, *18*, **19**, *19*;
    creativity defined 12; gender differences 22–23, *23*, *24*, 27; in loose
    parts play context 15–16, 19–20, *19*, *20*, 21–22, *21*, 23, *24*, 25–26; in
    manufactured play context *18*, 19–21, *20*, 22–23, *23*, 24–25; taxonomy of
    12–13, **14**; types of 13–16
Critical Ethnographic Participatory Action Research 169
Csikszentmihalyi, M. 126, 127
Cummins, E. 44, 45
Curriculum for Excellence (CfE), Scotland 2, 15, 108, 112, 124

daylight 94–95, 97, **98**, 101, 102, *102*, 104
Dearstyne, Howard 184
DeBord, K. **98**, **100**
Deci, E.L. 78, 127
deep play 80
Dehaene, M. 166–167, 168
Dempsey, N. 195
Denmark *see* child-friendliness of green space management
Devlin, A. S. **98**
directed attention 95, 127
disability *see* sensory gardens for children with special educational needs
divergent thinking 12, 13, 26
Dobson, T. B. 77
dramatic play 15
drawings, children's 150, *151*
Driscoll, C. 55
Duan, G. 211
Dundee Public Arts Projects 180
Dyment, J. E. 54, 56

Elkind, D. 59
Elliott, G. R. 214
Ellon, Aberdeenshire 189–190, *191*
environmental child-friendliness *see* child-friendliness of green space
    management
environmental motivation: functional 126–128, 133, 135, 137, 138; general
    model of 136–138, *136*
Erikson, E. H. 145
Estonia *see* playground design and play behaviour in Estonia
eudaimonic well-being 127, 135, 137, 138
Evaluation of Potential for Creativity tool 12, 13
experiential learning 125–126

Fang, W. 214, 217
Farrer, Noel 66
Fein, G. G. 13

Feldman, S. S. 214
Field of Action Theory 168, 174, 175, 176, 177
Fisher, A. 59
Fisher, E. P. 43
Fjørtoft, Ingunn 54
focus group discussions 149–150
forest schooling 54, 125
Foucault, Michel 165, 166, 167, 172, 173, 174, 175, 176, 177, 209, 218
free play 11
Freemantle, Chris 190
Froebel, Friedrich 96, 181–184, 192, 223
Frost, Joe L. 54, **98**
functional environmental motivation 126–128, 133, 135, 137, 138

Gao, S. 212
gardens 95; *see also* sensory gardens for children with special
    educational needs
Gaver, W. W. 147
gender differences: children's independent mobility 201–202; creative play
    22–23, *23*, *24*, 27; play behaviour in Estonia 56–57, *57*, *58*, *59*
General Service Administration (GSA), US 94, **98**, **100**
Geographical Information System (GIS) 44–45
Gibson, C. 210, 216
Gibson, E. 126
Gibson, J. J. 43, 113, 194
Giddens, A. 209
Gillespie, J. 165
Global Matrix 2.0 77
Goldstein, J. 54
Goličnik, B. 155
Goltsman, S. M. **98**
governmentality 165, 166, 167, 168
Gray, D. S. 121
Gray, Peter 11
green space management *see* child-friendliness of green space management
Gropius, Walter 184
group motivation 126
Groves, L. 57
Gulwadi, G. B. 97

Haikkola, L. 196
Handley-Schachler, M. 212
Hart, R. A. 150–151
Hathaway, W. E. 97
Hawkins, A. 79
He, B. 215
Healey, P. 209
Health Behaviour in School-Aged Children Study (HBSC) 77
Heft, H. 146
Henry Moore Institute, Leeds 188
Heschong, L. 94–95, **98**
heterotopia 165, 166–168, 172, 177; heterotopias of compensation 173–175;
    heterotopias of deviation 175–176; planning for 176–177
Hil, R. 214
Hillman, M. 173
Hofferth, S. L. 11
Hofstede, G. 212
Hogg, J. 64
Hopwood-Stephens, I. **98**

Horelli, L. 194
Husserl, Edmund 109

imperial exam system, China 32
independent mobility of children 31, 167, 172–173, **173**, 194–195, **197**, 201–202, *202*, 206
indoor–outdoor spatial relationships in early childhood classrooms 93–106; architectural interpretation of educational philosophies 95–96; attention restoration by nature 95, 102, *102*, 104; case study methods and site 97–101, **100**; child engagement 99, 104, *104*, **105**; daylight 94–95, 97, **98**, 101, 102, *102*, 104; literature review 96–97, **98**, **100**; nature-based learning 102–103, **105**; recommendations **105**; teacher motivation 99, 101–102, *102*, **105**; views 95, 96–97, **98**, 101–102, *102*, 104; window sills 102, *102*, *103*
interdisciplinary research 226–227
involuntary attention 95
Irwin, A. 93
Itten, Johannes 184

Jacobson, R. Dan 66
James, A. 153
Jansson, M. 195
Joachim, W. 93
John Muir Award 114
Johnson, L. M. 54
Johnson, P. 166, 175
joint attention 127, 135
Joshi, M. S. 172
Junk Playgrounds 15

Kahn, P. H. 113
Kaplan, R. 66, 95, **98**
Karmel, L. J. 97
Kellert, S. R. 118
Kelz, C. 153
Kemp, S. 217
Kentel, J. A. 77
Kim, P. 211
Kirkby, M. 15
Kretchmar, R.S. 79, 80
Küller, R. **98**
Kyttä, M. 146, 168, 174, 175, 176, 177

Lambe, L. 63
Lau, S. 216
Le Corbusier 183
Learning through Landscapes 64–65
Learning for Sustainability (LfS), Scotland 108, 124
learning and teaching in nature 108–122, 223–224; affiliation *114*, 118–119, *122*; definitions of nature 110–111; encounter *114*, 115–116, *115*, *122*; nature of knowing 112–113; seaweed vignettes 108, 115–119, *115*, *117*; surrender *114*, 119, *122*; touch *114*, 116–118, *117*, *122*; *see also* outdoor learning and natural richness
Lefebvre, H. 167
Lerner, Fern 183, 184
Lester, S. 167, 168
Li, D. 96–97, **98**, 211
Lieberman, G. A. **98**
lifeworld 109
Lindgren, T. 195

Lindsten, C. **98**
Liu, F. 216, 217
Logan, Frederick 183
Longhorn, F 64
loose parts play context 55, 156; creative play in 15–16, 19–20, *19*, *20*, 21–22, *21*, 23, *24*, 25–26
Louv, Richard 1, 96, 112
Loynes, C. 112
Lu, H. 211, 217, *217*
Lubart, T. I. 12, 13
Lyndale School, Liverpool 67, *67*, **68**, 70, 71–73, *72*

McGilchrist, Iain 126, 139
McKenzie, T. L. 44
McLinden, M. 66
McMillan, Margaret 96, 223
McNish, H. 57
Malaguzzi, Loris 113, 223
Malone, K. **98**, 195
manufactured play context: creative play in *18*, 19–21, *20*, 22–23, *23*, 24–25; *see also* playground design and play behaviour in Estonia
Marcus, Clare Cooper 75
Marshall, D. 26
Matsuoka, R. H. 97, **98**, **100**, 153
Maxwell, L. E. 15
memory, outdoor learning and 132–133
Mikkelsen, M.R . 167
model-making 150–151, *152*
Moholy-Nagy, Lazlo 184
Montessori, Maria 95–96, 97, 182, 223
Moore, R. C. **98**
Moore, R. C. 73
Moss, P. 148
motor competences 84–85, 86, 87–88
Mount, H. 65–66
multi-sensory environments *see* sensory gardens for children with special educational needs
Muñoz, S. A. 54
Mygind, E. 153

Nansen, B. 167
narrative analysis 81–85
National Institute of Child Health and Human Development (NICHD), US 93
Natural Learning Initiative (NLI) 99
natural light 94–95, 97, **98**, 101, 102, *102*, 104
natural playgrounds *see* playground design and play behaviour in Estonia
nature 1; *see also* indoor–outdoor spatial relationships in early childhood classrooms; learning and teaching in nature; outdoor learning and natural richness
nature deficit disorder 1, 96, 112
Neill, P. 15, 26
Nelson, L. J. 216
New Urban Agenda 165
Ngai, N. P. 213
Nicholson, S. 16, 26, 137
Norén-Björn, E. 25
North Carolina State University, Raleigh 99
novelty, of outdoor learning environment 137

O'Brien, M. 173
Ogbuigwe, Akpezi 112
Olds, A. 94, **98**, **100**
Oncu, E. C. 26
one-child policy, China 31, 32
open-air school movement 96
outdoor learning and natural richness 124–139, 223–224; case study
    methods and site 128–132, **129**, **130**, *131*, *132*; children's performance and
    engagement 132–135, *133*, *134*; experiential learning 125–126; functional
    environmental motivation 126–128, 133, 135, 137, 138; general model of
    environmental motivation 136–138, *136*; impacts on underachievers 135,
    223; teachers' experiences 136, 224; *see also* learning and teaching in nature
outdoor play: in summer holidays in Beijing 35, 38–39; worldwide decline of
    31; *see also* playground design and play behaviour in Estonia
Owens, T. J. 11

Paechter, C. 60
Palmer, Sue 11
parks: closures and spending cuts 223; as heterotopias of compensation
    173–175
Parten, M. B. 127
participant observation 154
Passini, R. 66
PECS (Picture Exchange Communication System) 69
Perceived Restorativeness Scale (PRS) 130, 133, 153
Percy-Smith, B. 206
Pestalozzi, Johann Heinrich 181, 184, 192
pets, as play companions 84, *84*
physical activity levels 53–54, 55–56, *55*, 77
physical activity promotion strategies 77, 78–79
physical literacy *see* active play and physical literacy
Piaget, Jean 144, 145, 147
Ping, L. 213
Pink, S. 113
A Place in Childhood 225
planning, for heterotopia 176–177
Planning Aid for Scotland (PAS) 209
Play England Charter for Children's Play 2
Play Scotland 225
playground design and play behaviour in Estonia 41–60; case study methods
    and sites 43–48, **45**, **46**, *47*, *48*; contemporary design guidance 42–43;
    Estonian pre-school education systems 41–42; favourite play areas 49–51,
    49, *50*, *51*; gender differences 56–57, *57*, *58*, *59*; physical activity levels
    53–54, 55–56, *55*; play types 51–55, *52*, *53*, *54*
playgrounds: adventure 15; closures and spending cuts 223; as heterotopias
    of compensation 173–174; traditional playground games 85, 87; *see also*
    school ground interventions
Podilchak, W. 79
positive interdependence 126
post-occupancy evaluation (POE) 143, 227–228
pretend play 13–15
privatisation of childhood space 171
Proulx, G. 66
Pudong, Shanghai 211, *211*
Pyle, R. M. 113

Quantum GIS (QGIS) 44–45
quasi-experimental action evaluation strategy 148, *148*
questionnaires 153

Rader, N. 126
Reed, Edward 126
Reggio Emilia philosophy 96, 113
Roe, J. 146–147
Röttger, Ernst 184
Rousseau, Jean-Jacques 181
Royal School for the Deaf and Communication Disorders (RSDCD),
    Manchester 67, **68**, *68*, 69, *69*, 70–71, *71*, 73, 74
Russ, S. W. 13–15
Russell, W. 168
Ryan, R. M. 78, 127

Sageie, Jostein 54
Santiago Theory of Cognition 130
Schiller, Friedrich 109, 181
school ground interventions 143–158; affordance theory 145–147;
    Bangladesh case study 143, *146*, 148, 149–158, *149*, *151*, *152*, **157**;
    behaviour settings theory 147; child development theories
    144–145; framework for data analysis 156, **157**; research methods
    147–156, *148*; *see also* playground design and play behaviour in Estonia
Scottish Curriculum for Excellence (CfE) 2, 15, 108, 112, 124
Scottish Sculpture Workshop, Lumsden 189–190
Sebba, J. 64
self-concept 145
semi-structured interviews 155–156
sensory gardens for children with special educational needs 63–75;
    case study methods and sites 66–69, *67*, **68**, *68*; design
    recommendations 74–75; most and least successful features
    69–74, *69*, *71*, *72*
Sensory Trust, UK 66, 75
sensory plants 199, *199*
shallow play 80
Shaw, B. 173
Shim, S. Y. **98**
Shim, S.-Y. 54
Shoemaker, C. 63
Siedentop, D. 79–80
social cognition 127
Sohn, H. 167
Somerville, M. 112
Sommer, D. 109
Sørensen, Carl Theodor 15
special educational needs *see* sensory gardens for children with special
    educational needs
Special Educational Needs Code of Practice, UK 65
Spencer, Herbert 145
sport vs. active play 81–82
Stalley, P. 216–217
standardised tests 153
Steiner, R. 113
Sterling, S. 112
Stoneham, Jane 66, 75
structuration theory 213–215
student environmental associations, China 217, *217*
Sullivan, W. C. 96–97, **98**
summer holiday activities in Beijing 31–40, **36**; academic pressures
    32–33; after-school classes 32–33, 35, 36–37; case study methods and
    site 33–35, *34*, *35*; home learning 36; outdoor play 35, 38–39; summer
    schools 35, 37

surplus energy theory 145
Sustainable Development Goals 225
Sutton, M. J. 15
Sweden *see* child-friendliness of green space management
System of Observing Play and Activity in Youth (SOPLAY) 44, 155
Szekely, I. 26

Tang, B. 215
Tanner, C. K. 97, **98**, **100**, 153
Tartu, Estonia *see* playground design and play behaviour in Estonia
Taylor, A. 95, **98**
Thelen, Esther 125
Theory of Loose Parts 16, 26, 137
thinking: convergent 12, 13; divergent 12, 13, 26
Thøgersen, S. 215
Thoreau, Henry David 180
traditional playground games 85, 87
trampolines 82, 83–84, *83*
Tranter, P. **98**, 195
trim trails 82–83, *83*
Tuul, M. 42
Tyrebagger Trust 188, *189*, *190*
Tyson, M. 66

Uggla, Y. 110
Ulrich, R. 95, **98**
UNICEF 11
United Nations Convention on the Rights of the Child (UNCRC) 1–2, 165, 177, 194, 209, 210, 211, 213, 216, 218
United Nations New Urban Agenda 165
United Nations Sustainable Development Goals 225
university entrance examination system, China 32
university environmental associations, China 217, *217*
unstructured and semi-structured active play 82–87, *83*, *84*, *85*, *86*
urban planning: child-friendliness of *198*, 201–203; *see also* youth participation in Chinese urban planning

urban population, China 211, *212*
utilitarian complexity, of outdoor learning environment 136–137

Veitch, J. 77
views from classrooms 95, 96–97, **98**, 101–102, *102*, 104
Vygotsky, Lev 80, 126, 145, 147

Walch, J. M. **98**
Waldorf Schools 113
Wang, X. J. 215
Ward, C. 167
Warwickshire County Council 223
Wells, N. M. 95, **98**
Whitehead, M. 77, 82
Wilkins, J. L. 214
Williams, C. 112
Wilson, E. O. 118
window sills 102, *102*, *103*
Winterbottom, D. 73
Wolzogen, Karoline von 181
Women's Sport and Fitness Foundation (WSFF) 79
Wong, S. W. 216
Wright, Frank Lloyd 182–183

Yang, D. 216–217
Yang, G. 217
youth participation in Chinese urban planning 209–219; challenges and opportunities for 216–218, *217*, **218**; civil engagement and 215–216; Confucianism and 211–213, *213*; institutional arrangements for 211–213, *213*, 215–216; socio-political context 210–211, *211*, *212*; young people's agency 213–215

Zamani, Z. 44, 45
Zeisel, J. 153
Zhao, Y. 215
zone of proximal development (ZPD) 80, 126, 135, 138, 145